# THE JERUSALEM BIBLE

*La Bible de Jérusalem*, originally published in France, was the culmination of decades of research and biblical scholarship. It was immediately recognized the world over as one of the great Bible achievements of our times. The publication of the English translation in 1966 was equally enthusiastically received by scholars and readers of all faiths as a translation that captures for contemporary man the vitality and immediacy that the Bible had for the first Christians. It is truly *the* modern Bible for the modern reader.

In preparing this translation, the translators made full use of the ancient Greek, Aramaic and Hebrew texts. How this was done while still retaining the interpretations and insights of the French edition is explained by Father Alexander Jones, the General Editor:

"The translation of the biblical text itself could clearly not be made from the French. In the case of a few books the initial draft was made from the French and then compared word for word with the Hebrew or Aramaic . . . and amended where necessary to ensure complete conformity with the ancient text. For the much greater part, the initial drafts were made from the Hebrew or Greek and simultaneously compared with the French when questions of variant reading arose. Whichever system was used, therefore, the same intended result was achieved, that is, an entirely faithful version of the ancient texts which, in doubtful points, preserves the text established and (for the most part) the interpretation adopted by the French scholars in the light of the most recent researches in the fields of history, archaeology and literary criticism."

D1245478

# The Old Testament

## OF THE JERUSALEM BIBLE

*READER'S EDITION*

———

Volume 4

## THE PROPHETS – MALACHI

*General Editor*
ALEXANDER JONES
L.S.S., S.T.L., I.C.B.

DOUBLEDAY & COMPANY, INC.
GARDEN CITY, NEW YORK

Image Books edition 1973
by special arrangement with Doubleday & Company, Inc.
Image Books edition published February 1973

The abridged introductions and notes of this Bible are based on those which appear in *La Bible de Jérusalem* (one volume edition) published by Les Editions du Cerf, Paris. The English text, though translated from the ancient texts, owes a large debt to the work of the many scholars who collaborated to produce *La Bible de Jérusalem,* which the publishers of this English Bible gratefully acknowledge.

ISBN: 0-385-07052-7

# EDITOR'S FOREWORD
## TO THE READER'S EDITION

When the Jerusalem Bible was first published in English in 1966, the Foreword to the complete Standard edition announced its objects: to serve two pressing needs facing the Church, the need to keep abreast of the times and the need to deepen theological thought. This double program was carried out by translating the ancient texts into the language we use today, and by providing notes to the texts which were neither sectarian nor superficial. In that Foreword also, the dependence of the translators on the original pioneer work of the School of Biblical Studies in Jerusalem was acknowledged, and the English version was offered as an entirely faithful rendering of the original texts which, in doubtful points, preserved the text established and (for the most part) the interpretation adopted by the School in the light of the most recent researches in the fields of history, archaeology and literary criticism. With the text, the Standard edition presents the full explanatory notes that would enable any student to confirm for himself the interpretations that were adopted, to appreciate the theological implications drawn from them, and to understand the complex relations between different parts of the Bible.

However the Bible is not only for students undergoing a formal course of study, and there has been an immediate demand for an edition of the Jerusalem Bible which would bring the modern clarity of the text before the ordinary reader, and open to him the results of modern researches without either justifying them at length in literary and historical notes or linking them with doctrinal studies. For this reason, the present Reader's Edition has been prepared. The full Introductions of the Standard edition are here greatly abridged, to serve simply as brief explanations of the character of each book or group of books, their dates and their authorship; and the full Notes of the Standard edition have been greatly reduced in number and length, to restrict them to the minimum which are necessary for understanding the primary, literal meaning of the text; to explain terms, places, people and customs; to specify dates, and to identify the sources of quotations. In short, the brief Introductions and Notes are here only to help the ordinary reader to understand what he is reading and do not assume in him any wide literary, historical or theological knowledge or interests.

ALEXANDER JONES

*Christ's College, Liverpool*
*March 1, 1968*

# CONTENTS

## VOLUME 4

*Some editions of the Bible have not admitted these deutero-canonical books (or parts of books: in the case of Esther the passages 1:1a–1r; 3:13a–13g; 4:17a–17z; 5:1a–1f,2a,2b; 8:12a–12v; 10:3a–31, which are here printed in italic type; and in Daniel the passages 3:*24–90* and ch. 13–14); or have included them only as Apocrypha.

# CONTENTS

# TYPOGRAPHICAL NOTE

### Chapter numbers

The beginning of a chapter is usually marked by a large bold numeral. A smaller bold numeral is used when a chapter begins inside a paragraph.

### Verse numbers

The beginning of each verse is indicated in the line by a dot · preceding the first word, except when a verse starts at the beginning of a line or begins a chapter. Where two verses begin in the same line, the verse numbers in the margin are placed one slightly above and the other slightly below the line. In a few places, the text adopted by the Editors differs from St. Jerome's famous Latin version, from which the Vulgate and indirectly the A.V. are derived, but for ease of reference the verse numbering of the previous versions has wherever possible been retained. Occasionally, however, where a verse is omitted or displaced, its number will not appear in the usual sequence, and where a large or lengthy divergence is inevitable from the Vulgate and the A.V. numbering, this previous numbering is printed in italic in addition to the new numbering necessitated by the text. Italic verse numbers are also used (e.g. in Dn. 3) for passages incorporated from the Greek Septuagint version where the verse numbering duplicates that of neighboring Hebrew material. Occasionally verse numbers are given a suffix letter a, b or c. This is generally to mark a rearrangement of parts of the verse, or to relate a reference from elsewhere in the Bible to a specific part of the verse.

### Italics in text

Italic type is used in the text to distinguish words which are quotations from or close allusions to another book of the Bible. The origins of such quotations or allusions are given as references in the footnotes (except in cases in which the source is obvious to any Bible reader), and are not necessarily repeated when the same passage is quoted more than once in a single book.

## Punctuation of biblical references

Chapter and verse are separated by a colon, e.g. Ex. 20:17. In a succession of references, items are separated by a semicolon, e.g. Ex. 20:17; Lv. 9:15. The same practice is followed in a succession of references to different chapters of one book, e.g. Ex. 20:17; 21:3 or Ex. 15;17;20.

## Brackets in the text

In the text, round brackets are used only to indicate that the words within them are considered to be a gloss.

# THE BOOKS OF THE BIBLE
## IN BIBLICAL ORDER

| | | | |
|---|---|---|---|
| Genesis | Gn. | Obadiah | Ob. |
| Exodus | Ex. | Jonah | Jon. |
| Leviticus | Lv. | Micah | Mi. |
| Numbers | Nb. | Nahum | Na. |
| Deuteronomy | Dt. | Habakkuk | Hab. |
| Joshua | Jos. | Zephaniah | Zp. |
| Judges | Jg. | Haggai | Hg. |
| Ruth | Rt. | Zechariah | Zc. |
| 1 Samuel | 1 S. | Malachi | Ml. |
| 2 Samuel | 2 S. | | |
| 1 Kings | 1 K. | Matthew | Mt. |
| 2 Kings | 2 K. | Mark | Mk. |
| 1 Chronicles | 1 Ch. | Luke | Lk. |
| 2 Chronicles | 2 Ch. | John | Jn. |
| Ezra | Ezr. | Acts | Ac. |
| Nehemiah | Ne. | Romans | Rm. |
| Tobit | Tb. | 1 Corinthians | 1 Co. |
| Judith | Jdt. | 2 Corinthians | 2 Co. |
| Esther | Est. | Galatians | Ga. |
| 1 Maccabees | 1 M. | Ephesians | Ep. |
| 2 Maccabees | 2 M. | Philippians | Ph. |
| Job | Jb. | Colossians | Col. |
| Psalms | Ps. | 1 Thessalonians | 1 Th. |
| Proverbs | Pr. | 2 Thessalonians | 2 Th. |
| Ecclesiastes | Qo. | 1 Timothy | 1 Tm. |
| Song of Songs | Sg. | 2 Timothy | 2 Tm. |
| Wisdom | Ws. | Titus | Tt. |
| Ecclesiasticus | Si. | Philemon | Phm. |
| Isaiah | Is. | Hebrews | Heb. |
| Jeremiah | Jr. | James | Jm. |
| Lamentations | Lm. | 1 Peter | 1 P. |
| Baruch | Ba. | 2 Peter | 2 P. |
| Ezekiel | Ezk. | 1 John | 1 Jn. |
| Daniel | Dn. | 2 John | 2 Jn. |
| Hosea | Ho. | 3 John | 3 Jn. |
| Joel | Jl. | Jude | Jude |
| Amos | Am. | Revelation | Rv. |

# THE BOOKS OF THE BIBLE IN
## ALPHABETICAL ORDER OF ABBREVIATION

| | | | |
|---|---|---|---|
| Ac. | Acts | Lk. | Luke |
| Am. | Amos | Lm. | Lamentations |
| Ba. | Baruch | Lv. | Leviticus |
| 1 Ch. | 1 Chronicles | 1 M. | 1 Maccabees |
| 2 Ch. | 2 Chronicles | 2 M. | 2 Maccabees |
| 1 Co. | 1 Corinthians | Mi. | Micah |
| 2 Co. | 2 Corinthians | Mk. | Mark |
| Col. | Colossians | Ml. | Malachi |
| Dn. | Daniel | Mt. | Matthew |
| Dt. | Deuteronomy | Na. | Nahum |
| Ep. | Ephesians | Nb. | Numbers |
| Est. | Esther | Ne. | Nehemiah |
| Ex. | Exodus | Ob. | Obadiah |
| Ezk. | Ezekiel | 1 P. | 1 Peter |
| Ezr. | Ezra | 2 P. | 2 Peter |
| Ga. | Galatians | Ph. | Philippians |
| Gn. | Genesis | Phm. | Philemon |
| Hab. | Habakkuk | Pr. | Proverbs |
| Heb. | Hebrews | Ps. | Psalms |
| Hg. | Haggai | Qo. | Ecclesiastes |
| Ho. | Hosea | Rm. | Romans |
| Is. | Isaiah | Rt. | Ruth |
| Jb. | Job | Rv. | Revelation |
| Jdt. | Judith | 1 S. | 1 Samuel |
| Jg. | Judges | 2 S. | 2 Samuel |
| Jl. | Joel | Sg. | Song of Songs |
| Jm. | James | Si. | Ecclesiasticus |
| Jn. | John | Tb. | Tobit |
| 1 Jn. | 1 John | 1 Th. | 1 Thessalonians |
| 2 Jn. | 2 John | 2 Th. | 2 Thessalonians |
| 3 Jn. | 3 John | 1 Tm. | 1 Timothy |
| Jon. | Jonah | 2 Tm. | 2 Timothy |
| Jos. | Joshua | Tt. | Titus |
| Jr. | Jeremiah | Ws. | Wisdom |
| Jude | Jude | Zc. | Zechariah |
| 1 K. | 1 Kings | Zp. | Zephaniah |
| 2 K. | 2 Kings | | |

# THE PROPHETS

# INTRODUCTION TO

# THE PROPHETS

## The nature of prophecy

The prophet in Israel is a mouthpiece; he has no doubt that "the word of God" has come to him and that he must pass it on to others. In whatever way the divine message comes to him, and whatever method he uses to convey it, he is a man to whom the holiness and the will of God have been revealed. He contemplates present and future through the eyes of God and is a man sent to remind the nation of its duty to God and to bring them back to obedience and love.

Moses is accounted the father of them all, and prophets play a part in the whole history of the nation, whether in confraternities or singly as influential persons. At times the prophet may be powerful enough to reprove a king or direct national policy; at other times he may be in lonely opposition and his message takes the form of a tissue of menaces and reproaches against the ruling powers.

## The prophetic books

Great prophets can be found in the historical books, but the men of whom we know most are those whose prophecies were collected into separate books bearing their names and sometimes including biographical incidents, and these books are grouped together in the Hebrew Scriptures. Traditionally, they are arranged without regard for chronological order: the four "Major Prophets" (distinguished only for the great length of their books)—Isaiah, Jeremiah, Ezekiel and Daniel —coming before the rest, who are called "Minor Prophets." With Jeremiah, the Greek Bible added Lamentations and Baruch as associated works, though the Hebrew Bible put Lamentations with "the Writings" and did not include Baruch; it is the order of the Greek which is followed here.

The great age of prophecy lasted less than two centuries, from the mid-eighth century to the Exile; it is dominated by the figures of Isaiah and Jeremiah, though it also saw the works of Amos, Hosea, Nahum, Zephaniah and Habakkuk. With Ezekiel, the prophet of Exile, spontaneity and verve decline, interest in "the last days" increases, and apocalyptic literary form is beginning to make its appearance. The great tradition of Isaiah is continued for a while by his disciples, but the other prophets of the Return from Exile are prepossessed by the rebuilding of the Temple. In later prophets, we find a greater literary freedom: there is apocalyptic writing and the parabolic teaching style known as midrash; there is also a growing note of messianic hope. In Daniel, images of past and future come together in one great vision, and at this point it seems that the high inspiration of the prophets is exhausted and Israel must await a new outpouring of the Spirit.

**Introductions**

Separate introductions to the four longer books of the "Major Prophets" are included in this edition of the Bible. Before the book of Hosea, there are short introductions to each of the books included in the "Minor Prophets."

# INTRODUCTION

## TO THE BOOK OF

# ISAIAH

Isaiah the prophet belongs to the last years of the kingdom of Judah. His vocation to prophecy came "in the year that King Uzziah died," 740 B.C., and it was his mission to announce the fall of Israel and of Judah as the due punishment for the whole nation's unfaithfulness. At this time, the kingdom of Judah, living under the threat of Assyrian invasion, was looking for military alliances to preserve its independence; Isaiah resisted all such human expedients as showing a lack of faith in God and his purposes. When eventually the armies under Sennacherib reached the walls of Jerusalem and called for the surrender of the city, Isaiah advised the king not to capitulate and in fact the city was saved without a battle. This is the background to the prophecies in the first part of the book, which ends with a history of the period written by his disciples, at chapter 39. The prophecies show Isaiah as a man of lofty vision with a strong sense of the transcendence of God; beyond the destined fall of his nation he sees a coming age in which a remnant of the people will survive to rebuild peace and justice under a future descendant of David.

In the same part of the book, some prophecies from the time of the Exile, about a hundred years later, have been included. These include oracles against Babylon (ch. 13–14), an apocalypse (ch. 24–27) and some poems (ch. 33–35).

Toward the end of Exile, some very fine and profound prophecies were made by an unnamed writer with a new depth of theology, looking forward to the coming time when God would comfort his people and restore them to Jerusalem. These prophecies in a collection known as "the Book of the Consolation of Israel," form chapters 40 to 55 of the book, and embedded in them are the four "Songs of the Servant of Yahweh" who suffers to atone for the sins of his people.

Chapters 56–66 contain prophecies which appear to date from different times throughout the whole age, from the call of Isaiah to the restoration in Jerusalem after the Exile.

# ISAIAH

## I. THE FIRST PART OF ISAIAH

### A. ORACLES BEFORE THE SYRO-EPHRAIMITE WAR

#### Title

¹ **1** The vision of Isaiah son of Amoz concerning Judah and Jerusalem, which he saw in the reigns of Uzziah, Jotham, Ahaz and Hezekiah, kings of Judah.

#### Against a thoughtless people

2
>Listen, you heavens; earth, attend
>for Yahweh is speaking,
>"I reared sons, I brought them up,
>but they have rebelled against me.

3
>The ox knows its owner
>and the ass its master's crib,
>Israel knows nothing,
>my people understands nothing."

#### The punishment of Judah

4
>A sinful nation, a people weighed down with guilt,
>a breed of wrongdoers, perverted sons.
>They have abandoned Yahweh, despised the Holy One of Israel,
>they have turned away from him.

5
>Where shall I strike you next,
>since you heap one betrayal on another?
>The whole head is sick, the whole heart grown faint;

6
>from the sole of the foot to the head there is not a sound spot:
>wounds, bruises, open sores
>not dressed, not bandaged,
>not soothed with oil.

7     Your land is desolate, your towns burned down,
      your fields—strangers lay them waste before your
                eyes;
      all is desolation, as after the fall of Sodom.[a]

8     The daughter of Zion is left
      like a shanty in a vineyard,
      like a shed in a melon patch,
      like a besieged city.
9     Had Yahweh not left us a few survivors,
      we should be like Sodom,
      we should now be like Gomorrah.

### Against religious hypocrisy

10    Hear the word of Yahweh,
      you rulers of Sodom;
      listen to the command of our God,
      you people of Gomorrah.

11    "What are your endless sacrifices to me?
      says Yahweh.
      I am sick of holocausts of rams
      and the fat of calves.
      The blood of bulls and of goats revolts me.
12    When you come to present yourselves before
                me,
      who asked you to trample over my courts?
13    Bring me your worthless offerings no more,
      the smoke of them fills me with disgust.
      New Moons, sabbaths, assemblies—
      I cannot endure festival and solemnity.
14    Your New Moons and your pilgrimages
      I hate with all my soul.
      They lie heavy on me,
      I am tired of bearing them.
15    When you stretch out your hands
      I turn my eyes away.
      You may multiply your prayers,
      I shall not listen.
      Your hands are covered with blood,
16    wash, make yourselves clean.

**1 a.** The occasion of this prophecy is probably the siege of Jerusalem, 735.

"Take your wrongdoing out of my sight.
Cease to do evil.
17    Learn to do good,
search for justice,
help the oppressed,
be just to the orphan,
plead for the widow.

18    "Come now, let us talk this over,
says Yahweh.
Though your sins are like scarlet,
they shall be as white as snow;
though they are red as crimson,
they shall be like wool.

19    "If you are willing to obey,
you shall eat the good things of the earth.
20    But if you persist in rebellion,
the sword shall eat you instead."
The mouth of Yahweh has spoken.

### Lament for Jerusalem

21    What a harlot she has become,
the faithful city,
Zion, that was all justice!
Once integrity lived there,
but now assassins.

22    Your silver has turned into dross,
your wine is watered.
23    Your princes are rebels,
accomplices of thieves.

All are greedy for profit
and chase after bribes.
They show no justice to the orphan,
the cause of the widow is never heard.

24    Therefore—it is the Lord Yahweh Sabaoth who
speaks,
the Mighty One of Israel,
"Ah, I will outdo my enemies,
avenge myself on my foes.

25    "I will turn my hand against you,

I will smelt away your dross in the furnace,
I will remove all your base metal from you.

26    "I will restore your judges as of old,
your counselors as in bygone days.
Then you will be called City of Integrity,
Faithful City."

27    Zion will be redeemed by justice,
and her penitents by integrity.
28    Rebels and sinners together will be shattered,
and those who abandon Yahweh will perish.

### Against tree worship[b]

29    Yes, you will be ashamed of the terebinths
which give you such pleasure;
you will blush for the gardens
that charm you.
30    Since you will be like a terebinth
with faded leaves,
like a garden
without water.
31    The man of high estate will be tinder,
his handiwork a spark.
Both will burn together
and no one put them out.

### Everlasting peace

1  2  The vision of Isaiah son of Amoz, concerning Judah
and Jerusalem.
2    In the days to come
the mountain of the Temple of Yahweh
shall tower above the mountains
and be lifted higher than the hills.
All the nations will stream to it,
3    peoples without number will come to it; and they
will say:
"Come, let us go up to the mountain of Yahweh,
to the Temple of the God of Jacob
that he may teach us his ways
so that we may walk in his paths;

**b.** A pagan practice; possibly the prophecy is against Samaria.

since the Law will go out from Zion,
and the oracle of Yahweh from Jerusalem."

4    He will wield authority over the nations
and adjudicate between many peoples;
these will hammer their swords into plowshares,
their spears into sickles.
Nation will not lift sword against nation,
there will be no more training for war.

5    O House of Jacob, come,
let us walk in the light of Yahweh.

### The coming of Yahweh

6    Yes, you have cast off your people,
the House of Jacob;
the land is full of soothsayers,
full of sorcerers like the Philistines;
they clap foreigners by the hand.

7    His land is full of silver and gold
and treasures beyond counting;
his land is full of horses
and chariots without number;

8    his land is full of idols . . .
They bow down before the work of their hands,
before the thing their fingers have made.

9    The mortal will be humbled, man brought low;
do not forgive them.

10   Get among the rocks,
hide in the dust,
at the sight of the terror of Yahweh,
at the brilliance of his majesty,
when he arises
to make the earth quake.

11   Human pride will lower its eyes,
the arrogance of men will be humbled.
Yahweh alone shall be exalted,
on that day.

12   Yes, that will be the day of Yahweh Sabaoth
against all pride and arrogance,
against all that is great, to bring it down,

13   against all the cedars of Lebanon

and all the oaks of Bashan,

14      against all the high mountains
        and all the soaring hills,

15      against all the lofty towers
        and all the sheer walls,

16      against all the ships of Tarshish[a]
        and all things of price . . .

17      Human pride will be humbled,
        the arrogance of men will be brought low.
        Yahweh alone will be exalted,
        on that day,

18      and all idols thrown down.

19      Go into the hollows of the rocks,
        into the caverns of the earth,
        at the sight of the terror of Yahweh,
        at the brilliance of his majesty,
        when he arises
        to make the earth quake.

20      That day man will fling to moles and bats the idols
of silver and the idols of gold that he made for worship.

21      and go into the crevices of the rocks
        and the rifts of the crag,
        at the sight of the terror of Yahweh,
        at the brilliance of his majesty,
        when he arises
        to make the earth quake.

22      Trust no more in man,
        he has but a breath in his nostrils.
        How much is he worth?

### Anarchy in Jerusalem

1 **3**   Yes, see how the Lord Yahweh Sabaoth
          is taking from Jerusalem and Judah
          support of every kind
          (support of bread and support of water):

2         hero, man-at-arms, judge, prophet,

3         diviner, elder, ·captain, noble,

2 a. Tarshish is Tartessos in Spain—"the ends of the earth."
"Ships of Tarshish" means "great ocean-going vessels."

4
counselor, sorcerer, soothsayer.
"I give them boys for princes,
raw lads to rule over them."

5
The people bully each other,
neighbor and neighbor;
a youth can insult his elder,
a lout abuse a noble,
6
so that everyone tries to catch his brother
in their father's house, to say,
"You have a cloak, so you be leader,
and rule this heap of ruins."

7
When that day comes the other will protest,
"I am no doctor,
in my house is neither bread nor cloak;
do not make me leader of the people."
8
Yes, Jerusalem is falling into ruins
and Judah is in collapse,
since their words and their deeds affront the
        Lord,
insulting his glory.

9
Their insolent airs bear witness against them,
they parade their sin like Sodom.
To their own undoing, they do not hide it,
they are preparing their own downfall.

10
Tell them, "Happy is the virtuous man,
for he will feed on the fruit of his deeds;
11
woe to the wicked, evil is on him,
he will be treated as his actions deserve."

12
O my people, oppressed by a lad,
ruled by women.[a]
O my people, your rulers mislead you
and destroy the road you walk on.

13
Yahweh rises from his judgment seat,
he stands up to arraign his people.
14
Yahweh calls to judgment
the elders and the princes of his people:

"You are the ones who destroy the vineyard
and conceal what you have stolen from the poor.

15      By what right do you crush my people
        and grind the faces of the poor?"
        It is the Lord Yahweh Sabaoth who speaks.

## A warning to the women of Jerusalem

16      Yahweh said: Because of the haughtiness
        of the daughters of Zion,
        the way they walk with their heads held high
        and enticing eyes,
        the way they mince along,
        tinkling the bangles on their feet,
17      the Lord will give the daughters of Zion itching
                heads
        and uncover their nakedness.

18      That day the Lord will take away the ankle orna-
19      ments, tiaras, ·pendants and bracelets, the veils, ·head-
20      bands, foot chains and belts, the scent bottles and amu-
21      lets, ·signet rings and nose rings, ·the expensive dresses,
22      mantles, cloaks and purses, ·the mirrors, linen gar-
23      ments, turbans and mantillas.

24      Instead of scent, a stink;
        instead of belt, a rope;
        instead of hair elaborately done, a shaven scalp,
        and instead of gorgeous dress, a sack;
        and brand marks instead of beauty.

## The widows of Jerusalem

25      Your men will fall by the sword,
        your heroes in the fight.
26      The gates will moan and mourn;
        you will sit on the ground desolate.

 1 **4** And seven women will fight
        over a single man that day[a]:
        "We will eat our own food,
        and wear our own clothing," they will say,
        "let us just bear your name;
        take our disgrace away."

**3 a.** The "lad" is possibly the young king Ahaz, at the start of
his reign, 736.
**4 a.** The army has been destroyed; the circumstances are those
of the first or second siege of Jerusalem, 735 or 701.

### The remnant of Jerusalem

2        That day, the branch of Yahweh
        shall be beauty and glory,
        and the fruit of the earth
        shall be the pride and adornment
        of Israel's survivors.

3        Those who are left of Zion
        and remain of Jerusalem
        shall be called holy
        and those left in Jerusalem, noted down for sur-
           vival.

### The future restoration

4        When the Lord has washed away
        the filth of the daughter of Zion
        and cleansed Jerusalem of the blood shed in her
        with the blast of judgment and the blast of de-
           struction,

5        Yahweh will come and rest
        on the whole stretch of Mount Zion
        and on those who are gathered there,
        a cloud by day, and smoke,
        and by night the brightness of a flaring fire.
        For, over all, the glory of Yahweh

6        will be a canopy ·and a tent
        to give shade by day from the heat,
        refuge and shelter from the storm and the rain.

### The song of the vineyard

1  **5**  Let me sing to my friend
        the song of his love for his vineyard.

        My friend had a vineyard
        on a fertile hillside.

2        He dug the soil, cleared it of stones,
        and planted choice vines in it.
        In the middle he built a tower,
        he dug a press there too.
        He expected it to yield grapes,
        but sour grapes were all that it gave.

3        And now, inhabitants of Jerusalem
        and men of Judah,

I ask you to judge
between my vineyard and me.
4    What could I have done for my vineyard
that I have not done?
I expected it to yield grapes.
Why did it yield sour grapes instead?

5    Very well, I will tell you
what I am going to do to my vineyard:
I will take away its hedge for it to be grazed on,
and knock down its wall for it to be trampled on.
6    I will lay it waste, unpruned, undug;
overgrown by the briar and the thorn.
I will command the clouds
to rain no rain on it.
7    Yes, the vineyard of Yahweh Sabaoth
is the House of Israel,
and the men of Judah
that chosen plant.
He expected justice, but found bloodshed,
integrity, but only a cry of distress.

### Curses

8    Woe to those who add house to house
and join field to field
until everywhere belongs to them
and they are the sole inhabitants of the land.
9    Yahweh Sabaoth has sworn this in my hearing,
"Many houses shall be brought to ruin,
great and fine, but left untenanted;
10    ten acres of vineyard will yield only one barrel,
ten bushel of seed will yield only one bushel."

11    Woe to those who from early morning
chase after strong drink,
and stay up late at night
inflamed with wine.
12    Nothing but harp and lyre,
tambourine and flute,
and wine for their drinking bouts.

Never a thought for the works of Yahweh,
never a glance for what his hands have done.
13    My people will go into exile,

for want of perception;
her dignitaries dying of hunger,
her populace parched with thirst.

14    *a*. . . Yes, Sheol opens wide his throat
and gapes with measureless jaw
to swallow up her thronging nobility
as they are shouting for joy.

15    The mortal humbled, man brought low,
proud eyes will be cast down.

16    Yahweh Sabaoth will increase his glory by his
       sentence,
the holy God will display his holiness by his
       integrity.

17    Lambs will graze as at pasture,
fatlings and kids browse in the ruins.

18    Woe to those who draw down punishment on
       themselves
with an ox's halter,
and sin
as with a chariot's traces:

19    and to those who say, "Quick! Let him hurry
       his work
so that we can see it;
these plans of the Holy One of Israel,
let them happen and come true
so that we can know what they are."

20    Woe to those who call evil good, and good evil,
who substitute darkness for light
and light for darkness,
who substitute bitter for sweet
and sweet for bitter.

21    Woe to those who think themselves wise
and believe themselves cunning.

22    Woe to the heroes of drinking bouts,
to the champions at preparing strong drinks.

23    Woe to those who for a bribe acquit the guilty
and cheat the good man of his due.

24    For this, as stubble is prey for the flames
and as straw vanishes in the fire,
so their root will rot,

their blossom be carried off like dust,
for rejecting the Law of Yahweh Sabaoth,
and despising the word of the Holy One of
    Israel.

### The anger of Yahweh

25          So, Yahweh aflame with anger against his
                people
        has raised his hand to strike them;
        he has killed the princes, their corpses lie
        like dung in the streets.
        Yet his anger is not spent,
        still his hand is raised to strike.

### The Assyrian invasion

26          He hoists a signal for a distant nation,
        he whistles it up from the ends of the earth;
        and look, it comes, swiftly, promptly.

27          None of them faint or weary,
        none sleeping or drowsy,
        none of them with belt loose,
        none with sandal straps broken.

28          Its arrows are sharpened,
        its bows all bent,
        the hoofs of its horses are like flint,
        its chariot wheels like tornadoes.

29          Its roar is the roar of a lioness,
        like a lion cub it roars,
        it growls and seizes its prey,
        it bears it off, and no one can snatch it back.

30          Growling against it, that day,
        like the growling of the sea.
        Only look at the country: darkness and distress,
        and the light flickers out in shadows.

---

**5 a.** Vv. 14–16 are out of place and should perhaps be read with
2:6–22.

## B. THE BOOK OF IMMANUEL

### The call of Isaiah

1 In the year of King Uzziah's death[a] I saw the Lord Yahweh seated on a high throne; his train filled 2 the sanctuary; ·above him stood seraphs, each one with six wings: two to cover its face, two to cover its feet and two for flying.

3
>     And they cried out one to another in this way,
>     "Holy, holy, holy is Yahweh Sabaoth.
>     His glory fills the whole earth."

4 The foundations of the threshold shook with the voice of the one who cried out, and the Temple was 5 filled with smoke. ·I said:

>     "What a wretched state I am in! I am lost,
>     for I am a man of unclean lips
>     and I live among a people of unclean lips,
>     and my eyes have looked at the King, Yahweh
>         Sabaoth."

6 Then one of the seraphs flew to me, holding in his hand a live coal which he had taken from the altar 7 with a pair of tongs. ·With this he touched my mouth and said:

>     "See now, this has touched your lips,
>     your sin is taken away,
>     your iniquity is purged."

8 Then I heard the voice of the Lord saying:

>     "Whom shall I send? Who will be our mes-
>         senger?"

9 I answered, "Here I am, send me." ·He said:

>     "Go, and say to this people,
>     'Hear and hear again, but do not understand;
>     see and see again, but do not perceive.'
10     Make the heart of this people gross,
>     its ears dull;

> shut its eyes,
> so that it will not see with its eyes,
> hear with its ears,
> understand with its heart,
> and be converted and healed."

11  Then I said, "Until when, Lord?" He answered:

> "Until towns have been laid waste and deserted,
> houses left untenanted,
> countryside made desolate,
12  > and Yahweh drives the people out.
> There will be a great emptiness in the country
13  > and, though a tenth of the people remain,
> it will be stripped like a terebinth
> of which, once felled, only the stock remains.
> The stock is a holy seed."

## The first warning to Ahaz

1  In the reign of Ahaz son of Jotham, son of Uzziah, king of Judah, Razon the king of Aram went up against Jerusalem with Pekah son of Remaliah, king of Israel, to lay siege to it; but he was unable to capture it.

2  The news was brought to the House of David. "Aram," they said, "has reached Ephraim." Then the heart of the king and the hearts of the people shuddered as the trees of the forest shudder in front 3 of the wind. ·Yahweh said to Isaiah, "Go with your son Shear-jashub,[a] and meet Ahaz at the end of the conduit of the upper pool on the Fuller's Field road, 4 and say to him:

> 'Pay attention, keep calm, have no fear,
> do not let your heart sink
> because of these two smoldering stumps of fire-
> brands,[b]
5  > or because Aram, Ephraim and the son of
> Remaliah
> have plotted to ruin you, and have said:
6  > Let us invade Judah and terrorize it

---

6 a. 740 B.C.
7 a. The name means "a remnant will return."
b. The kings of Damascus and Israel.

and seize it for ourselves,
and set up a king there,
the son of Tabeel.

7　The Lord Yahweh says this:
It shall not come true; it shall not be.

8a　The capital of Aram is Damascus,
the head of Damascus, Razon;

9a　the capital of Ephraim, Samaria,
the head of Samaria, the son of Remaliah.

8b　Six or five years more
and a shattered Ephraim shall no longer be a
　　　people.

9b　But if you do not stand by me,
you will not stand at all.' "

## The second warning to Ahaz. The sign of Immanuel

10
11　Once again Yahweh spoke to Ahaz and said, •"Ask
Yahweh your God for a sign for yourself coming either
from the depths of Sheol or from the heights above."

12　"No," Ahaz answered, "I will not put Yahweh to the
test."

13　Then he said:

Listen now, House of David:
are you not satisfied with trying the patience
　　　of men
without trying the patience of my God, too?

14　The Lord himself, therefore,
will give you a sign.
It is this: the maiden is with child
and will soon give birth to a son
whom she will call Immanuel.

15　On curds and honey will he feed
until he knows how to refuse evil
and choose good.

16　For before this child knows how to refuse evil
and choose good,
the land whose two kings terrify you
will be deserted.

17　Yahweh will bring times for you
and your people and your father's House,
such as have not come

since Ephraim broke away from Judah
(the king of Assyria).

18  That day Yahweh will whistle up mosquitoes
from the Delta of the Egyptian Niles,
and bees from the land of Assyria,

19  to come and settle
on the steep ravine, on the rocky cleft,
on the thorn bush and on every pasture.

20  On that day the Lord will shave
with a blade hired from beyond the River[c]
(the king of Assyria),
the head and hairs of the body,
and take off the beard, too.

21  That day each man will raise
one heifer and two sheep,

22  and because of the abundance of milk they give,
all who are left in the country
will feed on curds and honey.

23  That day, where a thousand vines used to be,
worth one thousand pieces of silver,
all will be briar and thorn.

24  Men will enter it with arrows and bow,
since the whole country will revert to briar and
thorn.

25  On any hillside hoed with the hoe
no one will come
for fear of briars and thorns;
it will be pasture for cattle and grazing for
sheep.

### The birth of a son to Isaiah

1  Yahweh said to me, "Take a large seal and scratch
8 on it in ordinary writing MAHER-SHALAL-HASH-BAZ.[a]

2  Then find me reliable witnesses, Uriah the priest and
Zechariah son of Jeberechiah."

3  I went to the prophetess, she conceived and gave
birth to a son. Yahweh said to me, "Call him Maher-

4  shalal-hash-baz, ·for before the child knows how to say
father or mother, the wealth of Damascus and the
booty of Samaria will be carried off before the king
of Assyria."

c. Euphrates.
8 a. "Speedy-spoil-quick-booty."

### Shiloah and the Euphrates

5    Yahweh spoke to me again and said:

6        Because this people has refused the waters of
Shiloah[b]
which flow in tranquility,
and trembles before Razon
and the son of Remaliah,

7        the Lord will bring up against you
the mighty and deep waters of the River
(the king of Assyria and all his glory),
and it will overflow out of its bed
bursting all its banks;

8        it will inundate Judah, flow over, pour out,
flooding it up to the neck,
and its wings will be spread
over the whole breadth of your country, O Immanuel.

### Terror for the invaders

9        Know this, peoples, you will be crushed;
listen, far-off nations,
arm yourselves, yet you will be crushed.

10       Devise a plan, it is thwarted;
put forward an argument, there is no substance
in it,
for God is with us.[c]

### Yahweh a stone in the way

11       Yes, Yahweh spoke to me like this
when his hand seized hold of me
to turn me from walking in the path
that this people follows.

12       Do not call conspiracy
all that this people calls conspiracy;
do not fear what they fear,
do not be afraid of them.

13       It is Yahweh Sabaoth,
whom you must hold in veneration,
him you must fear,
him you must dread.

14       He is the sanctuary and the stumbling stone
and the rock that brings down
the two Houses of Israel;

a trap and a snare
for the inhabitants of Jerusalem.

15      By it many will be brought down,
many fall and be broken,
be trapped and made captive.

## Isaiah addresses his disciples

16      I bind up this testimony,
I seal this revelation,
in the heart of my disciples.

17      I wait for Yahweh
who hides his face from the House of Jacob;
in him I hope.

18      I and the children whom Yahweh has given me
are signs and portents in Israel
from Yahweh Sabaoth
who dwells on Mount Zion.

19      And should men say to you, "Consult ghosts
and wizards that whisper and mutter"—
by all means a people must consult its gods
and, on behalf of the living, consult the dead.

20      To obtain a revelation and a testimony,
without doubt this is how they will talk,
since there is no dawn for them.

## Wandering in the night

21      Distressed and starving he will wander through
the country
and, starving, he will become frenzied,
blaspheming his king and his God;
turning his gaze upward,

22      then down to the earth,
he will find only distress and darkness,
the blackness of anguish,
and will see nothing but night.

23      Is not all blackness where anguish is?

## Epiphany

1      In days past he humbled the land of Zebulun
and the land of Naphtali, but in days to come he will

b. The only spring of water in Jerusalem.
c. The meaning of the name Immanuel.

confer glory on the Way of the Sea on the far side of
Jordan, province of the nations.

1    **9**    The people that walked in darkness
has seen a great light;
on those who live in a land of deep shadow
a light has shone.

2      You have made their gladness greater,
you have made their joy increase;
they rejoice in your presence
as men rejoice at harvest time,
as men are happy when they are dividing the
       spoils.

¾      For the yoke that was weighing on him,
the bar across his shoulders,
the rod of his oppressor,
these you break as on the day of Midian.

⅘      For all the footgear of battle,
every cloak rolled in blood,
is burned,
and consumed by fire.

⅚      For there is a child born for us,
a son given to us
and dominion is laid on his shoulders;
and this is the name they give him:
Wonder Counselor, Mighty God,
Eternal Father, Prince of Peace.

⁶⁄₇      Wide is his dominion
in a peace that has no end,
for the throne of David
and for his royal power,
which he establishes and makes secure
in justice and integrity.
From this time onward and for ever,
the jealous love of Yahweh Sabaoth will do this.

### The vengeance of Yahweh

⅞      The Lord hurls a word against Jacob,
it falls on Israel.

⁸⁄₉      All the people of Ephraim and all the inhabi-
       tants of Samaria know it.
In their pride they have said,

speaking in the arrogance of their heart,

9/10   "The bricks have fallen down, then we will build
with dressed stone;

the sycamores have been cut down, we will put
cedars in their place."

10/11   But Yahweh is marshaling his people's enemies
against them,

he is stirring up their foes:

11/12   to the east, Aram, to the west, the Philistines

devour Israel with gaping jaw.

Yet his anger is not spent,

still his hand is raised to strike.

12/13   But the people have not come back to him who
struck them,

they have not come looking for Yahweh Sabaoth;

13/14   hence Yahweh has cut head and tail from Israel,

palm branch and reed in a single day.

14/15   (The "head" is the elder and the man of rank;

the "tail," the prophet with lying vision.)

15/16   This people's leaders have taken the wrong
turning,

and those who are led are lost.

16/17   And so the Lord will not spare their young men,

will have no pity for their orphans and widows.

Since the whole people is godless and evil,

its speech is madness.

Yet his anger is not spent,

still his hand is raised to strike.

17/18   Yes, wickedness burns like a fire:

it consumes briar and thorn,

it sets the forest thickets alight

and columns of smoke go rolling upward.

18/19   The land is set aflame by the wrath of Yahweh
Sabaoth

and the people are food for the fire.

Not one spares his brother,

19b   each devours the flesh of his neighbor.

On the right side they carve and still are hungry,

on the left they devour and are not satisfied.

19a/20   Manasseh devours Ephraim, Ephraim Manasseh,

and both hurl themselves on Judah.

21      Yet his anger is not spent,
       still his hand is raised to strike.

**10**

1      Woe to the legislators of infamous laws,
       to those who issue tyrannical decrees,
2      who refuse justice to the unfortunate
       and cheat the poor among my people of their
          rights,
       who make widows their prey
       and rob the orphan.
3      What will you do on the day of punishment,
       when, from far off, destruction comes?
       To whom will you run for help?
       Where will you leave your riches?
4      Nothing for it but to crouch with the captives
       and to fall with the slain.
       Yet his anger is not spent,
       still his hand is raised to strike.

### Against a king of Assyria[a]

5      Woe to Assyria, the rod of my anger,
       the club brandished by me in my fury!
6      I sent him against a godless nation;
       I gave him commission against a people that
          provokes me,
       to pillage and to plunder freely
       and to stamp down like the mud in the streets.
7      But he did not intend this,
       his heart did not plan it so.
       No, in his heart was to destroy,
       to go on cutting nations to pieces without limit.
8      He said, "Are not my officers all kings?
9      Is not Calno like Carchemish,
       Hamath like Arpad,[b]
       Samaria like Damascus?
10     As my hand has reached out to the kingdoms
          of the idols,
       richer in sculptured images than Jerusalem and
          Samaria,
11     as I have dealt with Samaria and her idols,
       shall I not treat Jerusalem and her images the
          same?"

12     When the Lord has completed all his work on Mount

Zion and in Jerusalem, he will punish what comes from the king of Assyria's boastful heart, and his arrogant insolence.

13   For he has said:

"By the strength of my own arm I have done
    this
and by my own intelligence, for understanding
    is mine;
I have pushed back the frontiers of peoples
and plundered their treasures.
I have brought their inhabitants down to the
    dust.

14   As if they were a bird's nest, my hand has
    seized
the riches of the peoples.
As people pick up deserted eggs
I have picked up the whole earth,
with not a wing fluttering,
not a beak opening, not a chirp."

15   Does the ax claim more credit than the man
    who wields it,
or the saw more strength than the man who
    handles it?
It would be like the cudgel controlling the man
    who raises it,
or the club moving what is not made of wood!

16   And so Yahweh Sabaoth is going to send
a wasting sickness on his stout warriors;
beneath his plenty, a burning will burn
like a consuming fire.

17   The light of Israel will become a fire
and its Holy One a flame
burning and devouring thorns
and briars in a single day.

18   He will destroy the luxuriance of his forest
and his orchard, soul and body too;
that will be like a sick man passing away;

**10 a.** Probably Sennacherib at the end of his invasion, 701.
**b.** Calno (N. Syria) captured by Tiglath-pileser, 738; Carchemish (Hittite) taken by Sargon, 717; Hamath (Syria) captured by Sargon, 720; Arpad (near Aleppo) captured, 728.

19              the remnant of his forest trees will be so easy
                       to count
                that a child could make the list.

### The name Shear-jashub[o]

20              That day,
                the remnant of Israel and the survivors of the
                       House of Jacob
                will stop relying on the man who strikes them
                and will truly rely on Yahweh,
                the Holy One of Israel.
21              A remnant will return, the remnant of Jacob,
                to the mighty God.

### A prophecy of destruction

22      Israel, your people may be like the sand on the sea-
        shore, but only a remnant will return. A destruction
        has been decreed that will bring inexhaustible integrity.
23      Yes, throughout the country the Lord Yahweh Sabaoth
        will carry out the destruction he has decreed.

### Oracle

24              And so Yahweh Sabaoth says this:
                My people who live in Zion,
                do not be afraid of Assyria who strikes you with
                       the club
                and lifts up the rod against you.

25              A little longer, a very little,
                and fury will come to an end,
                my anger will destroy them.
26              Yahweh Sabaoth will whirl the whip against
                       him,
                like the time he struck Midian at the Rock of
                       Oreb,
                like the time he stretched out his rod against the
                       sea
                and raised it over the road from Egypt.
27              That day,
                his burden will fall from your shoulder,
                his yoke will cease to weigh on your neck.

### The invader[d]

                He advances from the district of Rimmon,
28              he reaches Aiath,

he passes through Migron,
he leaves his baggage train at Michmash.
29   They file through the defile,
they bivouac at Geba.
Ramah quakes,
Gibeah of Saul takes flight.
30   Bath-gallim, cry aloud!
Laishah, hear her!
Anathoth, answer her!
31   Madmenah is running away,
the inhabitants of Gebim are fleeing.
32   This very day he will halt at Nob.
He will shake his fist against the mount of the
        daughter of Zion,
against the hill of Jerusalem.
33   See, the Lord Yahweh Sabaoth
hews down the boughs with a crash.
The topmost heights are cut off,
the proudest are brought down.
34   The forest thickets fall beneath the ax.
Lebanon and its splendor collapse.

## The coming of the virtuous king

1 **11** A shoot springs from the stock of Jesse,
    a scion thrusts from his roots:
2   on him the spirit of Yahweh rests,
a spirit of wisdom and insight,
a spirit of counsel and power,
a spirit of knowledge and of the fear of Yahweh.
(The fear of Yahweh is his breath.)
3   He does not judge by appearances,
he gives no verdict on hearsay,
4   but judges the wretched with integrity,
and with equity gives a verdict for the poor of
        the land.
His word is a rod that strikes the ruthless,
his sentences bring death to the wicked.

5   Integrity is the loincloth around his waist,
faithfulness the belt about his hips.

c. See 7:3.
d. The invasion route of this Assyrian enemy is not actually the
way taken by Sennacherib in 701; the towns are chosen because
their names suggest appropriate puns or recall past battles.

6
The wolf lives with the lamb,
the panther lies down with the kid,
calf and lion cub feed together
with a little boy to lead them.

7
The cow and the bear make friends,
their young lie down together.
The lion eats straw like the ox.

8
The infant plays over the cobra's hole;
into the viper's lair
the young child puts his hand.

9
They do no hurt, no harm,
on all my holy mountain,
for the country is filled with the knowledge
of Yahweh
as the waters swell the sea.

### The return of the exiles

10
That day, the root of Jesse
shall stand as a signal to the peoples.
It will be sought out by the nations
and its home will be glorious.

11
That day, the Lord will raise his hand once more
to ransom the remnant of his people,
left over from the exile of Assyria, of Egypt,
of Pathros, of Cush, of Elam,
of Shinar, of Hamath, of the islands of the sea.[a]

12
He will hoist a signal for the nations
and assemble the outcasts of Israel;
he will bring back the scattered people of Judah
from the four corners of the earth.

13
Then Ephraim's jealousy will come to an end
and Judah's enemies be put down;
Ephraim will no longer be jealous of Judah
nor Judah any longer the enemy of Ephraim.

14
They will sweep down westward on the Philistine slopes,
together they will pillage the sons of the East,
extend their sway over Edom and Moab,
and make the Ammonites their subjects.

15
And Yahweh will dry up the gulf of the Sea of
Egypt
with the heat of his breath,
and stretch out his hand over the River,
and divide it into seven streams,

for men to cross dry-shod,
16    to make a pathway for the remnant of his people
left over from the exile of Assyria,
as there was for Israel
when it came up out of Egypt.

## Two hymns of thanksgiving

1  **12**  That day, you will say:
I give thanks to you, Yahweh,
you were angry with me
but your anger is appeased
and you have given me consolation.
2    See now, he is the God of my salvation
I have trust now and no fear,
for Yahweh is my strength, my song,
he is my salvation.
3    And you will draw water joyfully
from the springs of salvation.

4    That day, you will say:
Give thanks to Yahweh,
call his name aloud.
Proclaim his deeds to the people,
declare his name sublime.
5    Sing of Yahweh, for he has done marvelous
things,
let them be made known to the whole world.
6    Cry out for joy and gladness,
you dwellers in Zion,
for great in the midst of you
is the Holy One of Israel.

## C. ORACLES ON FOREIGN NATIONS

### Against Babylon

1  **13**  Oracle on Babylon, seen by Isaiah son of Amoz.

2    On a bare hill hoist a signal,
sound the war cry.
Beckon them to come
to the Nobles' Gate.

**11 a.** The places to which the inhabitants of the Jerusalem area
had dispersed after the destruction of the city.

3
I, for my part, issue orders
to my sacred warriors,
I summon my knights to serve my anger,
my proud champions.

4
Listen! A rumbling in the mountains
like a great crowd.
Listen! The din of kingdoms,
of nations mustering.
It is Yahweh Sabaoth
marshaling the troops for battle.

5
They come from a distant country,
from the far horizons,
Yahweh and the instruments of his fury
to lay the whole earth waste.

6
Howl! For the day of Yahweh is near,
bringing devastation from Shaddai.

7
At this, every arm falls limp . . .
The heart of each man fails him,

8
they are terrified,
pangs and pains seize them,
they writhe like a woman in labor.
They look at one another
with feverish faces.

9
The day of Yahweh is coming, merciless,
with wrath and fierce anger,
to reduce the earth to desert
and root out the sinners from it.

10
For the stars of the sky and Orion
shall not let their light shine;
the sun shall be dark when it rises,
and the moon not shed her light.

11
I will punish the world for its evil-doing,
and the wicked for their crimes,
to put an end to the pride of arrogant men
and humble the pride of despots.

12
I will make men scarcer than pure gold,
human life scarcer than the gold of Ophir.

13
This is why I am going to shake the heavens—
and make the earth reel from its place,
before the wrath of Yahweh Sabaoth,
the day when his anger flares.

14
Then like a startled gazelle,
like sheep that no one shepherds,

each man will return to his people,
each take flight to his native land.

15  All those caught are slaughtered,
all those captured fall by the sword,

16  their babies are dashed to pieces before their
eyes,
their houses plundered,
their wives raped.

17  See now, I stir up against them the Medes,
who think nothing of silver,
who take no pleasure in gold.

18  The baby boys all cut to pieces,
the baby girls all crushed.
They have no mercy on the fruit of the womb,
no pity in their eyes for children.

19  Babylon, that pearl of kingdoms,
the jewel and boast of Chaldaeans,
like Sodom and Gomorrah
shall be overthrown by God.

20  Never more will anyone live there or be born
there
from generation to generation.
No Arab will pitch his tent there,
nor shepherds feed their flocks.

21  But beasts of the desert will lie there,
and owls fill its houses.
Ostriches will make their home there
and satyrs have their dances there.

22  Hyenas will call to each other in its keeps,
jackals in the luxury of its palaces . . .
Its time is almost up,
its days will not last long.

### The return from the Exile

1  **14** Yes, Yahweh will have pity on Jacob, he will
choose Israel once more and settle them in their
own country. The foreigner will join them and attach
2  himself to the House of Jacob. ·Nations will take them
and lead them to the place they came from, and the
House of Israel will adopt them in the land of Yahweh
as slaves and slave girls. They will capture those who
captured them and master their oppressors.

### A satire on the death of a tyrant

3     The day Yahweh gives you rest after your suffering
and torment and the grim servitude to which you were
4 forcibly enslaved, ·you are to recite this satire on the
king of Babylon:

> What was the end of the tyrant?
> What was the end of his arrogance?
>
> 5 Yahweh has broken the staff of the wicked
> and the scepter of tyrants—
> 6 which angrily thrashed the peoples
> with blow after blow,
> which furiously tyrannized over the nations,
> persecuting without respite.
> 7 The whole earth is at rest, it is calm,
> shouting for joy.
> 8 The cypresses, the cedars of Lebanon
> rejoice at your fate,
> "Now that you have been laid low,
> no one comes up to fell us."
>
> 9 On your account Sheol beneath us
> is astir to greet your arrival.
> To honor you he rouses the ghosts
> of all the rulers of the world.
> He makes all the kings of the nations
> get up from their thrones.
> 10 Each has something to say
> and what they will say to you is this,
> "So you too have been brought to nothing, like
> ourselves.
> You, too, have become like us.
> 11 Your magnificence has been flung down to
> Sheol
> with the music of your harps;
> underneath you a bed of maggots,
> and over you a blanket of worms.
> 12 How did you come to fall from the heavens,
> Daystar, son of Dawn?
> How did you come to be thrown to the ground,
> you who enslaved the nations?
> 13 You who used to think to yourself,
> 'I will climb up to the heavens;

and higher than the stars of God
I will set my throne.
I will sit on the Mount of Assembly
in the recesses of the north.

14    I will climb to the top of thunderclouds,
I will rival the Most High.'

15    What! Now you have fallen to Sheol
to the very bottom of the abyss!"

16    All who see you will gaze at you,
will stare at you,
"Is this the man who made the earth tremble,
and overthrew kingdoms,

17    who made the world a desert
and leveled cities,
who never to his captives
opened the prison gates?"

18    All the kings of the nations lie honorably,
each in his tomb.

19    But you, you have been expelled from your
grave
like loathsome dung,
buried under the slaughtered,
under those cut down by the sword,
and thrown on the stones of the ditch
like a mangled carcass.

20    You are never going to rejoin them in the grave,
for you have brought your country to ruin
and destroyed your people.
The offspring of the wicked
will leave no name behind them.

21    Start slaughtering the sons
for the guilt of their fathers!
Never again must they rise to conquer the earth
and spread across the face of the world.

### Oracle against Babylon

22    I will rise against them—it is Yahweh Sabaoth who
speaks—and wipe out name and remnant from Babylon.
No offspring, no posterity—it is Yahweh who speaks.

23    I will turn it into marshland, into a place for hedgehogs.
I will sweep it with the broom of destruction—it is Yahweh Sabaoth who speaks.

### Assyria will be destroyed

24
> Yahweh Sabaoth has sworn it, saying: Yes,
> what I have planned shall happen,
> what I have decided shall be fulfilled—

25
> to break Assyria in my country,
> to crush him on my mountains.
> His yoke will slip from them,
> his burden from their shoulder.

26
> This is the decision taken
> against the whole world;
> this, the hand stretched out
> against all the nations.

27
> When Yahweh Sabaoth has made a decision,
> who would dare cancel it?
> When he stretches out his hand,
> who can make him withdraw it?

### A warning to the Philistines

28
> In the year Ahaz died[a] this oracle was pro-
> nounced:

29
> Do not rejoice, whole country of Philistia,
> because the rod that beat you has broken,
> since the serpent's stock can still produce a
> basilisk
> and the offspring of that will be a flying dragon.

30
> But the poor are going to feed in my pastures
> and beggars rest in safety,
> while I let your posterity die out through hunger,
> killing off any that survive.

31
> Howl, Gate; cry, City;
> shudder, whole country of Philistia!
> For a smoke is coming from the north,
> and there are no deserters in those battalions.

32
> What reply will be given then
> to the messengers of that nation?
> "Yahweh has laid the foundations of Zion,
> and there the poor of his people shall find
> refuge."

## Lament for Moab

1 **15** Oracle on Moab:

> The night when Ar was ravaged
> Moab collapsed.
> The night when Kir was ravaged
> Moab collapsed.

2
> People climb to the temple of Dibon,
> climb high places to weep;
> on Nebo and in Medeba
> Moab laments.

> Every head shaven,
> every beard clipped;
3
> they wear sackcloth in the streets,
> and wail on the housetops.

> All in the squares are lamenting
> and bursting into tears.
4
> Heshbon and Elealeh are howling,
> their noise can be heard as far as Jahaz.
> That is why the loins of Moab are shivering,
> why its soul is shuddering;
5
> why the heart of Moab is groaning,
> why its fugitives are as far afield as Zoar (Eglath
>     Shelishiyah).

> Ah, slopes of Luhith,
> they climb them weeping.
> On the road to Horonaim
> they utter heart-rending cries.

6
> Ah, the waters of Nimrim
> are a waste land,
> the grass dried up, the turf all withered,
> nothing green any more.

7
> That is why they are busily preparing . . .
> And they transport their possessions
> across the wadi of the Willows.

**14 a.** In spite of this heading, "the rod that beat" Philistia must
have been Sargon II (died 705).

8
Ah, the shrieking rings around
the whole territory of Moab;
its wailing resounds right to Eglaim,
echoes as far as Beer-elim.

9
Ah, the waters of Dibon are swollen with blood,
and worse disasters are still in store for Dibon,
a lion to pounce on anyone who escapes from
    Moab,
and on the few survivors of that country.

## The Moabites take refuge in Judah

1 **16**
Send lambs
to the king of the country
from Sela, by way of the desert,
to the mountain of the daughter of Zion.

2
Flying backward and forward
like bewildered nestlings,
such are the daughters of Moab
at the ford of the Arnon.

3
"Advise us what to do,
decide for us.

"Spread your shadow as if it were night
at the height of noon.
Hide those who have been driven out,
do not let the refugee be seen.

4
"Let those who have been driven out of Moab
stay with you;
be their refuge
against the destroyer."

Once the oppression is over,
and the destroyer is no more,
and those now trampling the country underfoot
    have gone away,
5
the throne will be made secure in gentleness,
and on it there will sit in all fidelity,
within the tent of David,
a judge careful for justice
and eager for integrity.

## Lament for Moab

6      We have heard of the pride of Moab,
       an excessive pride—
       of his conceit, his pride, his arrogance;
       his pretensions are empty.

7      And so the Moabites must mourn for Moab,
       all of them lamenting together.
       For the raisin cakes of Kir-hareseth
       they mourn, in their utter bewilderment.

8      For blighted are the fields of Heshbon,
       and the vine of Sibmah
       whose clusters proved too strong
       for the overlords of the nations;

       it once reached all the way to Jazer,
       had even wound its way into the desert,
       and its shoots had spread
       even beyond the sea.

9      And so I weep, as Jazer weeps,
       for the vine of Sibmah.
       I water you with my tears,
       Heshbon and Elealeh.

       For over your fruit and your vintage
       a cheer has been heard;
10     joy and gladness
       have vanished from the orchards.

       No more revelry in the vineyards,
       no more happy shouting;
       no more wine trodden out in the presses,
       the shouting all silenced.

11     And so for Moab my whole being
       quivers like lyre strings,
       my inmost self, for Kir-hareseth.

12     In vain may Moab go
       to wear himself out at high places,
       to come and pray in his temple;
       he can do nothing.

### Oracle on Moab

13  Such was the sentence once pronounced against
14 Moab by Yahweh. ·Now Yahweh proclaims, "Within
three years, as a wage earner reckons them, the glorious power of Moab, despite his teeming population, will
cease to command respect, and what remains of him
will be slight, feeble, impotent."

### Oracle on Damascus

1 **17** Oracle against Damascus:

    Damascus is going to cease to be a city,
    She will become a heap of ruins.
2     Her towns, abandoned for ever,
    will be pastures for flocks.
    There they will rest with no one to frighten
      them away.
3     Ephraim*a* will lose his defenses
    and Damascus her sovereignty;
    the remnant of Aram will be treated
    in the same way as the glory of the Israelites.
    It is Yahweh Sabaoth who speaks.

4     That day, the glory of Jacob will be diminished,
    from being fat he will grow lean;
5     as when a reaper hugs an armful of standing
      corn
    and slices off the ears,
    or when they glean the ears in the Valley of
      Rephaim:
6     nothing remains but gleanings;
    or when an olive tree is beaten:
    two or three berries left on the topmost bough,
    four or five on the branches of the tree.
    It is Yahweh, the God of Israel, who speaks.

### An end to idolatry

7  That day, man will look to his creator and his eyes
8 will turn to the Holy One of Israel. ·He will no longer
look after the altars, his own handiwork, nor gaze at
what his hands have made: the sacred poles and the
solar pillars.

### Against the gardens of Adonis

9              That day, your cities will be abandoned
                  as were those of the Amorites and the Hivites
                  in the path of the children of Israel.
                  They will be a desert
10            because you have forgotten the God of your
                      salvation,
                  and failed to keep in remembrance the Rock
                      of your strength.
                  For you are planting plants for Adonis,
                  you put in sprigs of foreign gods,
11            you make them flower the same day as you
                      plant them,
                  as soon as it is light your seedlings blossom,
                  but all that you pick will vanish on the day of
                      trouble,
                  and the evil will be incurable.

### The upsurge of the nations

12            Vast hordes thundering,
                  with thunder like thundering seas,
                  the roaring of nations roaring
                  like the roar of mighty waters.
13            (Nations roaring like the roar of many waters.)
                  He rebukes them
                  and far away they flee, driven off
                  like chaff on the mountains before the wind,
                  like an eddy of dust before the storm.

14            At evening all was terror;
                  before morning comes they are no more.
                  Such was the lot of our plunderers,
                  such, the fate of our despoilers.

### Oracle against Cush[a]

1  **18**  Country of whirring wings
                  beyond the rivers of Cush,
2            who send ambassadors by sea,
                  in papyrus skiffs over the waters.

                  Go, swift messengers

17 a. The kingdom of Israel.
18 a. Egypt, denounced under the ancient name for Ethiopia.

to a people tall and bronzed,
to a nation always feared,
a people mighty and masterful,
in the country crisscrossed with rivers.

3 All you who inhabit the world,
you who people the earth,
the signal is being hoisted on the mountains,
look!
The horn is being sounded, listen!

4 For thus Yahweh speaks to me:
From where I am I gaze, untroubled,
like the clear heat produced by light,
like a dewy mist in the heat of harvest.

5 For, before the vintage, once the flowering is
over
and blossom turns into ripening grape,
the tendrils are cut back with a pruning knife,
the shoots taken off, cut away.

6 They will all be abandoned together
to the birds of prey in the mountains
and to the beasts of the earth.
The birds of prey will summer on them,
and all the beasts of the earth winter on them.

7 At that time, offerings will be brought to Yahweh
Sabaoth on behalf of the tall and bronzed nation, on
behalf of the nation always feared, on behalf of the
mighty and masterful people in the country crisscrossed
with rivers, to the place where the name of Yahweh
Sabaoth dwells, on Mount Zion.

### Against Egypt[a]

1 19 Oracle against Egypt:

See! Yahweh, riding a swift cloud,
comes to Egypt.
The idols of Egypt tremble before him,
and the hearts of the Egyptians sink within
them.

2 I will stir up the Egyptians against each other

and they shall fight every man against his
  brother,
friend against friend, city against city,
kingdom against kingdom.

3      Egypt is going to be demoralized,
for I shall confound all their wits.
They will consult idols and wizards,
necromancers and sorcerers.

4      I mean to hand the Egyptians over
to a hard master;
a cruel king will rule them.
It is Yahweh Sabaoth who speaks.

5      The waters will ebb from the Nile,
the river bed be parched and dry,
6      the canals grow foul,
the Niles of Egypt sink and dry up.

Rush and reed will droop,
7      the plants on the banks of the Nile;
all the Nile vegetation will dry up,
blow away, and be seen no more.

8      The fishermen will groan,
all who cast hook in the Nile will mourn;
those who throw nets on the waters
will lament.

9      The flax workers will be baffled,
the carders too, and weavers of white cloth.
10      The weavers will be dismayed
and all the workmen dejected.

11      The princes of Zoan are utter fools,
and Pharaoh's wisest counselors are stupid;
how can you say to Pharaoh,
"I am a disciple of the sages,
a disciple of bygone kings?"

12      Where are these sages of yours?
Let them come forward now,

**19 a.** Isaiah preached against Egypt probably at the time (718–
701) when Egypt was seeking an alliance against Assyria.

let them explain to you
what Yahweh Sabaoth has decided
to do with Egypt

13　　　The princes of Zoan are fools,
the princes of Noph,[b] self-deceivers;

Egypt is led astray
by the governors of her provinces.

14　　　On them Yahweh has poured out
a spirit of giddiness.
They have Egypt slithering in all she undertakes
as a drunkard slithers in his vomit.

15　　　And Egypt will never succeed in anything
undertaken by head or by tail, by palm or reed.

## The conversion of Egypt and Assyria

16 That day, the Egyptians will become like women, fearful, terrified, when they see the uplifted hand that 17 Yahweh Sabaoth will raise against them. ·The land of Judah will become the terror of Egypt. Whenever Egypt is reminded of this, she will be terrified, because of the fate Yahweh Sabaoth has prepared for her. 18 That day, in the land of Egypt there will be five towns speaking the language of Canaan and swearing oaths in the name of Yahweh Sabaoth; Ir Haheres will be 19 one of them. ·That day, there will be an altar to Yahweh in the center of the land of Egypt and, close to the 20 frontier, a pillar to Yahweh, ·which will be both sign and witness of Yahweh Sabaoth in the land of Egypt. When in oppression the Egyptians cry to Yahweh he will send them a savior to protect and deliver them. 21 Yahweh will reveal himself to them, and that day the Egyptians will acknowledge Yahweh and worship him with sacrifices and offerings. They will make vows to 22 Yahweh and perform them. ·Then, though Yahweh has struck the Egyptians harshly, he will heal them. They will turn to Yahweh who will listen to them and 23 heal them. ·That day, there will be a road from Egypt to Assyria. Assyria will have access to Egypt and Egypt have access to Assyria. Egypt will serve Assyria. 24 That day, Israel, making the third with Egypt and Assyria, will be blessed in the center of the world.

25 Yahweh Sabaoth will give his blessing in the words,
"Blessed be my people Egypt, Assyria my creation, and
Israel my heritage."

## Prophecy of the capture of Ashdod[a]

1 **20** The year the cupbearer-in-chief, sent by Sargon
king of Assyria, came to Ashdod and stormed
2 and captured it: ·at that time Yahweh had spoken
through Isaiah son of Amoz. He had said to him, "Go
and undo the sackcloth around your waist and take
the sandals off your feet." The latter had done so, and
3 walked about, naked and barefoot. ·Yahweh then said,
"As my servant Isaiah has been walking about naked
and barefoot for the last three years—a sign and portent
4 for Egypt and Cush—·so will the king of Assyria lead
away captives from Egypt and exiles from Cush, young
and old, naked and barefoot, their buttocks bared, to
5 the shame of Egypt. ·You will be frightened and
ashamed about Cush in which you trusted, and about
6 Egypt of which you boasted. ·And the inhabitants of
this coast will say, 'Look what has happened to those
in whom we trusted and to whom we fled for help
and safety from the king of Assyria! And now, how are
we going to escape?' "

## The fall of Babylon

1 **21** Oracle on the maritime plain:

As whirlwinds
sweeping over the Negeb
come from the desert,
from a land of horror
2 —a harsh vision has been shown me—
the plunderer plunders,
the destroyer destroys.

"Go up, Elam,
lay siege, Media.
I am putting an end
to groaning."

**b.** Memphis.
**20 a.** A Philistine town captured in 711.

3
This is why my loins
are wracked with shuddering;
I am seized with pains
like the pains of a woman in labor;
I am too distressed to hear,
too afraid to see.

4
My heart flutters,
dread makes me tremble,
the twilight I longed for
has become my horror.

5
They spread the table,
cover it with a cloth;
they eat, they drink . . .
Up, captains,
grease the shield!

6
For this is what the Lord has said to me,
"Go and post the watchman,
and let him report what he sees.

7
"If he sees cavalry,
horsemen two by two,
men mounted on donkeys,
men mounted on camels,
let him observe,
closely observe."

8
The lookout shouts,
"On a watchtower, Lord,
I stand all day;
and at my post
I keep guard all night."

9
Look, here come the cavalry,
horsemen two by two.
They spoke to me; they said,
"Fallen, fallen is Babylon,
and all the images of her gods
are shattered on the ground."

10
You who are threshed,
you who are winnowed,
what I have learned
from Yahweh Sabaoth,
from the God of Israel,
I am telling you now.

### Answer to the Edomites

11    Oracle on Edom:

> Someone shouts to me from Seir,
> "Watchman, what time of night?
> Watchman, what time of night?"

12    The watchman answers,
> "Morning is coming, then night again.
> If you want to, why not ask,
> turn around, come back?"

### Oracle on the Arabs

13    Oracle in the wastelands.

> You who pass the night in the scrublands, in
>     the wastelands,
> you caravans of Dedanites,[a]
> bring water
14   for the thirsty.
> You inhabitants of Tema
> go and meet the fugitive
> and give him bread;
15   since these are fleeing from the swords,
> from biting swords,
> from bent bows,
> from the stress of battle.

### Against Kedar

16    Yes, the Lord said this to me, "In one year's time
as a wage earner reckons it, all the glorious power of
17  Kedar will be finished. ·Of the bowmen, of the hardi-
est sons of Kedar, hardly any will be left, for Yahweh
God of Israel has decreed this."

### Against untimely rejoicing in Jerusalem

1  **22**  Oracle against the Valley of Hinnom:

> What is the matter now that you are all climbing
> with one accord to the housetops,
2   you the uproarious, the boisterous town, the joy-
>     ful city?
> Your slain were not slain by the sword,

**21 a.** A tribe of Bedouin.

your dead have not fallen in battle;

3     your rulers have all fled away
and been captured before bending their bows;
and the bravest among you have been taken
    prisoner,
they have fled far away.

4     That is why I say, "Turn your eyes away from
    me,
let me weep bitterly;
do not try to comfort me
over the destruction of the daughter of my
    people."

5     For this, a day of panic and rout,
is from the Lord Yahweh Sabaoth.
In the Valley of Hinnom a wall is thrown down,
they are shouting for help on the mountains.

6     Elam takes up his quiver,
Aram mounts his horse
and Kir[a] fetches out his shield.

7     Your fairest valleys
are filled with chariots
and the horsemen take up positions at the gates;

8     thus falls the defense of Judah.

### Against military preparations

You turned your gaze that day
to the armory of the House of the Forest.

9     You saw how many breaches there were
in the Citadel of David.
You collected the waters
of the lower pool.

10     You counted
the houses of Jerusalem,
and you pulled down houses
to strengthen the wall.

11     In the middle you made a reservoir between
    the two walls
for the waters of the old pool.
But you had no thought for the Maker,
no eyes for him who shaped everything long
    ago.

12     The Lord Yahweh Sabaoth called you
that day
to weep and mourn,
to shave your heads, to put on sackcloth;
13     instead, there is joy and amusement,
killing of oxen, slaughtering of sheep,
eating of meat, drinking of wine,
"Let us eat and drink,
for tomorrow we may be dead."
14     My ears have had this revelation
from Yahweh Sabaoth:
"Most certainly this sin will not be atoned for,
until you die,"
says the Lord Yahweh Sabaoth.

### Against Shebna

15     Thus says the Lord Yahweh Sabaoth:
Now go to this steward,
to Shebna, the master of the palace,
16     who is hewing a tomb for himself high up,
carving out a room for himself in the rock,
"What right have you here, and what relatives
     have you here
for you to hew yourself a tomb in this place?
17     See, Yahweh hurls you down,
down with a single throw;
then with a strong grip he grips you,
18     and he winds you up into a ball
and hurls you into an immense country.
There you will die,
and there will be sent the chariots you were so
     proud of,
you, the disgrace of your master's palace."

### Another oracle against Shebna

19     I dismiss you from your office,
I remove you from your post,
20     and the same day I call on my servant
Eliakim son of Hilkiah.
21     I invest him with your robe,

**22 a.** Three nations defeated by Sennacherib are now providing
soldiers for his army.

gird him with your sash,
entrust him with your authority;
and he shall be a father
to the inhabitants of Jerusalem
and to the House of Judah.

22 I place the key of the House of David
on his shoulder;
should he open, no one shall close,
should he close, no one shall open.

23 I drive him like a peg
into a firm place;
he will become a throne of glory
for his father's house.

## The calamity of the family of Eliakim

24 On it they will hang all the glory of his father's
house, offspring and issue, all the least of vessels from
25 cups to pitchers. ·That day—it is Yahweh Sabaoth who
speaks—the peg driven into a firm place will give way.
It will be torn out and will fall. And the whole load
hanging on it will be shattered, for Yahweh has spoken.

## On Tyre and Sidon

1 **23** Oracle on Tyre:

Howl, ships of Tarshish,[a]
for your fortress has been destroyed.
They learn the news
on their way from the land of Kittim.[b]

2 Be struck dumb, you inhabitants of the coast,
you merchants of Sidon,
whose goods traveled over the sea,

3 over wide oceans.
The grain of Nile, the harvest of the river,
formed her revenues,
as she marketed it throughout the world.

4 Blush, Sidon,
for thus speaks the sea,
"I have not labored nor given birth,
not reared young men
nor brought up young girls."

5 When the Egyptians learn the fate of Tyre,
they will be appalled.

6    Take ship for Tarshish, howl,
     you inhabitants of the coast.

7    Is this your joyful city
     founded far back in the past?
     Whose footsteps led her abroad
     to found her own colonies?

8    Who took this decision
     against imperial Tyre,
     whose traders were princes,
     whose merchants, the great ones of the world?

9    Yahweh Sabaoth took this decision
     to humble the pride of all her beauty
     and humiliate the great ones of the world.

10   Till the soil, daughter of Tarshish,
     the harbor is no more.

11   He has stretched his hand over the sea
     to overthrow its kingdoms;
     Yahweh has ordained the destruction
     of the fortresses of Canaan.

12   He has said: Rejoice no more,
     ravished one,
     virgin daughter of Sidon.
     Get up and take ship for Kittim;
     no respite for you there, either.

13   Look at the land of Kittim . . .
     They have set up towers.
     They have demolished its bastions
     and reduced it to ruins.

14   Howl, ships of Tarshish,
     for your fortress has been destroyed.

### The subjection of Tyre

15   That day, Tyre will be forgotten for seventy years.
But in the reign of another king, at the end of the
seventy years, Tyre will become like the whore in the
song:

16       Take your lyre, walk the town,
         forgotten whore.
         Play your sweetest, sing your songs again,
         to make them remember you.

**23 a.** See note on 2:16.
**b.** Cyprus.

17    At the end of the seventy years Yahweh will visit Tyre. Once again she will begin to receive the pay for her whoring. She will play the whore with all the kingdoms on the surface of the earth. ·But her profits and
18 doms on the surface of the earth. ·But her profits and wages will be dedicated to Yahweh and not stored or hoarded. Her profits will go to buy abundant food and splendid clothes for those who live in the presence of Yahweh.

## D. APOCALYPSE

### The sentence

1
**24** See how Yahweh lays the earth waste,
     makes it a desert, buckles its surface,
     scatters its inhabitants,
2
     priest and people alike, master and slave,
     mistress and maid, seller and buyer,
     lender and borrower, creditor and debtor.
3
     Ravaged, ravaged the earth,
     despoiled, despoiled,
     as Yahweh has said.
4
     The earth is mourning, withering,
     the world is pining, withering,
     the heavens are pining away with the earth.
5
     The earth is defiled
     under its inhabitants' feet,
     for they have transgressed the law, violated the
        precept,
     broken the everlasting covenant.
6
     So a curse consumes the earth
     and its inhabitants suffer the penalty,
     that is why the inhabitants of the earth are
        burned up
     and few men are left.

### The city in ruins

7
     The wine is mourning, the vine is pining away,
     all glad hearts are sighing.
8
     The merry tambourines are silent,
     the sound of reveling is over,
     the merry lyre is silent.

9　　They no longer sing over their wine,
the drunkard finds strong drink revolting.

10　　The city of emptiness is in ruins,
the entrance to every house is shut.

11　　There is lamentation in the streets: no wine,
joy quite gone,
gladness banished from the country.

12　　Nothing but rubble in the city,
the gate smashed to pieces;

13　　and so it will be on earth,
among the peoples,
as at the beating of the olive trees,
as at the gleaning of the grapes
when the grape harvest is over.

14　　They lift up their voices, singing for joy;
they acclaim the majesty of Yahweh from the
sea.

15　　Therefore in the islands they give glory to
Yahweh,
in the islands of the sea, to the name of Yahweh,
the God of Israel.

16　　From remotest earth we hear songs, "Honor
to the upright one."

But "Enough, enough!" I say.
"Woe to the traitors who betray,
to the traitors who treacherously betray!"

17　　Terror, the pit, the snare
for you, inhabitants of the earth:

18　　the man who runs away at the city of terror
shall fall into the pit,
and the man who climbs out of the pit
shall be caught in the snare.

**Continuation of the poem on the sentence**

Yes, the sluice gates above will open,

19　　and the foundations of the earth will rock.
The earth will split into fragments,
the earth will be riven and rent.

20　　The earth will shiver and shake,
the earth will stagger like a drunkard,
sway like a shanty;

21 so heavy will be its sin on it, it will fall
never to rise again.
That day, Yahweh will punish
above, the armies of the sky,
below, the kings of the earth;

22 they will be herded together,
shut up in a dungeon,
confined in a prison
and, after long years, punished.

23 The moon will hide her face, the sun be
ashamed,
for Yahweh Sabaoth will be king
on Mount Zion, in Jerusalem,
and his glory will shine in the presence of his
elders.

## A prayer of thanksgiving

1 **25** Yahweh, you are my God,
I extol you, I praise your name;
for you have carried out your excellent design,
long planned, trustworthy, true.

2 For you have made the town a heap of stones,
the fortified city a ruin.
The citadel of the proud is a city no longer,
it will never be rebuilt.

3 Hence a mighty people gives you glory,
the city of pitiless nations holds you in awe;

4 for you are a refuge for the poor,
a refuge for the needy in distress,
a shelter from the storm,
a shade from the heat;
while the breath of pitiless men
is like the winter storm.

5 Like drought in a dry land
you will repress the clamor of the proud;
like heat by the shadow of a cloud
the singing of the despots will be subdued.

## The messianic banquet

6 On this mountain,
Yahweh Sabaoth will prepare for all peoples
a banquet of rich food, a banquet of fine wines,
of food rich and juicy, of fine strained wines.

7   On this mountain he will remove
the mourning veil covering all peoples,
and the shroud enwrapping all nations,

8   he will destroy Death for ever.
The Lord Yahweh will wipe away
the tears from every cheek;
he will take away his people's shame
everywhere on earth,
for Yahweh has said so.

9   That day, it will be said: See, this is our God
in whom we hoped for salvation;
Yahweh is the one in whom we hoped.
We exult and we rejoice
that he has saved us;

10   for the hand of Yahweh
rests on this mountain.
Moab is trodden down where he stands
as straw is trodden in the dung pit;

11   and there he stretches out his hands
like a swimmer stretching out his hands to swim.
But Yahweh curbs his pride
and whatever his hands attempt.

12   Your arrogant, lofty walls
he destroys, he overthrows,
he flings them in the dust.

### Song of victory

26 1   That day, this song will be sung in the land of
Judah:
We have a strong city;
to guard us he has set
wall and rampart about us.

2   Open the gates! Let the upright nation come in,
she, the faithful one

3   whose mind is steadfast, who keeps the peace,
because she trusts in you.

4   Trust in Yahweh for ever,
for Yahweh is the everlasting Rock;

5   he has brought low those who lived high up
in the steep citadel;
he brings it down, brings it down to the ground,
flings it down in the dust:

6 the feet of the lowly, the footsteps of the poor
trample on it.

**A psalm**

7 The path of the upright man is straight,
you smooth the way of the upright.
8 Following the path of your judgments,
we hoped in you, Yahweh,
your name, your memory are all my soul desires.

9 At night my soul longs for you
and my spirit in me seeks for you;
when your judgments appear on earth
the inhabitants of the world learn the meaning
of integrity.

10 If favor is shown to the wicked,
he does not learn the meaning of integrity.
He does evil in the land of uprightness,
he fails to see the majesty of Yahweh.

11 Yahweh, your hand is raised,
but they do not see it.
Let them see your jealous love for this people
and be ashamed,
let the fire prepared for your enemies consume
them.

12 Yahweh, you are giving us peace,
since you treat us
as our deeds deserve.

13 Yahweh our God,
other lords than you have ruled us,
but we acknowledge no one other than you,
no other name than yours.

14 The dead will not come to life,
their ghosts will not rise,
for you have punished them, annihilated them,
and wiped out their memory.

15 Enlarge the nation, Yahweh, enlarge it,
to the nation grant glory,
extend all the frontiers of the country.

16    Distressed, we search for you, Yahweh;
the misery of oppression was your punishment
    for us.

17    As a woman with child near her time
writhes and cries out in her pangs,
so are we, Yahweh, in your presence:

18    we have conceived, we writhe
as if we were giving birth;
we have not given the spirit of salvation to the
    earth,
no more inhabitants of the world are born.

19    Your dead will come to life,
their corpses will rise;
awake, exult,
all you who lie in the dust,
for your dew is a radiant dew
and the land of ghosts will give birth.

## Oracle

20    Go into your rooms, my people,
shut your doors behind you.
Hide yourselves a little while
until the wrath has passed.

21    For, see, Yahweh will soon come out of his
    dwelling,
to punish all the inhabitants of earth for their
    crimes.
The earth will reveal its blood
and no longer hide its slain.

1  **27**  That day, Yahweh will punish,
with his hard sword, massive and strong,
Leviathan the fleeing serpent,
Leviathan the twisting serpent:
he will kill the sea dragon.

## The vineyard of Yahweh

2    That day,
sing of the delightful vineyard!

3    I, Yahweh, am its keeper;
every moment I water it
for fear its leaves should fall;

night and day I watch over it.

4　　I am angry no longer.
If thorns and briars come
I will declare war on them,
I will burn them every one.

5　　Or if they would shelter under my protection,
let them make their peace with me,
let them make their peace with me.

## Pardon for Jacob; punishment for the oppressor

6　　In the days to come, Jacob will put out shoots,
Israel will bud and blossom
and fill the whole world with fruit.

7　　Has he beaten her as he beat those who beat
　　　her?
Has he murdered her as he murdered those who
　　　murdered her?

8　　You have punished it with expulsion and exile;
he pursued it with a blast as fierce as the wind
　　　from the east.

9　　Now here is how Jacob's guilt will be atoned for,
here is the ransom for its sin:
he treats all the altar stones
like lumps of chalk that are ground to powder.

10　　Sacred poles and solar pillars stand no longer,
for the fortified city is abandoned now,
it lies deserted,
forsaken as a wilderness.
There the herd grazes,
there it rests and browses on the branches.

11　　The boughs are dry and broken,
women come and use them for firewood;
for this is a nation without understanding
and so its Maker will have no pity for it,
he that shaped it will show it no favor.

## Oracle

12　　That day, Yahweh will start his threshing
from the course of the River to the wadi of
　　　Egypt,
and you will be gathered one by one,
sons of Israel.

13  That day, the great trumpet will be sounded,
and those lost in the land of Assyria will come,
and those exiled to the land of Egypt,
and they will worship Yahweh
on the holy mountain, in Jerusalem.


## E. POEMS ON ISRAEL AND JUDAH

### A warning to Samaria

1  **28**  Woe to the haughty crown of Ephraim's
drunkards,
to the fading flower of its proud splendor
overlooking the lush valley,
to those prostrated by wine!

2  See, a strong and mighty one, sent by the Lord,
like a storm of hail, a destroying tempest,
like a storm of torrential, overflowing waters;
with his hand he throws them to the ground.

3  There will be trampled underfoot
the haughty crown of Ephraim's drunkards,

4  and the faded flower of its proud splendor
overlooking the lush valley.
Just like a fig before summer comes:
whoever notices it, picks it,
no sooner in the hand than swallowed.


5  That day, Yahweh Sabaoth
will be a crown of glory
and a diadem of splendor
for the remnant of his people,

6  a spirit of justice
for him who sits in judgment,
and a spirit of courage
for him who thrusts back the attacker to the
gate.

### Against the priests and the false prophets

7  These, too, are reeling with wine,
staggering from strong drink.
Priest and prophet are reeling
from strong drink,
they are muddled with wine;

strong drink makes them stagger,
they totter when they are having visions,
they stumble when they are giving judgment.

8   Yes, all the tables are covered with vomit,
not a place left clean.

9   "Who does he think he is lecturing?
Who does he think his message is for?
Babies just weaned?
Babies just taken from the breast?

10   With his
*sav lasav, sav lasav,*
*kav lakav, kav lakav,*
*zeer sham, zeer sham!"* [a]

11   Yes, certainly with stammering lips
and in a foreign language,
he will talk to this nation,

12   he who once told them: Here is rest;
let the weary rest.
Here is repose.
—But they would not listen.

13   That is why Yahweh now says:
*kav lakav, kav lakav,*
*sav lasav, sav lasav,*
*zeer sham, zeer sham.*
So that when they walk they may fall over
     backward
and be broken, snared and made captive.

## Against evil counselors

14   Listen to the word of Yahweh,
you scoffers,
rulers of this people
in Jerusalem.

15   You say, "We have made
a covenant with Mot,[b]
and with Sheol
we have made a pact.
The destructive whip, as it goes by,
will not catch us,
for we have made lies our refuge,
and falsehood our shelter."

### Oracle

16      That is why the Lord Yahweh says this:
See how I lay in Zion
a stone of witness,
a precious cornerstone, a foundation stone:
The believer shall not stumble.

17      And I will make justice the measure,
integrity the plumb line.

### Continuation of the poem against evil counselors

But hail will sweep away the refuge of lies
and floods overwhelm the shelter;

18      your covenant with Mot will be broken
and your pact with Sheol annulled.
When the destructive whip goes by
it will crush you;

19      each time it goes by,
it will seize you.
It will go by, morning after morning,
both day and night;
what panic there would be
if you were to understand what it meant!

20      The bed is too short to stretch in,
the blanket too narrow for covering.

21      Yes, as Yahweh did on Mount Perazim, he is
going to rise,
as he did in the Valley of Gibeon he is going
to stir himself
to do the deed, his extraordinary deed,
to work the work, his mysterious work.

22      Stop scoffing, then,
or your bonds will be tightened further;
for I have listened to the warrant of destruction
issued against the whole country
by the Lord Yahweh Sabaoth.

### The parable of the farmer

23      Listen closely to my words,
be attentive and understand what I am saying.

---

**28 a.** Described in the next verse as "stammering and in a foreign language": the impression made by Isaiah's preaching on his hearers.
**b.** Phoenician god, known to the Egyptians as Osiris.

24    Does the plowman do nothing but plow
         and turn the soil and harrow it?
25    Will he not, after he has leveled it,
         scatter fennel, sow cummin,
         put in wheat and barley
         and, on the edges, spelt?
26    He has been taught this discipline
         by his God who instructs him.

27    For fennel must not be crushed,
         nor a drag be rolled over cummin;
         fennel must be beaten with a stick,
         and cummin with a flail.
28    Does a man crush wheat? No;
         he does not thresh it endlessly.
         When he has rolled the drag over it
         he winnows it without crushing it.
29    This too comes from Yahweh Sabaoth,
         whose advice is always admirable,
         whose deeds are very great.

## Oracle on Ariel[a]

**29**

1    Woe, Ariel, Ariel,
         city where David encamped.
         Let a year or two pass,
         let the feasts make their full round
2    then I will lay siege to Ariel,
         and there will be moaning and bemoaning.
         You will be an Ariel for me,
3    like David I will encamp against you,
         I will blockade you with palisades,
         and mount siegeworks against you.

4    Thrown down—you will speak from the ground,
         your words will come muffled by dust.
         Your voice will rise from the earth like a ghost's,
         you will speak from the dust in a whisper.

5c    Suddenly, unexpectedly,
6    you shall be visited by Yahweh Sabaoth
         with thunder, earthquake, mighty din,
         hurricane, tempest, flame of devouring fire.

5ab    The horde of your enemies shall be scattered
         like fine dust,

the tyrant horde like flying chaff;
the horde of all the nations at war with Ariel
7    shall vanish like a dream, like a vision at night.

And all those fighting against her,
the entrenchments besieging her,
8    shall be like the hungry man who dreams he
            eats,
and wakes with an empty belly,

like the thirsty man who dreams he drinks
and wakes exhausted, his throat parched;
so shall it be with the horde of all the nations
making war on Mount Zion.

9    Be stupefied and stunned,
go blind, unseeing,
drunk but not on wine,
staggering but not through liquor.

10    For on you has Yahweh poured
a spirit of lethargy,
he has closed your eyes (the prophets),
he has veiled your heads (the seers).

### Secrecy of the revelation

11    For you every vision has become like the words of
a sealed book. You give it to someone able to read and
say, "Read that." He replies, "I cannot, because the
12  book is sealed." ·Or else you give the book to someone
who cannot read, and say, "Read that." He replies, "I
cannot read."

### Oracle

13    Yahweh has said: Because this people
approaches me only in words,
honors me only with lip service
while its heart is far from me,
and my religion, as far as it is concerned,
is nothing but human commandment, a lesson
            memorized,
14    very well, I shall have to go on

**29 a.** Ariel is "lion of God": here it signifies Jerusalem.

being prodigal of prodigious prodigies with this
people.
The wisdom of its sages shall decay,
the intelligence of its intelligent men shall be
shrouded.

### Against evil counselors

15
Woe to those who hide from Yahweh
to conceal their plans,
who scheme in the dark
and say, "Who can see us? Who can recognize
us?"

16
What perversity this is!
Is the potter no better than the clay?
Can something that was made say of its maker,
"He did not make me?"
Or a pot say of the potter,
"He is a fool?"

17
In a short time, a very short time,
shall not Lebanon become fertile land
and fertile land turn into forest?
18
The deaf, that day,
will hear the words of a book
and, after shadow and darkness,
the eyes of the blind will see.

19
But the lowly will rejoice in Yahweh even more
and the poorest exult in the Holy One of Israel;
20
for tyrants shall be no more, and scoffers vanish,
and all be destroyed who are disposed to do evil:

21
those who gossip to incriminate others,
those who try at the gate to trip the arbitrator
and get the upright man's case dismissed for
groundless reasons.

22
Therefore Yahweh speaks,
the God of the House of Jacob,
Abraham's redeemer:
No longer shall Jacob be ashamed,
no more shall his face grow pale,
23
for he shall see what my hands have done in
his midst,

he shall hold my name holy.
They will hallow the Holy One of Jacob,
stand in awe of the God of Israel.
24    Erring spirits will learn wisdom
and murmurers accept instruction.

## Against the embassy to Egypt

1  **30**  Woe to those rebellious sons!
—it is Yahweh who speaks.
They carry out plans that are not mine
and make alliances not inspired by me,
and so add
sin to sin.
2    They have left for Egypt,
without consulting me,
to take refuge in Pharaoh's protection,
to shelter in Egypt's shadow.
3    Pharaoh's protection will be your shame,
the shelter of Egypt's shadow your confounding.
4    For his ministers have gone to Zoan,
his ambassadors have already reached Hanes.[a]
5    All are carrying gifts
to a nation that will be of no use to them,
that will bring them neither aid, nor help,
nothing but shame and disgrace.

## A second oracle against the embassy

6    Oracle on the beasts of the Negeb.

Through the land of distress and of anguish,
of lioness and roaring lion,
of viper and flying serpent,

they bear their riches on donkeys' backs,
their treasures on camels' humps,
to a nation that is of no use to them,

7    to Egypt who will prove futile and empty to
them;
and so I call her
Rahab-do-nothing.

**30 a.** Zoan and Hanes are Tanis and Anusis, in the Egyptian delta.

### The testament of Isaiah

8
> Now go and inscribe this on a tablet,
> write it in a book,
> that it may serve in the time to come
> as a witness for ever:

9
> This is a rebellious people,
> they are lying sons,
> sons who will not listen
> to Yahweh's orders.

10
> To the seers they say,
> "See no visions";
> to the prophets,
> "Do not prophesy the truth to us,

> "tell us flattering things;
> have illusory visions;

11
> turn aside from the way, leave the path,
> take the Holy One out of our sight."

12
> So the Holy One of Israel says:
> Since you reject this warning
> and prefer to trust in wile and guile
> and to rely on these,

13
> then your guilt will prove
> to be for you
> a breach on the point of collapse,
> the bulge at the top of the city wall

> which suddenly and all at once
> comes crashing down,

14
> irretrievably shattered,
> smashed like an earthenware pot
> —so that of the fragments not one shard remains
> big enough to carry
> a cinder from the hearth or scoop water from
> the cistern.

15
> For thus says the Lord Yahweh, the Holy One
> of Israel:
> Your salvation lay in conversion and tranquillity,
> your strength, in complete trust;
> and you would have none of it.

16    "No," you said, "we will flee on horses."
      So be it, flee then!
      And you add, "In swift chariots."
      So be it, your pursuers will be swift too.

17    A thousand will flee at the threat of one
      and when five threaten you will flee,
      until what is left of you will be
      like a flagstaff on a mountain top,
      like a signal on a hill.

18    But Yahweh is waiting to be gracious to you,
      to rise and take pity on you,
      for Yahweh is a just God;
      happy are all who hope in him.

## The coming prosperity

19    Yes, people of Zion, you will live in Jerusalem and
weep no more. He will be gracious to you when he
20 hears your cry; when he hears he will answer. ·When
the Lord has given you the bread of suffering and the
water of distress, he who is your teacher will hide no
longer, and you will see your teacher with your own
21 eyes. ·Whether you turn to right or left, your ears will
hear these words behind you, "This is the way, follow
22 it." ·You will regard your silvered idols and gilded
images as unclean. You will throw them away like the
polluted things they are, shouting after them, "Good
23 riddance!" ·He will send rain for the seed you sow
in the ground, and the bread that the ground provides
will be rich and nourishing. Your cattle will graze,
24 that day, in wide pastures. ·Oxen and donkeys that
till the ground will eat a salted fodder, winnowed with
25 shovel and fork. ·On every lofty mountain, on every
high hill there will be streams and watercourses, on
the day of the great slaughter when the strongholds
26 fall. ·Then moonlight will be bright as sunlight and
sunlight itself be seven times brighter—like the light
of seven days in one—on the day Yahweh dresses the
wound of his people and heals the bruises his blows
have left.

### Assyria will be sacrificed

27
See, the name of Yahweh comes from afar,
blazing is his anger, heavy his exaction.
His lips brim with fury,
his tongue is like a devouring fire.

28
His breath is like a river in spate
coming up to the neck.
He comes to sift the nations with the sieve of destruction,
to put the bit of his bridle between the jaws of the nations.

30
Yahweh will make his majestic voice be heard
and display his arm falling to strike,
in the ferocity of his anger, in the glare of a devouring fire,
in cloudburst, downpour, hailstones.

31
For at the voice of Yahweh Assyria will be battered
and beaten with the rod.

32a
Each time he will feel the punishing rod
that Yahweh will lay on him.

29
The song you sing will be like that on a festal night
when hearts are gay,
or when to the sound of flute men make
a pilgrimage to the mountain of Yahweh,
to the rock of Israel,

32b
with music of tambourine and harp
and with dancing . . .

33
For in Topheth there has been prepared beforehand,[b]
yes, made ready for Molech,
a pit deep and wide
with straw and wood in plenty.
The breath of Yahweh, like a stream of brimstone,
will set fire to it.

### Against Egypt

1
**31** Woe to those who go down to Egypt
to seek help there,

who build their hopes on cavalry,
who rely on the number of chariots
and on the strength of mounted men,
but never look to the Holy One of Israel
nor consult Yahweh.

2      Yet he too is skilled in working disaster,
and he has not gone back on his word;
he will rise against the house of the wicked,
and against the protectors of evil men.

3      The Egyptian is a man, not a god,
his horses are flesh, not spirit;
Yahweh will stretch out his hand
to make the protector stumble;
the protected will fall
and all will perish together.

## Yahweh wages war against Assyria

4      Yes, this is what Yahweh has said to me:
As a lion or lion cub
growls over its prey,
and even when a whole band of shepherds
gathers against him,
he is not frightened by their shouting
or alarmed by the noise they make,
just so will Yahweh Sabaoth descend to fight
on Mount Zion and on its hill.

5      Like hovering birds
so will Yahweh Sabaoth protect Jerusalem,
he will protect it, rescue it,
spare it and save it.

6      Come back to the one you have so wickedly
betrayed,
sons of Israel.

7      Yes, that day, every one of you will throw away the
silver idols and gold idols which you have made with
your guilty hands.

8      Assyria will fall by a sword that is not man's,

**b.** Topheth is the place where human sacrifice was offered to
Molech.

will be devoured by a sword that is more than
    human,
he will flee before the sword
and his young warriors will be enslaved.

9   In his terror he will abandon his rock,
and his panic-stricken leaders desert their
    standard.
It is Yahweh who speaks, whose fire is in Zion,
and his furnace in Jerusalem.

### The integrity of the king

1    **32**   A king reigns by integrity
and princes rule by law;

2   each is like a shelter from the wind,
a refuge from the storm,
like streams of water in dry places,
like the shade of a great rock in a thirsty land.

3   The eyes of those who see will no longer be
    closed.

4   the ears of those who hear will be alert,
the heart of the hasty will learn to judge,
the tongue of stammerers will speak clearly,

5   the fool will no more be called noble,
nor the villain be styled honorable.

### Contrasts between fool and noble

6   For the fool speaks folly,
and his heart meditates wickedness,
that he may practice godlessness
and speak wild words about Yahweh,
and leave the hungry man's craving unsatisfied,
and refuse drink to the thirsty.

7   And the villain—his villainies are evil;
he devises wicked plots
to ruin the poor with lies

8   even when the cause of these lowly ones is just;
but the noble man plans only noble things
and bears himself nobly.

### A warning to idle women

9   Stand up, you idle women,
listen to my words;

you overconfident daughters,
pay attention to what I say.

10    Within one year and a few days
you will tremble, you overconfident women;
the grape harvest will be over,
gathering will not come again.

11    Shudder, you idle women,
tremble, you overconfident women;
strip, undress,
put sackcloth around your waists.

12    Beat your breasts,
for the pleasant fields,
for the fruitful vine,
for the soil of my people
13    where thorns and briars grow,
for all the happy houses,
for the gay city.

14    Since the palace has been abandoned
and the noisy city deserted,
Ophel and Keep become
caverns for ever,
the playground of wild asses
and the pasture of flocks.

### Salvation from Yahweh

15    Once more there will be poured on us
the spirit from above;
then shall the wilderness be fertile land
and fertile land become forest.

16    In the wilderness justice will come to live
and integrity in the fertile land;
17    integrity will bring peace,
justice give lasting security.

18    My people will live in a peaceful home,
in safe houses,
in quiet dwellings
19    —the forest shall be beaten down and the city
laid low.
20    Happy will you be, sowing by every stream,
letting ox and donkey roam free.

## Psalm of hope in Yahweh

**33**

1 Woe to you, ravager never ravaged,
plunderer never plundered!
When your ravaging is over, you shall be
ravaged;
when your plundering is done, you shall be
plundered.

2 Yahweh, have pity on us,
we hope in you.
Be our strong arm each morning,
our salvation in time of distress.

3 At the sound of your threat peoples flee,
when you rise nations scatter,
4 they gather loot as the grasshopper gathers,
they leap on it as locusts leap.

5 Yahweh is exalted, for he is enthroned above,
and fills Zion with justice and integrity.

6 Your continuance is assured;
wisdom and knowledge are riches that save,
the fear of Yahweh is his treasure.

## The intervention of Yahweh

7 Look, Ariel is lamenting in the streets,
the ambassadors of peace weep bitterly.

8 The highways are deserted,
no travelers use the roads.
Treaties are broken, witnesses despised,
there is respect for no one.

9 The land mourns, it pines away,
Lebanon is withered with shame,
Sharon is a desert,
Bashan and Carmel are stripped bare.

10 "Now I stand up," says Yahweh
"now I rise to my full height.
11 You have conceived chaff, you will give birth
to straw,
my breath shall devour you like fire.

12      "The peoples will be reduced to lime,
     like cut thorns they will be burned in the fire.
13      You who are far away, listen to what I have
         done,
     and you who are near, realize my strength."

14      Sinners in Zion are struck with horror
     and fear seizes on the godless.
     Which of us can live with this devouring fire,
     which of us exist in everlasting flames?

15      —He who acts with integrity,
     who speaks sincerely
     and rejects extortionate profit,
     who waves away bribes from his hands,
     shuts suggestions of murder out of his ears
     and closes his eyes against crime;

16      this man will dwell in the heights,
     he will find refuge in a citadel built on rock,
     bread will be given him, he shall not want for
         water.

### The glorious future

17      Your eyes are going to look on a king in his
         beauty,
     they will see an immense country;
18      your heart will look back on its fears:
     where is he who counted,
     where is he who weighed out,
     where is he who counted the precious stones?
19      You will no longer see the overweening people,
     the people of obscure, unintelligible speech,
     of barbarous, senseless tongue.
20      Look on Zion, city of our feasts,
     your eyes will see Jerusalem
     as a home that is secure,
     a tent not to be moved:
     its pegs not pulled out,
     not one of its ropes broken.

21      There Yahweh is princely to us,
     on the banks of broad-spreading rivers,
     where there rows no galley,

23a
    there passes no majestic ship:
    its tackle hangs loose,
    it supports the mast no longer,
    it does not hoist the pennon.

22
    For Yahweh is our judge, Yahweh our lawgiver,
    Yahweh our King and our savior.

23b
    Then immense booty shall be shared out,
    even the lame fall to plundering,

24
    no one living there shall say, "I am sickly";
    the people who live there will be forgiven all
        their faults.

### The end of Edom

1
**34** Come near and listen all you races,
    pay attention all you nations,
    listen, earth and all that you hold,
    world and all that comes from you.

2
    Yahweh is angry with all the nations,
    enraged with all their hordes.
    He has vowed them to destruction,
    and marked them down for slaughter.

3
    Their dead are thrown into the streets,
    a stench comes up from their corpses,
    the mountains run with their blood,

4
    the armies of heaven rot.

    The heavens are rolled up like a scroll
    and their armies all drop like leaves,
    like vine leaves falling,
    like falling fig leaves.

5
    For my sword has drunk deep in the
        heavens . . .
    See now how it slashes through Edom,
    through the people I have condemned to be
        punished.

6
    The sword of Yahweh is gorged with blood,
    it is glutted with fat,
    the blood of lambs and goats,
    the fat of the saddle of rams.

    For Yahweh has a sacrifice in Bozrah,
    a great slaughter in the land of Edom.

7    But instead of wild oxen, nations fall,
     in place of bulls, a race of mighty men.

     Their land is drenched with blood,
     its dust is sodden with fat,
8    for this is the day of Yahweh's vengeance,
     the year of revenge for the defender of Zion.

9    Its streams turn into pitch,
     its dust into brimstone,
     its land becomes blazing pitch . . .

10   Never quenched night or day,
     its smoke goes up for ever,
     it shall lie waste age after age,
     no one will pass through it.

11   It will be the haunt of pelican and hedgehog,
     the owl and the raven will live there;
     over it Yahweh will stretch the measuring line
          of chaos
     and the plumb line of emptiness.

12   The satyrs will make their home there,
     its nobles will be no more,
     kings will not be proclaimed there,
     all its princes will be brought to nothing.

13   Thorns will grow in the palaces there,
     thistles and nettles in its fortresses,
     it will be a lair for jackals,
     a lodging for ostriches.

14   Wild cats will meet hyenas there,
     the satyrs will call to each other,
     there too will Lilith take cover
     seeking rest.

15   The viper will nest and lay eggs there,
     will brood and hatch its eggs;
     kites will gather there
16c  and make it their meeting place.

16ab Search in the book of Yahweh, and read,
     not one of these is missing;

for his mouth has ordained it,
and his spirit has brought them together.

17 He has drawn lots for the share of each,
his hand has divided the land with the line.
They shall possess it for ever,
and live there age after age.

## The judgment of God

1
35 Let the wilderness and the dry lands exult,
let the wasteland rejoice and bloom,
2 let it bring forth flowers like the jonquil,
let it rejoice and sing for joy.

The glory of Lebanon is bestowed on it,
the splendor of Carmel and Sharon;
they shall see the glory of Yahweh,
the splendor of our God.

3 Strengthen all weary hands,
steady all trembling knees
4 and say to all faint hearts,
"Courage! Do not be afraid.

"Look, your God is coming,
vengeance is coming,
the retribution of God;
he is coming to save you."

5 Then the eyes of the blind shall be opened,
the ears of the deaf unsealed,
6 then the lame shall leap like a deer
and the tongues of the dumb sing for joy;

for water gushes in the desert,
streams in the wasteland,
7 the scorched earth becomes a lake,
the parched land springs of water.

The lairs where the jackals used to live
become thickets of reed and papyrus . . .

8 And through it will run a highway undefiled
which shall be called the Sacred Way;
the unclean may not travel by it,
nor fools stray along it.

9    No lion will be there
     nor any fierce beast roam about it,
     but the redeemed will walk there,
10   for those Yahweh has ransomed shall return.

     They will come to Zion shouting for joy,
     everlasting joy on their faces;
     joy and gladness will go with them
     and sorrow and lament be ended.


## APPENDIX

### Sennacherib's invasion

1 **36** In the fourteenth year of King Hezekiah, Sennacherib king of Assyria attacked all the fortified
2 towns of Judah and captured them. ·From Lachish the king of Assyria sent the cupbearer-in-chief with a large force to King Hezekiah in Jerusalem. The cupbearer-in-chief took up a position near the conduit of the upper
3 pool on the road to the Fuller's Field. ·The master of the palace, Eliakim son of Hilkiah, Shebna the secretary and the herald Joah son of Asaph went out to him.
4 The cupbearer-in-chief said to them, "Say to Hezekiah, 'The great king, the king of Assyria, says to you: What
5 makes you so confident? ·Do you think empty words are as good as strategy and military strength? Who are
6 you relying on, to dare to rebel against me? ·We know you are relying on that broken reed—Egypt—which pricks and pierces the hand of the man who leans on it.—That is what Pharaoh, king of Egypt, is like to all
7 who rely on him.—·You may say to me: We rely on Yahweh our God, but are they not his high places and altars that Hezekiah has suppressed, saying to the people of Judah and Jerusalem: Here is the altar before which
8 you must worship? ·Come, make a wager with my lord the king of Assyria: I will give you two thousand horses
9 if you can find horsemen to ride them. ·How could you repulse a single one of the least of my master's servants? And yet you have relied on Egypt for chariots
10 and horsemen. ·And lastly, have I come up against this country to lay it waste without warrant from Yahweh?

Yahweh himself said to me: March against this country and lay it waste.' "

11     Eliakim, Shebna and Joah said to the cupbearer-in-chief, "Please speak to your servants in Aramaic, for we understand it; do not speak to us in the Judaean language within earshot of the people on the ramparts."

12 But the cupbearer-in-chief said, "Do you think my lord sent me here to say these things to your master or to you? On the contrary, it was to the people sitting on the ramparts who, like you, are doomed to eat their own dung and drink their own urine."

13     Then the cupbearer-in-chief stood erect and, shouting loudly in the Judaean language, called out, "Listen 14 to the words of the great king, the king of Assyria. ·The king says to you: 'Do not let Hezekiah delude you! He 15 will be powerless to save you. ·Do not let Hezekiah persuade you to rely on Yahweh by saying: Yahweh is sure to save us; this city will not fall into the power 16 of the king of Assyria.' ·Do not listen to Hezekiah, for 17 the king of Assyria says: Make peace with me, ·surrender to me, and every one of you will eat the fruit of his own vine and of his own fig tree and drink the water of his own cistern until I come and deport you to a country like your own, a land of corn and good 18 wine, a land of bread and of vineyards. ·Do not let Hezekiah delude you by saying: Yahweh will save you. Has any god of any nation saved his country from the 19 power of the king of Assyria? ·Where are the gods of Hamath and Arpad? Where are the gods of Sepharvaim? Where are the gods of the land of Samaria? Did 20 they save Samaria from me? ·Tell me which of all the gods of these countries have saved their countries from my hands, for Yahweh to be able to save Jerusalem?"

21     They kept silence and said nothing in reply, since this was the king's order: "Do not answer him," he 22 had said. ·The master of the palace, Eliakim son of Hilkiah, Shebna the secretary and the herald Joah son of Asaph, with their garments torn, went to Hezekiah and reported what the cupbearer-in-chief had said.

### The prophet Isaiah is consulted

1 37 On hearing this, King Hezekiah tore his garments, covered himself with sackcloth and went

2 to the Temple of Yahweh. ·He sent the master of the
palace, Eliakim, Shebna the secretary and the elders
of the priests, covered in sackcloth, to the prophet
3 Isaiah son of Amoz. ·They said to him, "This is what
Hezekiah says, 'Today is a day of suffering, of punishment, of disgrace. Children come to birth and there is
4 no strength to bring them forth. ·May Yahweh your
God hear the words of the cupbearer-in-chief whom
his master, the king of Assyria, has sent to insult the
living God, and may Yahweh your God punish the
words he has heard! Offer your prayer for the remnant
that is left.' "
5    When the ministers of King Hezekiah had come to
6 Isaiah, ·he replied, "Say to your master, 'Yahweh says
this: Do not be afraid of the words you have heard
or the blasphemies the minions of the king of Assyria
7 have uttered against me. ·I am going to put a spirit
in him, and when he hears a rumor he will return to
his own country and in that country I will bring him
down with the sword.' "

**The cupbearer returns to his master**

8    The cupbearer went back and rejoined the king of
Assyria at Libnah, which he was attacking. The cupbearer had already learned that the king of Assyria had
9 left Lachish, ·since he had received this news about
Tirhakah king of Cush: "He has set out to fight you."

**Second account of Sennacherib's activities**

   Sennacherib sent messengers to Hezekiah again, say-
10 ing, ·"Tell this to Hezekiah king of Judah, 'Do not let
your God on whom you are relying deceive you when
he says: Jerusalem shall not fall into the power of the
11 king of Assyria. ·You have learned by now what the
kings of Assyria have done to every country, putting
them all under the ban. Are you likely to be spared?
12 What power to help did the gods have of those nations
my fathers destroyed, Gozen, Haran, Rezeph and the
13 Edenites who were in Tel Basar? ·Where are the king
of Hamath, the king of Arpad, the kings of Sepharvaim, of Hena, of Ivvah?' "
14    Hezekiah took the letter from the hands of the messengers and read it; he then went up to the Temple of

15 Yahweh and spread it out before Yahweh. ·Hezekiah
16 said this prayer in the presence of Yahweh, ·"Yahweh
Sabaoth, God of Israel, enthroned on the cherubs, you
alone are God of all the kingdoms of the earth, you
have made heaven and earth.

17      "Give ear, Yahweh, and listen.
        Open your eyes, Yahweh, and see.
        Hear the words of Sennacherib
        who has sent to insult the living God.

18   "It is true, Yahweh, that the kings of Assyria have
19 exterminated all the nations and their countries, ·they
have thrown their gods on the fire, for these were not
gods but the work of men's hands, wood and stone,
20 and hence they have destroyed them. ·But now, Yahweh our God, save us from his hand, and let all the
kingdoms of the earth know that you alone are God,
Yahweh."

## Isaiah intervenes

21   Then Isaiah son of Amoz sent to Hezekiah. "This,"
he said, "is what Yahweh, the God of Israel, says in
answer to the prayer you have addressed to me about
22 Sennacherib king of Assyria. ·Here is the oracle that
Yahweh has pronounced against him:

23      'She despises you, she scorns you,
        the virgin, daughter of Zion;
        she tosses her head behind you,
        the daughter of Jerusalem.
        Whom have you insulted, whom did you
            blaspheme?
        Against whom raised your voice
        and lifted your insolent eyes?
        Against the Holy One of Israel.
24      Through your minions you have insulted the
            Lord;
        you have said: With my many chariots
        I have climbed the tops of mountains,
        the utmost peaks of Lebanon.
        I have felled its tall forest of cedars,
        its finest cypresses.

I have reached its furthest recesses,
its forest garden.

25    Yes I have dug wells and drunk
of alien waters;
I have put down my feet, and have dried up
all the rivers of Egypt.

26    'Do you hear? Long ago
I planned for it,
from days of old I designed it,
now I carry it out.
Your part was to bring down in heaps of ruins
fortified cities.

27    Their inhabitants, hands feeble,
dismayed, discomfited,
were like plants of the field,
like tender grass,
like grass of housetop and meadow,
under the east wind.

28    I know whenever you rise ·and whenever you
         sit,
your going out, your coming in.

29    Because you have raved against me
and your insolence has come to my ears,
I will put my ring through your nostrils,
my bit between your lips,
to make you return by the road
on which you came.

### A sign for Hezekiah

30    'This shall be the sign for you:
This year will be eaten the self-sown grain,
next year what sprouts in the fallow,
but in the third year sow and reap,
plant vineyards and eat their fruit.

31    The surviving remnant of the House of Judah
         shall bring forth
new roots below and fruits above.

32    For a remnant shall go out from Jerusalem,
and survivors from Mount Zion.
The jealous love of Yahweh Sabaoth will ac-
complish this.

### An oracle on Assyria

33 "This, then, is what Yahweh says about the king of Assyria:

> 'He will not enter this city,
> he will let fly no arrow against it,
> confront it with no shield,
> throw up no earthwork against it.

34
> By the road that he came on he will return;
> he shall not enter this city. It is Yahweh who
> speaks.

35
> I will protect this city and save it
> for my own sake and for the sake of my servant
> David.' "

### Sennacherib is punished

36      That same night the angel of Yahweh went out and struck down a hundred and eighty-five thousand men in the Assyrian camp. In the early morning, when it was time to get up, there they lay, so many corpses.

37      Sennacherib struck camp and left; he returned home
38 and stayed in Nineveh. ·One day when he was worshiping in the temple of his god Nisroch, his sons Adrammelech and Sharezer struck him down with the sword and escaped into the land of Ararat. His son Esarhaddon succeeded him.

### The illness and cure of Hezekiah

1 **38** In those days Hezekiah fell ill and was at the point of death. The prophet Isaiah son of Amoz came and said to him, "Yahweh says this, 'Put your affairs in order, for you are going to die, you will not
2 live.'" ·Hezekiah turned his face to the wall and ad-
3 dressed this prayer to Yahweh, ·"Ah, Yahweh, remember, I beg you, how I have behaved faithfully and with sincerity of heart in your presence and done what is right in your eyes." And Hezekiah shed many tears.

4
5      Then the word of Yahweh came to Isaiah, ·"Go and say to Hezekiah, 'Yahweh, the God of David your ancestor, says this: I have heard your prayer and seen your tears. I will cure you: in three days' time you shall go up to the Temple of Yahweh. I will add fifteen years

6 to your life. ·I will save you from the hands of the king
of Assyria, I will protect this city.' "

21 "Bring a fig poultice," Isaiah said, "apply it to the
22 ulcer and he will recover." ·Hezekiah said, "What is
the sign to tell me that I shall be going up to the Temple
7 of Yahweh?" ·"Here," Isaiah replied, "is the sign from
8 Yahweh that he will do what he has said. ·Look, I shall
make the shadow cast by the declining sun go back ten
steps on the steps of Ahaz." And the sun went back
the ten steps by which it had declined.

### The canticle of Hezekiah

9   Canticle of Hezekiah king of Judah after his illness
and recovery.

10      I said: In the noon of my life
        I have to depart
        for the gates of Sheol,
        I am deprived of the rest of my years.

11      I said: I shall never see Yahweh again
        in the land of the living,
        never again look on any man
        of those who inhabit the earth.

12      My tent is pulled up, and thrown away
        like the tent of a shepherd;
        like a weaver you roll up my life
        to cut it from the loom.

        From dawn to night you are compassing my
                end,
13      I cry aloud until the morning;
        like a lion he crushes all my bones,
        from dawn to night you are compassing my end.

14      I am twittering like a swallow,
        I am moaning like a dove,
        my eyes turn to the heights,
        take care of me, be my safeguard.

15      What can I say? Of what can I speak to him?
        It is he who is at work;
        I will give glory to you all the years of my life
        for my sufferings.

16      Lord, my heart will live for you,
        my spirit will live for you alone.
        You will cure me and give me life,
17      my suffering will turn to health.

        It is you who have kept my soul
        from the pit of nothingness,
        you have thrust all my sins
        behind your back.

18      For Sheol does not praise you,
        Death does not extol you;
        those who go down to the pit do not go on
                trusting
        in your faithfulness.

19      The living, the living are the ones who praise
                you,
        as I do today.
        Fathers tell their sons
        about your faithfulness.

20      Yahweh, come to my help
        and we will make our harps resound
        all the days of our life
        in front of the Temple of Yahweh.

## The Babylonian embassy

1  **39** At that time, the king of Babylon, Merodach-
          baladan son of Baladan, sent letters and a gift
to Hezekiah, for he had heard of his illness and re-
2  covery. ·Hezekiah was delighted at this and showed
the messengers his treasure house, the silver, gold,
spices, precious oil, his armory too, and everything
there was in his storehouses. There was nothing Hezekiah did not show them in his palace or in his whole
domain.
3      Then the prophet Isaiah came to King Hezekiah and
asked him, "What have these men said, and where have
they come from?" Hezekiah answered, "They have
4  come from a faraway country, from Babylon." ·Isaiah
said, "What have they seen in your palace?" "They
have seen everything in my palace," Hezekiah answered. "There is nothing in my storehouses that I have
not shown them."

5 Then Isaiah said to Hezekiah, "Listen to the word
6 of Yahweh Sabaoth, ·'The days are coming when everything in your palace, everything that your ancestors
have amassed until now, will be carried off to Babylon.
7 Not a thing will be left,' says Yahweh. ·'Sons sprung
from you, sons begotten by you, will be chosen to be
8 eunuchs in the palace of the king of Babylon.'" ·Heze-
kiah said to Isaiah, "This word of Yahweh that you
announce is reassuring," for he was thinking, "There
is going to be peace and security during my own lifetime."


## II. THE BOOK OF THE CONSOLATION OF ISRAEL


### The calling of the prophet

1  **40**  "Console my people, console them,"
            says your God.
2            "Speak to the heart of Jerusalem
             and call to her
             that her time of service is ended,
             that her sin is atoned for,
             that she has received from the hand of Yahweh
             double punishment for all her crimes."

3            A voice cries, "Prepare in the wilderness
             a way for Yahweh.
             Make a straight highway for our God
             across the desert.
4            Let every valley be filled in,
             every mountain and hill be laid low,
             let every cliff become a plain,
             and the ridges a valley;
5            then the glory of Yahweh shall be revealed
             and all mankind shall see it;
             for the mouth of Yahweh has spoken."
6            A voice commands: "Cry!"
             and I answered, "What shall I cry?"
             —"All flesh is grass
             and its beauty like the wild flower's.

7
The grass withers, the flower fades
when the breath of Yahweh blows on them.
(The grass is without doubt the people.)

8
The grass withers, the flower fades,
but the word of our God remains for ever."

### Prophecy of the theophany

9
Go up on a high mountain,
joyful messenger to Zion.
Shout with a loud voice,
joyful messenger to Jerusalem.
Shout without fear,
say to the towns of Judah,
"Here is your God."

10
Here is the Lord Yahweh coming with power,
his arm subduing all things to him.
The prize of his victory is with him,
his trophies all go before him.

11
He is like a shepherd feeding his flock,
gathering lambs in his arms,
holding them against his breast
and leading to their rest the mother ewes.

### The majesty of God

12
Who was it measured the water of the sea in
the hollow of his hand
and calculated the dimensions of the heavens,
gauged the whole earth to the bushel,
weighed the mountains in scales,
the hills in a balance?

13
Who could have advised the spirit of Yahweh,
what counselor could have instructed him?

14
Whom has he consulted to enlighten him,
and to learn the path of justice
and discover the most skillful ways?

15
See, the nations are like a drop on the pail's rim,
they count as a grain of dust on the scales.
See, the islands weigh no more than fine powder.

16
Lebanon is not enough for the fires
nor its beasts for the holocaust.

17
All the nations are as nothing in his presence,
for him they count as nothingness and emptiness.

18    To whom could you liken God?
      What image could you contrive of him?

19    A craftsman casts the figure,
      a goldsmith plates it with gold
      and casts silver chains for it.
20c   For it a clever sculptor seeks
20a   precious palm wood,
20b   selects wood that will not decay
20d   to set up a sturdy image.

21    Did you not know,
      had you not heard?
      Was it not told you from the beginning?
      Have you not understood how the earth was
         founded?
22    He lives above the circle of the earth,
      its inhabitants look like grasshoppers.
      He has stretched out the heavens like a cloth,
      spread them like a tent for men to live in.
23    He reduces princes to nothing,
      he annihilates the rulers of the world.
24    Scarcely are they planted, scarcely sown,
      scarcely has their stem taken root in the earth,
      than he blows on them. Then they wither
      and the storm carries them off like straw.

25    "To whom could you liken me
      and who could be my equal?" says the Holy
         One.
26    Lift your eyes and look.
      Who made these stars
      if not he who drills them like an army,
      calling each one by name?
      So mighty is his power, so great his strength,
      that not one fails to answer.

### The might of Providence

27    How can you say, Jacob,
      how can you insist, Israel,
      "My destiny is hidden from Yahweh,
      my rights are ignored by my God?"
28    Did you not know?
      Had you not heard?

Yahweh is an everlasting God,
he created the boundaries of the earth.
He does not grow tired or weary,
his understanding is beyond fathoming.

29     He gives strength to the wearied,
he strengthens the powerless.

30     Young men may grow tired and weary,
youths may stumble,

31     but those who hope in Yahweh renew their
strength,
they put out wings like eagles.
They run and do not grow weary,
walk and never tire.

## The calling of Cyrus[a]

1

41

Islands, keep silence before me,
let the people renew their strength.
Let them come forward and speak,
let us appear together for judgment.

2     "Who roused from the east
him that victory hails at every step?
Who presents him with nations,
subdues kings to him?

"His sword makes dust of them
and his bow scatters them like straw.

3     He pursues them and advances unhindered,
his feet scarcely touching the road.

4     "Who is the author of this deed
if not he who calls the generations from the
beginning?
I, Yahweh, who am the first
and shall be with the last."

5     The islands see him and take fright,
the limits of the earth tremble:
they approach, they are here.

6     Men help one another,
they say to each other, "Take heart!"

7     The craftsman encourages the goldsmith,
the man who beats out with the hammer encourages the man who strikes the anvil.

Of the soldering he says, "It is sound,"
and fastens the idol with nails
to keep it steady.[b]

## God is with Israel

8    You, Israel, my servant,
     Jacob whom I have chosen,
     descendant of Abraham my friend.

9    You whom I brought from the confines of the
               earth
     and called from the ends of the world;
     you to whom I said, "You are my servant,
     I have chosen you, not rejected you,"

10   do not be afraid, for I am with you;
     stop being anxious and watchful, for I am your
               God.
     I give you strength, I bring you help,
     I uphold you with my victorious right hand.

11   Yes, all those who raged against you,
     shall be put to shame and confusion;
     they who fought against you
     shall be destroyed, and perish.

12   You will seek but never find them,
     those enemies of yours.
     They shall be destroyed and brought to nothing,
     those who made war on you.

13   For I, Yahweh, your God,
     I am holding you by the right hand;
     I tell you, "Do not be afraid,
     I will help you."

14   Do not be afraid, Jacob, poor worm,
     Israel, puny mite.
     I will help you—it is Yahweh who speaks—
     the Holy One of Israel is your redeemer.

15   See, I turn you into a threshing sled,
     new, with doubled teeth;

**41 a.** The king who freed the people of Judah from their captivity
in the Babylonian exile.
**b.** V. 6 and 7 are in interpolation, and belong with 40:19–20.

you shall thresh and crush the mountains,
and turn the hills to chaff.

16
You shall winnow them and the wind will blow
them away,
the gale will scatter them.
But you yourself will rejoice in Yahweh,
and glory in the Holy One of Israel.

## Miracles of the new Exodus

17
The poor and needy ask for water, and there
is none,
their tongue is parched with thirst.
I, Yahweh, will answer them,
I, the God of Israel, will not abandon them.

18
I will make rivers well up on barren heights,
and fountains in the midst of valleys;
turn the wilderness into a lake,
and dry ground into waterspring.

19
In the wilderness I will put cedar trees,
acacias, myrtles, olives.
In the desert I will plant juniper,
plane tree and cypress side by side;

20
so that men may see and know,
may all observe and understand
that the hand of Yahweh has done this,
that the Holy One of Israel has created it.

## Yahweh is the only God

21
"Produce your defense," says Yahweh,
"present your case," says Jacob's king.

22
"Let them come forward and tell us
what is going to happen next.
What could they tell us of the past
to make it worth our notice?
Or will you discourse to us of future things
and let us know their outcome?

23
Tell us what is to happen in the future,
and so convince us you are gods.
Do something at least
so that we can note it and all see it.

24　　No, you are nothing and your works are
　　　　　nothingness;
　　to choose you would be an outrage."

### Yahweh foretells victory for Cyrus

25　　I roused him from the north to come,
　　from the rising sun I summoned him by name.
　　He has trampled the satraps like mortar,
　　like a potter treading clay.

26　　Who predicted this from the beginning so we
　　　　　might know it,
　　who foretold it long ago so we might say, "It
　　　　　is right?"
　　No one predicted it,
　　no, no one proclaimed it,
　　no, no one heard you speak.

27　　I had said in Zion beforehand, "Here they
　　　　　come!"
　　I had sent a bearer of good news to Jerusalem.

28　　I looked, but there was no one,
　　there was not a single counselor among them
　　who, if I asked, could give an answer.

29　　Taken altogether they are nothing;
　　their works are nothingess,
　　their images wind and emptiness.

### First song of the servant of Yahweh: part one

1　**42**　Here is my servant whom I uphold,
　　　　my chosen one in whom my soul delights.
　　I have endowed him with my spirit
　　that he may bring true justice to the nations.

2　　He does not cry out or shout aloud,
　　or make his voice heard in the streets.

3　　He does not break the crushed reed,
　　nor quench the wavering flame.

　　Faithfully he brings true justice;
4　　he will neither waver, nor be crushed
　　until true justice is established on earth,
　　for the islands are awaiting his law.

### Part two

5
    Thus says God, Yahweh,
    he who created the heavens and spread them
        out,
    who gave shape to the earth and what comes
        from it,
    who gave breath to its people
    and life to the creatures that move in it:

6
    I, Yahweh, have called you to serve the cause
        of right;
    I have taken you by the hand and formed you;
    I have appointed you as a covenant of the peo-
        ple and light of the nations,

7
    to open the eyes of the blind,
    to free captives from prison,
    and those who live in darkness from the
        dungeon.

8
    My name is Yahweh,
    I will not yield my glory to another,
    nor my honor to idols.

9
    See how former predictions have come true.
    Fresh things I now foretell;
    before they appear I tell you of them.

### Hymn of triumph

10
    Sing a new hymn to Yahweh!
    Let his praise resound from the ends of the
        earth,
    let the sea and all that it holds sing his praises,
    the islands and those who inhabit them.

11
    Let the desert and its cities raise their voice,
    the camp where Kedar lives.
    Let the inhabitants of Sela cry aloud
    and shout from the mountain tops.

12
    Let them give glory to Yahweh
    and let the people of the islands voice his praise.

13
    Yahweh advances like a hero,
    his fury is stirred like a warrior's.

He gives the war shout, raises the hue and cry,
marches valiantly against his foes.

14      "From the beginning I have been silent,
I have kept quiet, held myself in check.
I groan like a woman in labor,
I suffocate, I stifle.

15      "I will turn mountain and hill to desert,
wither all their greenery,
turn rivers to pools
and dry up lakes.

16      "But I will make the blind walk along the road
and lead them along paths.
I will turn darkness into light before them
and rocky places into level tracks.

"These things I will do,
and not leave them undone."

17      All who trust in idols
shall withdraw in shame,
all those who say to images of cast metal,
"You are our gods."

## The blinding of the people

18      Listen, you deaf!
Look and see, you blind!
19      Who so blind as my servant,
so deaf as the messenger I send?
(Who so blind as my envoy,
so deaf as the servant of Yahweh?)
20      You have seen many things but not observed
them;
your ears are open but you do not hear.
21      It is Yahweh's will, for the sake of his integrity,
to make his Law great and glorious.
22      But this is a people all pillaged and plundered,
trapped in caves,
hidden in dungeons.
They are looted, with no one to rescue them,
robbed, with no one to say, "Give it back!"
23      Which of you listening to this,

will pay attention and mark it, against the time
to come?

24
Who handed Jacob over to the robber,
Israel to the pillagers?
Was it not Yahweh? We had sinned against him,
we had refused to follow his ways
or obey his Law.

25
On him he poured out the blaze of his anger
and the furies of war.
It enveloped him in flames and he did not notice,
it burned him up, and he gave it no thought.

### The liberation of Israel

43
1
But now, thus says Yahweh,
who created you, Jacob,
who formed you, Israel:

Do not be afraid, for I have redeemed you;
I have called you by your name, you are mine.
2
Should you pass through the sea, I will be with
you;
or through rivers, they will not swallow you up.
Should you walk through fire, you will not be
scorched
and the flames will not burn you.
3
For I am Yahweh, your God,
the Holy One of Israel, your savior.

I give Egypt for your ransom,
and exchange Cush and Seba for you.
4
Because you are precious in my eyes,
because you are honored and I love you,
I give men in exchange for you,
peoples in return for your life.
5
Do not be afraid, for I am with you.

I will bring your offspring from the east,
and gather you from the west.
6
To the north I will say, "Give them up,"
and to the south, "Do not hold them."
Bring back my sons from far away,
my daughters from the end of the earth,
7
all those who bear my name,

whom I have created for my glory,
whom I have formed, whom I have made.

## Yahweh alone is God

8    Bring forward the people that is blind, yet has
         eyes,
     that is deaf and yet has ears.
9    Let all the nations muster
     and assemble with every race.
     Which of them ever declared this
     or foretold this in the past?
     Let them bring their witnesses to prove them
         right,
     let men hear them so that they may say, "It is
         true."
10   You yourselves are my witnesses—it is Yahweh
         who speaks—
     my servants whom I have chosen,
     that men may know and believe me
     and understand that it is I.
     No god was formed before me,
     nor will be after me.
11   I, I am Yahweh,
     there is no other savior but me.
12   It is I who have spoken, have saved, have made
         the proclamation,
     not any strangers among you.
     You are my witnesses—it is Yahweh who
         speaks—
13   and I, I am your God, ·I am he from eternity.
     No one can deliver from my hand,
     I act and no one can reverse it.

## Babylon will be destroyed

14   Thus says Yahweh,
     your redeemer, the Holy One of Israel:

     For your sake I send an army against Babylon;
     I will knock down the prison bars
     and the Chaldaeans will break into laments.
15   I am Yahweh, your Holy One,
     the creator of Israel, your king.

### Miracles of the new Exodus

16
    Thus says Yahweh,
    who made a way through the sea,
    a path in the great waters;

17
    who put chariots and horse in the field
    and a powerful army,
    which lay there never to rise again,
    snuffed out, put out like a wick:

18
    No need to recall the past,
    no need to think about what was done before.

19
    See, I am doing a new deed,
    even now it comes to light; can you not see it?
    Yes, I am making a road in the wilderness,
    paths in the wilds.

20
    The wild beasts will honor me,
    jackals and ostriches,
    because I am putting water in the wilderness
    (rivers in the wild)
    to give my chosen people drink.

21
    The people I have formed for myself
    will sing my praises.

### The ingratitude of Israel

22
    Jacob, you have not invoked me,
    you have not troubled yourself, Israel, on my
        behalf.

23
    You have not brought me your sheep for
        holocausts,
    nor honored me with sacrifices.
    I have never burdened you with oblations,
    nor troubled you for incense.

24
    You have spent no money on fragrant cane
        for me,
    you have not filled me with the fat of your
        sacrifices.
    Instead you have burdened me with your sins,
    troubled me with your iniquities.

25
    I it is, I it is, who must blot out everything
    and not remember your sins.

26
    Cast your mind back, let us judge this together;

state your own case and prove your innocence.
27  Your first father[a] sinned,
   your mediators have rebelled against me.
28  Your princes have profaned my sanctuary.
   So I have handed Jacob over to the ban,
   and Israel to insults.

## The blessing for Israel

1   But now listen, Jacob my servant,
2 **44** Israel whom I have chosen.
   Thus says Yahweh who made you,
   who formed you from the womb, who is your
      help:
   Do not be afraid, Jacob my servant,
   Jeshurun whom I have chosen.

3   For I will pour out water on the thirsty soil,
   streams on the dry ground.
   I will pour my spirit on your descendants,
   my blessing on your children.
4   They shall grow like grass where there is plenty
      of water,
   like poplars by running streams.

5   One man will say, "I belong to Yahweh,"
   another will call himself by Jacob's name.
   On his hand another will write "Yahweh"
   and be surnamed "Israel."

## Monotheism without compromise

6   Thus says Israel's king
   and his redeemer, Yahweh Sabaoth:
   I am the first and the last;
   there is no other God besides me.
7   Who is like me? Let him stand up and speak,
   let him show himself and argue it out before
      me.
   Who from the very beginning foretold the
      future?
   Let them tell us what is yet to come.
8   Have no fear, do not be afraid;
   have I not told you and revealed it long ago?

**43 a.** Jacob, Gn. 27:1–29.

You are my witnesses, is there any other God
    besides me?
There is no Rock; I know of none.

## A satire on idolatry

9 They are all makers of idols; they are nothing and
the works they prize are useless. Their servants see
nothing, they understand nothing, and so they will be
10 put to shame. ·Who ever fashioned a god or cast an
11 image without hope of gain? ·Watch how its devotees
will be put to shame, how its sculptors will blush. Let
them all come together, let them appear in court. They
will be both terrified and ashamed.

12 The blacksmith works on it over the fire and beats
it into shape with a hammer. He works on it with his
strong arm till he is hungry and tired; drinking no
water, he is exhausted.

13 The wood carver takes his measurements, outlines
the image with chalk, carves it with chisels, following
the outline with dividers. He shapes it to human pro-
portions, and gives it a human face, for it to live in a
14 temple. ·He cut down a cedar, or else took a cypress
or an oak which he selected from the trees in the forest,
or maybe he planted a cedar and the rain made it
15 grow. ·For the common man it is so much fuel; he
uses it to warm himself, he also burns it to bake his
bread. But this fellow makes a god of it and worships
it; he makes an idol of it and bows down before it.
16 Half of it he burns in the fire, on the live embers he
roasts meat, eats it and is replete. He warms himself
too. "Ah!" says he, "I am warm; I have a fire here!"
17 With the rest he makes his god, his idol; he bows down
before it and worships it and prays to it. "Save me,"
he says, "because you are my god."

18 They know nothing, understand nothing. Their eyes
19 are shut to all seeing, their heart to all reason. ·They
never think, they lack the knowledge and wit to say,
"I burned half of it on the fire, I baked bread on the
live embers, I roasted meat and ate it, and am I to
make some abomination of what remains? Am I to
bow down before a block of wood?"

20 A man who hankers after ashes has a deluded heart

and is led astray. He will never free his soul, or say,
"What I have in my hand is nothing but a lie!"

### Oracle

21      Remember these things, Jacob,
        and that you are my servant, Israel.
        I have formed you, you are my servant;
        Israel, I will not forget you.

22      I have dispelled your faults like a cloud,
        your sins like a mist.
        Come back to me, for I have redeemed you.

### Song of joy

23      Shout for joy, you heavens, for Yahweh has
                been at work!
        Shout aloud, you earth below!
        Shout for joy, you mountains,
        and you, forest and all your trees!
        For Yahweh has redeemed Jacob
        and displayed his glory in Israel.

### The might of Yahweh

24      Thus says Yahweh, your redeemer,
        he who formed you in the womb:
        I, myself, Yahweh, made all things,
        I alone spread out the heavens.
        When I gave the earth shape, did anyone help
                me?

25      I am he who foils the omens of wizards
        and makes fools of diviners,
        who makes sages recant
        and shows the nonsense of their knowledge,
26      who confirms the word of my servant
        and makes the plans of my envoys succeed.

        I am he who says of Jerusalem, "Let her be
                inhabited,"
        of the towns of Judah, "Let them be rebuilt,"
        and I will raise their ruins once more.
27      I am he who says to the ocean, "Be dry.
        I will dry up your rivers."

28      I am he who says of Cyrus, "My shepherd—
        he will fulfill my whole purpose,

saying of Jerusalem, 'Let her be rebuilt,'
and of the Temple, 'Let your foundation be
laid.' "

## Oracle in favor of Cyrus

**45**

1 Thus says Yahweh to his anointed, to Cyrus,
whom he has taken by his right hand
to subdue nations before him
and strip the loins of kings,*a*
to force gateways before him
that their gates be closed no more:

2 I will go before you
leveling the heights.
I will shatter the bronze gateways,
smash the iron bars.

3 I will give you the hidden treasures,
the secret hoards,
that you may know that I am Yahweh,
the God of Israel, who calls you by your name.

4 It is for the sake of my servant Jacob,
of Israel my chosen one,
that I have called you by your name,
conferring a title though you do not know me.

5 I am Yahweh, unrivaled;
there is no other God besides me.
Though you do not know me, I arm you

6 that men may know from the rising to the setting of the sun
that, apart from me, all is nothing.

## Oracle of salvation

I am Yahweh, unrivaled,

7 I form the light and create the dark.
I make good fortune and create calamity,
it is I, Yahweh, who do all this.

8 Send victory like a dew, you heavens,
and let the clouds rain it down.
Let the earth open
for salvation to spring up.
Let deliverance, too, bud forth
which I, Yahweh, shall create.

## The supreme power of Yahweh

9    Can it argue with the man who fashioned it,
     one vessel among earthen vessels?
     Does the clay say to its fashioner, "What are
          you making?"
     does the thing he shaped say, "You have no
          skill?"
10   Woe to him who says to a father, "What have
          you begotten?"
     or to a woman, "To what have you given birth?"

11   Thus says Yahweh,
     the Holy One, he who fashions Israel:
     Is it for you to question me about my children
     and to dictate to me what my hands should do?
12   I it was who made the earth,
     and created man who is on it.
     I it was who spread out the heavens with my
          hands
     and now give orders to their whole array.
13   I it was who roused him to victory,
     I leveled the way for him.
     He will rebuild my city,
     will bring my exiles back
     without ransom or indemnity,
     so says Yahweh Sabaoth.

## The heathen will rally to Yahweh

14   Thus says Yahweh:
     The peasants of Egypt and the traders of Cush,
     and the tall men of Seba,
     will submit to you and be yours;
     they will follow you in chains.
     They will bow down before you,
     they will pray to you:
     "With you alone is God, and he has no rival;
     there is no other god."
15   Truly, God is hidden with you,
     the God of Israel, the savior.
16   Those who opposed you will be disgraced and
          humiliated;

**45 a.** I.e. leaving them no weapons in their belts.

the makers of idols will go away confounded.

17 Israel will be saved by Yahweh,
saved everlastingly.
You will never be disgraced or humiliated
for ever and ever.

### Evidence of the work of Yahweh

18 Yes, thus says Yahweh,
creator of the heavens,
who is God,
who formed the earth and made it,
who set it firm,
created it no chaos,
but a place to be lived in:

19 "I am Yahweh, unrivaled,
I have not spoken in secret
in some corner of a darkened land.
I have not said to Jacob's descendants,
'Seek me in chaos.'
I, Yahweh, speak with directness
I express myself with clarity."

### Yahweh is the God of all

20 Assemble, come, gather together,
survivors of the nations.
They are ignorant, those who carry about
their idol of wood,
those who pray to a god
that cannot save.

21 Speak up, present your case,
consult with each other.
"Who foretold this
and revealed it in the past?
Am I not Yahweh?
There is no other god besides me,
a God of integrity and a savior;
there is none apart from me.

22 Turn to me and be saved,
all the ends of the earth,
for I am God unrivaled.

23 "By my own self I swear it;
what comes from my mouth is truth,

a word irrevocable:
before me every knee shall bend,
by me every tongue shall swear,
24　　saying, 'From Yahweh alone
come victory and strength.'
To him shall come, ashamed,
all who raged against him.
25　　Victorious and glorious through Yahweh shall
be
all the descendants of Israel."

## The fall of Bel

1　**46**　Bel is crouching. Nebo cringing.[a]
Their idols are being loaded on animals, on
beasts of burden,
carried off like bundles on weary beasts.
2　　They are cringing and crouching together,
powerless to save the ones who carry them,
as they themselves go off into captivity.

3　　"Listen to me, House of Jacob,
all you who remain of the House of Israel,
you who have been carried since birth,
whom I have carried since the time you were
born.

4　　"In your old age I shall be still the same,
when your hair is gray I shall still support you.
I have already done so, I have carried you,
I shall still support and deliver you."

## Yahweh is without equal

5　　To whom can you compare me, equate me,
to whom claim I am similar, or comparable?
6　　These prodigals weigh out gold from their
purses
and silver on the scales.
They engage a goldsmith to make a god
then worship and prostrate themselves before it.
7　　They lift it on their shoulders and carry it,
and put it where it is meant to stand.
It never moves from the spot.

46 a. Gods of the Babylonians, defeated by Cyrus.

You may invoke it, it never replies,
it never saves anyone in trouble.

## Yahweh is lord of the future

8  Remember this and be dismayed,
stir your memories again, you sinners,
9  remember things long past.
I am God unrivaled
God who has no like.
10  From the beginning I foretold the future,
and predicted beforehand what is to be.

I say: My purpose shall last;
I will do whatever I choose.
11  I call a bird of prey from the east,
my man of destiny from a far country.
No sooner is it said than done,
no sooner planned than performed.
12  Listen to me, faint hearts,
who feel far from victory.
13  I bring my victory near, already it is close,
my salvation will not be late.
I will give salvation to Zion,
my glory shall be for Israel.

## Lament for Babylon

1  **47** Down with you! Sit in the dust,
virgin, daughter of Babylon.
Sit on the ground, dethroned,
daughter of the Chaldaeans.
Never again will you be called
tender and delicate.
2  Take the millstones, grind the meal.
Remove your veil,
tie up your skirt, uncover your legs.
Wade through rivers.
3  Let your nakedness be seen,
and your shame exposed.
I am going to take vengeance
and no one can stop me.

4  Our redeemer, Yahweh Sabaoth his name,
the Holy One of Israel, says:
5  Sit in silence and creep into shadows,

daughter of the Chaldaeans,
for you will no longer be called
sovereign lady of the kingdoms.

6    I was angry with my people,
I had profaned my heritage.
I had surrendered it into your hands,
but you showed them no mercy.
On the aged you laid
your crushing yoke.

7    You said, "For ever
I shall be sovereign lady."
You never took these things to heart
or pondered on their outcome.

8    So listen now, voluptuous woman,
lolling at ease
and saying to yourself,
"I, and none besides me.
I shall never be widowed,
never know loss of children."

9    Yet both these things shall happen to you
both suddenly and on the same day.
Loss of children, widowhood, at once
will come to you;
in spite of all your witchcraft
and the power of all your spells.

10   You were bold in your wickedness and said,
"There is no one to see me."
That wisdom and knowledge of yours
led you astray.
You said to yourself,
"I, and none besides me."

11   A calamity shall fall on you
which you will not be able to charm away,
a disaster shall overtake you
which you will not be able to avert,
unforeseen ruin
will suddenly descend on you.

12   Keep to your spells then,
and all your sorceries,
for which you have worn yourself out since
your youth.

Do you think they will help you?
Do you think they will make anyone nervous?

13   You have spent weary hours with your many
        advisers.
Let them come forward now
and save you, these who analyze the heavens,
who study the stars
and announce month by month
what will happen to you next.

14   Oh, they will be like wisps of straw
and the fire will burn them.
They will not save their lives
from the power of the flame.
No embers these, for baking,
no fireside to sit by.

15   This is what your wizards will be for you,
those men for whom you have worn yourself
        out since your youth.
They will all go off, each his own way,
powerless to save you.

### Yahweh acts alone and is sole master of the future

1 **48** Listen to this, House of Jacob,
you who bear the name of Israel,
and have sprung from the seed of Judah;
you who swear by the name of Yahweh
and invoke the God of Israel

2   though not in good faith or uprightness—
calling yourselves after the holy city
and bolstering yourselves on the God of Israel,
whose name is Yahweh Sabaoth.

3   Things now past I once revealed long ago,
they went out from my mouth and I proclaimed
        them;
then suddenly I acted and they happened.

4   For I knew you to be obstinate,
your neck an iron bar,
your forehead bronze.

5   And so I revealed things beforehand,
before they happened I announced them to you,
so that you could not say, "My idol was the one
        that performed them,

   it was my carved image, my image of cast metal,
    that decreed them."
6  You have heard and seen all this,
   will you not admit it?

   Now I am revealing new things to you,
   things hidden and unknown to you,
7  created just now, this very moment,
   of these things you have heard nothing until
    now,
   so that you cannot say, "Oh yes, I knew all this."

8  You had never heard,
   you did not know,
   I had not opened your ear beforehand;
   for I knew how treacherous you were,
   and that you have deserved the name of rebel
    from your birth.

9  For the sake of my name I deferred my anger,
   for the sake of my honor I curbed it; I did not
    destroy you.
10  And now I have put you in the fire like silver,
   I have tested you in the furnace of distress.
11  For my sake and my sake only have I acted—
   is my name to be profaned?
   Never will I yield my glory to another.

### Cyrus is the beloved of Yahweh

12  Listen to me, Jacob,
   Israel whom I have called:
   I am the first,
   I am also the last.
13  My hand laid the foundations of earth
   and my right hand spread out the heavens.
   I summon them
   and they all come forward together.
14  Assemble, all of you, and listen;
   which of them has foretold this?
   "My beloved will perform my pleasure
   with Babylon and the offspring of the Chal-
    daeans."
15  I, yes I myself, have spoken and summoned him,
   brought him and prospered his plans.

16     Come near and listen to this:
from the beginning I have never spoken to you
    obscurely,
and all the time these things have been hap-
    pening, I have been present.
—And now the Lord Yahweh, with his spirit,
sends me.

## What Yahweh had intended for Israel

17     Thus says Yahweh, your redeemer, the Holy
    One of Israel:
I, Yahweh, your God, teach you what is good
    for you,
I lead you in the way that you must go.
18     If only you had been alert to my command-
    ments,
your happiness would have been like a river,
your integrity like the waves of the sea.
19     Your children would have been numbered like
    the sand,
your descendants as many as its grains.
Never would your name have been cut off or
    blotted out before me.

## A song of departure from Babylon

20     Go away from Babylon! Flee from the Chal-
    daeans!
Declare this with cries of joy and proclaim it,
send it out to the ends of the earth.
Say, "Yahweh has redeemed his servant Jacob."

21     Those he led through the deserts never went
    thirsty;
he made water spring for them from the rock,
he split the rock and water flowed.
22     There is no happiness, says Yahweh, for the
    wicked.

## Second song of the servant of Yahweh

1 **49**     Islands, listen to me,
pay attention, remotest peoples.
Yahweh called me before I was born,
from my mother's womb he pronounced my
    name.

2  He made my mouth a sharp sword,
    and hid me in the shadow of his hand.
  He made me into a sharpened arrow,
    and concealed me in his quiver.

3  He said to me, "You are my servant (Israel)
    in whom I shall be glorified";
4  while I was thinking, "I have toiled in vain,
    I have exhausted myself for nothing";

  and all the while my cause was with Yahweh,
    my reward with my God.
5b  I was honored in the eyes of Yahweh,
    my God was my strength.

5a  And now Yahweh has spoken,
    he who formed me in the womb to be his
      servant,
    to bring Jacob back to him,
    to gather Israel to him:

6  "It is not enough for you to be my servant,
    to restore the tribes of Jacob and bring back the
      survivors of Israel;
    I will make you the light of the nations
    so that my salvation may reach to the ends of
      the earth."

## The marvelous epic of the return

7  Thus says Yahweh,
    the redeemer of Israel and his Holy One,
    to him whose life is despised, whom the nations
      loathe,
    to the slave of despots:
  Kings will stand up when they see you,
    and princes will bow,
    for the sake of Yahweh who has been faithful,
    the Holy One of Israel who has chosen you.

8  Thus says Yahweh:
    At the favorable time I will answer you,
    on the day of salvation I will help you.
    (I have formed you and have appointed you
    as covenant of the people.)

9
> I will restore the land
> and assign you the estates that lie waste.
> I will say to the prisoners, "Come out,"
> to those who are in darkness, "Show yourselves."

10
> On every roadway they will graze,
> and each bare height shall be their pasture.
> They will never hunger or thirst,
> scorching wind and sun shall never plague them;
> for he who pities them will lead them
> and guide them to springs of water.

11
> I will make a highway of all the mountains,
> and the high roads shall be banked up.

12
> Some are on their way from afar,
> others from the north and the west,
> others from the land of Sinim.[a]

13
> Shout for joy, you heavens; exult, you earth!
> You mountains, break into happy cries!
> For Yahweh consoles his people
> and takes pity on those who are afflicted.

14
> For Zion was saying, "Yahweh has abandoned
> me,
> the Lord has forgotten me."

15
> Does a woman forget her baby at the breast,
> or fail to cherish the son of her womb?
> Yet even if these forget,
> I will never forget you.

16
> See, I have branded you on the palms of my
> hands,
> your ramparts are always under my eye.

17
> Your rebuilders make haste,
> and your destroyers and despoilers depart.

18
> Look around about you, look,
> All are assembling, coming to you.
> By my life—it is Yahweh who speaks—
> you will wear these as your jewels,
> they will adorn you as brides are adorned;

19
> for your desolate places and your ruins
> and your devastated country
> will now be too small for all your inhabitants,

now that your devourers are far away.

20 Once more they will speak in your hearing,
those sons you thought were lost,
"This place is too small for me,
give me more space to live in."

21 You will then say in your heart,
"Who has borne me these?
I was childless and barren,
who has brought these up?

I was left all alone,
and now, where do these come from?"

22 Thus speaks the Lord Yahweh:
I beckon to the nations
and hoist my signal for the peoples.
They will bring back your sons in the cloak,
they will take your daughters on their shoulders.

23 Kings will be your fosterfathers,
their queens your nursing mothers.
They will fall prostrate before you, faces to the
ground,
and lick the dust at your feet.
You shall then know that I am Yahweh;
and that those who hope in me will not be put
to shame.

24 Can spoil be snatched from heroes,
or captives escape from a soldier?

25 Yes, thus says Yahweh:
The hero's captive will be snatched away,
the soldier's spoil escape.
I myself will fight with those who fight you,
and I myself will save your children.

26 I will make your oppressors eat their own flesh,
they shall get as drunk on their own blood as on
new wine.
Then all mankind shall know
that I, Yahweh, am your savior
and that your redeemer is the Mighty One of
Jacob.

**49 a.** Assuan in southern Egypt.

### The offer of salvation remains open

**50** Thus says Yahweh:
Where is your mother's writ of divorce
by which I dismissed her?
Or to which of my creditors
have I sold you?
You were sold for your own crimes,
for your own faults your mother was dismissed.

2   Why did I find no one when I came?
Why did no one answer when I called?
Is my hand too short to redeem?
Have I not strength to save?
With one threat I can dry the sea,
and turn rivers to desert;
so that their fish shrivel up for want of water
and die of thirst.

3   I dress the heavens in black,
make sackcloth their covering.

### Third song of the servant of Yahweh
### a. The servant speaks

4   The Lord Yahweh has given me
a disciple's tongue.
So that I may know how to reply to the wearied
he provides me with speech.
Each morning he wakes me to hear,
to listen like a disciple.

5   The Lord Yahweh has opened my ear.

For my part, I made no resistance
neither did I turn away.

6   I offered my back to those who struck me,
my cheeks to those who tore at my beard;
I did not cover my face
against insult and spittle.

7   The Lord Yahweh comes to my help,
so that I am untouched by the insults.
So, too, I set my face like flint;
I know I shall not be shamed.

8   My vindicator is here at hand. Does anyone
start proceedings against me?

> Then let us go to court together.
> Who thinks he has a case against me?
> Let him approach me.

9
> The Lord Yahweh is coming to my help,
> who dare condemn me?
> They shall all go to pieces like a garment
> devoured by moths.

### b. Exhortation to follow the servant

10
> Let anyone who fears Yahweh among you
> listen to the voice of his servant!
> Whoever walks in darkness,
> and has no light shining for him,
> let him trust in the name of Yahweh,
> let him lean on his God.

11
> But you, you are all setting light to a fire,
> and fanning embers.
> Then in with you to the flames of your fire,
> to the embers that you are lighting.
> So will my hand deal with you
> and you shall lie down in torments.

### The salvation of the sons of Abraham

1 **51**
> Listen to me, you who pursue integrity,
> who seek Yahweh.
> Consider the rock you were hewn from,
> the quarry from which you were cut.

2
> Consider Abraham your father
> and Sarah who gave you birth.
> For he was all alone when I called him,
> but I blessed and increased him.

3
> Yes, Yahweh has pity on Zion,
> has pity on all her ruins;
> turns her desolation into an Eden,
> her wasteland into the garden of Yahweh.
> Joy and gladness shall be found in her,
> thanksgiving and the sound of music.

### Yahweh will soon judge the world

4
> Pay attention to me, you peoples,
> listen to me, you nations.

For from me comes the Law
and my justice shall be the light of the peoples,
5　　I will establish ·my integrity speedily,
my salvation shall come like the light,
my arm shall judge the peoples.
The islands put their hope in me,
put their trust in my strength.

6　　Lift up your eyes to the heavens,
look down at the earth.
The heavens will vanish like smoke,
the earth wear out like a garment,
and its inhabitants die like vermin,
but my salvation shall last for ever
and my justice have no end.

7　　Listen to me, you who know what integrity
　　　　means,
people who take my laws to heart:
do not fear the taunts of men,
nor be dismayed by their insults,
8　　for the moth shall eat them like garments,
the grub devour them like wool,
but my integrity will remain for ever,
and my salvation for all generations.

## The awakening of Yahweh

9　　Awake, awake! Clothe yourself in strength,
arm of Yahweh.
Awake, as in the past,
in times of generations long ago.
Did you not split Rahab in two,
and pierce the Dragon through?
10　　Did you not dry up the sea,
the waters of the great Abyss,
to make the seabed a road
for the redeemed to cross?

11　　Those whom Yahweh has ransomed return,
they come to Zion shouting for joy,
everlasting joy in their faces;
joy and gladness go with them,
sorrow and lament are ended.

### Yahweh is the all-powerful consoler

12      I, I am your consoler.
        How then can you be afraid
        of mortal man, of son of man,
        whose fate is the fate of grass?

13      You have forgotten Yahweh who made you,
        who spread out the heavens and laid the earth's
            foundations,
        why still go in daily dread
        of the oppressor's fury,
        when he sets out to destroy you?
        What has happened to the fury of oppressors?

### Salvation

14  The captive is soon to be set free; he will not die in
15  a deep dungeon nor will his bread run out. ·I am Yah-
    weh your God who stirs the sea, making its waves roar,
16  my name is Yahweh Sabaoth. ·I put my words into
    your mouth, I hid you in the shadow of my hand, when
    I spread out the heavens and laid the earth's founda-
    tions and said to Zion, "You are my people."

### The awakening of Jerusalem

17      Awake, awake!
        To your feet, Jerusalem!
        You who from Yahweh's hand have drunk
        the cup of his wrath.
        The chalice of stupor
        you have drained to the dregs.

18      She has not one to guide her
        of all the sons she has borne,
        not one to take her by the hand
        of all the sons she has reared.

19      These two calamities have befallen you
        —who is there to mourn for you?
        Devastation and ruin, famine and sword
        —who is there to console you?

20      Your sons lie helpless
        (at every street corner)
        like an antelope trapped in a net,

sodden with the wrath of Yahweh,
with the threats of your God.

21    Listen then to this, prostrated one,
drunk, though not with wine.
22    Thus says your Lord Yahweh,
your God, defender of your people.

See, I take out of your hand
the cup of stupor,
the chalice of my wrath;
you shall drink it no longer.
23    I will put it into the hand of your tormentors,
of those who said to you,
"Bow down that we may walk over you";
while of your back you made a pavement,
a street for them to walk on.

1 **52** Awake, awake!
Clothe yourself in strength, Zion.
Put on your richest clothes,
Jerusalem, holy city;
since no longer shall there enter you
either the uncircumcised or the unclean.
2    Shake off your dust; to your feet,
captive Jerusalem!
Free your neck from its fetters,
captive daughter of Zion.

## The nation in captivity

3 Yes, Yahweh says this: You were sold for nothing
4 and you will be redeemed without money. ·Yes, Yahweh says this: Once my people went to Egypt to settle
5 there, then Assyria bitterly oppressed them. ·But now what is there for me here?—it is Yahweh who speaks—now that my people have been carried off for nothing, and their masters shout their triumph—it is Yahweh who speaks—all day long my name is constantly blas-
6 phemed. ·My people will therefore know my name; that day they will understand that it is I who say, "I am here."

## The awakening of Yahweh and of Jerusalem

7    How beautiful on the mountains,
are the feet of one who brings good news,

who heralds peace, brings happiness,
proclaims salvation,
and tells Zion,
"Your God is king!"

8    Listen! Your watchmen raise their voices,
they shout for joy together,
for they see Yahweh face to face,
as he returns to Zion.

9    Break into shouts of joy together,
you ruins of Jerusalem;
for Yahweh is consoling his people,
redeeming Jerusalem.

10   Yahweh bares his holy arm
in the sight of all the nations,
and all the ends of the earth shall see
the salvation of our God.

11   "Go away, go away, leave that place,
touch nothing unclean.
Get out of her,[a] purify yourselves,
you who carry the vessels of Yahweh.

12   "But you are not to hurry away,
you are not to leave like fugitives.
No, Yahweh will go in front of you,
and the God of Israel will be your rearguard."

## Fourth song of the servant of Yahweh

13   See, my servant will prosper,
he shall be lifted up, exalted, rise to great
heights.

14   As the crowds were appalled on seeing him
—so disfigured did he look
that he seemed no longer human—
15   so will the crowds be astonished at him,
and kings stand speechless before him;
for they shall see something never told
and witness something never heard before:

**52 a.** Babylon; the returning exiles are to be ritually purified because they will carry with them the sacred vessels of the Temple, restored to them by Cyrus, Ezr. 1:7f.

**53** <sup></sup>1 "Who could believe what we have heard,
and to whom has the power of Yahweh been
revealed?"

2 Like a sapling he grew up in front of us,
like a root in arid ground.
Without beauty, without majesty (we saw him),
no looks to attract our eyes;

3 a thing despised and rejected by men,
a man of sorrows and familiar with suffering,
a man to make people screen their faces;
he was despised and we took no account of him.

4 And yet ours were the sufferings he bore,
ours the sorrows he carried.
But we, we thought of him as someone punished,
struck by God, and brought low.

5 Yet he was pierced through for our faults,
crushed for our sins.
On him lies a punishment that brings us peace,
and through his wounds we are healed.

6 We had all gone astray like sheep,
each taking his own way,
and Yahweh burdened him
with the sins of all of us.

7 Harshly dealt with, he bore it humbly,
he never opened his mouth,
like a lamb that is led to the slaughterhouse,
like a sheep that is dumb before its shearers
never opening its mouth.

8 By force and by law he was taken;
would anyone plead his cause?
Yes, he was torn away from the land of the
living;
for our faults struck down in death.

9 They gave him a grave with the wicked,
a tomb with the rich,
though he had done no wrong
and there had been no perjury in his mouth.

10 Yahweh has been pleased to crush him with
suffering.
If he offers his life in atonement,

he shall see his heirs, he shall have a long life
and through him what Yahweh wishes will be
done.

11    His soul's anguish over
he shall see the light and be content.
By his sufferings shall my servant justify many,
taking their faults on himself.

12    Hence I will grant whole hordes for his tribute,
he shall divide the spoil with the mighty,
for surrendering himself to death
and letting himself be taken for a sinner,
while he was bearing the faults of many
and praying all the time for sinners.

## The fertility of Jerusalem

1    **54** Shout for joy, you barren women who bore no
children!
Break into cries of joy and gladness, you who
were never in labor!
For the sons of the forsaken one are more in
number
than the sons of the wedded wife, says Yahweh.

2    Widen the space of your tent,
stretch out your hangings freely,
lengthen your ropes, make your pegs firm;
3    for you will burst out to right and to left.
Your race will take possession of the nations,
and people the abandoned cities.

## The love of Yahweh

4    Do not be afraid, you will not be put to shame,
do not be dismayed, you will not be disgraced;
for you will forget the shame of your youth
and no longer remember the curse of your
widowhood.
5    For now your creator will be your husband,
his name, Yahweh Sabaoth;
your redeemer will be the Holy One of Israel,
he is called the God of the whole earth.
6    Yes, like a forsaken wife, distressed in spirit,
Yahweh calls you back.

Does a man cast off the wife of his youth?
says your God.

7    I did forsake you for a brief moment,
     but with great love will I take you back.
8    In excess of anger, for a moment
     I hid my face from you.
     But with everlasting love I have taken pity on
          you,
     says Yahweh, your redeemer.

9    I am now as I was in the days of Noah
     when I swore that Noah's waters
     should never flood the world again.
     So now I swear concerning my anger with you
     and the threats I made against you;

10   for the mountains may depart,
     the hills be shaken,
     but my love for you will never leave you
     and my covenant of peace with you will never
          be shaken,
     says Yahweh who takes pity on you.

## The new Jerusalem

11   Unhappy creature, storm-tossed, disconsolate,
     see, I will set your stones on carbuncles
     and your foundations on sapphires.
12   I will make rubies your battlements,
     your gates crystal,
     and your entire wall precious stones.
13   Your sons will all be taught by Yahweh.
     The prosperity of your sons will be great.
14   You will be founded on integrity;
     remote from oppression, you will have nothing
          to fear;
     remote from terror, it will not approach you.
15   Should anyone attack you, that will not be my
          doing,
     and whoever attacks you, for your sake will fall.
16   I it was created the smith
     who blows on the coal fire
     and from it takes the weapons to work on.

But I also created the destroyer who renders
   them useless.
17    Not a weapon forged against you will succeed.
Every tongue that accuses you in judgment will
   be refuted.
Such will be the lot of the servants of Yahweh,
the triumphs I award them—it is Yahweh who
   speaks.

## The food of the poor

1  **55**  Oh, come to the water all you who are thirsty;
though you have no money, come!
Buy corn without money, and eat,
and, at no cost, wine and milk.
2    Why spend money on what is not bread,
your wages on what fails to satisfy?
Listen, listen to me, and you will have good
   things to eat
and rich food to enjoy.
3    Pay attention, come to me;
listen, and your soul will live.

## The covenant

With you I will make an everlasting covenant
out of the favors promised to David.
4    See, I have made of you a witness to the peoples,
a leader and a master of the nations.
5    See, you will summon a nation you never knew,
those unknown will come hurrying to you,
for the sake of Yahweh your God,
of the Holy One of Israel who will glorify you.

## The nearness and remoteness of Yahweh

6    Seek Yahweh while he is still to be found,
call to him while he is still near.
7    Let the wicked man abandon his way,
the evil man his thoughts.
Let him turn back to Yahweh who will take
   pity on him,
to our God who is rich in forgiving;
8    for my thoughts are not your thoughts,
my ways not your ways—it is Yahweh who
   speaks.

9          Yes, the heavens are as high above earth
             as my ways are above your ways,
             my thoughts above your thoughts.

### The word of Yahweh cannot fail

10    Yes, as the rain and the snow come down from the
heavens and do not return without watering the earth,
making it yield and giving growth to provide seed for
11  the sower and bread for the eating, ·so the word that
goes from my mouth does not return to me empty,
without carrying out my will and succeeding in what
it was sent to do.

### Conclusion of the Book of Consolation

12          Yes, you will leave with joy
             and be led away in safety.
             Mountains and hills will break into joyful cries
                before you
             and all the trees of the countryside clap their
                hands.
13          Cypress will grow instead of thorns,
             myrtle instead of briars.
             And this will make Yahweh famous,
             a sign for ever, ineffaceable.

## III. THIRD PART OF THE BOOK OF ISAIAH

### Yahweh welcomes converts from paganism

1    **56** Thus says Yahweh: Have a care for justice, act
         with integrity, for soon my salvation will come
and my integrity be manifest.
2    Blessed is the man who does this and the son of
man who clings to it: observing the sabbath, not profaning it, and keeping his hand from every evil deed.
3    Let no foreigner who has attached himself to Yahweh say, "Yahweh will surely exclude me from his
people." Let no eunuch say, "And I, I am a dried-up
tree."
4    For Yahweh says this: To the eunuchs who observe
my sabbaths, and resolve to do what pleases me and

5 cling to my covenant, ·I will give, in my house and within my walls, a monument and a name better than sons and daughters; I will give them an everlasting name that shall never be effaced.

6    Foreigners who have attached themselves to Yahweh to serve him and to love his name and be his servants—all who observe the sabbath, not profaning it, and

7 cling to my covenant—·these I will bring to my holy mountain. I will make them joyful in my house of prayer. Their holocausts and their sacrifices will be accepted on my altar, for my house will be called a house of prayer for all the peoples.

8    It is the Lord Yahweh who speaks, who gathers the outcasts of Israel: there are others I will gather besides those already gathered.

### The unworthiness of the leaders of Judah

9          Come and gorge, all you wild beasts,
           all you beasts of the forest.
10         Our watchmen are all blind,
           they notice nothing.

           Dumb watchdogs all,
           unable to bark,
           they dream, lie down,
           and love to sleep.

11         Greedy dogs that are never satisfied.
           Shepherds who know nothing.
           They all go their own way,
           each after his own interest.

12         "Come, let me fetch wine;
           we will get drunk on strong drink,
           tomorrow will be just as wonderful as today
           and even more so!"

1  **57** The upright perish
           and no one cares.
           Devout men are taken off
           and no one gives it a thought.

           Yes, on account of evil the upright man is taken
                off
2          to enter peace.

They lie on their beds
those who followed the right way.

3 But you, you sons of a witch, come here,
offspring of the adulterer and the whore.

4 At whom are you jeering, and making faces,
and sticking out your tongue?
Are you not the spawn of sin,
children of lies?

5 Lusting among the terebinths,
and under every spreading tree,
sacrificing children in the wadis
and in rocky clefts.

## Prophetic elegy against idolatry

6 The smooth stones of the wadis, these are your
share,
these, these your portion.
To these you pour libations,
bring oblations.
Can all this appease me?

7 On a mountain high and lofty
you have put your bed.
Thither, too, you have climbed
to offer sacrifice.

8 Behind door and doorpost
you have set up your sign.[a]
Yes, far, far removed from me, you unroll your
bedding,
climb into it and spread it wide.

You have struck a pact with those
whose bed you love,
whoring with them often
with your eyes on the sacred symbol.

9 With oil you made yourself look your best for
Molech,
lavishing your scents;
you sent your envoys far afield,
down to Sheol itself.[b]

10 Tired with so much journeying,
you never said, "I give up."

Finding your strength revived,
you never weakened.

11   Who was it you dreaded, and feared,
that you should disown me
and not remember me,
and refuse me a place in your heart?

Meanwhile I kept silent and shut my eyes, did
          I not?
So you cannot have been afraid of me.
12   But now I will expose this integrity of yours
and your futile actions.

13   When you cry, let your hateful idols save you!
The wind will carry them all away,
a breath will take them off.
But whoever trusts in me shall inherit the land
and own my holy mountain.

### A poem of consolation

14   It shall be said:
Open up, open up, clear the way,
remove all obstacles from the way of my people.
15   For thus speaks the Most High,
whose home is in eternity,
whose name is holy:

"I live in a high and holy place,
but I am also with the contrite and humbled
          spirit,
to give the humbled spirit new life,
to revive contrite hearts.

16   "For I will not quarrel for ever
nor be always angry,
for then the spirit would give way before me,
the very souls I have made.

17   "Angered by his wicked brutality,
I hid my face and struck him in anger.
Like a rebel he went the way of his choice;
18   but I have seen the way he went.

57 a. A domestic idol.
b. By sacrificing children.

"But I will heal him, and console him,
I will comfort him to the full,
both him and his afflicted fellows,

19
bringing praise to their lips.
Peace, peace to far and near,
I will indeed heal him," says Yahweh.

20
The wicked however are like the restless sea
that cannot be still,
and washes up mud and slime.

21
"No peace," says my God, "for the wicked."

## Fasting

1 **58** Shout for all you are worth,
raise your voice like a trumpet.
Proclaim their faults to my people,
their sins to the House of Jacob.

2
They seek me day after day,
they long to know my ways,
like a nation that wants to act with integrity
and not ignore the law of its God.

They ask me for laws that are just,
they long for God to draw near:

3
"Why should we fast if you never see it,
why do penance if you never notice?"

Look, you do business on your fast days,
you oppress all your workmen;

4
look, you quarrel and squabble when you fast
and strike the poor man with your fist.

Fasting like yours today
will never make your voice heard on high.

5
Is that the sort of fast that pleases me,
a truly penitential day for men?

Hanging your head like a reed,
lying down on sackcloth and ashes?
Is that what you call fasting,
a day acceptable to Yahweh?

6
Is not this the sort of fast that pleases me
—it is the Lord Yahweh who speaks—

to break unjust fetters
and undo the thongs of the yoke,

to let the oppressed go free,
and break every yoke,
7    to share your bread with the hungry,
and shelter the homeless poor,

to clothe the man you see to be naked
and not turn from your own kin?
8    Then will your light shine like the dawn
and your wound be quickly healed over.

Your integrity will go before you
and the glory of Yahweh behind you.
9    Cry, and Yahweh will answer;
call, and he will say, "I am here."

If you do away with the yoke,
the clenched fist, the wicked word,
10   if you give your bread to the hungry,
and relief to the oppressed,

your light will rise in the darkness,
and your shadows become like noon.
11   Yahweh will always guide you,
giving you relief in desert places.

He will give strength to your bones
and you shall be like a watered garden,
like a spring of water
whose waters never run dry.

12   You will rebuild the ancient ruins,
build up on the old foundations.
You will be called "Breach-mender,"
"Restorer of ruined houses."

### The sabbath

13   If you refrain from trampling the sabbath,
and doing business on the holy day,
if you call the sabbath "Delightful,"
and the day sacred to Yahweh "Honorable,"
if you honor it by abstaining from travel,
from doing business and from gossip,
14   then shall you find your happiness in Yahweh

and I will lead you triumphant over the heights
    of the land.
I will feed you on the heritage of Jacob your
    father.
For the mouth of Yahweh has spoken.

## A psalm

**59**

1  No, the hand of Yahweh is not too short to save,
    nor his ear too dull to hear.

2  But your iniquities have made a gulf
    between you and your God.
Your sins have made him veil his face
    so as not to hear you,

3  since your hands are stained with blood,
    your fingers with crime,
your lips utter lies,
    your tongues murmur treachery.

4  No one makes just accusations
    or pleads sincerely.
All rely on nothingness, utter falsehood,
    conceive harm and give birth to misery.

5  They are hatching adders' eggs
    and weaving a spider's web;
eat one of their eggs and you die,
    crush one and a viper emerges.

6  Their webs are no good for clothing,
    their plots no use for covering.
Their plans are sinful plots,
    violence is their only method.

7  Their feet run to do evil,
    are quick to shed innocent blood.
Their thoughts are sinful thoughts,
    wherever they go there is havoc and ruin.

8  They know nothing of the way of peace,
    there is no equity in their paths.
Twisty trails they clear for themselves
    and no one who follows them knows any peace.

9  So justice is removed far away from us,
    and integrity keeps its distance.
We looked for light and all is darkness,
    for brightness and we walk in the dark.

10    Like the blind we feel our way along walls
      and hesitate like men without eyes.
      We stumble as though noon were twilight
      and dwell in the dark like the dead.
11    We growl, all of us, like bears,
      and moan like doves,
      waiting for the justice that never comes,
      for salvation that is removed far away from us.

12    For our faults in your sight have been many
      and our sins are a witness against us.
      And indeed our faults are present to our minds,
      and we know our iniquities:
13    rebellion and denial of Yahweh,
      turning our back on our God,
      talking treachery and revolt,
      murmuring lies in our heart.
14    Justice is withheld
      and integrity stands aloof;
      in the public square sincerity is brought to its
          knees
      and uprightness forbidden to enter.

### Fragments of an apocalypse

15    Sincerity is missing
      and he who avoids evil is robbed.
      Yahweh has seen this, and is indignant
      that there is no justice to be seen.
16    He saw there was no one
      and wondered there was no one to intervene.
      So he made his own arm his mainstay,
      his own integrity his support.
17    He put integrity on like a breastplate,
      and on his head the helmet of salvation.
      He put vengeance on like a tunic
      and wrapped himself in ardor like a cloak.
18    To each he will pay his due,
      wrath to his enemies, reprisals on his foes.
19    In the west men will see the name of Yahweh
      and in the east his glory;
      for he shall come like a pent-up stream
      impelled by the breath of Yahweh.
20    But for Zion he will come as Redeemer,

for those of Jacob who turn from their faults.
It is Yahweh who speaks.

## Oracle

21    For my part, this is my covenant with them, says
Yahweh. My spirit with which I endowed you, and
my words that I have put in your mouth, will not disappear from your mouth, nor from the mouths of your
children, nor from the mouths of your children's children for ever and ever, says Yahweh.

## The glorious resurrection of Jerusalem

1    **60**    Arise, shine out, for your light has come,
                the glory of Yahweh is rising on you,
2               though night still covers the earth
                and darkness the peoples.

       Above you Yahweh now rises
       and above you his glory appears.
3      The nations come to your light
       and kings to your dawning brightness.

4      Lift up your eyes and look around:
       all are assembling and coming toward you,
       your sons from far away
       and your daughters being tenderly carried.

5      At this sight you will grow radiant,
       your heart throbbing and full;
       since the riches of the sea will flow to you,
       the wealth of the nations come to you;

6      camels in throngs will cover you,
       and dromedaries of Midian and Ephah;
       everyone in Sheba will come,
       bringing gold and incense
       and singing the praise of Yahweh.

7      All the flocks of Kedar will gather inside you,
       the rams of Nebaioth[a] will be at your service.
       They will come up, for acceptance, to my altar,
       to adorn the Temple of my glory.

8      Who are these flying like a cloud,
       like doves to their cote?

9      Yes, for me the ships are assembling,
       vessels of Tarshish in the front,

       to bring your sons from far away,
       and their silver and gold with them,
       for the sake of the name of Yahweh your God,
       for the sake of the Holy One of Israel who has
           made you glorious.

10     Foreigners will rebuild your walls
       and their kings will be your servants.
       For though I struck you in anger,
       in mercy I have pitied you.

11     And your gates will lie open continually,
       shut neither by day nor by night,
       for men to bring you the wealth of the nations
       with their kings leading them;
12     for the nation and kingdom that refuses to serve
           you shall perish,
       such nations shall be utterly ruined.

13     The glory of Lebanon[b] will come to you,
       with cypress and plane and box,
       to adorn the site of my sanctuary,
       to glorify the resting place of my feet.

14     The sons of your oppressors will come to you
           bowing,
       at your feet shall fall all who despised you.
       They will call you "City of Yahweh,"
       "Zion of the Holy One of Israel."

15     Though you have been abandoned,
       and hated and shunned,
       I will make you an eternal pride,
       a joy for ever and ever.

16     You will be suckled on the milk of nations,
       suckled on the riches of kings,
       and you shall know that I, Yahweh, am your
           savior,
       that your redeemer is the Mighty One of Jacob.

60 a. Kedar, a bedouin tribe; Nebaioth, a tribe of Arabia.
b. Cedar wood.

17
    For bronze I will bring gold;
    for iron, silver;
    and bronze for wood;
    and iron for stone;
    I will put Peace in as magistrate,
    and Integrity as the government.

18
    Violence will no longer be heard of in your
        country,
    nor devastation and ruin within your frontiers.
    You will call your walls "Salvation,"
    and your gates "Praise."

19
    No more will the sun give you daylight,
    nor moonlight shine on you,
    but Yahweh will be your everlasting light,
    your God will be your splendor.

20
    Your sun will set no more
    nor your moon wane,
    but Yahweh will be your everlasting light
    and your days of mourning will be ended.

21
    Your people will all be upright,
    possessing the land for ever;
    a shoot that Yahweh has planted,
    my handiwork, designed for beauty.

22
    The least among you will become a clan
    and the smallest a mighty nation.
    I, Yahweh, have spoken;
    in due time I shall act with speed.

## The mission of the prophet

1
**61**    The spirit of the Lord Yahweh has been given
        to me,
    for Yahweh has anointed me.
    He has sent me to bring good news to the poor,
    to bind up hearts that are broken;

    to proclaim liberty to captives,
    freedom to those in prison;
2
    to proclaim a year of favor from Yahweh,
    a day of vengeance for our God,

3      to comfort all those who mourn ·and to give
them
for ashes a garland;
for mourning robe the oil of gladness,
for despondency, praise.
They are to be called "terebinths of integrity,"
planted by Yahweh to glorify him.

4      They will rebuild the ancient ruins,
they will raise what has long lain waste,
they will restore the ruined cities,
all that has lain waste for ages past.

5      Strangers will be there to feed your flocks,
foreigners as your plowmen and vinedressers;
6      but you, you will be named "priests of Yahweh,"
they will call you "ministers of our God."
You will feed on the wealth of nations
and array yourselves in their magnificence.

7      For their shame was twofold,
disgrace and spitting their lot.
Twofold therefore shall they possess in their
land,
everlasting joy is theirs.

8      For I, Yahweh, love justice,
I hate robbery and all that is wrong.
I reward them faithfully
and make an everlasting covenant with them.

9      Their race will be famous throughout the
nations,
their descendants throughout the peoples.
All who see them will admit
that they are a race whom Yahweh has blessed.

10      "I exult for joy in Yahweh,
my soul rejoices in my God,
for he has clothed me in the garments of salvation,
he has wrapped me in the cloak of integrity,
like a bridegroom wearing his wreath,
like a bride adorned in her jewels.

11

"For as the earth makes fresh things grow,
as a garden makes seeds spring up,
so will the Lord Yahweh make both integrity
     and praise
spring up in the sight of the nations."

## Second poem on the glorious resurrection of Jerusalem

1
**62** About Zion I will not be silent,
about Jerusalem I will not grow weary,
until her integrity shines out like the dawn
and her salvation flames like a torch.

2

The nations then will see your integrity,
all the kings your glory,
and you will be called by a new name,
one which the mouth of Yahweh will confer.

3

You are to be a crown of splendor in the hand
     of Yahweh,
a princely diadem in the hand of your God;

4

no longer are you to be named "Forsaken,"
nor your land "Abandoned,"
but you shall be called "My Delight,"
and your land "The Wedded";
for Yahweh takes delight in you
and your land will have its wedding.

5

Like a young man marrying a virgin,
so will the one who built you wed you,
and as the bridegroom rejoices in his bride,
so will your God rejoice in you.

6

On your walls, Jerusalem,
I set watchmen.
Day or night
they must never be silent.

You who keep Yahweh mindful
must take no rest.

7

Nor let him take rest
till he has restored Jerusalem,
and made her
the boast of the earth.

8

Yahweh has sworn it by his right hand
and by his mighty arm:

Never again shall I give your corn
to feed your enemies.
Never again will foreigners drink your wine
that you labored for.

9       But those who gather the harvest will eat it
and praise Yahweh.
Those who gathered the grapes will drink
in the courts of my sanctuary.

## Conclusion

10      Pass through, pass through the gates.
Make a way for the people.
Bank up, bank up the highway,
clear it of stones.
Hoist the signal for the peoples.

11      This Yahweh proclaims
to the ends of the earth:

Say to the daughter of Zion, "Look,
your savior comes,
the prize of his victory with him,
his trophies before him."

12      They shall be called "The Holy People,"
"Yahweh's Redeemed."
And you shall be called "The-sought-after,"
"City-not-forsaken."

## An apocalyptic poem on the vengeance of Yahweh

1 **63** Who is this coming from Edom,
from Bozrah in garments stained with crimson,
so richly clothed,
marching so full of strength?
—It is I, who speak of integrity
and am powerful to save.

2       —Why are your garments red,
your clothes as if you had trodden the winepress?

3       —I have trodden the winepress alone.
Of the men of my people not one was with me.
In my anger I trod them down,
trampled them in my wrath.

Their juice spattered my garments,
and all my clothes are stained.

4      For in my heart was a day of vengeance,
my year of redemption had come.

5      I looked: there was no one to help;
aghast: not one could I find to support me.
My own arm then was my mainstay,
my wrath my support.

6      I crushed the people in my fury,
trampled them in my anger,
and made the juice of them run all over the
ground.

## A psalm

7      Let me sing the praises of Yahweh's goodness,
and of his marvelous deeds,
in return for all that he has done for us
and for the great kindness
he has shown us in his mercy
and in his boundless goodness.

8      He said, "Truly they are my people,
sons and no rogues."
He proved himself their savior

9      in all their troubles.
It was neither messenger nor angel
but his Presence that saved them.
In his love and pity
he redeemed them himself,
he lifted them up, carried them,
throughout the days of old.

10      But they rebelled, they grieved
his holy spirit.
Then he turned enemy,
and himself waged war on them.

11      They remembered the days of old,
of Moses his servant.
Where is he who brought out of the sea
the shepherd of his flock?
Where is he who endowed him
with his holy spirit,

12      who at the right hand of Moses
set to work with his glorious arm,

who divided the waters before them
to win himself everlasting renown,

13 who made them walk through the ocean
as easily as a horse through the desert?

14 They stumbled as little ·as an ox
going down to the plain.
The spirit of Yahweh led them to rest.
This is how you guided your people
to win yourself glorious renown.

15 Look down from heaven, look down
from your holy and glorious dwelling.
Where is your ardor, your might,
the yearning of your inmost heart?
Do not let your compassion go unmoved,

16 for you are our Father.
For Abraham does not own us
and Israel*a* does not acknowledge us;
you, Yahweh, yourself are our Father,
Our Redeemer is your ancient name.

17 Why, Yahweh, leave us to stray from your ways
and harden our hearts against fearing you?
Return, for the sake of your servants,
the tribes of your inheritance.

18 Why have the wicked set foot in your sanctuary,
why are our enemies trampling your sanctuary?

19 We have long been like people you do not rule,
people who do not bear your name.

*1* Oh, that you would tear the heavens open and
come down

*2* —at your Presence the mountains would melt,

*1* as fire sets brushwood alight,

# 64

as fire causes water to boil—
to make known your name to your enemies,
and make the nations tremble at your Presence,

*2* working unexpected miracles
*3* such as no one has ever heard of before.
*4*

No ear has heard,
no eye has seen
any god but you act like this
for those who trust him.

**63 a.** The patriarch Jacob.

$\frac{4}{5}$     You guide those who act with integrity
and keep your ways in mind.
You were angry when we were sinners;
we had long been rebels against you.

$\frac{5}{6}$     We were all like men unclean,
all that integrity of ours like filthy clothing.
We have all withered like leaves
and our sins blew us away like the wind.

$\frac{6}{7}$     No one invoked your name
or roused himself to catch hold of you.
For you hid your face from us
and gave us up to the power of our sins.

$\frac{7}{8}$     And yet, Yahweh, you are our Father;
we the clay, you the potter,
we are all the work of your hand.

$\frac{8}{9}$     Do not let your anger go too far, Yahweh,
or go on thinking of our sins for ever.
See, see, we are all your people;

$\frac{9}{10}$    your holy cities are a wilderness,
Zion a wilderness,
Jerusalem a desolation,

$\frac{10}{11}$   our holy and glorious Temple,
in which our fathers prayed to you,
is burned to the ground;
all that gave us pleasure lies in ruins.

$\frac{11}{12}$   Yahweh, can you go unmoved by all of this,
oppressing us beyond measure by your silence?

## A diatribe against idolatry; eschatological discourse

65 ¹ I was ready to be approached by those who did
not consult me, ready to be found by those who
did not seek me. I said, "I am here, I am here," to a
² nation that did not invoke my name. ·Each day I
stretched out my hand to a rebellious people who went
³ by evil ways, following their own whims, ·a people who
provoked me to my face incessantly, sacrificing in gar-
⁴ dens, burning incense on bricks, ·living in tombs,
spending nights in dark corners, eating the meat of
⁵ pigs, using unclean foods in their kitchens. ·"Keep off,"
they say, "do not come near me, or I might sanctify
you." Such men are smoke in my nostrils, an ever burn-
⁶ ing fire. ·See, it is inscribed in front of me; I will not
⁷ be silent until I have settled my account with them ·for

their sins and their fathers' sins, says Yahweh, those men who burned incense on the mountains and insulted me on the hills. I will pay them back in full all they deserve.

8    Yahweh says this: When new wine is found in a bunch of grapes people say, "Do not destroy it, it contains a blessing." I shall do the same for the sake of
9 those who serve me. I refuse to destroy the whole. ·I will create a race from Jacob, and heirs to my mountains from Judah. My chosen shall inherit them, my
10 servants live in them. ·Sharon will be a pasture for flocks, the Valley of Achor a feeding ground for oxen, for those of my people who have sought me.

11          But you who have abandoned Yahweh,
               and forgotten my holy mountain,
               who lay the table for Gad,
               who fill a cup for Meni,[a]
12          I commit you to the sword,
               all of you to fall in the slaughter.
               For I called and you would not answer,
               I spoke and you would not listen.
               You did what I consider evil,
               you chose to do what displeases me.
13          Therefore, thus speaks
               the Lord Yahweh:
               You shall see my servants eat
               while you go hungry.
               You shall see my servants drink
               while you go thirsty.
               You shall see my servants rejoice
               while you are put to shame.
14          You shall hear my servants sing
               for joy of heart,
               while you will moan
               for sadness of heart;
               you will wail for distress of spirit.

15    My chosen ones will use as a curse the name you leave behind: May the Lord Yahweh strike you dead.
16 But my servants are to be given a new name. ·Whoever

---

**65 a.** Gad and Meni are pagan gods.

asks to be blessed on earth will ask to be blessed by
the God of truth, and whoever takes oath on earth will
take oath by the God of truth, for past troubles will be
17 forgotten and hidden from my eyes. ·For now I create
new heavens and a new earth, and the past will not
be remembered, and will come no more to men's minds.
18 Be glad and rejoice for ever and ever for what I am
creating, because I now create Jerusalem "Joy" and
19 her people "Gladness." ·I shall rejoice over Jerusalem
and exult in my people. No more will the sound of
20 weeping or the sound of cries be heard in her; ·in her,
no more will be found the infant living a few days only,
or the old man not living to the end of his days. To
die at the age of a hundred will be dying young; not
21 to live to be a hundred will be the sign of a curse. ·They
will build houses and inhabit them, plant vineyards
22 and eat their fruit. ·They will not build for others to
live in, or plant so that others can eat. For my people
shall live as long as trees, and my chosen ones wear out
23 what their hands have made. ·They will not toil in
vain or beget children to their own ruin, for they will
be a race blessed by Yahweh, and their children with
24 them. ·Long before they call I shall answer; before
25 they stop speaking I shall have heard. ·The wolf and
the young lamb will feed together, *the lion eat straw
like the ox,* and dust will be the serpent's food. *They
will do no hurt, no harm on all my holy mountain,*
says Yahweh.[b]

**Oracle**

1
**66** Thus says Yahweh:
With heaven my throne
and earth my footstool,
what house could you build me,
what place could you make for my rest?
2          All of this was made by my hand
and all of this is mine—it is Yahweh who speaks.
But my eyes are drawn to the man
of humbled and contrite spirit,
who trembles at my word.

**Against the intrusion of idolatrous practice**

3          Some immolate an ox, some slaughter a man,
some sacrifice a lamb, some strangle a dog.

Some offer oblations of pig's blood,
    some burn memorial incense, some consecrate
        idols.
Since they elect to follow their own ways
    and their souls delight in their abominations,

4    I in my turn will select hardships for them
    and bring them what they dread;
    for I called and no one would answer,
    I spoke and they would not listen.
They did what I consider evil,
    they chose to do what displeases me.

## An apocalyptic poem

5    Listen to the word of Yahweh,
    you who tremble at his word.
    Your brothers say, who hate you,
    who reject you because of my name,
    "Let Yahweh show his glory,
    let us witness your joy!"
    But they shall be put to shame.

6    Listen. An uproar from the city!
    A voice from the Temple!
    The voice of Yahweh bringing
    retribution on his enemies.

7    Long before being in labor
    she has given birth.
    Before being overtaken by birth pangs,
    she has been delivered of a boy.

8    Who ever heard of such a thing,
    who ever saw anything like this?
    is a country born
    in one day?

    Is a nation brought forth
    all at once,
    that Zion only just in labor
    should bring forth sons?

9    Am I to open the womb and not bring to birth?
    says Yahweh.

b. The quotations from the poem which is ch. 11.

Or I, who bring to birth, am I to close it?
says your God.

10      Rejoice, Jerusalem,
        be glad for her, all you who love her!
        Rejoice, rejoice for her,
        all you who mourned her!

11      That you may be suckled, filled,
        from her consoling breast,
        that you may savor with delight
        her glorious breasts.

12      For thus says Yahweh:
        Now toward her I send flowing
        peace, like a river,
        and like a stream in spate
        the glory of the nations.

        At her breast will her nurslings be carried
        and fondled in her lap.
13      Like a son comforted by his mother
        will I comfort you.
        (And by Jerusalem you will be comforted.)

14      At the sight your heart will rejoice,
        and your bones flourish like the grass.
        To his servants Yahweh will reveal his hand,
        but to his enemies his fury.

15      For see how Yahweh comes in fire,
        his chariots like the tempest,
        to assuage his anger with burning,
        his threats with flaming fire.

16      For by fire will Yahweh execute judgment,
        and by his sword, against all mankind.
        The victims of Yahweh will be many.

## A fragment condemning pagan mysteries

17      As for those who sanctify themselves and purify
                themselves to enter the gardens,
        following the one in the center,
        who eat the flesh of pigs, reptiles, rats:

their deeds and their thoughts shall end all at
>    once
—it is Yahweh who speaks.

## An eschatological discourse

18  I am coming to gather the nations of every language.
19  They shall come to witness my glory. ·I will give them
a sign and send some of their survivors to the nations:
to Tarshish, Put, Lud, Moshech, Rosh, Tubal, and
Javan, to the distant islands[a] that have never heard of
me or seen my glory. They will proclaim my glory to
20  the nations. ·As an offering to Yahweh they will bring
all your brothers, on horses, in chariots, in litters, on
mules, on dromedaries, from all the nations to my holy
mountain in Jerusalem, says Yahweh, like Israelites
bringing oblations in clean vessels to the Temple of
21  Yahweh. ·And of some of them I will make priests
and Levites, says Yahweh.

22        For as the new heavens
and the new earth I shall make
will endure before me—it is Yahweh who
>        speaks—
so will your race and name endure.

23        From New Moon to New Moon,
from sabbath to sabbath,
all mankind will come to bow down
in my presence, says Yahweh.

24        And on their way out they will see
the corpses of men
who have rebelled against me.
Their worm will not die
nor their fire go out;
they will be loathsome to all mankind.

**66 a.** Of these distant places, Rosh is unknown; the other names
represent: Tartessos (Spain), Somaliland, Libya, two regions of
Asia Minor and Ionia.

INTRODUCTION TO THE BOOKS OF

# JEREMIAH, LAMENTATIONS AND BARUCH

### Jeremiah

Jeremiah, a man of peace, was called to prophesy strife and disaster. In the years which saw the ruin and the end of the kingdom of Judah, he contended against kings, priests, false prophets and the nation itself, maintaining that resistance to the Chaldaean invader was vain resistance to the inexorable will of Yahweh. As the biographical anecdotes included in the book show, he was not a popular figure in his own time and barely escaped the death penalty.

However the prophecies collected by his secretary Baruch continued to be studied, meditated and interpreted; and after his death he grew steadily in stature. The truth of his message was eventually proved by history; his book reflects a warm personal religion and a confidence that there will be a covenant written in the heart; and by the Maccabean period, we find Jeremiah considered a protector of the nation, almost a patron saint.

The various oracles in the book are not in their chronological order and they include certain prophecies of a later date altogether. Nevertheless, the body of the work is undoubtedly made up of the oracles dictated to Baruch in 605 (as recounted in the book) and rewritten and supplemented afterward, when the king had ordered the burning of the first scroll.

### Lamentations

The subject matter of this short book certainly reflects the lifetime of Jeremiah, to whom the Lamentations have traditionally been ascribed. Chapters 1, 2 and 4 take the form of a dirge for the dead, and were written in Palestine after the fall of Jerusalem in 587.

However, the conscious literary forms seem foreign to the direct sincerity of Jeremiah in his prophecies, and the poems contain judgments which contradict some of his decided views. The book remains a classic of repentance with a striking pathos.

## Baruch

This short collection testifies to the enduring reputation of Jeremiah. Commended under the name of Baruch, it actually contains a prayer, a "wisdom" poem, a prophetic passage, and a letter setting out the argument against idolatry. The letter is of the Greek period; the other sections are difficult to date and may be as late as the second or first century B.C.

# JEREMIAH

### Title

¹ 1 The words of Jeremiah son of Hilkiah, of a priestly
family living at Anathoth*a* in the territory of Ben-
² jamin. ·The word of Yahweh was addressed to him in
the days of Josiah son of Amon, king of Judah, in the
³ thirteenth year of his reign*b*; ·then in the days of Jehoiakim son of Josiah, king of Judah, until the end of
the eleventh year of Zedekiah son of Josiah, king of
Judah, until the deportation of Jerusalem which oc-
curred in the fifth month.*c*

## I. ORACLES AGAINST JUDAH AND JERUSALEM

### A. IN THE REIGN OF JOSIAH

#### The call of Jeremiah

⁴ The word of Yahweh was addressed to me, saying,

⁵ "Before I formed you in the womb I knew you;
before you came to birth I consecrated you;
I have appointed you as a prophet to the nations."

⁶ I said, "Ah, Lord Yahweh; look, I do not know how
to speak: I am a child!"

⁷ But Yahweh replied,
"Do not say, 'I am a child.'
Go now to those to whom I send you
and say whatever I command you.

1 a. Near Jerusalem.
b. 626 B.C.
c. That is, from 608 to July 587.

8 Do not be afraid of them,
for I am with you to protect you—
it is Yahweh who speaks!"

9 Then Yahweh put out his hand and touched my
mouth and said to me:

10 "There! I am putting my words into your mouth.
Look, today I am setting you
over nations and over kingdoms,
to tear up and to knock down,
to destroy and to overthrow,
to build and to plant."

11 The word of Yahweh was addressed to me asking,
"Jeremiah, what do you see?" "I see a branch of the
12 Watchful Tree,"[d] I answered. ·Then Yahweh said,
"Well seen! I too watch over my word to see it fulfilled."

13 A second time the word of Yahweh was spoken to
me, asking, "What do you see?" "I see a cooking pot
on the boil," I answered, "with its contents tilting from
14 the North." ·Then Yahweh said:

"The North is where disaster is boiling over
for all who live in this land;
15 since I am now going to summon all the kingdoms of the North—
it is Yahweh who speaks.
They are going to come, and each will set his
throne
in front of the gates of Jerusalem,
all around outside its walls,
and outside all the towns of Judah.
16 I am going to pronounce my judgments against
them
for all their wickedness; since they have abandoned me
to offer incense to other gods
and worship what their own hands have made.

17 "So now brace yourself for action.
Stand up and tell them
all I command you.
Do not be dismayed at their presence,

or in their presence I will make you dismayed.
18  I, for my part, today will make you
into a fortified city,
a pillar of iron,
and a wall of bronze
to confront all this land:
the kings of Judah, its princes,
its priests and the country people.
19  They will fight against you
but shall not overcome you,
for I am with you to deliver you—
it is Yahweh who speaks."

## The earliest preaching of Jeremiah: the apostasy of Israel

1  2  The word of Yahweh was addressed to me, saying,
2     "Go and shout this in the hearing of Jerusalem:

'Yahweh says this:
I remember the affection of your youth,
the love of your bridal days:
you followed me through the wilderness,
through a land unsown.
3  Israel was sacred to Yahweh,
the first fruits of his harvest;
anyone who ate of this had to pay for it,
misfortune came to them—
it is Yahweh who speaks.'
4  Listen to the word of Yahweh, House of Jacob,
and all you families of the House of Israel.
5  Thus says Yahweh,
"What shortcoming did your fathers find in me
that led them to desert me?
Vanity they pursued,
vanity they became.
6  They never said, 'Where is Yahweh,
who brought us out of the land of Egypt
and led us through the wilderness,
through a land arid and scored,
a land of drought and darkness,
a land where no one passes,
and no man lives?'

d. The almond, the earliest to flower.

7 I brought you to a fertile country
to enjoy its produce and good things;
but no sooner had you entered than you defiled
　　my land,
and made my heritage detestable.

8 The priests have never asked, 'Where is Yah-
　　weh?'
Those who administer the Law have no knowl-
　　edge of me.
The shepherds[a] have rebelled against me;
the prophets have prophesied in the name of
　　Baal,
following things with no power in them.

9 So I must put you on trial once more
—it is Yahweh who speaks—
and your children's children too.

10 Now take ship for the islands of Kittim[b]
or send to Kedar to inquire.
Take careful notice and observe
if anything like this has happened.

11 Does a nation change its gods?
—and these are not gods at all!
Yet my people have exchanged their Glory
for what has no power in it.

12 You heavens, stand aghast at this,
stand stupefied, stand utterly appalled
—it is Yahweh who speaks.

13 Since my people have committed a double
　　crime:
they have abandoned me,
the fountain of living water,
only to dig cisterns for themselves,
leaky cisterns
that hold no water.

14 "Is Israel then a slave,
or born to serfdom,
for him to be preyed on like this?

15 Lions have roared at him,
loudly they have roared.
They have reduced his land to a desert;
his towns lie burned and desolate.

16    The people of Noph and Tahpanhes
      have even shaved your skull!*c*

17    Have you not brought this on yourself,
      by abandoning Yahweh your God?

18    What is the good of going to Egypt now
      to drink the water of the Nile?
      What is the good of going to Assyria
      to drink the water of the river?

19    Your own wickedness is punishing you,
      your own apostasies are rebuking you:
      consider carefully
      how evil and bitter it is for you
      to abandon Yahweh your God
      and not to stand in awe of me
      —it is Yahweh Sabaoth who speaks.

20    "It is long ago now since you broke your yoke,
      burst your bonds
      and said, 'I will not serve!'
      Yet on every high hill
      and under every spreading tree
      you have lain down like a harlot.

21    Yet I had planted you, a choice vine,
      a shoot of soundest stock.
      How is it you have become a degenerate plant,
      you bastard Vine?

22    Should you launder yourself with potash
      and put in quantities of lye,
      I should still detect the stain of your guilt
      —it is the Lord Yahweh who speaks.

23    How dare you say, 'I am not defiled,
      I have not run after the Baals?'
      Look at your footprints in the Valley,
      and acknowledge what you have done.
      A frantic she-camel running in all directions

24    bolts for the desert,
      snuffing the breeze in desire;
      who can control her when she is on heat?

**2 a.** The rulers.
**b.** Probably Cyprus; but here the term must include the coasts
and islands of the Mediterranean, to the west of Palestine. *Kedar,*
in the next line, a Transjordanian tribe, represents the East.
**c.** Allusion to Egyptian intervention, 608–605; the two towns are
Egyptian.

Whoever looks for her will have no trouble,
he will find her with her mate!

25 Beware! Your own foot may soon go unshod,
your own throat may grow dry.
But 'Who cares?' you said.
'For I am in love with strangers
and they are the ones I follow.'

26 "Like a thief in the disgrace of being caught,
so will the House of Israel be:
they, their kings, their princes,
their priests and their prophets,

27 who say to a piece of wood, 'You are my father,'
to a stone, 'You have begotten me.'
They turn their backs to me,
never their faces;
but when trouble comes they shout,
'Get up! Save us!'

28 Where are those gods of yours you made for
yourself?
Let them get up to save you when trouble
comes!
For you have as many gods
as you have towns, Judah,
as many altars for Baal
as Jerusalem has streets.

29 What case can you make against me?
You have all apostatized from me
—it is Yahweh who speaks.

30 In vain I have struck down your sons,
you did not accept correction:
your sword devoured your prophets
like a destructive lion.

31 What a brood you are! Listen, this is the word
of Yahweh:
Have I been a desert for Israel
or a land of deepest gloom?
Then why do my people say,
'We will go our own way,
we will no longer come to you?'

32 Does a girl forget her ornaments,
a bride her sash?

And yet my people have forgotten me,
for days beyond number.

33     "How well you know the way
in pursuit of love!
Yes, you have even accustomed your steps
to walk with crime,
34     to the point when your hands display
the stains from the blood of innocent men.
—You never caught them trying to break and
enter!
Yes, for all these you will have to answer.
35     You say, 'I am blameless,
his anger has turned away from me.'
And here I am passing sentence on you
because you say, 'I have not sinned.'

36     "How frivolously you undertake
a change of course!
But you will be disappointed by Egypt
just as you were by Assyria.
37     You will have to leave there too
with your hands on your head,
for Yahweh has rejected those that you rely on,
you will come to no good with them."

### The conversion

1   **3** The word of Yahweh was addressed to me saying:

"If a man divorces his wife
and she leaves him
to marry someone else,
may she still go back to him?
Has not that piece of land
been totally polluted?
And you, who have prostituted yourself with so
many lovers,
you would come back to me?—it is Yahweh who
speaks.

2     "Lift your eyes to the bare heights and look!
Is there a single place where you have not offered your body?
You waited by the roadside for clients
like an Arab in the desert.

You have polluted the country
with your prostitution and your vices:
3    this is why the showers have been withheld,
the late rains have not come.

"And you maintained a prostitute's bold front,
never thinking to blush.
4    Even then did you not cry to me, 'My father!
You, the friend of my youth!
5    Will he keep his resentment for ever,
will he maintain his wrath to the end?'
That was what you said, and still you went on
sinning,
you were so obstinate."

## The Northern Kingdom urged to repent

6    In the days of King Josiah, Yahweh said to me,
"Have you seen what disloyal Israel has done? How
she has made her way up every high hill and to every
7 spreading tree, and has prostituted herself there? ·I
thought: After doing all this she will come back to me.
But she did not come back. Her faithless sister Judah
8 saw this. ·She also saw that I had repudiated disloyal
Israel for all her adulteries and given her her divorce
papers. Her faithless sister Judah, however, was not
9 afraid: she too went and played the whore. ·So shame-
less was her whoring that at last she polluted the country; she committed adultery with lumps of stone and
10 pieces of wood. ·Worse than all this: Judah, her faithless sister, has not come back to me in sincerity, but
only in pretense—it is Yahweh who speaks."
11    And Yahweh said to me, "Besides faithless Judah,
12 disloyal Israel seems virtuous. ·So go and shout these
words toward the North:

'Come back, disloyal Israel—it is Yahweh who
speaks—
I shall frown on you no more,
since I am merciful—it is Yahweh who speaks.
I shall not keep my resentment for ever.
13    Only acknowledge your guilt:
how you have apostatized from Yahweh your
God,
how you have flirted with strangers

and have not listened to my voice—it is Yahweh
who speaks.

## Zion in the messianic age

14   'Come back, disloyal children—it is Yahweh who
speaks—for I alone am your Master. I will take one
from a town, two from a clan, and bring you to Zion.
15   I will give you shepherds after my own heart, and these
16   shall feed you on knowledge and discretion. •And when
you have increased and become many in the land,
then—it is Yahweh who speaks—no one will ever say
again: Where is the ark of the covenant of Yahweh?
There will be no thought of it, no memory of it, no
17   regret for it, no making of another.[a] •When that time
comes, Jerusalem shall be called: The Throne of Yahweh; all the nations will gather there in the name of
Yahweh and will no longer follow the dictates of their
own stubborn hearts.
18   'In those days the House of Judah will unite with the
House of Israel; together they will come from the land
of the North to the land I gave your ancestors for a
heritage.

## Continuation of the poem on the conversion[b]

19             'And I was thinking:
             How I wanted to rank you with my sons,
             and give you a country of delights,
             the fairest heritage of all the nations!
             I had thought you would call me: My father,
             and would never cease to follow me.
20             But like a woman betraying her lover,
             the House of Israel has betrayed me—
             it is Yahweh who speaks.' "

21             A noise is heard on the bare heights:
             the weeping and entreaty of the sons of Israel,
             because they have gone so wildly astray,
             and forgotten Yahweh their God.
22             "Come back, disloyal sons,
             I want to heal your disloyalty."

**3 a.** The ark was destroyed with the Temple by the Chaldaeans
in 587.
**b.** Continued from v.5.

> "We are here, we are coming to you,
> for you are Yahweh our God.

23
> The heights are a delusion after all,
> so is the tumult of the mountains.

> "Yahweh our God is, after all,
> the saving of Israel.

24
> The Thing of Shame[c] has devoured what our
>     ancestors worked for
> since our youth
> (their flocks and herds, their sons and daugh-
>     ters).

25
> Let us lie down in our shame, let our dishonor
>     be our covering,
> for we have sinned against Yahweh our God.

("we and our ancestors since our youth until today;
and we have not listened to the voice of Yahweh our
God.")

1
> "If you wish to come back, Israel—it is Yahweh
>     who speaks—
> it is to me you must return.
> Do away with your abominations
> and you will have no need to avoid me.

2
> If you swear, 'As Yahweh lives!'
> truthfully, justly, honestly,
> the nations will bless themselves by you,
> and glory in you.

3
> For thus speaks Yahweh
> to the men of Judah and to the inhabitants of
>     Jerusalem:
> Clean your ground thoroughly,
> sow nothing among thorns.

4
> Circumcise yourselves for Yahweh; off with the
>     foreskin of your hearts
> (men of Judah and inhabitants of Jerusalem),
> lest my wrath should leap out like a fire,
> and burn with no one to quench it,
> in return for the wickedness of your deeds."

### Invasion from the North

5
> Announce it in Judah,
> proclaim it in Jerusalem!

Sound the trumpet in the countryside,
shout the message aloud:
Mobilize!
Take to the fortified towns!

6    Signpost the way to Zion;
Run! Do not delay!
I am bringing you disaster from the North,
an immense calamity.

7    The lion is up from his thicket,
the destroyer of nations is on his way,
he has come from his home
to reduce your land to a desert;
your towns will be in ruins, deserted.

8    So wrap yourselves in sackcloth,
lament and wail,
since the burning anger of Yahweh
has not turned away from us.

9    "That day—it is Yahweh who speaks—
the king's heart will fail him,
the princes' hearts will fail them too,
the priests will stand aghast,
the prophets stupefied.

10   People will say, 'Ah, Lord Yahweh,
how utterly you deceived us
by saying: You will have peace,[a]—
even when the sword is at our throats!'

11   When that time comes, this will be said
to this people and to Jerusalem:
From the bare heights a scorching wind
blows from the desert on the daughter of my
        people
—and not to winnow or to cleanse!

12   A wind, full of threats, comes at my command.
Now I myself am going to pronounce
sentence on them!

13   'Look, he is advancing like the clouds,
his chariots like a hurricane,
his horses swifter than eagles.
Trouble is coming! We are lost!'

c. The false god, Baal.
4 a. The promise of the false prophets. See 6:14.

14  Wash your heart clean of wickedness, Jerusalem,
and so be saved.
How long will you harbor in your breast
your pernicious thoughts?

15  For a voice from Dan shouts the news,
proclaims disaster from the highlands of Ephraim.

16  Give warning of it, announce it in Judah,
proclaim it to Jerusalem:
'Enemies are coming from a distant country,
shouting their war cry against the towns of Judah;

17  they surround Jerusalem like watchmen around a field
because she has apostatized from me—it is Yahweh who speaks.

18  Your own behavior and actions
have brought this on you.
This is your fate! How bitter!
How it pierces your heart!' "

19  I am in anguish! I writhe with pain!
Walls of my heart!
My heart is throbbing!
I cannot keep quiet,
for I have heard the trumpet call
and the cry of war.

20  Ruin on ruin is the news:
the whole land is laid waste,
my tents are suddenly destroyed,
in one moment all that sheltered me is gone.

21  How long must I see the standard
and hear the trumpet call?

22  "This is because my people are stupid,
they do not know me,
they are slow-witted children,
they have no understanding:
they are clever enough at doing wrong,
but do not know how to do right."

23  I looked to the earth, to see a formless waste;
to the heavens, and their light had gone.

24   I looked to the mountains, to see them quaking
and all the heights astir.

25   I looked, to see no man at all,
the very birds of heaven had fled.

26   I looked, to see the wooded country a wilderness,
all its towns in ruins,
at the presence of Yahweh,
at the presence of his burning anger.

27   Yes, thus speaks Yahweh,
"The whole land shall be laid waste,
I will make an end of it once for all;

28   at which the earth will go into mourning,
and the heavens above grow dark.
For I have spoken and will not change my mind,
I have decided and will not go back on it."

29   At the cry "Horsemen and bowmen!"
the whole country takes flight:
some plunge into the thickets,
others scale the rocks;
every town is abandoned,
no one is left there.

30   And you, what are you going to do?
You may dress yourself in scarlet,
put on ornaments of gold,
enlarge your eyes with paint
but you make yourself pretty in vain.
Your lovers disdain you,
your life is what they are seeking.

31   Yes, I hear screams like those of a woman in labor,
anguish like that of a woman giving birth to her first child;
they are the screams of the daughter of Zion, gasping,
hands outstretched,
"Ah, I despair! I am fainting away
with murderers surrounding me."

### The invasion well deserved

1   **5**   "Rove to and fro through the streets of Jerusalem,

> look, now, and learn,
> search her squares;
> if you can find a man,
> one man who does right
> and seeks the truth,
> then I will pardon her,
> says Yahweh."

3a     Yahweh, do not your eyes desire to look on truth?

2     But though they say, "As Yahweh lives,"
they are, in fact, uttering a false oath.

3b     You have struck them; they have not felt it.
You have crushed them; they have ignored the lesson.
They have set their faces harder than rock,
they have refused to repent.

4     "Only the ordinary people," I thought, "behave stupidly,
because they do not know what Yahweh requires,
nor the ruling of their God.

5     I will approach the men in power
and speak to them,
for these will know what Yahweh requires,
and the ruling of their God."
But these, too, had broken the yoke,
had burst the bonds.

6     And this is why a lion from the forest strikes them down,
a desert wolf makes havoc of them,
a leopard lurks around their towns:
whoever goes out is torn to pieces—
because of their countless crimes,
their ever increasing apostasies.

7     "Why should I pardon you?
Your sons have abandoned me,
to swear by gods that are not gods at all.
I fed them full, and they became adulterers,
they haunted the brothel.

8   They were well-fed, lusty stallions,
    each neighing for his neighbor's wife.

9   And am I not to punish them for such things
    —it is Yahweh who speaks—
    or from such a nation
    exact my vengeance?

10  Scale her terraces! Destroy!
    Make an end of her!
    Strip off her branches,
    Yahweh does not own them.

11  Treacherously indeed has she betrayed me,
    this House of Israel—it is Yahweh who speaks.

12  "They have disowned Yahweh:
    they have said, "He is nothing;
    no evil will overtake us,
    we shall not see sword or famine.

13a And the prophets? Nothing but wind;
    the word is not in them!'

14a Hence—so says Yahweh,
    the God of Sabaoth—

13b this is what is going to happen to them
14b for saying this:
    now I will make my words
    a fire in your mouth,
    and make this people wood,
    for the fire to devour.

15  Now I will bring on you all
    a nation from afar, House of Israel
    —it is Yahweh who speaks—
    an invincible nation,
    an ancient nation,
    a nation whose tongue you do not know,
    whose language you cannot understand.

16  Their quiver is an open tomb;
    heroes all of them.

17  They will devour your harvest and your food,
    devour your sons and daughters,
    devour your flocks and herds,
    devour your vines and fig trees,
    bring down your fortified towns
    in which you put your trust.

### Two supplementary paragraphs

18    "Yet even in those days—it is Yahweh who speaks—
I shall not completely destroy you.
19    "And when they ask, 'Why has Yahweh our God
done all this to us?' you are to give them this answer,
'As you abandoned me to serve alien gods in your own
land, so you must serve aliens in a land that is not your
own.'

### In a time of famine (?)

20          "Announce this in the House of Jacob,
            proclaim it in Judah, and say:
21          'Now listen to this,
            stupid and thoughtless people
            —they have eyes and do not see,
            they have ears and do not hear!
22          Have you no fear of me?—it is Yahweh who
                speaks—
            Will you not tremble at my presence,
            who set the sands as limit to the sea,
            as an everlasting barrier it can not pass?
            It storms but can do nothing,
            its waves may roar but do not pass beyond.
23          But this people
            has a rebellious, unruly heart;
            they have rebelled—being good at this!
24          They have not said in their hearts:
            Come, we must fear Yahweh our God
            who gives the rain, the early rain
            and the later, at the right time of year,
            who assures us
            of weeks appointed for harvest.
25          Your crimes have made all this go wrong,
            your sins have deprived you of these favors.

### Resumption of the theme of the invasion

26          'Yes, there are wicked men among my people
            who spread their nets;
            like fowlers they set snares,
            but it is men they catch.
27          Like a cage full of birds
            so are their houses full of loot;

they have grown rich and powerful because of
    it,
28    fat and sleek.
Yes, in wickedness they go to any lengths,
they have no respect for rights,
for orphans' rights, to support them;
they do not uphold the cause of the poor.
29    And must I not punish them for such things
—it is Yahweh who speaks—
or from such a nation
exact my vengeance?
30    Monstrous, horrible things
are happening in the land:
31    the prophets prophesy falsely,
the priests teach whatever they please.
And my people love it!
But when the end comes, what will you do?

## More about the invasion

1  **6**  'Save yourselves, men of Benjamin,
from the heart of Jerusalem!
Sound the trumpet in Tekoa![a]
Set up a standard on Beth-hac-cherem!
For disaster threatens from the North,
an immense calamity.
2    Shall we compare the daughter of Zion
to a tender pasture?
3    Shepherds advance on her
with their flocks.
They have pitched their tents all around her,
each grazes the part he chooses.
4    Prepare for battle against her!
To arms! We will launch the attack in broad
    daylight.
Despair! The daylight is fading already,
the evening shadows lengthen.
5    To arms! We will launch the attack under
    cover of dark
and destroy her palaces.
6    For thus says Yahweh Sabaoth:
Cut down the trees,

**6** a. Five miles south of Bethlehem.

throw up an earthwork outside Jerusalem:
she is the City of Falsehood,
with nothing but oppression in her.

7　As a well keeps its water fresh
so she keeps her wickedness fresh.
Violence and ruin are what you hear in her,
diseases and wounds are always before me.

8　Be warned, Jerusalem,
lest I should turn away from you,
and reduce you to a desert,
a land without people.

9　'Yahweh Sabaoth says this:
Glean, glean, as a vine is gleaned,
what is left of Israel;
like a grape picker pass your hand again
over the branches!' "

10　To whom am I to speak,
whom can I urge to hear?
Plainly their ears are uncircumcised,
they cannot listen.
Plainly the word of Yahweh is for them some-
　　　thing contemptible,
they have no taste for it.

11　But I am full of the wrath of Yahweh,
I am weary of holding it in.
"Then pour it on the children in the streets,
and where young men gather, too.
All shall be taken: husband and wife,
the graybeard and the man weighed down with
　　　years.

12　Their houses shall pass to other men,
so also their fields and their wives.
Yes, I will stretch my hand
over those living in this land—it is Yahweh who
　　　speaks.

13　For all, least no less than greatest,
all are out for dishonest gain;
prophet no less than priest,
all practice fraud.

14　They dress my people's wound
without concern: 'Peace! Peace!' they say,
but there is no peace.

15    They should be ashamed of their abominable
        deeds
But not they! They feel no shame,
they have forgotten how to blush.
And so as others fall, they too shall fall;
they shall be thrown down when I come to deal
        with them
—says Yahweh.

16    "Yahweh says this:
Put yourselves on the ways of long ago
inquire about the ancient paths:
which was the good way? Take it then,
and you shall find rest.
Instead they have said, 'We will not take it.'

17    I posted lookouts on their behalf:
Listen to the sound of the trumpet!
But they answered, 'We will not listen.'

18    Then hear, you nations,
and know, assembly,
what I will do to them.

19    Hear, earth!
I am bringing a disaster
on this people:
it is the fruit of their apostasy,
since they have not listened to my words
and, as for my Law, they have rejected that.

20    What do I care about incense
imported from Sheba,
or fragrant cane
from a distant country?
Your holocausts are not acceptable,
your sacrifices do not please me.

21    Therefore—thus says Yahweh:
In front of this people I will now lay blocks
for them to stumble over;
father as well as son,
neighbor and friend, all shall perish.

22    "Yahweh says this:
Now a people is coming from the land of the
        North,
from the far ends of the earth a mighty nation
        stirs:

23      they are armed with bow and spear,
they are cruel and pitiless;
their noise is like the roaring of the sea;
they are riding horses,
each man equipped for war
on you, daughter of Zion!

24      We have heard the news,
our hands fall limp,
anguish has gripped us,
pain like a woman's labor.

25      Do not go out into the countryside,
do not venture on the roads,
for the enemy's sword is there,
there is terror on every side.

26      Wrap yourself in sackcloth, daughter of my
          people,
roll in ashes;
mourn as for an only son,
a very bitter dirge.
For on us suddenly
the destroyer is coming.

27      "I have appointed you as assayer of my people,
to learn and to assay how they behave.

28      They are apostates, all of them, promiscuous
          slanderers,
all of them corrupt.

29      The bellows blast away
to make the fire burn away the lead.
In vain: the smelter does his work,
but the dross is not purged out.

30      Silver reject, men call them,
and indeed Yahweh has rejected them!"

## B. ORACLES MAINLY IN THE REIGN OF JEHOIAKIM

### True worship
#### a. Against the Temple

1   7 The word that was addressed to Jeremiah by Yah-
2      weh, ·"Go and stand at the gate of the Temple of
Yahweh and there proclaim this message. Say, 'Listen
to the word of Yahweh, all you men of Judah who
3 come in by these gates to worship Yahweh. ·Yahweh

Sabaoth, the God of Israel, says this: Amend your behavior and your actions and I will stay with you here
4 in this place. ·Put no trust in delusive words like these: This is the sanctuary of Yahweh, the sanctuary of Yah-
5 weh, the sanctuary of Yahweh! ·But if you do amend your behavior and your actions, if you treat each other
6 fairly, ·if you do not exploit the stranger, the orphan and the widow (if you do not shed innocent blood in this place), and if you do not follow alien gods, to your
7 own ruin, ·then here in this place I will stay with you, in the land that long ago I gave to your fathers for
8 ever. ·Yet here you are, trusting in delusive words, to
9 no purpose! ·Steal, would you, murder, commit adultery, perjure yourselves, burn incense to Baal, follow
10 alien gods that you do not know?—·and then come presenting yourselves in this Temple that bears my name, saying: Now we are safe—safe to go on committing all
11 these abominations! ·Do you take this Temple that bears my name for a robbers' den? I, at any rate, am not blind—it is Yahweh who speaks.

12     Now go to my place in Shiloh*a* where at first I gave my name a home; see what I have done to it because
13 of the wickedness of my people Israel! ·And now, since you have committed all these sins—it is Yahweh who speaks—and have refused to listen when I spoke so urgently, so persistently, or to answer when I called you,
14 I will treat this Temple that bears my name, and in which you put your trust, and the place I have given
15 to you and your ancestors, just as I treated Shiloh. ·I will drive you out of my sight, as I drove all your kinsmen, the entire race of Ephraim.'

### b. Alien gods

16     "You, for your part, must not intercede for this people, nor raise either plea or prayer on their behalf;
17 do not plead with me, for I will not listen to you. ·Cannot you see what they are doing in the towns of Judah
18 and in the streets of Jerusalem? ·The children collect the wood, the fathers light the fire, the women knead the dough, to make cakes for the Queen of Heaven*b*;
19 and, to spite me, they pour libations to alien gods. ·Is

---

7 a. The shrine at Shiloh had been destroyed by Philistines.
b. Ishtar, the Assyrian goddess of fertility.

it really me they spite—it is Yahweh who speaks—is it
20 not in fact themselves, to their own confusion? ·There-
fore, the Lord Yahweh says this: My anger and my
wrath shall be poured out on this place, over man and
beast, trees of the countryside, fruits of the soil; it shall
burn, and not be quenched.

### c. Worship without sincerity

21    "Yahweh Sabaoth, the God of Israel, says this: Add
your holocausts to your sacrifices and eat all the meat.
22 For when I brought your ancestors out of the land of
Egypt, I said nothing to them, gave them no orders,
23 about holocaust and sacrifice. ·These were my orders:
Listen to my voice, then I will be your God and you
shall be my people. Follow right to the end the way
24 that I mark out for you, and you will prosper. ·But
they did not listen, they did not pay attention; they
followed the dictates of their own evil hearts, refused to
25 face me, and turned their backs on me. ·From the
day your ancestors came out of the land of Egypt until
today, day after day I have persistently sent you all
26 my servants the prophets. ·But they have not listened
to me, have not paid attention; they have grown stub-
27 born and behaved worse than their ancestors. ·You
may say all these words to them: they will not listen
to you; you may call them: they will not answer.
28 So tell them this, 'Here is the nation that will not listen
to the voice of Yahweh its God nor take correction.
Sincerity is no more, it has vanished from their mouths.

### d. More about idolatrous worship: a threat of exile

29          'Cut off your tresses, throw them down.
         On the bare heights raise a dirge.
         For Yahweh has rejected, has abandoned,
         a brood that he detests.'

30    "Yes, the sons of Judah have done what displeases
me—it is Yahweh who speaks. They have put their
abominations in the Temple that bears my name, to
31 defile it; ·they have built the high place of Topheth
in the Valley of Benhinnom, to burn their sons and
daughters; a thing I never commanded, a thing that
32 never entered my thoughts. ·So now the days are coming—it is Yahweh who speaks—when people will no

longer talk of Topheth or of the Valley of Ben-hinnom,
but of the Valley of Slaughter. Topheth will become a
33 burial ground, for lack of other space; ·the corpses of
this people will feed the birds of heaven and the beasts
of the earth, and there shall be no one to drive them
34 away. ·I will silence the shouts of rejoicing and mirth,
the voices of bridegroom and bride, in the towns of
Judah and in the streets of Jerusalem, for the whole
1 land will be reduced to desert. **8** When that time comes
—it is Yahweh who speaks—the bones of the kings of
Judah, and of the princes, of the priests, of the prophets,
of the inhabitants of Jerusalem, will be taken from their
2 tombs. ·They will be spread out before the sun, the
moon, the whole array of heaven, whom they have
loved and served, followed, consulted and worshiped.[a]
They will not be gathered or reburied but stay lying on
3 the surface like dung. ·And death will seem preferable
to life to all the survivors of this wicked race, wherever
I have driven them—it is Yahweh Sabaoth who speaks.

### Threats, lamentations, advice. The perversity of Israel

4        "You are to tell them, 'Yahweh says this:
         If you fall, can you not stand up again,
         if you stray can you never find your way back?
5        Why does this people persist in apostasy,
         in continuous apostasy?
         They cling to illusion,
         they refuse to come back.
6        I have listened attentively,
         they are not saying what they ought to:
         not one repents of his wickedness
         saying: What have I done?
         All go astray as they pursue their course
         like a horse charging into battle.
7        Even the stork in the sky
         knows the appropriate season;
         turtledove, swallow, crane,
         observe their time of migration.
         And my people do not know
         the ruling of Yahweh!

**8 a.** Worship of the heavenly bodies was practiced in the reigns
of Manasseh and Amon.

---

### The Law as administered by the priests

8    'How dare you say: We are wise,
and we possess the Law of Yahweh?
But look how it has been falsified
by the lying pen of the scribes!

9    The wise shall be shamed,
caught out, confounded.
Look how they have rejected the word of
     Yahweh!
So what use is their wisdom to them?

### Repetition of an earlier threat

10    'So I will give their wives to other men,
their fields to new masters,
for all, least no less than greatest,
all are out for dishonest gain;
prophet no less than priest,
all practice fraud.

11    They dress my people's wound
without concern: Peace! Peace! they say,
but there is no peace.

12    They should be ashamed of their abominable
     deeds.
But not they! They feel no shame,
they have forgotten how to blush.
And so as others fall, they too shall fall;
they shall be thrown down when I come to deal
     with them
—says Yahweh.

### Threats against Judah the Vine

13    'I would like to go harvesting there, says
     Yahweh.
But there are no grapes on the vine,
no figs on the fig tree:
even the leaves are withered.
This is because I have brought them
ravagers to ravage them.'"

14    "Why do we sit still?
Mobilize!
Let us take to the fortified towns
and perish there,

since Yahweh our God wants us to perish:
giving us poisoned water to drink
because we have sinned against him.

15  We were hoping for peace—no good came of it!
For the time of healing—nothing but terror!

16  From Dan you can hear
the snorting of their horses;
at the sound of their stallions' neighing
the whole countryside quakes:
they come to devour the land and all it holds,
the town and those that live in it."

17  "Yes, now I send you
serpents, adders,
against which no charm exists;
they will bite you—it is Yahweh who speaks—

18  incurably.

## A lamentation of the prophet during a famine

"Sorrow overtakes me,
my heart fails me.

19  Listen, the cry of the daughter of my people
sounds throughout the land,
'Yahweh no longer in Zion?
Her King no longer in her?'
(Why have they provoked me with their carved
images,
with these Nothings from foreign countries?)

20  'The harvest is over, summer at an end,
and we have not been saved!'

21  The wound of the daughter of my people wounds
me too,
all looks dark to me, terror grips me.

22  Is there not balm in Gilead any more?
Is there no doctor there?
Then why does it make no progress,
this cure of the daughter of my people?

23
1   Who will turn my head into a fountain,
and my eyes into a spring for tears,
so that I may weep all day, all night,
for all the dead out of the daughter of my
people?

### The moral corruption of Judah

**9** ¹⁄₂ "Who will find me a wayfarer's shelter
in the desert,
for me to quit my people,
and leave them far behind?
For all of them are adulterers,
a conspiracy of traitors.

²⁄₃ They bend their tongue like a bow;
not truth but falsehood
predominates in the land;
yes, they go from crime to crime.
But Yahweh, they do not acknowledge him.

³⁄₄ Let each be on his guard against his friend,
be mistrustful of your brother,
for every brother is a very Jacob,
and every friend a diligent slanderer.

⁴⁄₅ Each deceives the other,
they do not speak the truth,
they have accustomed their tongues to lying,

⁵⁄₆ they are corrupt, incapable of ·repentance.
Fraud after fraud! Deceit after deceit!
They refuse to acknowledge Yahweh.

⁶⁄₇ And so—Yahweh Sabaoth says this:
Look, I will now test them in the crucible
—but how am I to deal with their wickedness?

⁷⁄₈ Their tongue is a deadly arrow,
the words they utter are deceitful;
'Peace!' each says to his neighbor,[a]
while in his heart plotting a trap for him.

⁸⁄₉ And am I not to punish them for such things
—it is Yahweh who speaks—
or from such a nation
exact my vengeance?

### Lamentation in Zion

⁹⁄₁₀ "Raise the wail and lamentation for the mountains,
the dirge for the desert pastures,
for they have been burned: no one passes there,
the sound of flocks is heard no more.
Birds of the sky and animals,
all have fled, all are gone.

10
11
> I mean to make Jerusalem a heap of ruins,
> a jackal's lair,
> and the towns of Judah
> an uninhabited wasteland."

11
12
Who is wise enough to understand this? Who has been charged by Yahweh's own mouth to tell.

> why the land lies in ruins,
> burned like the desert where no one passes?

12
13
Yahweh has said, "This is because they have forsaken my Law which I put before them and have not listened

13
14
to my voice or followed it, ·but have followed the dictates of their own stubborn hearts, followed the Baals

14
15
as their ancestors taught them. ·And so this is what Yahweh Sabaoth, the God of Israel says: Now I am going to give this people wormwood for their food and

15
16
poisoned water to drink. ·I am going to scatter them throughout nations unknown to their ancestors or to them; and I am going to pursue them with the sword until I have exterminated them."

16
17
> You, there! Call the mourning women! Let them
>     come!
> Send for those who are best at it! Let them
>     come!

17
18
> Let them lose no time in raising the lament for
>     us!
> Let our eyes rain tears,
> our eyelids run with weeping!

18
19
> Yes, the wail is to be heard from Zion,
> "What ruin is ours,
> what utter shame!
> For we must leave the land,
> abandon our homes!"

19
20
> And you, women, now hear the word of
>     Yahweh,
> let your ears take in the word his own mouth
>     speaks.
> Teach your daughters how to wail,
> teach one another what dirge to sing,

20
21
> "Death has climbed in at our windows,

**9 a.** The customary greeting.

and made its way into our palaces;
it has cut down the children in the street,
the youths in the square.

21
22    Men's corpses lie
like dung in the open field,
like sheaves left by the reaper,
with no one to gather them."

## True wisdom

22
23          Thus says Yahweh,
"Let the sage boast no more of his wisdom,
nor the valiant of his valor,
nor the rich man of his riches!

23
24          But if anyone wants to boast, let him boast of
this:
of understanding and knowing me.
For I am Yahweh, I rule with kindness,
justice and integrity on earth;
yes, these are what please me
—it is Yahweh who speaks."

## Circumcision, a false guarantee

24
25    "See, the days are coming—it is Yahweh who speaks
—when I am going to punish all who are circumcised
25
26 only in the flesh: ·Egypt, Judah, the sons of Ammon,
Moab, and all the Crop-Heads[b] who live in the desert. For all these nations, and the whole House of Israel
too, are uncircumcised at heart."

## Idols and the true God

1
2  **10** Listen, House of Israel, to the word that Yahweh
addresses to you. ·Thus says Yahweh:

"Do not adopt the ways of the nations
or take alarm at the heavenly signs,
alarmed though the nations may be at them.
3          Yes, the Dread of the peoples is a nothing,
wood, nothing more, cut out of a forest,
worked with a blade by a carver's hand,
4a         then embellished with silver and gold
9          —silver leaf from Tarshish,
and gold from Ophir—
work of a carver and a goldsmith's hand:

all some craftsman's work;
they dress them up in violet and purple;
4b  they fix them with nail and hammer
to prevent them from falling.
5  Scarecrows in a melon patch, and dumb as
these,
they have to be carried, cannot walk themselves.
Have no fear of them: they can do no harm
—nor any good either!"

6  Yahweh, there is no one like you,
so great are you,
so great your mighty name.
7  Who would not revere you, King of nations?
Yes, this is your due.
Since of all the wise among the nations,
and in all their kingdoms,
there is not a single one like you.

8  The whole lot of them are brutish and stupid:
the teaching given by these Nothings is void of
sense.
10  But Yahweh is the true God.
He is the living God,
the everlasting King.
The earth quakes when he is wrathful,
the nations cannot endure his fury.

11  ("Tell them this, 'The gods who did not make the
heavens and the earth, will vanish from the earth and
from under the heavens.'")

12  By his power he made the earth,
by his wisdom set the world firm,
by his discernment spread out the heavens.
13  When he thunders
there is a tumult of water in the heavens;
he raises clouds from the boundaries of earth,
makes the lightning flash for the downpour,
and brings the wind from his storehouse.
14  At this all men stand stupefied, uncomprehending,
every goldsmith blushes for the idol he has made,

b. Arabs.

since his images are nothing but delusion,
with no breath in them.

15    They are a Nothing, a laughable production;
when the time comes for them to be punished,
     they will vanish.

16    "The Portion of Jacob" is not like these,
for he is the maker of everything,
and Israel is the tribe that is his heritage.
His name is Yahweh Sabaoth.

### Panic in the country

17    Pack up! Flee the country,
you the besieged!

18    For Yahweh says this,
"Now I will throw out
the inhabitants of the land
this time,
and bring distress on them,
to see if they will find me then!"

19    I despair for this wound of mine!
My injury is incurable!
I told myself
this was an affliction that could be borne,

20    but now my tent is destroyed,
all my ropes are snapped,
my sons have left me and are no more;
no one is left to put my tent up again,
or to hang the side cloths.

21    The shepherds are the ones who have been
     stupid:
they have not searched for Yahweh.
This is why they have not prospered
and why their whole flock has been dispersed.

22    News! News has come!
A mighty uproar coming from the land of the
     North
to reduce the towns of Judah
to desert, to a jackal's lair.

### A prayer of Jeremiah

23    Well you know, Yahweh,
the course of man is not in his control,
nor is it in man's power as he goes his way
to guide his steps.

24　　Correct us, Yahweh, gently,
　　　　not in your anger or you will reduce us to
　　　　　　nothing.

25　　Pour out your anger on the pagans,
　　　　who do not acknowledge you,
　　　　and on those races
　　　　that do not call on your name,
　　　　for they have devoured Jacob and made an end
　　　　　　of him,
　　　　and reduced his home to desolation.

## Jeremiah and observance of the covenant

1　11 The word that was addressed to Jeremiah by Yah-
2　　　 weh, ·"Speak to the men of Judah and to the in-
3　habitants of Jerusalem. ·Tell them, 'Yahweh, the God of
Israel, says this: Cursed be the man who will not listen
4　to the words of this covenant ·which I ordained for
your ancestors when I brought them out of the furnace
of iron, out of the land of Egypt. Listen to my voice,
I told them, carry out all my orders, then you shall be
5　my people and I will be your God, ·to confirm the
oath I swore to your fathers, that I would give them
a land where milk and honey flow—as it still does to-
6　day.' " I replied, "Yahweh, I will." ·Then Yahweh said
to me, "Proclaim all this in the towns of Judah and
in the streets of Jerusalem: 'Listen to the words of
7　this covenant and obey them. ·For when I brought
your ancestors out of the land of Egypt, I solemnly
warned them, and have persistently warned them until
8　today: Listen to my voice. ·But they did not listen,
did not pay attention; everyone followed the dictates
of his own evil heart. So, I fulfilled against them all the
words of this covenant which I had ordained for them
to obey and which they have not obeyed.' "
9　　Yahweh said to me, "Plainly there is conspiracy
among the men of Judah and the citizens of Jerusalem.
10　They have reverted to the crimes of their ancestors who
refused to listen to my words: they too are following
alien gods and serving them. The House of Israel and
the House of Judah have broken my covenant which
11　I made with their ancestors. ·And so—Yahweh says
this—I will now bring them a disaster which they cannot escape; if they invoke me I will not listen to them.

12 The towns of Judah and the citizens of Jerusalem can go and invoke the gods to whom they burn incense, but these will be no help at all to them in the time of their distress.

13
> "For you have as many gods
> as you have towns, O Judah.
> You have built as many incense altars to Baal
> as Jerusalem has streets.

14 "You, for your part, must not intercede for this people, nor raise either plea or prayer on their behalf, for I will not listen when they call to me in the time of their distress.

## Rebuke to the frequenters of the Temple

15
> "What is my beloved doing in my house?
> She is playing the hypocrite!
> Can vows and consecrated meat
> rid you of your guilt?
> Am I to make you clean because of this?

16
> A spreading olive tree so fair, so sturdy,
> was Yahweh's name for you.
> With the roar of a great wind
> he sets its foliage on fire;
> its branches burn.

17 "And Yahweh Sabaoth, who planted you, has decreed disaster for you because of the crime the House of Israel and the House of Judah have committed, provoking me by burning incense to Baal."

## Jeremiah persecuted in his own town

18 Yahweh revealed it to me; I was warned. Yahweh, that was when you opened my eyes to their scheming.
6 12 "Yes, even your own brothers and your own family play you false. Behind your back, they too criticize you openly. Put no reliance on them when they seem to be
19 friendly." 11 I for my part was like a trustful lamb being led to the slaughterhouse, not knowing the schemes they were plotting against me, "Let us destroy the tree in its strength, let us cut him off from the land of the living, so that his name may be quickly forgotten!"

20          But you, Yahweh Sabaoth, who pronounce a
                  just sentence,
            who probe the loins and heart,
            let me see the vengeance you will take on them,
            for I have committed my cause to you.

21      This is how Yahweh has spoken against the men of
      Anathoth who are determined to kill me and have
      warned me, "Do not prophesy in the name of Yahweh
22    or you will die at our hands!" ·This is how I will
      punish them. Their young men shall die by the sword,
23    their sons and daughters by famine. ·No one will be
      left when I bring disaster on the men of Anathoth,
      when the year comes for their punishment."

### The prosperity of the wicked

1  12    You have right on your side, Yahweh,
            when I complain about you.
            But I would like to debate a point of justice
                  with you.
            Why is it that the wicked live so prosperously?
            Why do scoundrels enjoy peace?
2           You plant them, they take root,
            and flourish, and even bear fruit.
            You are always on their lips,
            yet so far from their hearts.
3           You know me, Yahweh, you see me,
            you probe my heart, it is in your hands.
            Drag them off like sheep for the slaughterhouse,
            reserve them for the day of butchery.

4       (How long will the land be in mourning, and the
      grass wither all over the countryside? The animals and
      birds are dying as a result of the wickedness of the
      inhabitants.)

            For they say,
            "God does not see our behavior."
5           If you find it exhausting to race against men
                  on foot,
            how will you compete against horses?
            If you are not secure in a peaceful country,
            how will you manage in the thickets along the
                  Jordan?

### Yahweh laments his ravaged inheritance

7
"I have abandoned my house,
left my heritage,
I have delivered what I dearly loved
into the hands of its enemies.

8
For me my heritage has become
a lion in the forest,
it roars at me ferociously:
so I now hate it.

9
Or is my heritage a speckled bird
for the birds to flock on her thus from all directions?
Come on, all you wild beasts, gather around,
fall on the quarry!

10
Many shepherds have laid my vineyard waste,
have trampled down my inheritance,
reducing my pleasant inheritance
to a deserted wilderness.

11
They have made it a mournful, desolate place,
desolate before me.
The whole land has been devastated
and no one takes it to heart.

12
The devastators have arrived
on all the bare heights of the desert
(for Yahweh wields a sword that devours):
from end to end of the land
there is no peace for any living thing.

13
Wheat they have sown, thorns they reap:
they have worn themselves out, to no profit.
They are disappointed in their harvests,
through the fury of Yahweh.

### The neighboring peoples: their judgment and salvation

14 "Thus says Yahweh: As for all my evil neighbors who have laid hands on the heritage I granted my people Israel I will now tear them from their countries. (But I will tear the House of Judah out of their hands.) 15 But, once torn out, I will take pity on them again and bring them back each to his heritage, each to his own 16 country. ·And if they take care to learn my people's way and to swear by my name, 'As Yahweh lives,' as my people learned from them to swear by Baal, then

17 they shall have a place among my people. ·But if any nation refuses to listen, I will tear it up by the roots and destroy it—it is Yahweh who speaks."

## The symbol of the loincloth

1 13 Yahweh said this to me, "Go and buy a linen loincloth and put it around your waist. But do 2 not dip it in water." ·And so, as Yahweh had ordered, 3 I bought a loincloth and put it around my waist. ·A second time the word of Yahweh was spoken to me, 4 "Take the loincloth that you have bought and are wearing around your waist; up! Go to the Euphrates and 5 hide it in a hole in the rock." ·So I went and hid it 6 near the Euphrates as Yahweh had ordered me. ·Many days afterward Yahweh said to me, "Get up and go to the Euphrates and fetch the loincloth I ordered you 7 to hide there." ·So I went to Euphrates, and I searched, and I took the loincloth from the place where I had hidden it. The loincloth was spoiled, good for nothing. 8 Then the word of Yahweh was addressed to me, 9 "Thus says Yahweh: In the same way I will spoil the 10 arrogance of Judah and Jerusalem. ·This evil people who refuse to listen to my words, who follow the dictates of their own hard hearts, who have followed alien gods, and served them and worshiped them, let them 11 become like this loincloth, good for nothing. ·For just as a loincloth clings to a man's waist, so I had intended the whole House of Judah to cling to me—it is Yahweh who speaks—to be my people, my glory, my honor and my boast. But they have not listened.

## The symbol of the shattered wine jugs

12    "Tell this people, 'Any jug can be filled with wine.' And if they answer you, 'Do you think we do not 13 know that any jug can be filled with wine?' ·you are to say, 'Thus says Yahweh: I am now going to fill all the inhabitants of this land with drunkenness, the kings who occupy the throne of David, the priests and the proph- 14 ets, and all the citizens of Jerusalem. ·And I will smash them one against the other, father and son together— it is Yahweh who speaks. Mercilessly, relentlessly, pitilessly, I will destroy them.'"

### A vision of exile

15
Listen, pay attention, away with pride—
Yahweh is speaking!

16
Give glory to Yahweh our God
before he brings darkness down
and your feet stumble
on the darkened mountains.
You hope for light,
but he will turn it into deep shadow,
change it into gloom.

17
If you do not listen to this warning,
I will bewail your pride in secret,
tears will flood my eyes,
for Yahweh's flock is led into captivity.

### Jehoiachin threatened

18
Tell the king and the queen mother,
"Sit in a lower place,
since your glorious crown
has fallen from your head."

19
The towns of the Negeb are shut off[a]
with no one to give access to them.
All Judah has been deported,
deported wholesale.

### An admonition to impenitent Jerusalem

20
"Raise your eyes, Jerusalem, and look at these
now coming from the North.
Where is the flock once entrusted to you,
the flock that was your boast?

21
What will you say when they descend on you
as conquerors,
those you yourself taught
to be your friends?
Will not anguish grip you
like a woman in labor?

22
You may ask yourself,
'Why has all this happened to me?'
Because of your great wickedness your skirts
have been pulled up,[b]
and you have been manhandled.

23      Can the Ethiopian change his skin,
        or the leopard his spots?
        And you, can you do what is right,
        you so accustomed to wrong?
24      I will scatter you like chaff
        driven by the desert wind.
25      This is your share, the wage of your apostasy.
        This comes from me—it is Yahweh who speaks—
        because you have forgotten me
        and put your trust in a Delusion.
26      I will also pull your skirts up as high as your
                face
        and let your shame be seen.
27      Oh! Your adulteries, your shrieks of pleasure,
        your vile prostitution!
        On the hills, in the countryside,
        I have seen your Abominations.
        Woe to you, Jerusalem, unclean still!
        How much longer will you go on like this?"

## The great drought

1  **14** The word of Yahweh that was addressed to Jere-
        miah on the occasion of the drought.

2       "Judah is in mourning,
        her towns are disconsolate,
        they sink to the ground;
        a cry goes up from Jerusalem.
3       The nobles send the lesser men for water,
        they come to the cisterns,
        and find no water,
        and return with their pitchers empty.
4       The ground refuses its yield,
        for the country has had no rain;
        in dismay the plowmen
        cover their heads.[a]
5       Even the doe abandons her newborn fawn in
                open country,
        for there is no grass;
6       the wild donkeys standing on the bare heights

13 a. Probably by the Edomites.
b. Men were led naked into captivity, women with their skirts
above their knees.
14 a. Sign of mourning.

> gasp for air like jackals:
> their eyes grow dim
> for lack of pasture."

7　　If our crimes are witness against us,
　　then, Yahweh, for your name's sake act!
　　Yes, our apostasies have been many,
　　we have sinned against you!

8　　Yahweh, hope of Israel,
　　its savior in time of distress,
　　why are you like a stranger in this land,
　　like a traveler who stays only for a night?

9　　Why are you like someone bemused,
　　like a warrior who has no power to rescue?
　　Yet, Yahweh, you are in our midst,
　　we are called by your name.
　　Do not desert us!

10　Yahweh says this regarding this people, "They take such pleasure in wandering, they cannot control their feet!" But Yahweh accepts them no longer; now he 11 recalls their crime and will punish their sins. ·Yahweh said to me, "Do not intercede for this people or their 12 welfare. ·If they fast, I will not listen to their plea; if they offer holocaust and oblation, I will not accept them. Rather, I mean to exterminate them by sword, famine and pestilence."

13　"Ah, Lord Yahweh," I answered, "here are the prophets telling them, 'You will not see the sword, famine will not touch you; I promise you unbroken peace in this place.'"

14　Then Yahweh said to me, "The prophets are prophesying lies in my name; I have not sent them, I gave them no orders, I never spoke to them. Delusive visions, hollow predictions, daydreams of their own, that is 15 what they prophesy to you. ·Therefore, Yahweh says this: The prophets who prophesy in my name when I have not sent them, and tell you there will be no sword or famine in this land, these same prophets are doomed 16 to perish by sword and famine. ·And as for the people to whom they prophesy, they will be tossed into the streets of Jerusalem, victims of famine and the sword, with not a soul to bury them: neither them nor their wives, nor their sons, nor their daughters. I will pour down on them their own wickedness.

17    "Say this word to them,
      'Tears flood my eyes
      night and day, unceasingly,
      since a crushing blow falls on the daughter of
            my people,
      a most grievous injury.
18    If I go into the countryside,
      there lie men killed by the sword;
      if I go into the city,
      I see people sick with hunger;
      even prophets and priests
      plow the land: they are at their wit's end.'"

19    "Have you rejected Judah altogether?
      Does your very soul revolt at Zion?
      Why have you struck us down without hope of
            cure?
      We were hoping for peace—no good came of
            it!
      For the moment of cure—nothing but terror!
20    Yahweh, we do confess our wickedness
      and our fathers' guilt:
      we have indeed sinned against you.
21    For your name's sake do not reject us,
      do not dishonor the throne of your glory.
      Remember us; do not break your covenant with
            us.
22    Can any of the pagan Nothings make it rain?
      Can the heavens produce showers?
      No, it is you, Yahweh.
      O our God, you are our hope,
      since it is you who do all this."

1  **15** Yahweh said to me, "Even if Moses and Samuel
      were standing in my presence I could not warm
   to this people! Drive them out of my sight; away with
2  them! ·And if they ask you, 'Where shall we go?' tell
   them this, 'Yahweh says this:

            Those for the plague, to the plague;
            those for the sword, to the sword;
            those for famine, to famine;
            those for captivity, into captivity!'

3  Four kinds of doom I consign them to: the sword to

kill, the dogs to drag away, the birds of heaven and
4 beasts of earth to devour and to destroy. ·I will make
them an object of horror to all the kingdoms of the
earth, because of Manasseh son of Hezekiah, king of
Judah, for his misdeeds in Jerusalem.

## The horrors of war

5
> "Who is there to pity you, Jerusalem,
> who to grieve for you,
> who to pause
> and ask how you are?

6
> You yourself have rejected me—it is Yahweh
>      who speaks—
> you have turned your back on me;
> so I have stretched my hand over you to destroy
>      you.
> I am tired of relenting.

7
> And so I have winnowed them with a fork
> in the towns of their land.
> I deprive my people of children, I exterminate
>      them
> since they refuse to leave their ways.

8
> Their widows have become more
> than the sand of the seas.
> On the mothers of young warriors
> I bring the destroyer in broad daylight.
> Suddenly I bring down
> anguish and terror on them.

9
> The mother of seven sons grows faint,
> and breathes her last.
> It is still day, but already her sun has set,
> shame and disgrace are hers . . .
> And the remainder of them I shall hand over
>      to their enemies
> to be cut to pieces—it is Yahweh who speaks."

## The call of Jeremiah renewed

10
> Woe is me, my mother, for you have borne me
>      to be a man of strife and of dissension for all
>      the land.
> I neither lend nor borrow,
> yet all of them curse me.

11  Truthfully, Yahweh, have I not done my best
        to serve you,
    interceded with you for my enemy
    in the time of his disaster, his distress?
15a You know I have!

12  Can a man break iron,
    iron from the north, or bronze?
13  "Your wealth and your treasures
    I will hand over to plunder,
    as payment for all your sins
    throughout your territory.
14  I will enslave you to your enemies
    in a country which you do not know,
    for my anger has kindled a fire
    that will burn you up."

15b Yahweh, remember me, take care of me,
    and avenge me on my persecutors.
    Your anger is very slow: do not let me be
        snatched away.
    Realize that I suffer insult for your sake.
16  When your words came, I devoured them:
    your word was my delight
    and the joy of my heart;
    for I was called by your name,
    Yahweh, God of Sabaoth.
17  I never took pleasure in sitting in scoffers' com-
        pany;
    with your hand on me I held myself aloof,
    since you had filled me with indignation.
18  Why is my suffering continual,
    my wound incurable, refusing to be healed?
    Do you mean to be for me a deceptive stream
    with inconstant waters?

19  To which Yahweh replied,
    "If you come back,
    I will take you back into my service;
    and if you utter noble, not despicable, thoughts,
    you shall be as my own mouth.
    They will come back to you,
    but you must not go back to them.
20  I will make you

a bronze wall fortified against this people.
They will fight against you
but they will not overcome you,
because I am with you
to save you and to deliver you
—it is Yahweh who speaks.

21    I mean to deliver you from the hands of the
          wicked
      and redeem you from the clutches of the
          violent."

### The prophet's life is itself symbolic

1 **16** The word of Yahweh was addressed to me as
              follows:
2 "You must not take a wife or have son or daughter in
3 this place. ·For Yahweh says this regarding the sons
  and daughters to be born in this place, about the mothers who give birth to them, and about the fathers who
4 beget them in this land: ·They will die of deadly diseases, unlamented and unburied; they will be like dung
  spread on the ground; they will meet their end by sword
  and famine, and their corpses will be food for the
  birds of heaven and the beasts of earth.

5    "Yes, Yahweh says this: Go into no house where
  there is mourning, do not go to lament or grieve with
  them; for I have withdrawn my peace from this people
  —it is Yahweh who speaks—have withdrawn love and
6 pity. ·High or low, they will die in this land, without
  burial or lament; there will be no gashing, no shaving
7 of the head for them. ·No bread will be broken for the
  mourner to comfort him for the dead; no cup of consolation will be offered him for father or for mother.

8    "And do not enter a house where there is feasting,
9 to sit with them and eat and drink. ·For Yahweh Sabaoth, the God of Israel, says this: Now before your
  eyes, in your own days, I will silence the shouts of
  rejoicing and mirth, and the voices of bridegroom and
  bride.

10   "When you tell this people all these words and they
  ask you, 'Why has Yahweh decreed this appalling disaster for us? What is our crime? What sin have we
11 committed against Yahweh our God?' ·then you are
  to answer, 'It is because your ancestors abandoned me

—it is Yahweh who speaks—and followed alien gods,
and served and worshiped them. They abandoned me
12 and did not keep my Law. ·And you for your part have
behaved even worse than your ancestors. Look, each
of you follows the dictates of his hardened, wicked
13 heart and will not listen to me. ·And so, I am going to
eject you from this land into a country unknown to
you and to your ancestors; there you will serve alien
gods, day and night, for I shall show you no more
favor.'

### The return of the scattered Israelites

14    "See, then, that the days are coming—it is Yahweh
who speaks—when people will no longer say, 'As Yahweh lives who brought the sons of Israel out of the
15 land of Egypt!' ·but, 'As Yahweh lives who brought the
sons of Israel out of the land of the North and back
from all the countries to which he had dispersed them.'
I will bring them back to the very soil I gave their
ancestors.

### The invasion foretold

16    "I will now send many fishermen—it is Yahweh who
speaks—and these will fish them up; next, I will send
many huntsmen, and these will hunt them out of every
17 mountain, every hill, out of the holes in the rocks. ·For
my eyes watch all their ways, these are not hidden from
18 me, and their guilt does not escape my gaze. ·I will
requite their guilt and their sin twice over, since they
have polluted my land with the corpses of their Horrors, and filled my heritage with their Abominations."

### The conversion of the nations

19          Yahweh, my strength, my stronghold,
          my refuge in the day of distress!
          To you the nations will come
          from the confines of earth and say,
          "Our fathers inherited nothing but Delusion,
          Nothings void of all power.
20        Can man make his own gods?
          If so, these are not gods!"
21        "Now listen, I am going to make them acknowl-
               edge,

this time I am going to make them acknowledge
my hand and my might;
and then they will know that Yahweh is my
name.

## Judah's contaminated worship

¹ **17** "The sin of Judah is written
with an iron pen,
engraved with a diamond point
on the tablet of their heart
and on the horns of their altars,
² as evidence against them

(their altars and their sacred poles, by every spreading
³ tree, on the high hills, ·on the mountains, in the open
countryside).

"Your wealth and your treasures
I will hand over to plunder
as payment for all your sins
throughout your territory.
You will have to relinquish your heritage
which I gave you;
⁴ I will enslave you to your enemies
in a country which you do not know,
for my anger has kindled a fire
that will burn for ever.

## A group of wisdom sayings

⁵ "Yahweh says this:

"A curse on the man who puts his trust in man,
who relies on things of flesh,
whose heart turns from Yahweh.
⁶ He is like dry scrub in the wastelands:
if good comes, he has no eyes for it,
he settles in the parched places of the wilderness,
a salt land, uninhabited.

⁷ "A blessing on the man who puts his trust in
Yahweh,
with Yahweh for his hope.
⁸ He is like a tree by the waterside

that thrusts its roots to the stream:
when the heat comes it feels no alarm,
its foliage stays green;
it has no worries in a year of drought,
and never ceases to bear fruit.

9 "The heart is more devious than any other
   thing,
 perverse too: who can pierce its secrets?
10 I, Yahweh, search to the heart,
 I probe the loins,
 to give each man what his conduct
 and his actions deserve.

11 "The partridge will hatch eggs it has not laid.
 Similarly, the man who wins his wealth unjustly:
 his days half done, he must leave it,
 proving a fool after all."

### Confidence in the Temple and in Yahweh

12 A glorious throne, set high from the beginning,
 such is our Holy Place.
13 Hope of Israel, Yahweh!
 All who abandon you will be put to shame,
 those who turn from you will be uprooted from
   the land,
 since they have abandoned the fountain of living water.

### A prayer for vengeance

14 Heal me, Yahweh, and I shall be really healed,
 save me, and I shall be saved,
 for you alone are my hope.
15 Look, they keep saying to me,
 "Where is the word of Yahweh? Let it come
   true then!"
16 But I, I have never urged you to do evil,
 the day of disaster was no desire of mine,
 this you know;
 what came from my lips was not concealed
   from you.
17 Do not be a terror to me,
 you, my refuge in the day of disaster.

18     Let my persecutors be confounded, not I,
       let them, not me, be terrified.
       On them bring the day of disaster,
       destroy them, destroy them twice over!

## Observance of the sabbath

19     Yahweh said this to me, "Go and stand at the Gate
of the Sons of the People by which the kings of Judah
20 go in and out—and at all the gates of Jerusalem. ·Say
to them, 'Listen to the word of Yahweh, you kings of
Judah, all you people of Judah too, and all you citi-
21 zens of Jerusalem who pass through these gates. ·Yah-
weh says this: As you value your lives, on no account
carry a burden on the sabbath day or bring it in
22 through the gates of Jerusalem. ·Bring no burden out
of your houses on the sabbath day, and do no work.
Keep the sabbath day holy, as I commanded your an-
23 cestors. ·They would not hear, would not pay attention, grew so stubborn they would not listen, and would
24 not accept instruction. ·But if you listen carefully to
me—it is Yahweh who speaks—and bring no burden in
through the gates of this city on the sabbath day, if
you keep the sabbath holy and do no work on that day,
25 then, through the gates of this city, kings occupying the
throne of David will continue to make their entry,
mounted on chariots and horses, they and their ministers, with the men of Judah and the citizens of Jeru-
26 salem. And this city will be inhabited for ever. ·They
will come from the towns of Judah, from the districts
around Jerusalem, from the land of Benjamin, from
the lowlands, from the highlands, from the Negeb, to
offer holocaust and sacrifice, oblation, incense and
27 thanksgiving sacrifice in the Temple of Yahweh. ·But
if you do not listen to my command to keep the sabbath day holy, and not to enter the gates of Jerusalem
with burdens on the sabbath day, then I will set fire to
its gates; it shall devour the palaces of Jerusalem and
not be quenched.' "

## Jeremiah visits the potter

1  **18** The word that was addressed to Jeremiah by Yah-
2       weh, ·"Get up and make your way down to the
potter's house; there I shall let you hear what I have

3 to say." ·So I went down to the potter's house; and
4 there he was, working at the wheel. ·And whenever
the vessel he was making came out wrong, as happens
with the clay handled by potters, he would start afresh
5 and work it into another vessel, as potters do. ·Then
6 this word of Yahweh was addressed to me, ·"House of
Israel, can not I do to you what this potter does?—it is
Yahweh who speaks. Yes, as the clay is in the potter's
7 hand, so you are in mine, House of Israel. ·On occasion, I decree for some nation, for some kingdom, that
8 I will tear up, knock down, destroy; ·but if this nation,
against which I have pronounced sentence, abandons
its wickedness, I then change my mind about the evil
9 which I had intended to inflict on it. ·On another occasion, I decree for some nation, for some kingdom,
10 that I will build up and plant; ·but if that nation does
what displeases me, refusing to listen to my voice, I
then change my mind about the good which I had in-
11 tended to confer on it. ·So now, say this to the men of
Judah and the citizens of Jerusalem, 'Yahweh says this:
Listen, I have been preparing a disaster for you, I have
been working out a plan against you. So now, each one
of you, turn back from your evil ways, amend your
12 conduct and actions.' ·They, however, will say, 'What
is the use of talking? We prefer to do as we please; we
mean to behave, each of us, as his wicked heart
dictates.'

### Israel repudiates Yahweh

13        "Therefore—Yahweh says this:
         Ask, if you will, among the nations
         if anyone has heard anything like this.
         She has done a deed of horror,
         the Virgin of Israel.
14       Does the snow of Lebanon
         vanish from the lofty crag?
         Do the proud waters run dry,
         so coolly flowing?
15       And yet my people have forgotten me!
         They burn their incense to a Nothing!
         They have lost their footing in their ways,
         on the roads of former times,
         to walk in tortuous paths,

a way unmarked.

16  They will make their country desolate,
everlastingly derided:
every passer-by will be appalled at it
and shake his head.

17  Like the east wind, I will scatter them
before the enemy.
I will turn my back to them and not my face
on the day of their disaster."

## A plot against Jeremiah

18  "Come on," they said, "let us concoct a plot against
Jeremiah; the priest will not run short of instruction
without him, nor the sage of advice, nor the prophet
of the word. Come on, let us hit at him with his own
tongue; let us listen carefully to every word he says."

19  Listen to me, Yahweh,
hear what my adversaries are saying.

20  Should evil be returned for good?
(For they are digging a pit for me.)
Remember how I stood in your presence
to plead on their behalf,
to turn your wrath away from them.

21  Then hand their sons over to famine,
abandon them to the edge of the sword.
May their wives become
childless and widowed.
May their husbands die of plague,
their young men be cut down by the sword in
battle.

22  Let cries re-echo from their houses
as you bring raiders suddenly on them.
For they have dug a pit to catch me,
they have laid snares to trap my feet.

23  But you, Yahweh,
know all their murderous plots against me.
Do not forgive their crime,
do not efface their sin from your sight.
Keep their destruction always in mind,
when the time for your anger comes deal with
them.

**The broken jug and the altercation with Pashhur**

1 **19** Then Yahweh said to Jeremiah, "Go and buy an earthenware jug. Take some of the elders of the 2 people and some priests with you. ·Go out toward the Valley of Ben-hinnom, as far as the entry of the Gate of the Potsherds. There proclaim the words I shall 3 speak to you. ·You are to say, 'Kings of Judah, citizens of Jerusalem! Listen to the word of Yahweh! Yahweh Sabaoth, the God of Israel, says this: I am bringing down such a disaster on this place that the ears of 4 every one who hears of it will ring. ·This is because they have abandoned me, have profaned this place, have offered incense here to alien gods which neither they, nor their ancestors, nor the kings of Judah, ever knew before. They have filled this place with the blood 5 of the innocent. ·They have built high places for Baal to burn their sons there, which I had never ordered or 6 decreed; which had never entered my thoughts. ·So now the days are coming—it is Yahweh who speaks— when people will no longer call this place Topheth, or the Valley of Ben-hinnom, but Valley of Slaughter. 7 Because of this place, I mean to drain[a] Judah and Jerusalem of sound advice; I will make them fall by the sword before their enemies, fall by the hand of people determined to kill them; I will give their corpses as food 8 to the birds of heaven and the beasts of earth. ·And I will make this city a desolation, a derision; every passer-by will be appalled at it, and whistle in amaze- 9 ment at such calamity. ·I will make them eat the flesh of their own sons and daughters: they shall eat each other during the siege, in the shortage to which their enemies, in their determination to kill them, will reduce them.'

10    "You are to break this jug in front of the men who 11 are with you, ·and say to them, 'Yahweh Sabaoth says this: I am going to break this people and this city just as one breaks a potter's pot, irreparably.

    "'Topheth will become a burial ground, for lack of 12 other space. ·That is how I will treat this place—it is Yahweh who speaks. And I mean to make this city like

**19 a.** In Hebrew "drain" has a similar sound to "jug"; this is another association of the jug parable.

¹³ Topheth; ·the houses of Jerusalem and those of the kings of Judah will be unclean,ᵇ like this place Topheth: all these houses on the roofs of which they offered incense to the whole array of heaven and poured their libations to alien gods.'"

¹⁴ When Jeremiah came back from Topheth where Yahweh had sent him to prophesy, he went and stood in the court of the Temple of Yahweh and addressed

¹⁵ all the people. ·"Yahweh Sabaoth, the God of Israel, says this, 'Yes, I am going to bring down every disaster I have threatened on this city and on all its outlying towns, since they have grown so stubborn and refused to listen to my words.'"

¹ **20** Now the priest Pashhur son of Immer, who was in charge of the police in the Temple of Yahweh,

² heard Jeremiah making this prophecy. ·Pashhur had Jeremiah the prophet beaten and then put in the stocks at the Gate of Benjamin, the upper gate leading into

³ the Temple of Yahweh. ·Next day, Pashhur had Jeremiah taken out of the stocks; Jeremiah said to him, "Not Pashhur but Terror is Yahweh's name for you.

⁴ For Yahweh says this, 'I am going to hand you over to terror, you and all your friends; they shall fall by the sword of their enemies; your own eyes shall see it. The whole of Judah, too, I will hand over to the king of Babylon; he will carry them off captives to Babylon

⁵ and put them to the sword. ·And all the wealth of this city, all its stores, all its valuables, all the treasures of the kings of Judah, I will hand over to their enemies who will plunder them, round them up and carry them

⁶ off to Babylon. ·As for you, Pashhur, and your whole household, you shall go into captivity; you shall go to Babylon; there you will die, and there be buried, you and all your friends to whom you have prophesied lies.'"

### Selections from the "Confessions" of Jeremiah

⁷         You have seduced me, Yahweh, and I have let
           myself be seduced;
        you have overpowered me: you were the
           stronger.
        I am a daily laughingstock,
        everybody's butt.

8 Each time I speak the word, I have to howl
  and proclaim: "Violence and ruin!"
  The word of Yahweh has meant for me
  insult, derision, all day long.

9 I used to say, "I will not think about him,
  I will not speak in his name any more."
  Then there seemed to be a fire burning in my
        heart,
  imprisoned in my bones.
  The effort to restrain it wearied me,
  I could not bear it.

10 I hear so many disparaging me,
   " 'Terror from every side!'
   Denounce him! Let us denounce him!"
   All those who used to be my friends
   watched for my downfall,
   "Perhaps he will be seduced into error.
   Then we will master him
   and take our revenge!"

11 But Yahweh is at my side, a mighty hero;
   my opponents will stumble, mastered,
   confounded by their failure;
   everlasting, unforgettable disgrace will be theirs.

12 But you, Yahweh Sabaoth, you who probe with
        justice,
   who scrutinize the loins and heart,
   let me see the vengeance you will take on them,
   for I have committed my cause to you.

13 Sing to Yahweh,
   praise Yahweh,
   for he has delivered the soul of the needy
   from the hands of evil men.

14 A curse on the day when I was born,
   no blessing on the day my mother bore me!

15 A curse on the man who brought my father the
        news,
   "A son, a boy has been born to you!"
   making him overjoyed.

16 May this man be like the towns
   that Yahweh overthrew without mercy;

b. Polluted by the presence of corpses.

may he hear alarms in the morning,
the war cry in broad daylight,

17 since he did not kill me in the womb;
my mother would have been my tomb
while her womb was swollen with me.

18 Why ever did I come out of the womb
to live in toil and sorrow
and to end my days in shame!

## C. ORACLES MAINLY LATER THAN THE REIGN OF JEHOIAKIM

### Jeremiah answers the envoys of Zedekiah[a]

1 **21** The word that was addressed to Jeremiah by Yahweh when King Zedekiah sent Pashhur son of Malchiah to him, with the priest Zephaniah son of 2 Maaseiah, to say this, ·"Please consult Yahweh for us, since Nebuchadnezzar king of Babylon is making war on us: perhaps Yahweh will work all his wonders on our behalf, so that the enemy will have to withdraw." 3 Jeremiah said to them, "Take this answer to Zedekiah, 4 'Yahweh, the God of Israel, says this: I am going to bring back the weapons of war which you are now carrying, and with which you are fighting the king of Babylon and the Chaldaeans now besieging your walls; 5 I am going to stack them in the center of this city. ·And I am going to fight against you myself with outstretched hand and mighty arm, in anger, fury and great wrath. 6 I am going to strike the inhabitants of this city, man 7 and beast, with a frightful plague: they will die. ·After which—it is Yahweh who speaks—I am going to deliver Zedekiah king of Judah with his servants and the people of this city who escape the plague, the sword, or the famine, into the hands of Nebuchadnezzar king of Babylon, into the hands of their enemies and of those determined to kill them; mercilessly, relentlessly, pitilessly, he will put them to the sword.'

8 "And you are to say to this people, 'Yahweh says this: Look, I now set in front of you the way of life 9 and the way of death. ·Those who stay in this city will die by sword, by famine, or by plague; but anyone who

leaves it and surrenders to the Chaldaeans now be-
10 sieging it will live; he shall escape with his life. ·For I
have turned my face against this city for its ruin, not
for its prosperity—it is Yahweh who speaks. It is to be
delivered into the hands of the king of Babylon, and he
will burn it down.'"

### Address to the royal family of Judah

11　　To the royal House of Judah. Listen to the word of
12　Yahweh, ·House of David! Yahweh says this:

> "Each morning give sound judgment,
> rescue the man who has been wronged
> from the hands of his oppressor,
> or else my wrath will leap out like a fire,
> it will burn and no one will be able to quench
> it.

13
> My quarrel is with you,
> you that have gone to live at Rock-in-the-Plain[b]
> —it is Yahweh who speaks—
> with you that say, 'Who would dare attack us
> and penetrate our fastness?'

14
> (I will punish you as your actions deserve
> —it is Yahweh who speaks.)
> I will set fire to its forest;
> it will devour the whole district."

1 **22** Yahweh said this, "Go down to the palace of the
king of Judah and there deliver this message,
2 'Listen to the word of Yahweh, king of Judah sitting
on the throne of David, you, your servants too, and
3 your people who go through these gates. ·Yahweh says
this: Practice honesty and integrity; rescue the man
who has been wronged from the hands of his oppressor; do not exploit the stranger, the orphan, the widow;
do no violence; shed no innocent blood in this place.
4 For if you are scrupulous in obeying this command,
then kings occupying the throne of David will continue
to make their entry through the gates of this palace
mounted on chariots and horses, they, their servants
5 and their people. ·But if you do not listen to these

---

21 **a.** During the siege of Jerusalem, 588.
**b.** Probably the royal palace built on Ophel.

words, then I swear by myself—it is Yahweh who speaks—this palace shall become a ruin!' "

6 "Yes, this is what Yahweh says about the royal palace of Judah:

'You were like a Gilead to me,
like a peak of Lebanon.
All the same, I will reduce you to a desert,
to an uninhabited town.

7 I have dedicated men to destroy you,
each man with his ax;
they will cut down your finest cedars
and throw them on the fire.

8 'When the hordes of the nations pass this city, they will say to each other: Why has Yahweh treated such
9 a great city like this? ·And the answer will be: Because they abandoned the covenant of Yahweh their God to worship alien gods and serve them.' "

### Oracles against various kings: against Jehoahaz

10 Do not weep for the man who is dead,[a]
do not raise the dirge for him.
Weep bitterly for the man who has gone away,
since he will never come back,
never see his native land again.

11 For this is what Yahweh has said about Shallum son of Josiah, king of Judah, who succeeded Josiah his father and was forced to leave this place, "He will never
12 come back to it ·but will die in the place to which he has been taken captive; and he will never see this country again.

### Against Jehoiakim

13 "Doom for the man who founds his palace on anything but integrity,
his upstairs rooms on anything but honesty,
who makes his fellow man work for nothing,
without paying him his wages,

14 who says, 'I will build myself an imposing palace with spacious rooms upstairs,'
who pierces lights in it,
panels it with cedar, and paints it vermilion.

15 Are you more of a king
  for outrivaling others with cedar?
 Your father ate and drank, like you,
  but he practiced honesty and integrity,
  so all went well for him.

16 He used to examine the cases of poor and
   needy,
  then all went well.
 Is not that what it means to know me?—it is
  Yahweh who speaks.

17 You on the other hand have eyes and heart for
   nothing
  but your own interests,
 for shedding innocent blood
  and perpetrating violence and oppression."

18 So Yahweh has said this about Jehoiakim son of
Josiah, king of Judah:

   "Doom for that man!
   Raise no dirge for him,
   'Mourn for my brother! Mourn for my sister!'
   Raise no dirge for him,
   'Mourn for his highness. Mourn for his maj-
    esty'

19 He will receive the funeral honors of a donkey,
  —dragged away and thrown
  out of the gates of Jerusalem.

### Against Jehoiachin

20  "Go up to Lebanon and shriek,
   let your voice be heard on Bashan,
   shriek from Abarim,[b]
  for all your lovers[c] have been ruined!

21  I spoke to you in your prosperity,
   but you said, 'I will not listen!'
  from your youth this has been how you behaved,
   refusing to listen to my voice.

**22 a.** Josiah; "the man who has gone away" is Jehoahaz, summoned by the Pharaoh Neco, and exiled in Egypt.
**b.** The mountain range to the east of Jordan.
**c.** The kings and leaders of Judah are the "lovers" of Jerusalem.

22      The wind will blow all your shepherds away to
                other pastures,
        your lovers will go into captivity.
        Yes, now you may well be ashamed and con-
                founded
        at the thought of all your wickedness.

23      You who made Lebanon your home,
        who made your nest among the cedars,
        how you will groan when anguish overtakes
                you,
        and pain like that of a woman in labor!

24      "As I live—it is Yahweh who speaks—even if Coniah
        son of Jehoiakim, king of Judah, were the signet ring
25      on my right hand, I would still wrench him off. ·I will
        deliver you into the hands of those determined to kill
        you, into the hands of those you dread, the hands of
        Nebuchadnezzar king of Babylon, the hands of the
26      Chaldaeans. ·You and the mother who bore you, I
        will thrust you both out into another country; you were
27      not born there but you will both die there. ·They will
        not return to the country to which they so long to
        return."

28      Is he a shoddy broken pot,
        this man Coniah,
        a crock that no one wants?
        Why are they ejected, he and his descendants,
        thrown into a country
        they know nothing of?
29      O land, land, land,
        listen to the word of Yahweh!
30      Yahweh says this,
        "List this man as: Childless;
        a man who made a failure of his life,
        since none of his descendants will have the for-
                tune
        to sit on the throne of David,
        or to rule in Judah again.

## Messianic oracles. The future king

1       **23** "Doom for the shepherds who allow the flock
                of my pasture to be destroyed and scattered—it
2       is Yahweh who speaks! ·This, therefore, is what Yah-

weh, the God of Israel, says about the shepherds in
charge of my people: You have let my flock be scattered and go wandering and have not taken care of
them. Right, I will take care of you for your misdeeds
3 —it is Yahweh who speaks! •But the remnant of my
flock I myself will gather from all the countries where
I have dispersed them, and will bring them back to
their pastures: they shall be fruitful and increase in
4 numbers. •I will raise up shepherds to look after them
and pasture them; no fear, no terror for them any
more; not one shall be lost—it is Yahweh who speaks!

5       "See, the days are coming—it is Yahweh who
          speaks—
        when I will raise a virtuous Branch for David,
        who will reign as true king and be wise,
        practicing honesty and integrity in the land.
6       In his days Judah will be saved
        and Israel dwell in confidence.
        And this is the name he will be called:
        Yahweh-our-integrity.

7   "So, then, the days are coming—it is Yahweh who
speaks—when people will no longer say, 'As Yahweh
lives who brought the sons of Israel out of the land of
8 Egypt!' •but, 'As Yahweh lives who led back and
brought home the descendants of the House of Israel
out of the land of the North and from all the countries
to which he had dispersed them, to live on their own
soil.' "

**A tract against the false prophets**

9   On the prophets.

        My heart is broken within me,
        I tremble in all my bones
        I am like a drunken man,
        a man overcome with wine—
        because of Yahweh
        and his holy words,
10        "The land is full of adulterers

(yes, because of these men the land is in mourning and
the desert pastures have dried up);

"they are quick only at doing wrong
and powerful only in crime.

11

Yes, even prophet and priest are godless,
I have found their wickedness even in my own
House
—it is Yahweh who speaks.

12

Because of this their way will prove
treacherous going for them;
in the darkness where they are driven,
there they will fall.
For I will bring disaster down on them
when the year comes for me to deal with them—
it is Yahweh who speaks.

13

"In the prophets of Samaria
I have seen nauseating things:
they prophesied in the name of Baal
and led my people Israel astray.

14

But in the prophets of Jerusalem
I have seen horrors:
adultery, persistent lying,
such abetting of evil men,
that no one renounces his evil-doing;
to me they are all like Sodom,
its inhabitants all like Gomorrah.

15

So this is what Yahweh Sabaoth says about the
prophets:
Now I will give them wormwood for their food,
and poisoned water to drink,
since from the prophets of Jerusalem
godlessness has spread throughout the land.

16

"Yahweh Sabaoth says this:
Do not listen to what those prophets say:
they are deluding you,
they retail visions of their own,
and not what comes from the mouth of Yahweh;

17

to those who reject the word of Yahweh they
say,
'Peace will be yours,'
and to those who follow the dictates of a hardened heart,
'No misfortune will touch you.'"

18    (But who has been present at the council of Yahweh? Who has seen it and heard his word? Who has
paid attention to his word in order to proclaim it?)

19              Now a storm of Yahweh breaks,
                a tempest whirls,
                it bursts over the head of the wicked;
20              the anger of Yahweh will not turn aside
                until he has performed, and has carried out,
                the decision of his heart.

You will understand this clearly in the days to come.

21              "I have not sent those prophets,
                yet they are running;
                I have not spoken to them,
                yet they are prophesying.
22              Have they been present at my council?
                If so, let them proclaim my words to my people
                and turn them from their evil way
                and from the wickedness of their deeds!

23              "Am I a God when near—it is Yahweh who
                      speaks—
                and not one when far away?
24              Can anyone hide in a dark corner
                without my seeing him?—it is Yahweh who
                      speaks.
                Do I not fill
                heaven and earth?—it is Yahweh who speaks.

25    "I have heard what the prophets say who make their
lying prophecies in my name. 'I have had a dream,'
26 they say, 'I have had a dream!' ·How long will they
retain this notion in their hearts, these prophets prophesying lies, who announce their private delusions as pro-
27 phetic? ·They hope, by means of the dreams that they
keep telling each other, to make my people forget my
name, just as their fathers forgot my name in favor of
28 Baal. ·Let the prophet who has had a dream tell his
dream as his own! And let him who receives a word
from me, deliver it accurately!

              "What have straw and wheat in common?
              —it is Yahweh who speaks.

29   Does not my word burn like fire
     —it is Yahweh who speaks—
     is it not like a hammer shattering a rock?

30  "So, then, I have a quarrel with the prophets—it is
Yahweh who speaks—that steal my words from one
31 another. ·I have a quarrel with the prophets—it is Yahweh who speaks—who have only to move their tongues
32 to utter oracles. ·I have a quarrel with the prophets
who make prophecies out of lying dreams—it is Yahweh who speaks—who recount them, and lead my people astray with their lies and their pretensions. I certainly never sent them or commissioned them, and they
serve no good purpose for this people—it is Yahweh
who speaks.

33  "And when these people, either a prophet or a priest,
ask you, 'What is the Burden of Yahweh?'ᵃ you are to
answer, 'You, you are the burden of Yahweh; yes, you,
and I mean to be rid of you! It is Yahweh who speaks.'
34  "And the prophet, priest, or anyone else, who says,
'Burden of Yahweh,' I will punish that man, and his
35 household too. ·This is the way you ought to talk,
neighbor to neighbor, brother to brother, 'What answer
36 has Yahweh given?' or 'What has Yahweh said?' ·But
do not go on using the expression burden of Yahweh
or, for the man who uses it, burdensome it will certainly
prove, since you twist the words of the living God, of
37 Yahweh Sabaoth, our God. ·This is the way to speak
to a prophet, 'What answer has Yahweh given?' or
38 'What has Yahweh said?' ·But if you say, 'Burden of
Yahweh,' then thus speaks Yahweh: Since you use
these words, 'Burden of Yahweh,' when I have warned
39 you to stop saying, 'Burden of Yahweh,' ·I myself will
pick you up and fling you out of my sight, both you
40 and the city I gave to you and to your ancestors. ·I will
bring down everlasting shame on you, everlasting and
unforgettable disgrace."

### The two baskets of figs

1 **24** Yahweh gave me a vision: placed in front of the
    Temple of Yahweh stood two baskets of figs.ᵃ
This was after Nebuchadnezzar king of Babylon had
led away Jeconiah son of Jehoiakim, king of Judah, into

exile from Jerusalem, with all the nobles of Judah, and the blacksmiths and metalworkers, and had taken them
2 to Babylon. ·One basket contained excellent figs, like those that ripen first; the other contained very bad figs,
3 so bad they were uneatable. ·Yahweh said to me, "What do you see, Jeremiah?" "Figs," I answered, "the good ones excellent, the bad ones very bad, so bad as
4 to be uneatable." ·Then the word of Yahweh was ad-
5 dressed to me, ·"Yahweh, the God of Israel, says this: As these figs are good, so I mean to concern myself with the welfare of the exiles of Judah whom I have
6 sent from this place to the land of the Chaldaeans. ·My eyes will watch over them for their good, to bring them back to this land, to build them up and not to break
7 them down, to plant them and not to tear them up. ·I will give them a heart to acknowledge that I am Yah-weh. They shall be my people and I will be their God,
8 for they will return to me with all their heart. ·As for the bad figs, the figs so bad as to be uneatable—yes, Yahweh says this—that is how I will treat Zedekiah king of Judah, his nobles and the remnant of Jerusalem: those who have stayed in this land, as also those living
9 in the land of Egypt. ·I will make them an object of horror to all the kingdoms of the earth, a thing of shame, a byword, a laughingstock, a curse in every
10 place where I shall disperse them. ·Sword, famine and plague I will send against them until they have van-ished from the soil I gave to them and to their an-cestors."

## D. BABYLON THE SCOURGE OF YAHWEH[a]

1 **25** The word that was addressed to Jeremiah about all the people of Judah in the fourth year of Jehoiakim son of Josiah, king of Judah (that is to say the first year of Nebuchadnezzar king of Babylon).

**23 a.** *Massa*, a burden, also means "an oracle." The second sense is distinguished here by a capital initial.
**24 a.** Offered to the Temple as first fruits.
**25 a.** The brackets in this section, and in the four chapters which follow, indicate passages which appear to be glosses and additions by a later hand; several of these are absent from the Greek text.

2 The prophet Jeremiah proclaimed it before all the people of Judah and all the citizens of Jerusalem:

3 "For twenty-three years, from the thirteenth year of Josiah son of Amon, king of Judah, until today, the word of Yahweh has been addressed to me and I have persistently spoken to you (but you have not listened. 4 Furthermore, Yahweh has persistently sent you all his servants the prophets, but you have not listened, or 5 paid attention). ·The message was this, 'Turn back, each of you, from your evil behavior and your evil actions, and you will stay on the soil Yahweh long ago 6 gave to you and to your ancestors for ever. ·(And do not follow alien gods to serve and worship them, do not provoke me by what your own hands have made; 7 then I will not harm you.) ·But you have not listened to me (it is Yahweh who speaks—so that you have now provoked me by what your own hands have made, and thus harmed yourselves).

8 'So—this is what Yahweh Sabaoth says: Since you 9 have not listened to my words, ·I will now send for all the clans of the North (it is Yahweh who speaks—referring to Nebuchadnezzar king of Babylon, my servant) and bring them down on this land and its inhabitants (and on all these surrounding nations): I will lay the ban on them and make them an object of hor- 10 ror, of scorn, of lasting shame. ·I will put an end for them to the shouts of rejoicing and mirth, to the voices of bridegroom and bride, to the sound of the millstone 11 and to the light of the lamp. ·The whole land shall be devastated and reduced to a desert, while they will stay 12 in slavery among the nations for seventy years. ·(But when the seventy years are over, I will punish the king of Babylon and that nation—it is Yahweh who speaks—for the wrong they have done; and punish the land of 13 the Chaldaeans too, and make it a desert for ever.) ·I will bring down on that country all the words I have pronounced against it, all that is written in this book.'"

# II. ORACLES AGAINST THE NATIONS

## A. INTRODUCTION

**The vision of the cup**                    (LXX 33:13–38)

What Jeremiah prophesied against all the nations.

14 ("For these in their turn are to be enslaved to powerful nations and great kings, and I will pay them back as their deeds and their handiwork deserve.")

15 Yahweh the God of Israel said this to me, "Take this cup of wine from my hand and make all the nations 16 to whom I send you drink it, ·let them drink and reel and lose their wits at the sword I am sending among 17 them." ·I took the cup from the hand of Yahweh and made all the nations to whom Yahweh sent me drink it 18 (Jerusalem and the towns of Judah, its kings and its nobles, to make them into a desolation and a waste, a 19 thing of scorn, a curse, as is so today): ·Pharaoh king of Egypt, with his servants, his nobles, and all his peo-20 ple, ·the whole crowd of foreigners besides (all the kings of the land of Uz); all the kings of the country of the Philistines, Ashkelon, Gaza, Ekron and what 21 still remains of Ashdod; ·Edom, Moab and the sons of 22 Ammon; ·(all) the kings of Tyre, (all) the kings of 23 Sidon, the kings of the islands across the sea; ·Dedan, 24 Tema, Buz, all the Crop-Heads, ·all the kings of Arabia 25 who live in the desert; ·(all the kings of Zimri) and 26 all the kings of Elam, and all the kings of Media; ·all the kings of the north, near and far, one after another; and all the kingdoms that are on the face of the earth. (As for the king of Sheshak, he shall drink last of all.)

27 "You are to say to them, 'Yahweh Sabaoth, the God of Israel, says this: Drink! Get drunk! Vomit! Fall, never to rise, at the sword that I am sending among 28 you!' ·If they refuse to take the cup from your hand and drink, you are to say to them, 'Yahweh Sabaoth 29 says this: You must drink! ·Since I am now making a beginning of disaster with the city that bears my name, do you think you are likely to go unpunished? You

certainly shall not, for I will next summon a sword against all the inhabitants of the earth—it is Yahweh Sabaoth who speaks.'

30 "Let your prophecy to them contain all these words, and tell them:

'Yahweh roars from on high,
he makes his voice heard from his holy dwelling
    place,
he roars loud against his sheepfold,
he shouts aloud like those who tread the grape.
The sound reaches all the inhabitants of the
    earth,
31     to the far end of the world.
For Yahweh is indicting the nations,
arraigning all flesh for judgment;
the wicked he abandons to the sword
—it is Yahweh who speaks.
32     Yahweh Sabaoth says this:
See! The disaster spreads
from nation to nation,
a mighty tempest rises
from the far ends of the world.

33 'Those slaughtered by Yahweh that day will be scattered across the world from end to end. No dirge will be raised for them; no one will gather them or bury them; they will stay lying on the surface like dung.

34     'Howl, shepherds, shriek,
roll on the ground, you lords of the flock,
for the days have arrived for your slaughter,
like the finest rams you will fall.
35     No refuge now for the shepherds,
no escape for the lords of the flock!
36     Listen! A shout from the shepherds,
a howl from the lords of the flock!
For Yahweh has laid their pastures waste,
37     their quiet sheepfolds are in ruins.
38     The lion has left his lair,
their land is a wasteland now,
thanks to the destroying sword,
and the fierce anger of Yahweh.'"

# III. PROPHECIES OF HAPPINESS

## A. INTRODUCTION: JEREMIAH THE TRUE PROPHET

### Jeremiah's discourse against the Temple: his arrest and condemnation (LXX 33)

1 26 At the beginning of the reign of Jehoiakim son of Josiah, king of Judah, this word was addressed
2 to Jeremiah by Yahweh, ·"Yahweh says this: Stand in the court of the Temple of Yahweh. To all the people of the towns of Judah who come to worship in the Temple of Yahweh you must speak all the words I have commanded you to tell them; do not omit one syllable.
3 Perhaps they will listen and each turn from his evil way: if so, I shall relent and not bring the disaster on
4 them which I intended for their misdeeds. ·Say to them, 'Yahweh says this: If you will not listen to me by follow-
5 ing my Law which I put before you, ·by paying attention to the words of my servants the prophets whom I send so persistently to you, without your ever listen-
6 ing to them, ·I will treat this Temple as I treated Shiloh, and make this city a curse for all the nations of the earth.'"
7 The priests and prophets and all the people heard Jeremiah say these words in the Temple of Yahweh.
8 When Jeremiah had finished saying everything that Yahweh had ordered him to say to all the people, the priests and prophets seized hold of him and said, "You
9 shall die! ·Why have you made this prophecy in the name of Yahweh, 'This Temple will be like Shiloh, and this city will be desolate, and uninhabited?'" And the people were all crowding around Jeremiah in the Tem-
10 ple of Yahweh. ·Hearing of this, the officials of Judah went up from the royal palace to the Temple of Yahweh and took their seats at the entry of the New Gate of the Temple of Yahweh.
11 The priests and prophets then addressed the officials and all the people, "This man deserves to die, since he has prophesied against this city, as you have heard with

¹² your own ears." ·Jeremiah, however, replied to the
people as follows, "Yahweh himself sent me to say all
the things you have heard against this Temple and this
¹³ city. ·So now amend your behavior and actions, listen
to the voice of Yahweh your God: if you do, he will
relent and not bring down on you the disaster he has
¹⁴ pronounced against you. ·For myself, I am as you see
in your hands. Do whatever you please or think right
¹⁵ with me. ·But be sure of this, that if you put me to
death, you will be bringing innocent blood on yourselves, on this city and on its citizens, since Yahweh has
truly sent me to you to say all these words in your
hearing."

¹⁶     The officials and all the people then said to the
priests and prophets, "This man does not deserve to
die: he has spoken to us in the name of Yahweh our
¹⁷ God." ·Some of the elders of the land had risen to
¹⁸ address all the assembled people. ·"Micah of Moresheth," they said, "who prophesied in the days of Hezekiah king of Judah, had this to say to all the people
of Judah, 'Yahweh says this:

> Zion will become plowland,
> Jerusalem a heap of rubble,
> and the mountain of the Temple a wooded
>     height.'ᵃ

¹⁹    "Did Hezekiah king of Judah and all of Judah put
him to death for this? Did they not rather, fearing
Yahweh, entreat his favor, to make him relent and not
bring the disaster on them which he had pronounced
against them? Are we now to burden our souls with
such a crime?"

²⁰    There was another man, too, who used to prophesy
in the name of Yahweh, Uriah son of Shemaiah, from
Kiriath-jearim. He prophesied exactly the same things
²¹ against this city and this land as Jeremiah. ·When King
Jehoiakim with all his ministers and officials heard what
he said, he wished to put him to death. Learning this,
²² Uriah took fright and escaped to Egypt. ·King Jehoiakim, however, sent Elnathan son of Achbor to Egypt
²³ with others, ·who brought Uriah back from Egypt and
took him to King Jehoiakim, who had him put to the
sword and his body thrown into the common burying

24 ground. ·But Jeremiah had a protector in Ahikam son of Shaphan,[b] so he was not handed over to the people to be put to death.

## B. THE PAMPHLET FOR THE EXILES

### The symbolic yoke and the message to the kings of the west

1 27 (At the beginning of the reign of Zedekiah son of Josiah, king of Judah, this word was addressed 2 to Jeremiah by Yahweh:) ·Yahweh said this to me, "Make yourself ropes and a yoke and put them on 3 your neck. ·Then send word to the king of Edom, the king of Moab, the king of the Ammonites, the king of Tyre, and the king of Sidon, through their envoys ac- 4 credited to Zedekiah king of Judah in Jerusalem. ·Give them the following message for their masters, 'Yahweh Sabaoth, the God of Israel, says this: You must tell 5 your masters this: ·I by my great power and out-stretched arm made the earth, man and the animals that are on earth. And I can give it to whom I please. 6 For the present, I have handed all these countries over to Nebuchadnezzar king of Babylon, my servant; I have 7 even put the wild animals at his service. ·(All the nations will be subject to him, to his son and to his grandson, until the time for his own country comes in its turn, when mighty nations and great kings will en- 8 slave him.) ·Any nation or kingdom that will not sub-mit to Nebuchadnezzar king of Babylon, and will not bow its neck to the yoke of the king of Babylon, I shall punish with sword, famine and plague—it is Yahweh who speaks—until I have delivered it into his power. 9 For your own part, do not listen to your prophets, your diviners, dreamers, soothsayers, or sorcerers, who tell you: You will not be subjects of the king of Baby- 10 lon. ·They prophesy lies to you, the result of which will be that you will be banished from your soil, that

26 a. Mi. 3:12.
b. The king's scribe, who had supported the reform under Josiah. His grandson, Gedaliah, was also to be a protector of Jeremiah, Jr. 40:5–6.

¹¹ I shall expel you, and you will perish. ·The nation, however, that bends its neck to the yoke of the king of Babylon and submits to him, I shall leave in peace on its own soil—it is Yahweh who speaks—to farm it and stay in it.' "

¹² To Zedekiah king of Judah I had the same to say. "Bend your necks," I told him, "to the yoke of the king of Babylon; submit to him and to his people and ¹³ you will live. ·(Why so anxious to die, you and your people, by sword, famine and plague, with which Yahweh has threatened the nation that will not submit to ¹⁴ the king of Babylon?) ·Do not listen to the words the prophets say to you, 'You will not be subjects of the ¹⁵ king of Babylon.' They prophesy lies to you. ·Since I have not sent them—it is Yahweh who speaks—they prophesy untruths in my name. The result will be that I shall expel you, you will perish, and so will the prophets who prophesy to you."

¹⁶ Next I spoke to the priests and all the people as follows, "Yahweh says this, 'Do not listen to the words of your prophets who prophesy to you as follows: Look, the vessels of the Temple of Yahweh will (soon) be brought back from Babylon: they prophesy lies to you. ¹⁷ (Do not listen to them; submit to the king of Babylon and you will live; why should this city become a waste?) ¹⁸ If they were prophets, if they had the word of Yahweh, they would now be praying to Yahweh Sabaoth that the remaining vessels in the Temple of Yahweh, in the royal palace of Judah and in Jerusalem should not go ¹⁹ to Babylon. ·For this is what Yahweh Sabaoth says about (the pillars, the Sea, the stands and) the other ²⁰ vessels still remaining in this city, ·those not carried off by Nebuchadnezzar king of Babylon when he led away Jeconiah son of Jehoiakim, king of Judah, into exile from Jerusalem to Babylon (with all the leading men ²¹ of Judah and Jerusalem). ·Yes, this is what Yahweh Sabaoth, the God of Israel, says about the vessels still remaining in the Temple of Yahweh, in the royal pal- ²² ace of Judah, and in Jerusalem: ·They will be carried off to Babylon (and stay there until the day I fetch them)—it is Yahweh who speaks. (Then I shall bring them back and restore them to this place.)' "

### The dispute with Hananiah     (LXX 35)

1 **28** That same year, at the beginning of the reign of Zedekiah king of Judah in the fifth month of the fourth year, the prophet Hananiah son of Azzur, a Gibeonite, spoke as follows to Jeremiah in the Temple of Yahweh in the presence of the priests and of all the 2 people. ·"Yahweh, the God of Israel, says this, 'I have 3 broken the yoke of the king of Babylon. ·In two years' time I will bring back all the vessels of the Temple of Yahweh which Nebuchadnezzar king of Babylon car- 4 ried off from this place and took to Babylon. ·And I will also bring back Jeconiah son of Jehoiakim, king of Judah, and all the exiles of Judah who have gone to Babylon—it is Yahweh who speaks. Yes, I am going to break the yoke of the king of Babylon.'"

5 The prophet Jeremiah then replied to the prophet Hananiah in front of the priests and all the people 6 there in the Temple of Yahweh. ·"I hope so," the prophet Jeremiah said. "May Yahweh do so. May he fulfill the words that you have prophesied and bring the vessels of the Temple of Yahweh and all the exiles 7 back to this place from Babylon. ·Listen carefully, however, to this word that I am now going to say for 8 you and all the people to hear: ·From remote times, the prophets who preceded you and me prophesied war, famine and plague for many countries and for great 9 kingdoms; ·but the prophet who prophesies peace can only be recognized as one truly sent by Yahweh when his word comes true."

10 The prophet Hananiah then took the yoke off the 11 neck of the prophet Jeremiah and broke it. ·In front of all the people Hananiah then said, "Yahweh says this, 'This is how, two years hence, I will break the yoke of Nebuchadnezzar king of Babylon and take it off the necks of all the nations.'" At this, the prophet Jeremiah went away.

12 After the prophet Hananiah had broken the yoke which he had taken off the neck of the prophet Jere- miah the word of Yahweh was addressed to Jeremiah, 13 "Go to Hananiah and tell him this, 'Yahweh says this: You can break wooden yokes? Right, I will make 14 them iron yokes instead! ·For Yahweh Sabaoth, the

God of Israel, says this: An iron yoke is what I now
lay on the necks of all these nations to subject them
to Nebuchadnezzar king of Babylon. (They will be subject to him; I have even given him the wild animals.)'"

15 The prophet Jeremiah said to the prophet Hananiah,
"Listen carefully, Hananiah: Yahweh has not sent you;
and thanks to you this people are now relying on what
16 is false. ·Hence—Yahweh says this, 'I am going to throw
you off the face of the earth: you are going to die this
year (since you have preached apostasy from Yahweh).'"

17 The prophet Hananiah died the same year, in the
seventh month.

## The letter to the exiles (LXX 36:1-23)

1 29 This is the text of the letter that the prophet
Jeremiah sent from Jerusalem to those elders carried off into exile, to the priests, the prophets and all
the people whom Nebuchadnezzar had led away into
2 exile from Jerusalem to Babylon. ·This was after King
Jeconiah had left Jerusalem with the queen mother,
the eunuchs, the nobility of Judah and Jerusalem, and
3 the blacksmiths and metalworkers. ·The letter was entrusted to Elasah son of Shaphan and to Gemariah son
of Hilkiah, whom Zedekiah king of Judah had sent to
Babylon, to Nebuchadnezzar king of Babylon. The letter said:

4 "Yahweh Sabaoth, the God of Israel, says this to all
5 the exiles deported from Jerusalem to Babylon, ·Build
houses, settle down; plant gardens and eat what they
6 produce; ·take wives and have sons and daughters;
choose wives for your sons, find husbands for your
daughters so that these can bear sons and daughters in
their turn; you must increase there and not decrease.
7 Work for the good of the country to which I have
exiled you; pray to Yahweh on its behalf, since on its
10 welfare yours depends. ·For Yahweh says this: Only
when the seventy years granted to Babylon are over,
will I visit you and fulfill my promise in your favor
11 by bringing you back to this place. ·I know the plans
I have in mind for you—it is Yahweh who speaks—plans
for peace, not disaster, reserving a future full of hope

12 for you. ·Then when you call to me, and come to
13 plead with me, I will listen to you. ·When you seek
me you shall find me, when you seek me with all your
14 heart; ·I will let you find me (—it is Yahweh who
speaks. I will restore your fortunes and gather you
from all the nations and all the places where I have
dispersed you—it is Yahweh who speaks. I will bring
you back to the place from which I exiled you).

15    'You may say: Yahweh has raised up prophets for
 8 us in Babylon, ·but thus says Yahweh Sabaoth, the
God of Israel: Do not be deceived by the prophets
among you or by your diviners; do not listen to the
 9 dreams they dream, ·since they prophesy lies to you
in my name. I have not sent them—it is Yahweh who
speaks.

16    'For this is what Yahweh says about the king now
seated on the throne of David and all the people who
live in this city, your brothers who did not go with you
17 into exile: ·Thus says Yahweh Sabaoth: I am now going to send them sword, famine and plague; I will make
18 them like rotten figs, so bad as to be uneatable. ·I will
pursue them with sword, famine and plague, and make
them an object of horror to all the kingdoms of the
earth, a curse, a thing of wonder, scorn, derision, for
19 all the nations where I have dispersed them; ·because
they have refused to listen to my words—it is Yahweh
who speaks—although I have persistently sent them all
my servants the prophets. However, they would not lis-
20 ten—it is Yahweh who speaks. ·But all you exiles, whom
I have sent from Jerusalem to Babylon, listen to the
word of Yahweh.

21    'This is what Yahweh Sabaoth, the God of Israel,
says about Ahab son of Kolaiah, and Zedekiah son of
Maaseiah, who prophesy lies to you in my name: I
shall hand them over now to Nebuchadnezzar king of
22 Babylon who will strike them before your eyes. ·This
curse, based on their fate, will be used by all the exiles
of Judah in Babylon: May Yahweh treat you like Zedekiah and Ahab, roasted alive by the king of Babylon!
23 Such is the fate of those who perpetrate infamies in
Israel, committing adultery with other men's wives,

speaking words in my name without orders from me.
I know all the same; I see—it is Yahweh who speaks.' "

### An exile objects to Jeremiah's letter    (LXX 36:24–32)

24
25      Shemaiah of Nehelam sent a letter of his own (to
all the people in Jerusalem) to the priest Zephaniah
son of Maaseiah (and to all the priests), which said:
26 "Yahweh has appointed you priest in succession to
Jehoiada to keep order in the Temple of Yahweh; in
the case of a madman who acts the prophet, your duty
27 is to put him in the stocks and iron collar. ·This being
the case, why have you not disciplined Jeremiah of
28 Anathoth, who poses as a prophet to you? ·—since on
the strength of this pretension he has sent a message to
us in Babylon to say, 'It will be a long time. Build
houses, settle down; plant gardens and eat what they
produce.' "

29      The priest Zephaniah read this letter aloud to the
30 prophet Jeremiah. ·The word of Yahweh, however, was
31 addressed to Jeremiah, ·"Send this message to all the
exiles, 'This is what Yahweh says about Shemaiah of
Nehelam: Since Shemaiah has prophesied to you without my sending him, and since it is due to him that you
32 are now relying on what is false, ·now therefore—thus
says Yahweh—I will punish Shemaiah of Nehelam and
his descendants; no male member of his family shall
survive among this people to see the happiness that I
will bestow on my people (—it is Yahweh who speaks
—since he has preached apostasy from Yahweh).' "


### C. THE BOOK OF CONSOLATION

### Promise of recovery for the northern kingdom of Israel      (LXX 37:1–38:22)

1
2 **30** The word addressed to Jeremiah by Yahweh:
Yahweh, the God of Israel says this: Write all
3 the words I have spoken to you in a book. ·For see,
the days are coming—it is Yahweh who speaks—when
I will restore the fortunes of my people Israel (and
Judah), Yahweh says, and bring them back to possess
the land I gave to their ancestors.

4        These are the words Yahweh spoke about Israel (and
Judah):

5                Yahweh says this:
                 I have heard a cry of panic,
                 of terror, not of peace.
6                Now ask, consider:
                 can men bear children?
                 Then why do I see each man
                 with his hands on his loins like a woman in
                       labor?
                 Why has every face changed,
                 turned pale?
7                This is indeed a great day,
                 no other like it:
                 a time of distress for Jacob;
                 but he will be freed from it.

8        On that day—it is Yahweh Sabaoth who speaks—I
will break the yoke on their necks, and snap their
chains. They will be no longer the servants of aliens,
9 but will serve Yahweh their God, and David their king
whom I will raise up for them.

10               So do not be afraid, my servant Jacob
                 —it is Yahweh who speaks—
                 Israel, do not be alarmed:
                 look, I will rescue you from distant countries
                 and your descendants from the country where
                       they are captive.
                 Jacob will have quiet again
                 and live at ease, with no one to trouble him.
11               For I am with you to save you:
                 I will make an end of all the nations
                 where I have scattered you;
                 I will not make an end of you,
                 only discipline you in moderation,
                 so as not to let you go entirely unpunished.

12               Yes, Yahweh says this:
                 Your wound is incurable,
                 your injury past healing.
13               There is no one to care for your sore,
                 no medicine to make you well again.

14     All your lovers have forgotten you,
    they look for you no more.
    Yes, I have struck you as an enemy strikes,
    with harsh punishment
    (so great is your guilt, so many your sins).

15     Why bother to complain about your wound?
    Your pain is incurable.
    So great is your guilt, so many your sins,
    that I have done all this to you.

16     But all those who devoured you shall them-
        selves be devoured,
    all your oppressors go into captivity,
    those who despoiled you shall be despoiled,
    and all who preyed on you I will make into prey.

17b     For they used to call you "The Outcast,"
    "Our booty whom no one cares about!"

17a     But I will restore you to health
    and heal your wounds—it is Yahweh who speaks.

18     Yahweh says this:
    Now I will restore the tents of Jacob,
    and take pity on his dwellings:
    the city shall be rebuilt on its ruins,
    the citadel restored on its site.

19     From them will come thanksgiving
    and shouts of joy.
    I will make them increase, and not diminish
        them,
    make them honored, and not disdained.

20     Their sons shall be as once they were,
    their community fixed firm in my presence,
    and I will punish all their oppressors.

21     Their prince will be one of their own,
    their ruler come from their own people.
    I will let him come freely into my presence and
        and he can come close to me;
    who else, indeed, would risk his life
    by coming close to me?—it is Yahweh who
        speaks.

22     And you shall be my people and I will be your
    God.

23     Now a storm of Yahweh breaks,
    a tempest whirls,

it bursts over the head of the wicked;
24      the anger of Yahweh will not turn aside
until he has performed and carried out,
the decision of his heart.
You will understand this in the days to come.

1  **31** When that time comes—it is Yahweh who speaks
—I will be the God of all the clans of Israel: they
shall be my people.

2       Yahweh says this:
They have found pardon in the wilderness,
those who have survived the sword.
Israel is marching to his rest.

3       Yahweh has appeared to him from afar:
I have loved you with an everlasting love,
so I am constant in my affection for you.

4       I build you once more; you shall be rebuilt,
virgin of Israel.
Adorned once more, and with your tambourines,
you will go out dancing gaily.

5       You will plant vineyards once more
on the mountains of Samaria
(the planters have done their planting: they will
gather the fruit).

6       Yes, a day will come when the watchmen shout
on the mountains of Ephraim,
"Up! Let us go up to Zion,
to Yahweh our God!"

7       For Yahweh says this:
Shout with joy for Jacob!
Hail the chief of nations!
Proclaim! Praise! Shout:
"Yahweh has saved his people,
the remnant of Israel!"

8       See, I will bring them back
from the land of the North
and gather them from the far ends of earth;
all of them: the blind and the lame,
women with child, women in labor:
a great company returning here.

9       They had left in tears,
I will comfort them as I lead them back;

I will guide them to streams of water,
by a smooth path where they will not stumble.
For I am a father to Israel,
and Ephraim is my first-born son.

10   Listen, nations, to the word of Yahweh.
Tell this to the distant islands,
"He who scattered Israel gathers him,
he guards him as a shepherd guards his flock."
11   For Yahweh has ransomed Jacob,
rescued him from a hand stronger than his own.
12   They will come and shout for joy on the heights
          of Zion,
they will throng toward the good things of
          Yahweh:
corn and oil and wine,
sheep and oxen;
their soul will be like a watered garden,
they will sorrow no more.
13   The virgin will then take pleasure in the dance,
young men and old will be happy;
I will change their mourning into gladness,
comfort them, give them joy after their troubles,
14   refresh my priests with rich food,
and see my people have their fill of my good
          things
—it is Yahweh who speaks.
15   Thus speaks Yahweh:
A voice is heard in Ramah,
lamenting and weeping bitterly:
it is Rachel[a] weeping for her children,
refusing to be comforted for her children,
because they are no more.
16   Yahweh says this:
Stop your weeping,
dry your eyes,
your hardships will be redressed:
they shall come back from the enemy country.
17   There is hope for your descendants:
your sons will come home to their own lands.
18   I plainly hear the grieving of Ephraim,
"You have disciplined me, I accepted the
          discipline

like a young bull untamed.
Bring me back, let me come back,
for you are Yahweh my God!

19    Yes, I turned away, but have since repented;
I understood, I beat my breast.
I was deeply ashamed, covered with confusion;
yes, I still bore the disgrace of my youth."

20    Is Ephraim, then, so dear a son to me,
a child so favored,
that after each threat of mine
I must still remember him,
still be deeply moved for him,
and let my tenderness yearn over him?
It is Yahweh who speaks.

21    Set up signposts,
raise landmarks;
mark the road well,
the way by which you went.
Come home, virgin of Israel,
come home to these towns of yours.

22    How long will you hesitate, disloyal daughter?
For Yahweh is creating something new on
      earth:
the Woman sets out to find her Husband again.

### Promise of restoration to Judah

23    Yahweh Sabaoth, the God of Israel, says this: In the
land of Judah and in its towns, they will use these words
again, once I have restored their fortunes:

"Yahweh grant you his blessing,
you pasture of justice,
you holy mountain!"

24 Judah and all his towns, the farmers and those who
25 tend the flock will live in this land. ·For I refresh the
26 wearied soul and satisfy every sorrowing soul. ·And
hence: [b]

I awoke and was refreshed,
and my sleep was peaceful.

**31 a.** The grandmother of Ephraim and Manasseh; her tomb was
at Bethlehem, Gn. 35:19.
**b.** A quotation, probably from a song.

### Israel and Judah                                    (LXX 38:27–28)

27    See, the days are coming—it is Yahweh who speaks
—when I am going to sow the seed of men and cattle
on the House of Israel and on the House of Judah.
28 And as I once watched them to tear up, to knock down,
to overthrow, destroy and bring disaster, so now I shall
watch over them to build and to plant. It is Yahweh
who speaks.

### Individual retribution

29    In those days people will no longer say:

> "The fathers have eaten unripe grapes;
> the children's teeth are set on edge."

30 But each is to die for his own sin. Every man who eats
unripe grapes is to have his own teeth set on edge.

### The new covenant                                  (LXX 38:31–34)

31    See, the days are coming—it is Yahweh who speaks—
when I will make a new covenant with the House of
32 Israel (and the House of Judah), ·but not a covenant
like the one I made with their ancestors on the day I
took them by the hand to bring them out of the land
of Egypt. They broke that covenant of mine, so I had
to show them who was master. It is Yahweh who speaks.
33 No, this is the covenant I will make with the House of
Israel when those days arrive—it is Yahweh who speaks.
Deep within them I will plant my Law, writing it on
their hearts. Then I will be their God and they shall be
34 my people. ·There will be no further need for neighbor
to try to teach neighbor, or brother to say to brother,
"Learn to know Yahweh!" No, they will all know me,
the least no less than the greatest—it is Yahweh who
speaks—since I will forgive their iniquity and never call
their sin to mind.

### Israel will endure                                (LXX 38:35–37)

35         Yahweh who provides the sun for light by day,
           the moon and stars for light by night,
           who stirs the sea, making its waves roar,
              he whose name is Yahweh Sabaoth, says this:
36         Were this established order ever to pass away

from my presence—it is Yahweh who speaks—
only then would the race of Israel also cease
to be a nation in my presence for ever.

37 Were the heavens above ever to be measured,
the foundations of the earth below ever to be
    fathomed,
only then would I reject the race of Israel
for all that they have done. It is Yahweh who
    speaks.

## Jerusalem magnificently rebuilt

38 See, the days are coming—it is Yahweh who speaks
—when the city of Yahweh will be rebuilt from the
39 Tower of Hananel to the Gate of the Corner. ·Then
once again the measuring line will stretch straight to
40 the Hill of Gareb, turning then to Goah.ᶜ ·And the
whole valley, with its dead and its ashes, and all the
fields beside the wadi Kidron as far as the corner of
the Horse Gate, eastward, will be consecrated to Yahweh. It shall never again be destroyed, or laid under
the ban.


## D. ADDITIONS TO THE BOOK OF CONSOLATION


## Jeremiah buys a field in token of his confidence in the
## future of Judah                              (LXX 39)

1  32 The word that was addressed to Jeremiah by
       Yahweh in the tenth year of Zedekiah king of
Judah, which was the eighteenth year of Nebuchadnez-
2 zar. ·The army of the king of Babylon was at that time
besieging Jerusalem, and the prophet Jeremiah was confined to the Court of the Guard in the royal palace of
3 Judah, ·where Zedekiah king of Judah had imprisoned
him. "Why," he had asked, "do you make a prophecy
like this, 'Yahweh says this: I am now going to deliver
this city into the hands of the king of Babylon, for him
4 to capture it; ·and Zedekiah king of Judah will not
escape the power of the Chaldaeans, but will inevitably
be delivered into the hands of the king of Babylon,

c. The same measurements of those of the old city destroyed by
the Chaldaeans.

5 speak to him personally and see him face to face. ·He will take Zedekiah to Babylon and he will stay there (until I visit him—it is Yahweh who speaks. If you fight the Chaldaeans you will not succeed!)'?"

6 Jeremiah said, "The word of Yahweh has been ad-
7 dressed to me as follows, ·'Look, Hanamel the son of your uncle Shallum will come to you and say: Buy my field at Anathoth, for you have the right of redemp-
8 tion*a* to purchase it.' ·And, as Yahweh had said, my cousin Hanamel came to me, in the Court of the Guard. He said to me, 'Buy my field at Anathoth, for you have the right of inheritance and redemption; buy it.'
9 I knew then that this was Yahweh's order. ·Accordingly, I bought the field from my cousin Hanamel of Anathoth and paid him the price: seventeen silver
10 shekels. ·I drew up the deed and sealed it, called in witnesses and weighed out the money on the scales.
11 I then took both the sealed deed of purchase and its open copy, in accordance with the requirements of the
12 law, ·and handed over the deed of purchase to Baruch son of Neriah, son of Mahseiah, in the presence of my cousin Hanamel, of the witnesses who had signed the deed of purchase, and of all the Jews who then hap-
13 pened to be in the Court of the Guard. ·In their pres-
14 ence I gave Baruch these instructions: ·Take these deeds, the sealed deed of purchase and its open copy, and put them in an earthenware pot, so that they may
15 be preserved for a long time. ·For Yahweh Sabaoth, the God of Israel, says this, 'People will buy fields and vineyards in this land again.'

16 "After I had entrusted the deed of purchase to
17 Baruch son of Neriah, I prayed thus to Yahweh: ·Ah, Lord Yahweh, you have made the heavens and the earth with your great power and outstretched arm. To
18 you nothing is impossible. ·You show kindness to thousands but repay the fathers' guilt in full to their children after them. Great and mighty God, whose name is Yah-
19 weh Sabaoth! ·Great in purpose, mighty in execution, whose eyes are open on all the ways of men, rewarding each man as his ways and the results of his actions
20 deserve! ·You performed signs and wonders in the land of Egypt and do the same today, in Israel and among mankind. You have won the name that is yours today.

21 You brought your people Israel out of the land of
Egypt with signs and wonders, with mighty hand and
22 outstretched arm and fearsome terror; ·then you gave
them this land which you promised on oath to their
23 ancestors, a land where milk and honey flow; ·and in
due course they entered it and took possession. But
they would not listen to your voice or follow your Law:
they would do nothing you ordered them to do; and
24 so you made all these disasters happen to them. ·See
how the earthworks grow nearer to the city for the
assault! Sword, famine, and plague will deliver the city
into the hands of the attacking Chaldaeans. What you
25 have said is now fulfilled, as you see. ·Yet you yourself,
Lord Yahweh, told me, 'Buy the field with money in
front of witnesses'—and even now the city is falling
into the hands of the Chaldaeans!

26 "The word of Yahweh was addressed to me as fol-
27 lows, ·'See, I am Yahweh, the God of all mankind:
is anything impossible to me?

28 'Therefore—Yahweh says this: I am now putting this
city into the power of the Chaldaeans, into the power
of Nebuchadnezzar king of Babylon, and he will cap-
29 ture it; ·the Chaldaeans attacking this city will come
and set fire to it; they will burn the houses on the roofs
of which incense was offered to Baal and libations were
30 poured to alien gods, to provoke me. ·For the sons of
Israel and of Judah have done nothing but displease
me from their youth up (the sons of Israel in fact have
done nothing but provoke me by their actions—it is
31 Yahweh who speaks). ·Yes, from the day when it was
built until today, this city has been such cause of anger
and of wrath to me that I mean to remove it from my
32 sight, ·because of all the wickedness the sons of Israel
and the sons of Judah have committed to provoke me:
they, their kings, their nobles, their priests and their
prophets, the men of Judah and the citizens of Jerusa-
33 lem. ·They turned their backs to me, never their faces;
and though I taught them so urgently, so persistently,
34 they would not listen and learn the lesson. ·They have
put their abominations in the Temple that bears my
35 name to defile it. ·They have built the high places of

32 a. By blood relationship with the late owner.

Baal in the Valley of Ben-hinnom, there to make their
sons and daughters pass through fire in honor of
Molech—something I never ordered, for it never entered my thoughts that they would do such detestable
things—and so they have led Judah into sin.

36    'But now, and for the same reason, this is what Yahweh, the God of Israel, says about this city of which
you say: Sword, famine and plague will deliver it into
37    the hands of the king of Babylon: ·I mean to gather
them from all the countries where I have driven them
in my anger, my fury and great wrath. I will bring
them back to this place and make them live in safety.
38    Then they shall be my people, and I will be their God.
39    I will give them a different heart and different behavior
so that they will always fear me, for the good of them-
40    selves and their children after them. ·I will make an
everlasting covenant with them; I will not cease in my
efforts for their good, and I will put respect for me into
41    their hearts, so that they turn from me no more. ·It
will be my pleasure to bring about their good, and I
will plant them firmly in this land, with all my heart and
42    soul. ·For Yahweh says this: As I have brought this
great disaster on this people, so I am going to bring
43    them all the good I promise them. ·People will buy
fields in this land of which you say: It is a wasteland
without man or beast, it is given over into the power of
44    the Chaldaeans. ·People will buy fields, pay money,
draw up deeds and seal them, and witness them in the
land of Benjamin, in the districts around Jerusalem,
in the towns of Judah, of the highlands, of the Lowlands and of the Negeb. For I am going to restore
their fortunes—it is Yahweh who speaks.' "

## Another promise of recovery for Jerusalem and Judah (LXX 40)

1    **33** Jeremiah was still confined to the Court of the
Guard when the word of Yahweh was addressed
2    to him a second time, ·"Yahweh, who made the earth,
who formed it and set it firm—Yahweh is his name—
3    says this, ·Call to me and I will answer you; I will tell
4    you great mysteries of which you know nothing. ·For
this is what Yahweh, the God of Israel, says about the
houses of this city and the royal palaces of Judah which

are to be destroyed. Against the earthworks and the
5 palisades ·they will join battle with the Chaldaeans,
only to fill the city with the corpses of those I strike
down in my anger and my wrath, of those from whom
I turned my face because of all their wickedness.

6    "But look, I will hasten their recovery and their
cure; I will cure them and let them know peace and
7 security in full measure. ·I will restore the fortunes of
Judah and Jerusalem, and build them again as they
8 were before. ·I will cleanse them of every sin they have
committed against me; the sins by which they offended
me and apostatized from me, all these I will forgive.
9 And Jerusalem shall be my theme of joy, my honor
and my boast, before all the nations of the earth: these,
when they hear of all the prosperity that I shall grant,
will be seized with fear and trembling at all the prosperity and the peace that I provide for it.

10    "Yahweh says this: In this place of which you say,
'It is a waste without man or beast,' in the towns of
Judah and in the ruined streets of Jerusalem where
there is neither man nor beast, once more will be heard
11 shouts of rejoicing and mirth, the voices of bridegroom
and bride, and the singing of those who bring thanksgiving sacrifices to the Temple of Yahweh, 'Give thanks
to Yahweh Sabaoth, for Yahweh is good, for his love
is everlasting.' For I will restore the fortunes of this
land as they were before. Yahweh declares it!

12    "Yahweh Sabaoth says this: In this place, this waste
without man or beast, and in all its towns, once again
there will be pastures for the shepherds to rest their
13 flocks. ·In all the towns of the highlands, of the Lowlands and the Negeb, in the land of Benjamin, in the
districts around Jerusalem and in the towns of Judah,
once again the flocks shall pass under the hand of him
who counts them. Yahweh declares it!

### The institutions of the future

14    "See, the days are coming—it is Yahweh who speaks
—when I am going to fulfill the promise I made to the
House of Israel and the House of Judah:

15            "In those days and at that time,
            I will make a virtuous Branch grow for David,

who shall practice honesty and integrity in the
land.

<sup>16</sup> In those days Judah shall be saved
and Israel shall dwell in confidence.
And this is the name the city will be called:
Yahweh-our-integrity.

<sup>17</sup> For Yahweh says this: David shall never lack a male descendant to sit on the throne of the House of Israel. <sup>18</sup> And the levitical priests shall never lack a male descendant to stand in my presence and offer holocaust, to burn the oblation and offer sacrifice every day."

<sup>19</sup> The word of Yahweh was addressed to Jeremiah, <sup>20</sup> "Yahweh says this: If you could break my covenant with the day and my covenant with the night so that <sup>21</sup> day and night do not come at their due time, ·then my covenant with David my servant might also be broken and he would have no son to reign on his throne, and so might my covenant with the levitical priests, who <sup>22</sup> are my ministers. ·As the array of heaven is past counting, the sand on the seashore beyond all reckoning, so will I increase the heirs of David my servant and the Levites, who, with these heirs, minister to me."

<sup>23</sup> The word of Yahweh was addressed to Jeremiah, <sup>24</sup> "Have you not noticed what these people say, 'The two families which Yahweh chose he has now rejected?' So they despise my people, whom they no longer think <sup>25</sup> of as a nation. ·Yahweh says this: If I have not created day and night and have not laid down laws for the <sup>26</sup> heavens and the earth, ·why, then I reject the descendants of Jacob and of David my servant and cease to choose rulers from his descendants for the heirs of Abraham, Isaac and Jacob! For I mean to restore their fortunes and take pity on them."


## E. MISCELLANEOUS PASSAGES

### The fate of Zedekiah                    (LXX 41:1–7)

<sup>1</sup> **34** The word addressed to Jeremiah by Yahweh when Nebuchadnezzar king of Babylon and his whole army, with all the kingdoms of the earth under his dominion and all the peoples, were waging war on <sup>2</sup> Jersualem and its outlying towns, ·"Yahweh, the God

of Israel, says this: Go and speak to Zedekiah king of
Judah. Say this to him, 'Yahweh says this: I am now
handing over this city into the power of the king of
3 Babylon, and he will burn it down. ·And you yourself
will not escape his power but will inevitably be captured
and delivered into his hands. You will see the king of
Babylon face to face and speak to him personally. Then
4 you will go to Babylon. ·Even so, listen to the word of
Yahweh, Zedekiah king of Judah, and you will not die
5 by the sword; ·you will die in peace. And as spices
were burned for your fathers, the kings who in times
past preceded you, so they will also burn spices for you
and raise this dirge for you: Mourn for his highness!
I myself declare it—it is Yahweh who speaks.' "
6     The prophet Jeremiah repeated all these words to
7 Zedekiah king of Judah, in Jerusalem, ·while the army
of the king of Babylon was attacking Jerusalem and
the towns of Judah which still held out, namely Lachish
and Azekah, these being the only towns of Judah that
still held out, since they were fortified.

## The episode of the liberated slaves    (LXX 41:8–22)

8     The word addressed to Jeremiah by Yahweh after
King Zedekiah had made a pact with all the people in
9 Jerusalem to free their slaves: ·each man was to free
his Hebrew slaves, men and women, and no one was
10 any longer to keep a brother Jew in slavery. ·All the
nobles and all the people who had entered into the
pact had agreed that everyone should free his slaves,
men or women, and no longer keep them as slaves:
11 they had agreed on this and set them free. ·Afterward,
however, they changed their minds, recovered the
slaves, men and women, whom they had set free, and
12 reduced them to slavery again. ·So the word of Yahweh
13 was addressed to Jeremiah, ·"Yahweh, the God of Israel, says this: I made a covenant with your ancestors
when I brought them out of Egypt, out of the house of
14 slavery; it said: ·At the end of seven years each one of
you is to free his brother Hebrew who has sold himself
to you: he may be your slave for six years, then you
must send him away free. But your ancestors did not
15 listen to me and would not pay attention. ·Now, today
you took a different attitude and did what pleases me
by proclaiming freedom for your neighbor; you made a

covenant in my presence in the Temple that bears my
16 name. ·And then you changed your mind and, profaning my name, each of you has recovered his slaves,
men and women, whom you had sent away free to live
their own lives, and has forced them to become your
slaves again.

17      "Therefore—Yahweh says this: You have disobeyed
me, by not each granting freedom to his brother and
his neighbor. Very well, I in my turn—it is Yahweh
who speaks—leave sword, famine and plague free to
deal with you; I will make you an object of horror to
18 all the kingdoms of the earth. ·And these men who
have infringed my covenant, who have not observed
the terms of the covenant made in my presence, I will
treat these men like the calf they cut in two to pass
19 between the parts of it.ᵃ ·As for the nobles of Judah
and of Jerusalem, the eunuchs and the priests, and all
the people of the country who have passed between
20 the parts of the calf, ·I will put them into the power
of their enemies and into the power of men determined
to kill them: their corpses will feed the birds of heaven
21 and the beasts of the earth. ·As for Zedekiah king of
Judah and his nobles, these too I will hand over to
their enemies and to men determined to kill them, and
to the army of the king of Babylon which has just
22 withdrawn. ·Listen, I will give the order—it is Yahweh
who speaks—and bring them back to this city to attack
it and capture it and burn it down. I am going to make
an uninhabited desert of the towns of Judah."

## The example of the Rechabites        (LXX 42)

1 **35** The word addressed to Jeremiah by Yahweh in
the days of Jehoiakim son of Josiah, king of
2 Judah, ·"Go to the clan of the Rechabites and speak
to them; bring them into one of the apartments of the
3 Temple of Yahweh and offer them wine to drink." ·So
I brought Jaazaniah son of Jeremiah, son of Habazzin-
iah, with his brothers and all his sons: the whole
4 Rechabite clan. ·I took them to the Temple of Yahweh
into the apartment of Ben-johanan son of Igdaliah, a
man of God, a room near that of the officials, over the
apartment of Maaseiah son of Shallum, guardian of the
5 threshold. ·I then set pitchers full of wine, and some

cups, before the men of the Rechabite clan and said, "Drink some wine."

6 They replied, "We do not drink wine, because our ancestor Jonadab son of Rechab gave us this order: 'You must never drink wine neither you nor your sons;
7 nor must you build houses, sow seed, plant vineyards, or own property; but you must live in tents all your lives, so that you may live long on the soil to which
8 you are alien.' ·We have punctiliously obeyed the orders of our ancestor, Jonadab son of Rechab, never drinking wine ourselves, nor our wives, our sons or
9 our daughters, ·not building houses to live in, owning
10 neither vineyard nor field to sow, ·living in tents. We have obeyed the orders of our ancestor Jonadab, re-
11 specting them in every particular. ·However, when Nebuchadnezzar king of Babylon invaded this country, we decided, 'We must get away! We will go to Jerusalem to escape the army of the Chaldaeans and the army of Aram.' So here we are, living in Jerusalem."

12 Then the word of Yahweh was addressed to Jere-
13 miah, ·"Thus says Yahweh Sabaoth, the God of Israel: Go and say to the men of Judah and the inhabitants of Jerusalem, 'Will you not learn the lesson and listen
14 to my words? It is Yahweh who speaks. ·The word of Jonadab son of Rechab ordering his sons to drink no wine has been kept; obedient to their ancestor's command, they drink none even today. But to me, who spoke to you so urgently, so persistently, you have not
15 listened. ·I have sent you all my servants the prophets so persistently, so often, to say: Each of you turn from your evil way, and amend your actions, do not follow alien gods and serve them; then you will be able to stay on the soil I gave to you and your ancestors. But you
16 would not listen to me. ·The sons of Jonadab son of Rechab have kept the command their ancestor gave
17 them, but this people has not listened to me. ·And so— Yahweh, the God of Sabaoth, the God of Israel, says this: I will bring down on Judah and the citizens of Jerusalem all the disasters with which I have threatened them, because I spoke to them and they would not listen, called to them and they would not answer.'"

**34 a.** The ancient ritual of covenant, Gn. 15:17.

18 Then Jeremiah said to the Rechabite clan, "Yahweh Sabaoth, the God of Israel, says this, 'Because you have obeyed the orders of Jonadab and kept all his rules 19 and done all that he ordered you, ·for this—thus says Yahweh Sabaoth, the God of Israel—Jonadab son of Rechab shall never lack a male descendant to stand in my presence.'"

## IV. THE SUFFERINGS OF JEREMIAH

### The scroll written in 605–604                    (LXX 43)

1 **36** In the fourth year of Jehoiakim[a] son of Josiah, king of Judah, this word was addressed to Jere- 2 miah by Yahweh, ·"Take a scroll and write on it all the words I have spoken to you about Jerusalem and Judah and all the nations, from the day I first spoke to 3 you, in the time of Josiah, until today. ·Perhaps when the House of Judah hears of all the evil I have in mind for them, each man will turn from his evil way, and 4 then I can forgive their misdeeds and their sin." ·Jere- miah therefore summoned Baruch son of Neriah, who at his dictation wrote down on the scroll all the words Yahweh had spoken to him.

9 Now in the fifth year of Jehoiakim son of Josiah, king of Judah, in the ninth month,[b] there was a sum- mons to a fast in the presence of Yahweh for the whole population of Jerusalem and for all the people who could come to Jerusalem from the towns of Judah. 5 Jeremiah then gave Baruch this order: "As I am pre- 6 vented from entering the Temple of Yahweh, ·you yourself must go and, from the scroll you wrote at my dictation, read all the words of Yahweh to the people in his Temple on the day of the fast; read them also in the hearing of all the men of Judah who come in from 7 the towns. ·Perhaps they will offer their prayers to Yah- weh and each one turn from his evil way, for great is the anger and wrath with which Yahweh has threat- 8 ened this people." ·Baruch son of Neriah duly carried out the order that the prophet Jeremiah had given him, to read all the words of Yahweh from the book in his 10 Temple. ·He read the words of Jeremiah from the book;

this happened in the apartment of Gemariah, son of Shaphan the secretary, in the upper court at the entry of the New Gate of the Temple of Yahweh, where all the people could hear.

11 Micaiah son of Gemariah, son of Shaphan, had heard all the words of Yahweh read from the book, 12 and he went down to the royal palace and into the secretary's room. All the officials were in session there: Elishama the secretary, Delaiah son of Shemaiah, Elnathan son of Achbor, Gemariah son of Shaphan, Zedekiah son of Hananiah and all the other officials. 13 Micaiah reported to them all the words he had heard 14 as Baruch was reading the book to the people. ·The officials then by common consent sent Jehudi son of Nethaniah to Baruch, with Shelemiah son of Cushi, to give him this message, "Come, and bring the scroll with you which you were reading to the people." Bringing the scroll with him, Baruch son of Neriah appeared 15 before them. ·"Sit down," they said, "and read it out." 16 So Baruch read it to them. ·When they had heard all the words they turned to one another in alarm and said, "We must certainly inform the king of all this." 17 They then questioned Baruch: "Tell us," they said, 18 "how you came to write all these words." ·"Jeremiah dictated them to me," Baruch replied, "and I wrote 19 them down in ink in this book." ·The officials then said to Baruch, "You and Jeremiah had better go into hid- 20 ing; and do not tell anyone where you are." ·Whereupon they went off to the king in the palace court, depositing the scroll in the room of Elishama the secretary. And they informed the king of the whole affair.

21 The king sent Jehudi for the scroll, and he brought it from the room of Elishama the secretary and read it out to the king and all the officials standing around 22 the king. ·The king was seated in his winter apartments —it was the ninth month—with a fire burning in a brazier 23 in front of him. ·Each time Jehudi had read three or four columns, the king cut them off with a scribe's knife and threw them into the fire in the brazier until the whole of the scroll had been burned in the brazier fire. 24 But even after hearing all these words, neither the king

**36 a.** He had just capitulated to Nebuchadnezzar.
**b.** December 604.

nor any of his servants took alarm or tore their gar-
25 ments; ·and although Elnathan and Delaiah and
Gemariah had urged the king not to burn the scroll
26 he would not listen to them. ·He ordered Prince
Jerahmeel and Seraiah son of Azriel and Shelemiah
son of Abdeel to arrest the scribe Baruch and the
prophet Jeremiah. But Yahweh had hidden them.

27    And then the word of Yahweh was addressed to
Jeremiah, after the king had burned the scroll con-
taining the words Baruch had written at the dictation
28 of Jeremiah, ·"Take another scroll and write down all
the words that were written on the first scroll burned
29 by Jehoiakim king of Judah. ·And as regards Jehoiakim
king of Judah, say, 'Yahweh says this: You have
burned this scroll, saying: Why have you written down:
The king of Babylon will certainly come and lay this
30 country waste and leave it without man or beast? ·And
so, this is what Yahweh says about Jehoiakim king of
Judah: He will have no one to sit on the throne of
David, and his corpse will be tossed out to the heat of
31 the day and the frost of the night. ·I will punish him,
his heirs and his servants for their misdeeds; on them,
on the citizens of Jerusalem and on the men of Judah
I will bring down all the disasters with which I have
threatened them, though they have not listened.' "

32    Jeremiah then took another scroll and gave it to the
scribe Baruch son of Neriah, and at the dictation of
Jeremiah he wrote down all the words of the book
that Jehoiakim king of Judah had burned, with many
similar words in addition.

## A verdict on Zedekiah                      (LXX 44:1-2)

1 **37** Zedekiah son of Josiah became king, succeeding
Coniah son of Jehoiakim: Nebuchadnezzar king
of Babylon had made him king of the land of Judah.
2 But neither he nor his servants nor the people of the
country paid any attention to the words Yahweh spoke
through the prophet Jeremiah.

## Zedekiah consults Jeremiah during the respite of 588
## (LXX 44:3-10)

3    King Zedekiah sent Jehucal son of Shelemiah and
the priest Zephaniah son of Maaseiah to the prophet

Jeremiah with this message, "Intercede for us with Yah-
4 weh our God." ·Now Jeremiah was still moving freely
among the people: he had not yet been put in prison.
5 Meanwhile Pharaoh's army was on the move from
Egypt and the Chaldaeans besieging Jerusalem had
raised the siege when they heard the news.
6    Then the word of Yahweh was addressed to the
7 prophet Jeremiah, ·"Yahweh, the God of Israel, says
this: To the king of Judah who sent you to consult
me make this reply, 'Is Pharaoh's army marching to
your aid? It will withdraw to its own country, Egypt.
8 The Chaldaeans will return to attack this city; they
9 will capture it and burn it down. ·Do not deceive yourselves and say: The Chaldaeans are leaving us for good.
10 They are not leaving. ·Even if you cut to pieces the
whole Chaldaean army now fighting against you until
there were only the wounded left, they would stand up
again, each man in his tent, to burn this city down.' "

## The arrest of Jeremiah. Improvement in his treatment
### (LXX 44:11–21)

11    At the time when the Chaldaean army, threatened
by the army of Pharaoh, had raised the siege of Jerusa-
12 lem, ·Jeremiah started to leave Jerusalem and go to
the land of Benjamin, there among his own people to
13 divide his property. ·He was at the Benjamin Gate
when a sentry on duty there, Irijah son of Shelemiah,
son of Hananiah, arrested the prophet Jeremiah. "You
14 are deserting to the Chaldaeans!" he said. ·"It is a lie!"
Jeremiah answered. "I am not deserting to the Chaldaeans." But Irijah would not listen to Jeremiah and
15 took him under arrest to the officials. ·The officials,
furious with Jeremiah, had him beaten and shut up in
the house of Jonathan the secretary which had been
16 turned into a prison. ·Thus Jeremiah found himself in
an underground cell. And there for a long time he
stayed.
17    King Zedekiah had him sent for, and he questioned
him privately in his palace. "Is there any word from
Yahweh?" he asked. "There is," Jeremiah answered.
" 'You will be handed over,' he said, 'into the power
18 of the king of Babylon.' " ·Jeremiah then said to King
Zedekiah, "What wrong have I done to you or your

servants or this people, for you to put me in prison?
<sup>19</sup> Where are your prophets now who prophesied, 'The king of Babylon will not attack you or this country?'
<sup>20</sup> Let my lord king be pleased to listen to me now; let my request meet your favor. Do not have me taken back to the house of Jonathan the secretary, or I shall die
<sup>21</sup> there." ·King Zedekiah then gave an order, and Jeremiah was confined in the Court of the Guard and given a loaf of bread a day from the Street of the Bakers as long as there was bread left in the city. So Jeremiah stayed in the Court of the Guard.

**Jeremiah is thrown into the cistern. Ebed-melech inter-venes**     **(LXX 45:1-13)**

<sup>1</sup> 38 But Shephatiah son of Mattan, Gedaliah son of Pashhur, Jucal son of Shelemiah and Pashhur son of Malchiah heard the words which Jeremiah was
<sup>2</sup> saying to all the people, ·"Yahweh says this, 'Anyone who stays in this city will die by sword, famine or plague; but anyone who leaves it and surrenders to the Chaldaeans will live; he will escape with his life.
<sup>3</sup> Yahweh says this: This city will certainly be delivered into the power of the army of the king of Babylon, who will capture it.'"
<sup>4</sup> These leading men accordingly spoke to the king. "Let this man be put to death: he is unquestionably disheartening the remaining soldiers in the city, and all the people too, by talking like this. The fellow does not have the welfare of this people at heart so much
<sup>5</sup> as its ruin." ·"He is in your hands as you know," King Zedekiah answered, "for the king is powerless against
<sup>6</sup> you." ·So they took Jeremiah and threw him into the well of Prince Malchiah in the Court of the Guard, letting him down with ropes. There was no water in the well, only mud, and into the mud Jeremiah sank.
<sup>7</sup> But Ebed-melech the Cushite, a eunuch attached to the palace, heard that Jeremiah had been put into the well. As the king was sitting at the Benjamin Gate,
<sup>8</sup> Ebed-melech came out from the palace and spoke to
<sup>9</sup> the king. ·"My lord king," he said, "these men have done a wicked thing by treating the prophet Jeremiah like this: they have thrown him into the well where he
<sup>10</sup> will die." ·At this the king gave Ebed-melech the

Cushite the following order: "Take three men with you from here and pull the prophet Jeremiah out of
11 the well before he dies." ·Ebed-melech took the men with him and went into the palace to the storehouse wardrobe; out of it he took some torn, worn-out rags which he lowered on ropes to Jeremiah in the well.
12 Ebed-melech the Cushite then said to Jeremiah, "These torn, worn-out rags are for you to put under your arm-
13 pits to pad the ropes." Jeremiah did this. ·They then hauled Jeremiah up with the ropes and pulled him out of the well. And Jeremiah stayed in the Court of the Guard.

### The last conversation between Jeremiah and Zedekiah (LXX 45:14–28)

14    King Zedekiah had the prophet Jeremiah summoned to him at the third entrance to the Temple of Yahweh. "I want to ask you for a word," the king said to Jere-
15 miah, "keep nothing back from me." ·Jeremiah answered Zedekiah, "If I tell you, surely you will have me put to death? And if I give you advice, you will not
16 listen to me." ·King Zedekiah then swore this oath in secret to Jeremiah, "As Yahweh lives, giver of this life of ours, I will neither have you put to death nor handed over into the power of these men who are
17 determined to kill you." ·Jeremiah then said to Zedekiah, "Yahweh, the God of Sabaoth, the God of Israel, says this, 'If you go out and surrender to the officers of the king of Babylon, your life will be safe and this city will not be burned down; you and your family will
18 survive. ·But if you do not go out and surrender to the officers of the king of Babylon, this city will be handed over into the power of the king of the Chaldaeans who will burn it down; and you yourself will not escape
19 their hands.'" ·King Zedekiah then said to Jeremiah, "I am afraid of the Jews who have already gone over to the Chaldaeans: I might be handed over to them and
20 they would ill-treat me." ·"You will not be handed over to them," Jeremiah replied, "just listen to the voice of Yahweh, in obedience to which I have spoken, and all
21 will go well with you and your life will be safe. ·But if you refuse to go, this is what Yahweh has shown me:
22 a vision of all the women left in the palace of the king

of Judah being led off to the officers of the king of Babylon and singing:

> 'They have misled you, they have overreached you,
> your fine friends!
> Are your feet sinking in the mud?
> They are up and away!'

23 Yes, all your wives and children will be led off to the Chaldaeans, and you yourself will not escape their hands, but will be a prisoner in the clutches of the king of Babylon. And as for this city, it will be burned down."

24 Zedekiah then said to Jeremiah, "Do not let anyone
25 else hear these words or you will die. ·If the officials hear that I have been talking to you, and come to you and say, 'Tell us what you said to the king and what the king said to you; keep nothing back from us, or
26 we will put you to death,' ·you must reply, 'I presented this request to the king: that he would not have me sent back to the house of Jonathan to die there.'"

27 All the officials did in fact come to Jeremiah to question him. He told them exactly what the king had ordered him to say. They then left him in peace, since no
28 part of the conversation had been overheard. ·Jeremiah stayed in the Court of the Guard until the day Jerusalem was captured.

## The fall of Jerusalem: the treatment Jeremiah received (LXX 45:28; 46:14)

Now when Jerusalem was captured . . .

1 **39** In the ninth year of Zedekiah king of Judah, in the tenth month,[a] Nebuchadnezzar king of Babylon came with his whole army to attack Jerusalem
2 and besieged it. ·In the eleventh year of Zedekiah, in the fourth month,[b] a breach was made in the city wall.
3 . . . all the officers of the king of Babylon marched in and took up their quarters at the Middle Gate: Nergal-sharezer, prince of Sin-magir, the chief officer, Nebushazban, the high official, and all the other officers of the king of Babylon . . .
4 Seeing this, Zedekiah king of Judah fled under cover of dark, with all the fighting men, leaving the city by

way of the king's garden through the gate between the two walls, and making their way toward the Arabah.[c]

5 The Chaldaean troops pursued them and caught up with Zedekiah in the plains of Jericho. They captured him and took him up to Nebuchadnezzar king of Babylon at Riblah in the land of Hamath, who passed sen-
6 tence on him. ·The king of Babylon had the sons of Zedekiah slaughtered before his eyes at Riblah; the king of Babylon also had all the leading men of Judah
7 put to death. ·He then put out Zedekiah's eyes and, loading him with chains, carried him off to Babylon.
8 The Chaldaeans burned down the royal palace and the private houses, and demolished the walls of Jerusalem.
9 Nebuzaradan, commander of the guard, deported the remainder of the population left behind in the city, the deserters who had gone over to him, and the rest of
10 the artisans to Babylon. ·Nebuzaradan, commander of the guard, left some of the humbler people who had nothing, in the land of Judah, at the same time giving them vineyards and fields.

11 Nebuchadnezzar king of Babylon had given the following orders to Nebuzaradan, commander of the
12 guard, about Jeremiah: ·"Take him, look after him; do him no harm, but treat him as he wishes."
13 Whereupon (Nebuzaradan, commander of the guard), Nebushazban, the high official, Nergal-sharezer, the chief officer, and all the officers of the king of Babylon dispatched men.
14 . . . and they dispatched men to take Jeremiah from the Court of the Guard, and allowed him to move about freely. And so he lived among the people.

### An oracle assuring the safety of Ebed-melech
(LXX 46:15–18)

15 While Jeremiah was confined in the Court of the Guard, the word of Yahweh was addressed to him,
16 "Go and say to Ebed-melech the Cushite, 'Yahweh, the God of Israel, says this: See, I am bringing disaster, not prosperity, on this city, as I said I would. That day,
17 when this comes true before your eyes, ·I will rescue

**39** a. January–February 588.
b. August 587.
c. The Jordan valley.

you that day—it is Yahweh who speaks—and you will
not be delivered into the hands of the men you fear.
18 I will see that you escape: you are not going to fall
to the sword; you will escape with your life, because
you have put your trust in me—it is Yahweh who
speaks.' "

## Further details about the treatment of Jeremiah
### (LXX 47:1–6)

1    **40** The word addressed to Jeremiah by Yahweh
    after Nebuzaradan, commander of the guard,
had released him from Ramah; there he had him singled out, chained as he was with all the other captives
from Jerusalem and Judah who were being deported
2 to Babylon. ·Then taking Jeremiah aside, the commander of the guard said to him, "Yahweh your God
3 foretold calamity for this country, ·and now he has
brought it. He has done what he threatened to do,
because you had sinned against Yahweh and would
not listen to his voice; so all this has happened to you.
4 Look, today I am having your hands unchained. If
you like to come with me to Babylon, then come: I
will look after you. If you do not want to come with
me to Babylon, never mind. Look, you have the whole
country to choose from: you may go where you please,
5 wherever you choose. ·You can, for instance, go back
to Gedaliah son of Ahikam, son of Shaphan, whom
the king of Babylon has appointed governor of the
towns of Judah, and stay with him and live with the
people; or you can go anywhere else you choose."
With that, the commander of the guard provided him
with food and gave him a present and sent him on his
6 way. ·Jeremiah went to Mizpah to Gedaliah son of
Ahikam and stayed with him, living with the people
still left in the country.

## Gedaliah the governor; his assassination
### (LXX 47:7–48:18)

7    When all the commanders of the troops, who with
their men were still roaming the countryside, heard
that the king of Babylon had appointed Gedaliah son
of Ahikam as governor of the country, making him
responsible for the men, women and children, and those

humbler people of the country who had not been de-
8 ported to Babylon, ·they went to Gedaliah at Mizpah:
Ishmael son of Nethaniah, Johanan son of Kareah,
Seraiah son of Tanhumeth, the sons of Ephai the
Netophathite, Jezaniah son of the Maacathite, they and
9 their men. ·To them and to their men Gedaliah son
of Ahikam, son of Shaphan, swore an oath. "Do not
be afraid," he said, "of submitting to the Chaldaeans;
but live in the country, and obey the king of Babylon,
10 and all will go well with you. ·I for my part, as the
man answerable to the Chaldaeans when they come to
us, am going to live here at Mizpah; but you can
harvest your wine, summer fruits and oil, fill your stor-
age jars and settle down in those towns which you
care to occupy."

11    Similarly, when all the Judaeans living in Moab and
among the Ammonites, and in Edom, heard that the
king of Babylon had left a remnant in Judah and had
appointed Gedaliah son of Ahikam, son of Shaphan,
12 as their governor, ·they all came back from all the
places to which they had been dispersed. On their return to the land of Judah, to Gedaliah at Mizpah, they
harvested an immense quantity of wine and summer
fruits.

13    Now Johanan son of Kareah, and all the army
leaders still roaming in the countryside, went to
14 Gedaliah at Mizpah ·and said to him, "Are you aware
that Baalis king of the Ammonites has sent Ishmael
son of Nethaniah to murder you?" But Gedaliah son
15 of Ahikam would not believe them. ·Johanan son of
Kareah had even told Gedaliah secretly at Mizpah,
"Let me go and kill Ishmael son of Nethaniah, and no
one will know who did it. Why should he murder you?
It would mean that all the Judaeans who have rallied
around you would be scattered again. Why should the
16 remnant of Judah perish?" ·But Gedaliah son of
Ahikam replied to Johanan son of Kareah, "You must
not do this; what you say about Ishmael is false."

1  **41** But in the seventh month, Ishmael son of Nethaniah, son of Elishama, who was of royal descent, and ten men with him, came to Gedaliah son
of Ahikam at Mizpah. And as they were taking their
2 meal together, there at Mizpah, ·Ishmael son of Ne-

thaniah stood up with his ten men, and attacking Gedaliah son of Ahikam, son of Shaphan, with their swords, murdered the man whom the king of Babylon 3 had made governor of the country. ·And all the Judaeans who were with him at the feast, and those of the Chaldaeans who happened to be there—they were fighting men—Ishmael killed too.

4 On the day after the murder of Gedaliah, before the 5 news had become known, ·eighty men arrived from Shechem, Shiloh and Samaria, with their beards shaved off, their garments torn and their bodies gashed; they had oblations and incense with them to take to the 6 Temple of Yahweh. ·Ishmael son of Nethaniah left Mizpah to meet them as they approached, weeping as they went. When he met them he said, "Come to 7 Gedaliah son of Ahikam." ·But once they were well inside the town, Ishmael son of Nethaniah slaughtered them, with the help of his men, and threw them into a 8 cistern. ·There were ten of them, however, who said to Ishmael, "Do not kill us: we have stocks of wheat and barley, oil and honey, hidden away in the fields." So he spared them and did not kill them with their 9 brothers. ·The cistern into which Ishmael threw the corpses of all the men he had killed was a large cistern which King Asa had built as a precaution against Baasha king of Israel. Ishmael son of Nethaniah filled 10 it with the bodies of his victims. ·Then Ishmael led the entire remnant of the people at Mizpah away, and the royal princesses whom Nebuzaradan, commander of the guard, had left in the care of Gedaliah son of Ahikam. Ishmael son of Nethaniah set out early to cross to the Ammonites.

11 When Johanan son of Kareah and all the army leaders who were with him heard about all the crimes 12 committed by Ishmael son of Nethaniah, ·mustering all their men, they set out to attack Ishmael son of Nethaniah. They caught up with him at the great Pool 13 of Gibeon. ·At the sight of Johanan son of Kareah and all the army leaders with him, all the people with 14 Ishmael were beside themselves with joy. ·All the people whom Ishmael had led away from Mizpah turned 15 about and rallied to Johanan son of Kareah. ·Ishmael son of Nethaniah escaped from Johanan with eight of

16 his men and fled to the Ammonites. ·Johanan son of
Kareah and all the army leaders with him then rallied
the entire remnant of the people whom Ishmael son of
Nethaniah had led away from Mizpah after the murder
of Gedaliah son of Ahikam: men, women and children,
and eunuchs, whom Johanan brought back from
17 Gibeon. ·They set out, making a halt at Khan Kimham
near Bethlehem. Their plan was to make for Egypt,
18 away from the Chaldaeans, of whom they were now
terrified because Ishmael son of Nethaniah had killed
Gedaliah son of Ahikam whom the king of Babylon
had made governor of the country.

## The flight to Egypt
### (LXX 49:1–18; 50:1–3; 49:19–22; 50:4–7)

1    42 Then all the army leaders, with Johanan son of
Kareah and Azariah son of Hoshaiah, and all
2 the people from least to greatest, approached ·the
prophet Jeremiah and said, "May it please you to hear
our request! Intercede with Yahweh your God for all
this remnant—and how few we are who once were so
3 many, your own eyes can now see—·so that Yahweh
your God may show us the way we are to go and what
4 we must do." ·The prophet Jeremiah replied, "I hear
you; and I will indeed pray to Yahweh your God as
you ask; and every word Yahweh your God replies I
5 will tell you, keeping nothing back from you." ·They
in their turn said to Jeremiah, "May Yahweh be a true
and faithful witness against us, if we do not follow the
instructions that Yahweh your God sends us through
6 you. ·Whether we like it or not, we mean to obey the
voice of Yahweh our God to whom we send you to
speak for us, and by thus obeying the voice of Yahweh
our God we will prosper."

7    Ten days later the word of Yahweh was addressed to
8 Jeremiah. ·He then summoned Johanan son of Kareah
and all the army leaders who were with him, and all
9 the people from least to greatest. ·He said, "Yahweh,
the God of Israel, to whom you delegated me to offer
10 your request says this: ·'If you are willing to remain
peaceably in this country, I will build you and not
overthrow you; I will plant you, not tear you up. For
11 I am sorry for the evil I have done you. ·Do not be

afraid of the king of Babylon any longer; do not fear him—it is Yahweh who speaks—for I am with you to
12 save you and deliver you from his hands. ·I will take pity on you, and move him to pity you and let you
13 return to your native soil. ·But if you say: We do not want to stay in this country; if you disobey the voice
14 of Yahweh your God, ·and say: No, the land of Egypt is where we want to go, where we shall not see war nor hear the sound of trumpet, nor lack for bread;
15 that is where we want to live; ·in that case, remnant of Judah, listen to the word of Yahweh. Yahweh Sab-
16 aoth, the God of Israel, says this: If ·you are deter- mined to go to Egypt, and if you do go and settle there, the sword you fear will overtake you, there in the land of Egypt; the famine you dread will follow on your heels, right into Egypt; you shall die there.
17 All the men who are determined to go to Egypt and settle there shall die by sword, famine and plague: not one survivor will escape the disaster I mean to bring
18 them. ·Yes, Yahweh Sabaoth, the God of Israel, says this: Just as my anger and my fury have been poured out on the citizens of Jerusalem, so will my fury be poured out on you if you go to Egypt: you will become an object of execration and horror, a curse, a laugh- ingstock; and you will never see this place again.' "

1 **43** However, when Jeremiah had finished telling all the people all the words of Yahweh their God, with which Yahweh had entrusted him for them—all the
2 words quoted above—·Azariah son of Hoshaiah, and Johanan son of Kareah, and all those arrogant and apostate men, said to Jeremiah, "You are lying. Yah- weh did not instruct you to say, 'Do not go to Egypt
3 and settle there.' ·It is Baruch son of Neriah who keeps encouraging you to thwart us, to hand us over into the power of the Chaldaeans, who will either put us to death or deport us to Babylon!"

19 **42** "Remnant of Judah!" Jeremiah answered, "Yahweh himself tells you, 'Do not go into Egypt.' Understand this clearly: today I have given you my solemn warning.
20 You were playing with your own lives when you made me your envoy to Yahweh your God and said, 'Inter- cede for us with Yahweh our God; tell us what Yahweh
21 our God orders and we will do it.' ·And now that I have told you, you have not obeyed the voice of Yah-

weh your God today, or any part of the message he
22 gave me for you. ·So understand this clearly: you are
going to die by sword, famine and plague in the place
where you have been wanting to go and settle."

4 **43** Despite this, Johanan son of Kareah and all the
army leaders and all the people would not obey
the voice of Yahweh and stay in the land of Judah.
5 Johanan son of Kareah and all the army leaders led
off the entire remnant of Judah, those who had come
back from all the nations into which they had been
6 dispersed, to live in the land of Judah: ·men, women,
children, the royal princesses too, and every single person entrusted to Gedaliah son of Ahikam, son of Shaphan, by Nebuzaradan, commander of the guard; they
also led off the prophet Jeremiah and Baruch son of
7 Neriah. ·And so, disregarding the voice of Yahweh,
they reached the land of Egypt and arrived at Tahpanhes.

**Jeremiah foretells the invasion of Egypt by Nebuchad-
nezzar                                    (LXX 50:8–13)**

8    At Tahpanhes the word of Yahweh was addressed
9 to Jeremiah, ·"Take some large stones and bury them
in the presence of the men of Judah in the cement on
the square outside the entrance of Pharaoh's palace in
10 Tahpanhes. ·Then say to them, 'Yahweh, the God of
Israel, says this: I am sending for Nebuchadnezzar,
king of Babylon, my servant; he will place his throne
over these stones that I have buried, and spread his
11 canopy above them. ·He is coming to strike the land
of Egypt:

> Those for the plague, to the plague;
> those for captivity, into captivity;
> those for the sword, to the sword!

12 He will set fire to the temples of the gods of Egypt;
he will burn these gods or carry them off; as a shepherd
picks his cloak clean of vermin, so will he pick Egypt
13 clean and leave without interference.[a] ·He will break
the obelisks of the temple of the Sun at On[b] and burn
down the temples of the gods of Egypt.' "

**43 a.** This successful expedition took place in 568–567.
**b.** Heliopolis.

**The last episode of Jeremiah's ministry: the Jews and the Queen of Heaven** (LXX 51:1–30)

1 **44** The word that was addressed to Jeremiah for all the Jews living in the land of Egypt with homes in Migdol, Tahpanhes, Noph and the land of Pathros.[a]

2 "Yahweh Sabaoth, the God of Israel, says this: You have seen all the misery I have brought down on Jerusalem and the towns of Judah; today they lie in ruins 3 and uninhabited. ·This was because of the wicked deeds which they committed to provoke me, offering incense and serving alien gods which neither they, nor you, nor 4 your ancestors ever knew. ·I persistently sent you all my servants the prophets; I sent them to say, 'Do not 5 commit this abomination that I find so hateful.' ·But they would not listen, would not pay attention and so turn from their wicked deeds and no longer offer in-6 cense to alien gods. ·And so my fury and my anger overflowed, burning down the towns of Judah and the streets of Jerusalem, which were reduced to ruins and 7 wasteland, as they still are today. ·And now, Yahweh, the God of Sabaoth, the God of Israel, says this: Why bring the same disaster on yourselves? Do you want to destroy all the men, women, children and babes in arms, out of Judah, and leave yourselves no remnant, 8 by provoking me with the work of your own hands, offering incense to alien gods in the land of Egypt where you have come to settle, thus working for your own destruction, to become a curse and a laughingstock 9 for all the nations of the earth? ·Have you forgotten the crimes of your ancestors, of the kings of Judah and of their wives, your own crimes, the crimes of your own wives, committed in the land of Judah and in the 10 streets of Jerusalem? ·To this day they have felt neither contrition nor fear; they have not observed my Law nor the statutes I proclaimed before you, as before your 11 ancestors. ·Therefore—Yahweh Sabaoth, the God of Israel, says this: Now I mean to turn my face against you to bring disaster, and exterminate the whole of 12 Judah. ·The remnant of Judah who resolved to come to the land of Egypt and to settle there, I will remove: they will all perish in the land of Egypt; they will fall to the sword or perish of famine, from least to greatest;

by sword and famine they will die; they will be an object of execration and horror, a curse, a laughing-
13 stock. ·I will deal as severely with these who have made their home in the land of Egypt, as I dealt with
14 Jerusalem, with sword, famine and plague. ·Of the remnant of Judah settled in the land of Egypt, not one survivor is going to escape to return to the land of Judah where they long to live once again. For none of them are going to return, except for a few refugees."

15 At this, all the men who knew that their wives offered incense to alien gods, and all the women who were standing there, a large assembly (with all the people living in Pathros in the land of Egypt), answered
16 Jeremiah as follows, ·"We have no intention of listening to this word you have spoken to us in Yahweh's
17 name, ·but intend to go on doing all we vowed to do: offering incense to the Queen of Heaven and pouring libations in her honor, as we used to do, we and our fathers, our kings and our leaders, in the towns of Judah and in the streets of Jerusalem: we had food in plenty then, we lived well, we suffered no disasters.
18 But since we gave up offering incense to the Queen of Heaven and pouring libations in her honor, we have been destitute and have perished either by sword or by
19 famine." ·The women added, "When we offer incense to the Queen of Heaven and pour libations in her honor, do you think we make cakes for her with her features on them, and pour libations to her, without our husbands' knowledge?"

20 To all the people, men and women; all those who
21 had made this answer, Jeremiah retorted, ·"The incense you offered in the towns of Judah and in the streets of Jerusalem, you, your fathers, your kings, your leaders, and the people of the country—is not this what
22 Yahweh remembered, what came to his mind? ·Yahweh could no longer endure your misdeeds and your detestable practices; this is why your country has today become a desert, an object of horror and a curse, unin-
23 habited. ·And this has happened because you offered incense, because you sinned against Yahweh, refusing

---

**44 a.** Migdol, Tahpanhes, Noph (Memphis) are in Lower Egypt; "the land of Pathros" is Upper Egypt.

to listen to the voice of Yahweh, or to observe his Law,
his statutes and his decrees; this is the cause of the
disaster that has overtaken you—as is the case today."

24 Then Jeremiah spoke to all the people, and particu-
larly to all the women, "Listen to the word of Yahweh:
25 Yahweh Sabaoth, the God of Israel, says this, 'You
women, what your mouth promises, your hands should
certainly perform! You have said: We will perform the
vows we have made without fail and offer incense to
the Queen of Heaven and pour libations in her honor.
26 Very well, keep your vows, make your libations! ·But
listen to the word of Yahweh, all you Judaeans living
in the land of Egypt: I swear by my great name, Yahweh says, that my name shall be spoken no more by any
man of Judah throughout the land of Egypt; not one
27 shall say: As the Lord Yahweh lives.[b] ·Yes, I will watch
over them for their ruin, not for their good; all the men
of Judah in the land of Egypt shall perish either by
28 the sword or by famine until they are wiped out. ·Yet,
though few in number, those who escape the sword
will return to the land of Judah from the land of Egypt.
Then the entire remnant of Judah who have come to
settle in the land of Egypt will know whose word came
true, mine or theirs.

29 'And here is the proof for you—it is Yahweh who
speaks—that I mean to deal with you in this place:
so that you may know that the words with which I
30 threaten you will come true: ·Yahweh says this: I will
hand the pharaoh Hophra,[c] king of Egypt, over to his
enemies and to those determined to kill him, just as I
handed Zedekiah king of Judah over to Nebuchadnezzar king of Babylon, his enemy who was bent on killing
him.' "

## An oracle of comfort for Baruch (LXX 51:31–35)

1 **45** The word that the prophet Jeremiah addressed
to Baruch son of Neriah when the latter wrote
these words down in a book at the dictation of Jeremiah in the fourth year of Jehoiakim[a] son of Josiah,
2 king of Judah, ·"This is what Yahweh, the God of
3 Israel, says about you, Baruch! ·Since you have said,
'I despair, for Yahweh has added sorrow to my ordeals!
4 I am worn out with groaning, and find no relief!' ·Yah-

weh says this, 'Now I am knocking down what I have
built, tearing up what I have planted: I am going to
5 strike the whole earth. ·And here you are asking for
special treatment! Do not ask, for I am now going
to bring down disaster on all mankind—it is Yahweh
who speaks. As for you, I will let you escape with your
own life, wherever you may go.' "

## II (continued). ORACLES AGAINST THE NATIONS

### B. THE ORACLES IN DETAIL

1 **46** The words of Yahweh which were addressed to
the prophet Jeremiah against the nations.

**Oracles against Egypt. The defeat at Carchemish
(LXX 26, 2–12)**

2    On Egypt.
Against the army of Pharaoh Neco, king of Egypt,
which took up position near the river Euphrates by Carchemish,*a* when it was defeated by Nebuchadnezzar
king of Babylon in the fourth year of Jehoiakim son
of Josiah, king of Judah.

3        Have buckler ready, and shield:
        onward to battle!
4        Harness the horses:
        into the saddle, horsemen!
        To your ranks! On with your helmets!
        Sharpen your spears,
        put on your breastplates! . . .
5        What do I see?
        They are panic-stricken,
        in full retreat!

**b.** The worshipers of Ishtar, queen of heaven, also made a show
of invoking Yahweh.
**c.** Hophra succeeded Neco in 588; he was dethroned and exe-
cuted in 569.
**45 a.** 605 B.C.
**46 a.** 605 B.C.

Their heroes, beaten back,
are fleeing headlong
with not a look behind.
Terror from every side!
—it is Yahweh who speaks.

6    The fastest cannot escape,
nor the bravest save himself:
there in the north, there by the river Euphrates,
they have collapsed, have fallen.

7    Who was it rose like the Nile,
its waters foaming like a torrent?

8    Why, Egypt rose like the Nile,
its waters foaming like a torrent.
"I will rise," he said, "and drown the earth;
sweep towns and their inhabitants away!

9    Charge, horses!
Crash on, chariots!
Advance, warriors,
you men from Cush and Put with shield in hand,
you men from Lud who bend the bow!"[b]

10    Now, this is the day of the Lord Yahweh,
a day of vengeance for his revenge on his
         enemies:
his sword will eat them up and have its fill,
will grow drunk with their blood.
Yes, the Lord Yahweh Sabaoth has a sacrifice
         to make
in the north country, by the river Euphrates.

11    Go up to Gilead in search of balm,
virgin daughter of Egypt!
You multiply remedies in vain,
nothing can cure you.

12    The nations have heard of your shame,
the dirge raised for you fills the earth:
for warrior has stumbled against warrior,
and both have fallen.

## The invasion of Egypt      (LXX 26:13–28)

13    The word that Yahweh addressed to the prophet Jeremiah when Nebuchadnezzar king of Babylon set out to attack the land of Egypt.

14    Publish it in Migdol,
      proclaim it in Noph.
      Say, "To your posts! At the ready!"
      for the sword is devouring around you.

15    What! Has Apis[c] fled?
      Has your Strong One not stood firm?

16    Yes, Yahweh has knocked him ·flat!
      He tottered, and now he has fallen down!
      Then they said to each other,
      "Up! Let us go back to our own people,
      to the country where we were born,
      far from the destroying sword!"

17    Give this name to Pharaoh:
      "Much-noise-but-he-lets-the-chance-slip-by!"

18    As I live—it is the King who speaks
      whose name is Yahweh Sabaoth—
      someone will come, a Tabor among mountains,
      a Carmel high above the sea.

19    Get your bundle ready for exile,
      daughter of Egypt, so safe in your home!
      Noph will be reduced to a desert,
      desolate, uninhabited.

20    Egypt was a splendid heifer,
      but a gadfly from the North has settled on her.

21    The mercenaries she had with her, these too
      were as sleek as fattened calves:
      but they too have taken to their heels,
      they all run at once and cannot hold their
          ground.
      For on them comes the day of their disaster,
      their time of reckoning.

22    Listen: a sound like a serpent hissing!
      Yes, they are coming in force
      to fall on her with their axes,
      with woodcutters,

23    they will fell her forest—it is Yahweh who
          speaks.
      Yes, they are past counting,
      outnumbering the locusts,
      innumerable.

b. Cush is Ethiopia; Put is Somaliland and the "men from Lud"
are a neighboring African people.
c. The sacred bull of Ptah, god of Memphis.

24
> The daughter of Egypt is put to shame,
> handed over to a people from the North.

25 Yahweh Sabaoth, the God of Israel, has said: Now
I mean to punish Amon of No,[d] with Pharaoh and
26 those who put their trust in him. ·I will hand him over
to those who are determined to kill him, over to Nebuchadnezzar king of Babylon, over to his servants. But
in later days, Egypt will be inhabited again as in the
past—it is Yahweh who speaks.

27
> But do not be afraid, my servant Jacob,
> Israel, do not be alarmed:
> look, I will rescue you from distant countries
> and your descendants from the country where
>     they are captive.
> Jacob will have quiet again
> and live at ease, with no one to trouble him.
28
> Do not be afraid, my servant Jacob
> —it is Yahweh who speaks—for I am with you:
> I will make an end of all the nations
> where I have scattered you;
> I will not make an end of you,
> only discipline you in moderation,
> so as not to let you go entirely unpunished.

### Oracle against the Philistines       (LXX 29:1–7)

1 **47** The word of Yahweh that was addressed to Jeremiah against the Philistines before Pharaoh took
2 Gaza by storm. ·Yahweh says this:

> See how the waters rise from the North,
> and become an overflowing torrent,
> overflowing the country and all it contains,
> the towns and their inhabitants!
> Men shout aloud, and there is wailing
> from all the inhabitants of the country,
3
> at the thunder of his stallions' hoofs,
> the crash of his chariots, the grinding of his
>     wheels.
> Fathers forget about their children,
> their hands fall limp
4
> because the day has come
> on which all the Philistines are to be destroyed,

on which Tyre and Sidon are to be stripped
to the last of their auxiliaries.
Yes, Yahweh is destroying the Philistines,
the remnant from the Isle of Caphtor.

5    A shaven scalp for Gaza!
Silence over Ashkelon!
Ashdod, all that is left of the Anakim,
how long will you gash yourselves?[a]

6    Oh, sword of Yahweh,
how long before you rest?
Back into your scabbard,
stop, keep still!

7    Yet how can it rest
when Yahweh has given it an order?
Ashkelon and the sea coast,
these are the targets assigned to it.

## Oracles against Moab                    (LXX 31)

1  **48** On Moab. Yahweh, the God of Israel, says this:

Woe to Nebo, for it has been ravaged,
Kiriathaim has been taken,
all is confusion and alarm in the fortress:

2       it is no longer the boast of Moab!
At Heshbon[a] they plotted her downfall,
"Come on! Let us blot her out from the nations!"
And you too, Madmen, you will be subdued,
the sword is close on you.

3    Hark! From the Abarim a shout,
"Devastation! Dire calamity!"

4    "Moab is shattered"
the cry echoes as far as Zoar.

5    Ah, slopes of Luhith,
they go up them weeping.
At the descent of Horonaim
cries of distress are heard,

6    "Away! Flee for your lives!

d. Thebes, the god of which was Amon.
**47 a.** Self-inflicted wounds, like the shaven head, were a sign of mourning.
**48 a.** There are Hebrew puns on the similar sounds of "Heshbob" and "plotted"; and "Madmen" and "subdued."

Run like the wild asses in the desert!"

7   Yes, since you trusted in your strongholds
    you will be captured too.
    Chemosh[b] will go into exile,
    with all his priests and his nobles.

8   The destroyer will descend on every town,
    no one will escape;
        the Valley will be despoiled, the Plain be
            plundered:
    Yahweh proclaims it!

9   Give Moab a tomb,
    since she is totally destroyed;
    her towns are in ruins,
    with no one to live in them.

10  (Cursed be he who does the work of Yahweh half-
    heartedly! Cursed be he who grudges blood to his
    sword!)

11      From his youth Moab lived at ease,
        he settled on his lees,
        never having been decanted,
        never having gone into exile:
        and so he kept his own flavor,
        his aroma was unchanged.[c]

12  And so the days are coming—it is Yahweh who speaks
    —when I shall send him decanters to decant him; they
    will empty his storage jars and break his amphorae to
13  bits. ·Moab will blush for Chemosh then, as the House
    of Israel blushed for Bethel[d] in whom they put their
    trust.

14      How can you say, "We are heroes,
        sturdy fighting men?"

15      The destroyer of Moab has advanced on him:
            the flower of his youth goes down to the
                slaughter.

16      Moab's ruin is coming soon,
        his downfall comes at top speed.

17      Grieve for him, all you living near him,
        all you who knew his name.
        Say, "Imagine it being broken, that mighty rod,
        that splendid scepter!"

18 Come down from your glory, sit in the dung,
daughter of Dibon, so safe in your home:
the destroyer of Moab has advanced on you,
he has stormed your strongholds.

19 Stand by the roadside, keep watch,
inhabitants of Aroer.
Question fugitive and runaway,
ask, "What has happened?"

20 Moab is shattered and shamed.
Wail and shriek!
Shout across the Arnon,
"Moab has been laid waste!"

21 Judgment has also come on the land of the Plain, on
22 Holon, Jahzah, Mephaath, ·Dibon, Nebo, Beth-
23 diblathaim, ·Kiriathaim, Beth-gamul, Beth-meon,
24 Kerioth, Bozrah, and all the towns in the land of Moab,
far and near.

25 The horn of Moab has been cut off,
and his arm broken.

26 Make him drunk! He has set himself up against Yahweh: Moab will wallow in his vomit, become a laugh-
27 ingstock in his turn. ·Was not Israel a laughingstock to
you? Was he caught red-handed with the thieves, for
you to shake your head whenever you mention him?

28 Leave the towns, make the rocks your home,
inhabitants of Moab.
Learn from the dove that makes its nest
in the walls of the gaping gorge.

29 We have heard of the pride of Moab,
excessive pride!
What arrogance! What pride! What conceit!
What a haughty heart!

30 —I know all about his presumption—it is Yahweh who speaks—
his empty boasting,
those empty deeds of his!

b. God of Moabites.
c. Moab was famous for wine.
d. The sanctuary of the Northern Kingdom, a rival to Jerusalem.

31      —And so I lament for Moab,
for all Moab I cry aloud,
and mourn for the men of Kir-heres.[e]

32      More than for Jazer I weep for you,
vine of Sibmah:
your shoots stretched beyond the sea,
they reached all the way to Jazer.
On your harvest, on your vintage,
the destroyer has descended.

33      Gladness and joy have vanished
from the land of Moab.
There is no longer wine in the presses,
the treader of grapes treads no more,
no more do shouts of joy ring out.

34    The howling of Heshbon and Elealeh can be heard
as far as Jahaz. The shrieks resound from Zoar to
Horonaim and Eglath-shelishiyah, for the waters of
Nimrim too are now becoming desolation.

35    And I shall make an end—it is Yahweh who speaks
—of any man in Moab who offers sacrifice and incense
to his god on the high places.

36    That is why my heart sobs like a flute for Moab,
sobs like a flute for the men of Kir-heres: that accu-
37 mulated treasure all lost! ·Yes, every head is shorn,
every beard cut off, gashes are on the hands of all,
38 sackcloth around all their loins. ·On all the housetops of Moab and in its squares there is nothing but
lamenting, for I have broken Moab like a crock that no
39 one wants—it is Yahweh who speaks. ·What! Broken?
What! Moab so shamefully in retreat? What! Moab
become a laughingstock, a thing of horror to all its
neighbors?

40      For Yahweh says this:
(Here is one who hovers like an eagle,
who will spread his wings over Moab.)

41      The towns will be captured,
the strongholds seized.

(And the heart of Moab's warriors that day will be like
the heart of a woman in labor pains.)

42      Moab will be destroyed, no longer a people,
for setting itself up against Yahweh.

43    Terror, the pit, the snare,
      are for you, inhabitant of Moab—
      it is Yahweh who speaks:
44    the man who takes flight from the terror
      shall fall into the pit,
      climbing out of the pit,
      he shall be caught in the snare.
      Yes, these are the scourges I mean to inflict on
            Moab
      when the year comes to punish them—
      it is Yahweh who speaks.
45    In the shelter of Heshbon the fugitives
      have paused, exhausted.
      But a fire has come out from Heshbon,
      a flame from the palace of Sihon,
      consuming the brows of Moab,
      the head of a turbulent brood.
46    Woe to you, Moab!
      People of Chemosh, you are lost!
      For your sons have been taken into exile,
      and your daughters into captivity.
47    But I will restore the fortunes of Moab
      in the days to come. It is Yahweh who speaks.

Thus far the judgment on Moab.

**Oracle against Ammon**              (LXX 30:17–21)

1   **49** On the sons of Ammon.

      Yahweh says this:
      Has Israel no sons?
      Has he no heir?
      Why should Milcom have inherited Gad
      and his people have settled in its towns?
2     And so the days are coming
      —it is Yahweh who speaks—
      when I will make the war cry ring out
      for Rabbath-of-the-Ammonites:
      she will become a deserted ruin,
      her daughter towns burned down.
      Israel will then despoil his despoilers,
      Yahweh proclaims.

e. The capital of Moab, now Kerak.

3
> Heshbon lament! The destroyer is on the march.
> Cry aloud, daughters of Rabbah!
> Wrap yourself in sackcloth, raise the dirge,
> walk about with your bodies gashed.
> For Milcom is going into exile,
> with all his priests and his nobles.

4
> So you boast of your valley,
> thoughtless girl!
> Confident of your resources, you say,
> "Who will dare to attack me?"

5
> But I will bring down on you
> terror from every side;
> you shall be driven away, each man making his
> own way,
> with no one to rally the fugitives.

6 (But later I will restore the fortunes of the sons of Ammon. It is Yahweh who speaks.)

### Oracle against Edom

7 On Edom.

> Yahweh says this:
> Is there no wisdom left in Teman?
> Have the shrewd run out of commonsense,
> has their wisdom gone stale?

8
> Away! Take to your heels! Go into hiding,
> inhabitants of Dedan!
> For I will bring down ruin on Esau,
> at the time when I must punish him.

9
> If grape gatherers come to you,
> they will leave no gleanings behind them;
> if robbers come at night,
> they will loot to their heart's content.

10
> For I myself am despoiling Esau,
> I lay his hiding places bare
> until he has no cover left.
> His race is destroyed: it is no more!
> Of his neighbors, not one will say,

11
> "Leave your orphans, I will keep them alive,
> your widows can rely on me."

12 For Yahweh says this: Those who were not bound to drink the cup have to drink it now; so why should you

go unpunished? You will not go unpunished: you too
13 must drink! ·For by my own self I have sworn it—it is
Yahweh who speaks: Bozrah[a] is to become an object
of horror, a laughingstock, a desert, a curse, and all
its towns ruins for ever.

14        I have received a message from Yahweh,
        a herald has been sent throughout the nations,
        "Muster! March against this people!
        Prepare for battle!"
15        For now I will reduce you among the nations,
        make you despised among mankind:
16        your reputation for ferocity,
        your pride of heart, have led you astray,
        you whose home is in the holes in the rocks,
        who cling to the topmost peaks!
        Though you made your nest high as the eagle,
        I would still fling you down again—it is Yahweh
        who speaks.

17 Edom will become a desolation; every passer-by will be
appalled at it, and whistle in amazement at such calam-
18 ity. ·As at the overthrow of Sodom and Gomorrah
and their neighboring towns, no one will live there any
more, Yahweh proclaims, no man will make his home
there ever again.

19        See how the lion climbs from the thickets of the
                Jordan
        to a perennial pasture!
        So shall I chase them suddenly away,
        and place there whom I please.
        For who is there like me?
        Who can hale me into court?
        Name me the shepherd
        who can stand up to me.
20        So now hear the plan
        that Yahweh has made for Edom,
        the schemes he has in mind
        for the inhabitants of Teman:
        yes, even the weakest of the flock will be dragged
                away.

49 a. The principal Edomite stronghold, north of Petra.

> At such a sight their pastures will shudder with
>     dread.

21
> Earth trembles at the crash of their downfall,
> the sound of it echoes as far as the Sea of Reeds.

22
> Here is someone who soars and hovers like an
>     eagle,
> who will spread his wings over Bozrah.
> And the heart of Edom's warriors that day
> will be like the heart of a woman in labor pains.

## Oracle against the towns of Syria    (LXX 30:29–33)

23
On Damascus:

> Hamath is in confusion, so is Arpad[b];
> they have heard bad news.
> Their heart is faint with fear
> and cannot be calmed.

24
> Damascus is unmanned, she prepares for flight,
> she is seized with trembling

(anguish and sorrow have laid hold on her as on a
woman in labor).

25
> What now! That famous town deserted,
> that city of gaiety?

26
And so in her squares her young men will fall, and
all her fighting men will perish, that day. It is Yahweh
Sabaoth who speaks.

27
> I will light a fire inside the walls of Damascus,
> it shall devour the palaces of Ben-hadad.

## Oracle against the Arab tribes    (LXX 30:23–28)

28
On Kedar and the kingdoms of Hazor, which were
conquered by Nebuchadnezzar king of Babylon. Yahweh says this:

> Up! March on Kedar,
> destroy the sons of the East!

29
> Let their tents and their flocks be captured,
> their fabrics, all their gear,
> and their camels too.
> Let the shout be raised for them: "Terror on
>     every side!"

30    Away! Get into hiding as fast as you can,
      citizens of Hazor! It is Yahweh who speaks.
      For Nebuchadnezzar has made a plan for you,
      he has a scheme in mind for you:

31    "Up! March on a nation at its ease,
      that dwells in confidence,
      that has no gates, no bars,
      that lives in a remote place!

32    Their camels will be the plunder,
      their countless sheep the spoil."
      I will scatter them to the winds,
      those Crop-Heads,
      and bring disaster down on them from every
            side,
      it is Yahweh who speaks.

33    Hazor will become a lair for jackals,
      a desert for ever.
      No one will live there any more,
      no man make his home there ever again.

### Oracle against Elam                    (LXX 25:14–20)

34    The word of Yahweh that was addressed to the
prophet Jeremiah about Elam, at the beginning of the
35 reign of Zedekiah king of Judah. ·Yahweh Sabaoth
says this:

      I am going to break the bow of Elam,
      the source of all his might.

36    I will bring four winds down on Elam
      from the four corners of the sky,

and I will scatter the Elamites to the winds: there will
not be a single nation into which the Elamites have not
been driven for refuge.

37    I will make the Elamites tremble before their
            enemies,
      before those determined to kill them.
      I will bring down disaster on them,
      my own fierce anger.
      I will pursue them with the sword
      until I have destroyed them all.

b. Hamath is on the river Orontes, Arpad to the north of Aleppo.

38
    I will set up my throne in Elam,
      and purge it of king and nobles.
      It is Yahweh who speaks.

39    But in the days to come I will restore the fortunes of
Elam. It is Yahweh who speaks.

### Oracle against Babylon         (LXX 27:1)

1 **50** The word that Yahweh spoke against Babylon,
against the country of the Chaldaeans, through
the prophet Jeremiah.

### The fall of Babylon and the liberation of Israel
###                     (LXX 27:2–20)

2
    Publish it among the nations, proclaim it;
      make no secret of it, say:
      "Babylon is captured, Bel disgraced,
    Merodach shattered.[a]
      (Her idols are disgraced,
      her Obscenities shattered.)"

3
    For a nation is marching on her from the North,
      to turn her country into a desert:
      no one will live there any more;
      man and beast have fled and gone.

4
    In those days and at that time
      the sons of Israel will return:
      they will come weeping
      in search of Yahweh their God.

5
    They will ask the way to Zion,
      their faces will turn in that direction:
      "Come," they say, "let us bind ourselves to
           Yahweh
      by an everlasting covenant never to be for-
           gotten!"

6
    Lost sheep, such were my people;
      their shepherds led them astray, left them wan-
           dering in the mountains;
      from mountain to hill they went,
      forgetful of their fold.

7
    Whoever came across them devoured them,
      their enemies said, "No blame to us;

it is because they have sinned against Yahweh
their true fold and the hope of their fathers."

8
Escape out of Babylon,
from the country of the Chaldaeans.
Go! Act like the he-goats,
be leaders of the flock.

9
See, I am raising a league
of mighty nations against Babylon.
They will come from the land of the North,
    will draw up the battle line against her:
there she will be captured;
their arrows are like a victorious warrior,
never returning empty-handed.

10
Chaldaea will be plundered,
all who plunder her will have their fill.

11
Rejoice, if you like! Have your triumph,
you plunderers of my heritage!
Be playful like calves let out to grass!
Neigh like stallions!

12
But your mother is covered with shame,
disgraced is the woman who bore you;
she is the least of nations now;
a wilderness, a parched land, a desert.

13
The fury of Yahweh will leave her uninhabited,
she will become an empty solitude.
All who pass by Babylon will be appalled at it,
and whistle in amazement at such calamity.

14
Draw yourself up against Babylon, surround
    her,
all you who bend the bow.
Shoot! Do not spare your arrows.

15
Raise the war cry against her from all sides.
She surrenders! Her bastions fall!
Her walls collapse!
This is the vengeance of Yahweh. Take revenge
    on her.
Treat her as she has treated others.

16
Deprive Babylon of the man who sows,
of the man who wields the sickle at harvest.

---

**50 a.** Bel and Marduk (Merodach) are two names of the tutelary
god of Babylon.

> Escape from the destroying sword,
> let everyone return to his own people,
> let everyone escape to his own country!

17
> Israel was a straying sheep
> hunted by lions.

First, the king of Assyria devoured him; next, Nebu-
18 chadnezzar king of Babylon crunched his bones. ·There-
fore—Yahweh, the God of Israel, says this: Now I will
punish the king of Babylon and his country as I punished the king of Assyria.

19
> I will bring Israel back to his pastures
> to browse on Carmel and in Bashan,
> and on the highlands of Ephraim and in Gilead
> to eat his fill.
20
> In those days and at that time
> you may look for Israel's iniquity, it will not be
> there,
> for Judah's sins, you will not find them.
> For I will pardon the remnant that I leave.

### The fall of Babylon proclaimed to Jerusalem
### (LXX 27:21–28)

21
> March up to the land of Merathaim;
> march against it
> and against the inhabitants of Pekod;
> follow them;
> brandish the sword, let their destruction be com-
> plete,
> it is Yahweh who speaks.
> Do everything I have ordered![b]
22
> The din of battle fills the country,
> immense destruction.

23
> What! Broken to pieces
> that hammer of the whole world?
> What! Babylon become a thing of horror,
> throughout the nations?
24
> A snare was set for you, and you were caught
> before you knew it.
> You have been found out and overpowered,
> because you defied Yahweh.

25       Yahweh has opened his armory
          and taken out the weapons of his fury.
          For the Lord Yahweh has work to do
          in the country of the Chaldaeans.

26       Fall on her, one and all,
          break her granaries open,
          pile the plunder up like heaps of grain, put her
              under the ban
          until nothing is left of her.

27       Slaughter all her bulls,
          down to the slaughterhouse with them!
          Woe to them, their day has come,
          their time of reckoning.

28       Listen! Fugitives and runaways come
          from the land of Babylon
          to proclaim in Zion
          the vengeance of Yahweh our God.

### The sin of arrogance          (LXX 27:29–32)

29       Call up the archers against Babylon!
          All you who bend the bow,
          encamp around her:
          leave her no way of escape.
          Repay her as her deeds deserve;
          treat her as she has treated others,
          to repay her arrogance against Yahweh,
          against the Holy One of Israel.

30 And so in her squares her young men will fall, and
her fighting men will perish, that day. It is Yahweh who
speaks.

31       My quarrel is with you, "Arrogance!"
          It is the Lord Yahweh Sabaoth who speaks:
          your day has come,
          the time when I must punish you.

32       "Arrogance" will stumble, she will fall,
          no one will lift her up:
          I will light a fire inside her towns;
          it shall devour all her surroundings.

**b.** The orders are addressed to the invaders of Babylon. Merathaim is the Tigris delta region; Pekod a region east of Babylon.

### Yahweh the redeemer of Israel     (LXX 27:33–40)

33
> Yahweh Sabaoth says this:
> The sons of Israel are oppressed,
> all those who have taken them captive hold them
> fast,
> they will not let them go.

34
> But their redeemer is strong:
> Yahweh Sabaoth is his name.
> He has taken up their cause:
> he will bring peacefulness to the world
> but trembling to the inhabitants of Babylon.

35
> A sword for the Chaldaeans,
> for the inhabitants of Babylon,
> for her leaders and her sages!

36
> A sword for her diviners: may they lose their
> wits!
> A sword for her men of war: may they be dis-
> comfited!

37
> A sword for the whole crowd of foreigners
> within her: may they be like women!
> A sword for her treasures: may they be
> plundered!

38
> A sword for her waters: may they dry up!

For it is a country of idols: they are mad, they and
their bogies.

39
> Hence wild cats and jackals will live there,
> and ostriches make their home there.
> She will never be inhabited again,
> but remain uninhabited age after age.

40
> As when God overthrew Sodom and Gomorrah,
> with their neighboring towns
> —it is Yahweh who speaks—
> no one will live there any more,
> no man will make his home there ever again.

### The enemy from the north and the lion of Jordan
### (LXX 27:41–46)

41
> Now a people is coming from the North,
> a mighty nation;
> from the far ends of the earth
> great kings are stirring:

42    they fight with bow and spear,
    they are cruel and pitiless;
    their noise is like the roaring of the sea;
    they ride horses,
    each man equipped for war
    on you, daughter of Babylon.

43    But the king of Babylon has heard the news
        of them,
    his hands fall limp,
    anguish has seized him,
    pain like that of a woman in labor.

44    See how the lion climbs from the thickets of the
        Jordan
    to a perennial pasture!
    So shall I chase them suddenly away,
    and place there whom I please.
    For who is there like me?
    Who can hale me into court?
    Name me the shepherd
    who can stand up to me.

45    So now hear the plan
    that Yahweh has made for Babylon,
    the schemes he has in mind
    for the country of the Chaldaeans:
    yes, even the weakest of the flock will be dragged
        away.
    At such a sight their pastures will shudder with
        dread.

46    Earth trembles at the sound of the capture of
        Babylon,
    the dirge for her is heard throughout the
        nations.

### Yahweh makes war on Babylon    (LXX 28:1–19)

1 **51**    Yahweh says this:
    *a*Against the citizens of Leb-kamai I will rouse
    a destroying spirit;

2    I will send winnowers to Babylon to winnow her
        and leave her country bare:
    for they will beleaguer her from every side
    in the day of disaster.

**51 a.** Cryptogram for "Kashdim" (Chaldaeans).

3　Let no archer bend his bow!
Let no man swagger in his coat of mail!
—No quarter for her young warriors!
Vow her whole army to the ban!

4　In the country of the Chaldaeans the slaughtered
will fall,
in the streets of Babylon, those whom the sword
runs through.

5b　This is because their country was full of sin
against the Holy One of Israel.

5a　But Israel is not bereft
of his God, Yahweh Sabaoth.

6　Escape out of Babylon
(save your lives, each one of you);
do not perish yourselves in her punishment,
for this is the time of Yahweh's vengeance:
he is paying her her reward!

7　Babylon was a golden cup in Yahweh's hand,
she made the whole world drunk,
the nations drank her wine
and then went mad.

8　Babylon has suddenly fallen, is broken:
lament for her!
Go and fetch balm for her wounds,
perhaps she can be cured!

9　—"We tried to cure Babylon; she has got no
better.
Leave her alone and let us each go to his own
country."
Yes, her sentence reaches to the sky,
rises to the very clouds.

10　Yahweh has vindicated our integrity.
Come, let us tell in Zion
what Yahweh our God has done.

11　Sharpen the arrows,
fill the quivers!

Yahweh has roused the spirit of the king of the Medes,[b]
because he has a plan against Babylon to destroy it;
this is the vengeance of Yahweh, the revenge for his
Temple.

12　Against the walls of Babylon display the
standard!

> Strengthen the guard!
> Post the sentries!
> Take up concealed positions!

For Yahweh made a plan, and he has treated the citizens of Babylon as he promised he would.

13 　　Enthroned beside abundant waters,
　　　rich in treasures,
　　　you now meet your end,
　　　the finish of your pillaging.

14 By his own self Yahweh Sabaoth has sworn: had I filled you with men as plentiful as locusts, the war cry would still have been raised against you!

15 　　By his power he made the earth,
　　　by his wisdom set the world firm,
　　　by his discernment spread out the heavens.

16 　　When he thunders
　　　there is a tumult of water in the heavens;
　　　he raises clouds from the boundaries of earth,
　　　makes the lightning flash for the downpour,
　　　and brings the wind from his storehouse.

17 　　At this all men stand stupefied, uncomprehending,
　　　every goldsmith blushes for the idol he has made,
　　　since his images are nothing but delusion,
　　　with no breath in them.

18 　　They are a Nothing, a laughable production,
　　　when the time comes for them to be punished,
　　　they will vanish.

19 　　"The portion of Jacob" is not like these,
　　　for he has formed everything,
　　　and Israel is the tribe that is his heritage.
　　　His name is Yahweh Sabaoth.

## The hammer of Yahweh and the giant mountain
(LXX 28:20–26)

20 　　You were my mace,
　　　a weapon of war.

**b.** This later prose gloss names the Medes, meaning Persians; the poem speaks only of an enemy from the North.

With you I crushed the nations,
struck kingdoms down,

21
with you crushed horse and rider,
chariot and charioteer,

22
with you crushed man and woman,
old man and young,
youth and maid,

23
with you crushed shepherd and flock,
plowman and team,
governors and nobles,

24 but I will let you see how I make Babylon and all the
inhabitants of Chaldaea pay for all the wrongs they
have done to Zion. It is Yahweh who speaks.

25
My quarrel is with you,
Mountain of destruction
—it is Yahweh who speaks—
destroyer of the whole world!
I will stretch out my hand against you
and send you tumbling from the crags
and make you a mountain scorched.

26
Never a cornerstone will be taken from you,
never a foundation stone either,
for you will be a desert for ever,
it is Yahweh who speaks.

### The end of Babylon is imminent    (LXX 28:27–33)

27
Display the standard throughout the world,
sound the trumpet among the nations!
Prepare nations to make war on her;
summon kingdoms against her:
Ararat, Minni, Ashkenaz[c];
call the roll of her enemies, officer!
Bring up the cavalry, bristling like locusts.

28 Prepare nations to make war on her: the king of
Media with his governors and dignitaries and the whole
territory under his rule.

29
Then the earth trembled and writhed,
for Yahweh's plan against Babylon was going
forward:
to change the country of Babylon
into an unpopulated desert.

30     The warriors of Babylon have done with
           fighting,
       they have taken to their strongholds;
       their strength has gone:
       they are like women now.
       Her houses are on fire,
       her gates are shattered.

31     Courier follows close on courier,
       messenger on messenger,
       to tell the king of Babylon
       that his city has been stormed from every side:

32     the fords occupied,
       the bastions burned down,
       the fighting men thrown into panic.

33     For Yahweh Sabaoth, the God of Israel, says
           this:
       The daughter of Babylon is like a threshing floor
       when it is being trodden:
       a little while, and there the grain will lie
       that has been harvested.

## The vengeance of Yahweh          (LXX 28:34–40)

34     "He has devoured, consumed me, that king of
           Babylon;
       he has left me like an empty dish,
       like a dragon he has swallowed me whole,
       he has filled his belly with my delicacies."

35     "May her violence to me, and all my sufferings,
           be avenged on Babylon!"
       say the people of Zion;
       "On the inhabitants of Chaldaea be my blood!"
       says Jerusalem.

36     Therefore—Yahweh says this:
       See, I myself am taking up your cause
       to make sure you are avenged.
       I will dry her river up,
       make her springs run dry,

37     and turn Babylon into a heap of stones,
       a lair for jackals,
       a thing of horror and of scorn,
       with no one living in it.

c. Kingdoms near Armenia.

38       Like lions they roar together,
      they growl like lions' whelps.

39       Are they feverish? I will prepare them a drink
      and make them drink until they grow drowsy
      and fall into an everlasting sleep,
      never to wake up;
      it is Yahweh who speaks.

40       I will take them down to the slaughterhouse like
          lambs,
      like rams and he-goats.

### An elegy for Babylon       (LXX 28:41–43)

41       What! Is she captured and conquered,
      the admiration of all the world?
      What! Babylon become a thing of horror,
      throughout the nations?

42       The sea has risen over Babylon,
      she sinks under its boisterous waves.

43       Her towns have been turned into desert,
      a parched land, a wilderness:
      no one lives in them,
      no man goes that way.

### Yahweh punishes the idols       (LXX 28:44–57)

44       I will punish Bel in Babylon
      and take from his mouth what he has swallowed.
      In future the nations
      will stream to him no more.
      The wall of Babylon has fallen.

45       Go out of her, my people;
      save your lives, each one of you,
      from the fierce anger of Yahweh.

46 But do not be fainthearted! Do not take fright at ru-
mors hawked around the country: one rumor spreads
one year, next year another follows; violence rules on
earth and one tyrant cancels out another.

47       See, the days are coming
      when I am going to punish the idols of Babylon.
      Her whole country shall be put to shame,
      with all her slaughtered lying in her midst.

48       Then heaven and earth and all within them
      shall shout for joy over Babylon,
      because the destroyers from the North

are coming against her—it is Yahweh who
    speaks.

49    Babylon in her turn must fall
    because of those who were slaughtered in Israel,
    just as through Babylon there fell
    men slaughtered over all the world.

50    You who have escaped her sword,
    get away, do not wait there!
    Remember Yahweh in that distant country,
    let Jerusalem be in your mind.

51    —"We were ashamed when we heard of the out-
        rage,
    our face was covered with confusion:
    because foreigners had entered
    the holy places of the Temple of Yahweh."

52    —See, the days are coming,
    it is Yahweh who speaks,
    when I will punish her idols,
    and the stricken shall groan throughout her
        country.

53    Were Babylon to scale the heavens,
    or reinforce her towering citadel,
    destroyers would still fall on her at my com-
        mand,
    it is Yahweh who speaks.

54    Listen to the shouting from Babylon,
    the mighty crash from the country of the
        Chaldaeans!

55    That is Yahweh as he lays Babylon waste
    and silences her monstrous din;
    well may her waves roar like mighty waters
    and their tumultuous voice resound:

56    for a destroyer is sweeping down on Babylon,
    her warriors are taken captive, their bows are
        broken.
    Yes, Yahweh is a God of retribution,
    he pays in full.

57    I will make her nobles and her sages drink,
    her governors, her officials and her warriors;
    they shall fall into an everlasting sleep
    and not wake up;

it is the King who speaks,
whose name is Yahweh Sabaoth.

### Babylon razed to the ground          (LXX 28, 58)

58          Yahweh Sabaoth says this:
The wide ramparts of Babylon
will be razed to the ground,
and her high gates
will be burned down.
Thus the laboring of the peoples comes to
nothing
the toiling of the nations ends in fire.

### The written oracle thrown into the Euphrates
### (LXX 28:59–64)

59          This is the order that the prophet Jeremiah gave to
Seraiah son of Mahseiah when the latter left for Babylon at the command of Zedekiah king of Judah, in the
60 fourth year of his reign. ·Now Jeremiah had written
down the entire disaster that was to befall Babylon in
a special book, all these words recorded here as regards
61 Babylon. ·Jeremiah then said to Seraiah, "When you
reach Babylon, make a point of reading out every one
62 of these words. ·Then say, 'Yahweh, you yourself have
proclaimed that this place will be destroyed, that no one
will live here ever again, neither man nor beast, but
63 that it will remain desolate for ever.' ·When you have
finished reading this book, tie a stone to it and throw
64 it into the middle of the Euphrates, ·with the words,
'So shall Babylon sink, never to rise again from the
disaster with which I am going to overwhelm her.' "
Here end the words of Jeremiah.

# V. APPENDIX[a]

### The destruction of Jerusalem and the pardon of Jehoiachin

1  **52** Zedekiah was twenty-one years old when he came
to the throne, and he reigned for eleven years
in Jerusalem. His mother's name was Hamital, daughter

2 of Jeremiah, from Libnah. ·He did what is displeasing
3 to Yahweh, just as Jehoiakim had done. ·That this happened in Jerusalem and Judah was due to the anger
of Yahweh, with the result that in the end he cast them
away from him.

4     Zedekiah rebelled against the king of Babylon. ·In
the ninth year of his reign, in the tenth month,[b] on the
tenth day of the month, Nebuchadnezzar king of Babylon came with his whole army to attack Jerusalem; he
pitched camp in front of the city and threw up earth-
5 works around it. ·The city lay under siege till the elev-
6 enth year of King Zedekiah. ·In the fourth month, on
the ninth day of the month, when famine was raging
in the city and there was no food for the populace,
7 a breach was made in the city wall. Seeing this, the
king fled under cover of dark, with all the fighting men,
leaving the city by way of the gate between the two
walls, which is near the king's garden—the Chaldaeans
had surrounded the city—and making his way toward
8 the Arabah. ·The Chaldaean troops pursued the king
and caught up with Zedekiah in the plains of Jericho,
9 where all his troops deserted. ·The Chaldaeans captured the king and took him to the king of Babylon at
Riblah in the land of Hamath, who passed sentence
10 on him. ·He had the sons of Zedekiah slaughtered before his eyes; he also had all the leading men of Judah
11 put to death at Riblah. ·He then put out Zedekiah's
eyes. Loading him with chains, the king of Babylon
carried him off to Babylon where he kept him prisoner
until his dying day.

12     In the fifth month, on the tenth day of the month
—it was in the nineteenth year of Nebuchadnezzar king
of Babylon—Nebuzaradan, commander of the guard,
13 one of the king's ministers, entered Jerusalem. ·He
burned down the Temple of Yahweh, the royal palace
14 and all the houses in Jerusalem. ·The Chaldaean troops
who accompanied the commander of the guard demolished all the walls surrounding Jerusalem.

15     Nebuzaradan, commander of the guard, deported

---

52 a. An expanded version of the narrative in 2 K. 24–25, partly
paralleled in Jr. 39.
b. January–February 588.

the remainder of the population left behind in the city,
the deserters who had gone over to the king of Baby-
16 lon, and the remainder of the artisans. ·Nebuzaradan,
commander of the guard, left some of the humbler
country people as vineyard workers and plowmen.
17    The Chaldaeans broke up the bronze pillars from
the Temple of Yahweh, the wheeled stands and the
bronze Sea that were in the Temple of Yahweh, and
18 took all the bronze away to Babylon. ·They also took
the ash containers, the scoops, the knives, the sprinkling bowls, the incense boats, and all the bronze fur-
19 nishings used in worship. ·The commander of the
guard also took the bowls, the censers, the sprinkling
bowls, the ash containers, the lampstands, the goblets
and the saucers: everything that was made of gold and
20 everything made of silver. ·As regards the two pillars,
the one Sea and the twelve bronze oxen supporting the
Sea, and the wheeled stands, which King Solomon had
made for the Temple of Yahweh, there was no reckon-
21 ing the weight of bronze in all these objects. ·As regards the pillars, the height of one pillar was eighteen
cubits, its circumference was twelve cubits, it was four
22 fingers thick, and hollow inside; ·on it stood a capital
of bronze, the height of the capital being five cubits;
around the capital were filigree and pomegranates, all
23 in bronze. So also for the second pillar. ·There were
ninety-six pomegranates which hung down, making a
hundred pomegranates around the filigree in all.
24    The commander of the guard took prisoner Seraiah
the chief priest, Zephaniah the priest next in rank, and
25 the three guardians of the threshold. ·In the city he
took prisoner a eunuch who was in command of the
fighting men, seven of the king's personal friends who
were discovered in the city, the secretary of the army
commander, responsible for military conscription, and
26 sixty men of distinction discovered in the city. ·Nebu-
zaradan, commander of the guard, took these men and
27 brought them to the king of Babylon at Riblah, ·and
at Riblah, in the land of Hamath, the king of Babylon
had them put to death.
28    Thus Judah was deported from its land. ·The num-
—    ber of people deported by Nebuchadnezzar was as
follows. In the seventh year: three thousand and

29 twenty-three Judaeans; ·in the eighteenth year of Nebuchadnezzar, eight hundred and thirty-two persons were
30 deported from Jerusalem; ·in the twenty-third year*c* of
Nebuchadnezzar, Nebuzaradan, commander of the
guard, deported seven hundred and forty-five Judaeans.
In all: four thousand six hundred persons.

31   But in the thirty-seventh year of the exile of Jehoiachin king of Judah, in the twelfth month, on the
twenty-fifth day of the month, Evil-merodach king of
Babylon, in the year he came to the throne,*d* pardoned
Jehoiachin king of Judah and released him from
32 prison. ·He treated him kindly and allotted him a seat
above those of the other kings who were with him in
33 Babylon. ·So Jehoiachin laid aside his prisoner's garb,
and for the rest of his life always ate at the king's table.
34 And his upkeep was permanently ensured by the king
for the rest of his life day after day until his dying day.

c. 582 B.C.
d. 562 B.C.

# LAMENTATIONS

## FIRST LAMENTATION

*Aleph*

**1**

Oh, how lonely she sits,
 the city once thronged with people,
as if suddenly widowed.
 Though once great among the nations,
she, the princess among provinces,
 is now reduced to vassalage.

*Beth*

**2**

She passes her nights weeping;
 the tears run down her cheeks.
Not one of all her lovers
 remains to comfort her.
Her friends have all betrayed her
 and become her enemies.

*Ghimel*

**3**

Judah is exiled after her downfall
 and harsh enslavement.
She dwells among the nations now,
 but finds no relief there.
Her pursuers all overtake her
 in places where there is no way out.

*Daleth*

**4**

The roads to Zion are in mourning;
 no one comes to her festivals now.
Her gateways are all deserted;
 her priests groan;
her virgins are grief-stricken;
 she suffers bitterly.

*He*

**5**

Her oppressors now have the upper hand,
 her enemies enjoy prosperity;

Yahweh himself has made her suffer
　　for her many, many sins;
her little children have left her as prisoners
　　driven in front of the oppressor.

*Waw*

6

From the daughter of Zion
　　all her glory has departed.
Her leaders were like rams
　　that find no pasture.
Listlessly they took the road,
　　driven by the drover.

*Zain*

7

Jerusalem remembers
　　her days of misery and distress,
when her people fell before the enemy
　　and no one came to help her.
Her oppressors looked at her
　　and laughed at her downfall.

*Heth*

8

Jerusalem has sinned grievously
　　and she has become a thing unclean.
All those who used to honor her despise her;
　　they have seen her nakedness.
While she herself groans
　　and turns her face away.

*Teth*

9

Her filth clings to the hem of her clothes.
　　She had never thought of ending like this,
sinking as low as this.
　　She has no one to comfort her.
"Yahweh, look on my degradation;
　　my enemy is triumphant."

*Yod*

10

The oppressor has laid his hands
　　on all she treasured;
she has seen the pagans
　　enter her sanctuary,
men whom you had forbidden
　　to attend your Assembly.

*Kaph*

11

All her people groan
　　as they search for bread;

they barter their valuables for food,
  to keep life in them.
"Look, Yahweh, and mark
  how despised I am."

*Lamed*

12  All you who pass this way,
    look and see:
  is any sorrow like the sorrow
    that afflicts me,
  with which Yahweh has struck me
    on the day of his burning anger?

*Mem*

13  He has sent a fire from on high
    down into my bones;
  he has laid a snare underneath my feet;
    he has brought me down;
  he has left me deserted,
    and ill all day long.

*Nun*

14  The yoke of my sins weighs down on me,
    his, the hand that knotted them;
  their yoke is on my neck,
    he makes my energy fail.
  The Lord has put me at their mercy,
    I have no strength left to resist.

*Samek*

15  Yahweh has spurned
    the bravest fighters I had;
  he has summoned a host against me
    to destroy the flower of my army.
  In his winepress the Lord has trampled
    the virgin daughter of Judah.

*Ain*

16  And that is why I weep;
    my eyes dissolve in tears,
  since the comforter who could revive me
    is far away.
  My sons are in despair,
    the enemy has proved too strong.

*Pe*

17  Zion stretches out her hands;
    no one is there to comfort her.

Yahweh has summoned against Jacob
　　foes from every side;
Jerusalem has become
　　an unclean thing to them.

*Sade*

18　　Yahweh is acting rightly,
　　for I had rebelled against his order.
Listen therefore, all you nations,
　　and see my sorrow.
My virgins and my young men
　　have gone into exile.

*Qoph*

19　　I called for help to my lovers;
　　they failed me.
My priests and my elders
　　were perishing inside the city,
as they searched for food
　　to keep life in them.

*Resh*

20　　Look, Yahweh. How great my anguish!
　　My entrails shudder;
my heart turns over inside me.
　　Alas! I have always been a rebel—
and now, outside, the sword has robbed me of
　　　　　　　　　　　　　　　[my children,
　　and inside, there is death.

*Shin*

21　　Listen to my groaning;
　　there is no one to comfort me.
All my enemies gloat over my disaster:
　　this is your doing.
Bring the day you once foretold,
　　so that they may be as I am.

*Tau*

22　　Let all their wickedness come before you;
　　treat them
as you have treated me
　　for all my sins.
Many indeed are my groans,
　　my heart is sick.

## SECOND LAMENTATION

*Aleph*

**1 2** Oh, how Yahweh in his wrath
    has brought darkness on the daughter of
                       [Zion!

He has flung the glory of Israel
    from heaven to the ground,
no more remembering his footstool[a]
    on the day of his wrath.

*Beth*

**2** The Lord has pitilessly destroyed
    all the homes of Jacob;
in his displeasure he has shattered
    the strongholds of the daughter of Judah;
he has thrown to the ground, he has left
                    [accursed
    the kingdom and its rulers.

*Ghimel*

**3** In his burning anger
    he has broken every horn in Israel,
withdrawn the strength of his right hand
    at the coming of the enemy,
and kindled in Jacob a fire
    that burns up everything near it.

*Daleth*

**4** Like an enemy he has bent his bow,
    holding his right hand steady;
like a foe, he has slaughtered
    everything that delights the eye;
on the tent of the daughter of Zion
    he has poured his anger out like fire.

*He*

**5** The Lord has been like an enemy;
    he has destroyed Israel;
he has destroyed every one of her palaces,
    laid low her strongholds,

**2 a.** The Temple.

and for the daughters of Judah has multiplied
    wailing on wailing.

*Waw*

6    He has wrecked his own domain like a garden,
    shattered his own gathering place;
Yahweh has wiped out the memory
    of festivals and sabbaths in Zion;
in the heat of his wrath he has repudiated
    king and priest.

*Zain*

7    The Lord has grown weary of his altar,
    has come to loathe his sanctuary,
and handed her palace walls
    over to the enemy;
from the uproar in the Temple of Yahweh
    it might have been a day of festival.

*Heth*

8    Yahweh resolved to ruin
    the city wall of the daughter of Zion;
with a line he measured it, and did not withdraw
                       [his hand
    until he had completely overthrown it,
bringing mourning on city wall and rampart;
    now they are crumbling down together.

*Teth*

9    Her gates have sunk into the ground;
    he has shattered their bars.
Her king, her nobles, are now with the pagans,
    the Law is no more.
Even her prophets receive
    no further vision from Yahweh.

*Yod*

10   Mutely they sit on the ground,
    the elders of the daughter of Zion;
they have put dust on their heads,
    and wrapped themselves in sackcloth.
The virgins of Jerusalem hang their heads
    down to the ground.

*Kaph*

11   My eyes wasted away with weeping,
    my entrails shuddered,

my liver spilled on the ground
    at the ruin of the daughters of my people,
as children, mere infants, fainted
    in the squares of the Citadel.

*Lamed*

12    They kept saying to their mothers,
        "Where is the bread?"
as they fainted like wounded men
    in the squares of the City,
as they poured out their souls
    on their mothers' breasts.

*Mem*

13    How can I describe you, to what compare you,
        daughter of Jerusalem?
Who can rescue and comfort you,
    virgin daughter of Zion?
For huge as the sea is your affliction;
    who can possibly cure you?

*Nun*

14    The visions your prophets had on your behalf
        were delusive, tinsel things,
they never pointed out your sin,
    to ward off your exile.
The visions they proffered you were false,
    fallacious, misleading.

*Samek*

15    All who pass your way
        clap their hands at the sight;
they whistle and shake their heads
    over the daughter of Jerusalem.
"Was this the loveliest of all,
    this, the joy of the whole world?"

*Pe*

16    Your enemies open their mouths
        in chorus against you;
they whistle and grind their teeth;
    they say, "We have swallowed her up.
This is the day we were waiting for;
    now we can touch it, see it."

*Ain*

17    Yahweh has accomplished his intention,
    he has carried out his word

decreed in the days of old;
    he has destroyed without pity,
giving your enemy cause to gloat over you
    and raising his horn.

*Sade*

18    Cry aloud, then, to the Lord,
    groan, daughter of Zion;
let your tears flow like a torrent,
    day and night;
give yourself no relief,
    grant your eyes no rest.

*Qoph*

19    Up, cry out in the nighttime,
    in the early hours of darkness;
pour your heart out like water
    before Yahweh.
Stretch out your hands to him
    for the lives of your children.

*Resh*

20    Look, Yahweh, and consider:
    whom have you ever treated like this?
Why, women have eaten their little ones,
    the children they had nursed in their arms!
Why, priest and prophet have been slaughtered
    in the sanctuary of Yahweh!

*Shin*

21    Children and old men are lying
    on the ground in the streets;
my virgins and my young men
    have fallen by the sword;
you have killed on the day of your wrath,
    you have slaughtered pitilessly.

*Tau*

22    As though to a festival you have summoned
    terrors from every side;
on the day of your wrath, no one escaped,
    no one survived.
Those whom I had nursed and reared,
    my enemy has murdered them all.

## THIRD LAMENTATION

*Aleph*

1  3  I am the man familiar with misery
           under the rod of his anger;

2  I am the one he has driven and forced to walk
           in darkness, and without any light.

3  Against me alone he turns his hand,
           again and again, all day long.

*Beth*

4  He has wasted my flesh and skin away,
           has broken my bones.

5  He has made a yoke for me,
           has encircled my head with weariness.

6  He has forced me to dwell in darkness
           with the dead of long ago.

*Ghimel*

7  He has walled me in; I cannot escape;
           he has made my chains heavy;

8  and when I call and shout,
           he shuts out my prayer.

9  He has blocked my ways with cut stones,
           he has obstructed my paths.

*Daleth*

10  For me he has been a lurking bear,
           a lion on the watch.

11  He has filled my paths with briars and torn me,
           he has made me a thing of horror.

12  He has bent his bow and taken aim,
           making me the target for his arrows.

*He*

13  In my back he has planted his darts,
           the children of his quiver.

14  I have become the laughingstock of my whole
                        [nation,
           their butt all day long.

15  He has given me my fill of bitterness,
           he has made me drunk with wormwood.

*Waw*

16 He has broken my teeth with gravel,
    he has given me ashes for food.

17 My soul is shut out from peace;
    I have forgotten happiness.

18 And now I say, "My strength is gone,
    that hope which came from Yahweh."

*Zain*

19 Brooding on my anguish and affliction
    is gall and wormwood.

20 My spirit ponders it continually
    and sinks within me.

21 This is what I shall tell my heart,
    and so recover hope:

*Heth*

22 the favors of Yahweh are not all past,
    his kindnesses are not exhausted;

23 every morning they are renewed;
    great is his faithfulness.

24 "My portion is Yahweh" says my soul
    "and so I will hope in him."

*Teth*

25 Yahweh is good to those who trust him,
    to the soul that searches for him.

26 It is good to wait in silence
    for Yahweh to save.

27 It is good for a man to bear the yoke
    from youth onwards,

*Yod*

28 to sit in solitude and silence
    when the Lord fastens it on him,

29 to put his lips to the dust
    —perhaps there still is hope—

30 to offer his cheek to the striker,
    to be overwhelmed with insults.

*Kaph*

31 For the Lord does not reject mankind
    for ever and ever.

32 If he has punished, he has compassion
    so great is his kindness;

33 since he takes no pleasure in abasing
    and afflicting the human race.

*Lamed*

34   When all the prisoners in a country
      are crushed and trampled underfoot,

35   when a man's rights are overridden
      in defiance of the Most High,

36   when a man is deprived of justice,
      does not the Lord see it?

*Mem*

37   Who has only to speak to make things exist?
      Who commands, if not the Lord?

38   From where, if not from the mouth of the Most
                                  [High,
      do evil and good come?

39   Why then should man complain?
      Better for him to be bold against his sins.

*Nun*

40   Let us examine our path, let us ponder it
      and return to Yahweh.

41   Let us stretch out our hearts and hands
      to God in heaven.

42   We are the ones who have sinned, who have
                                  [rebelled,
      and you have not forgiven.

*Samek*

43   You have wrapped yourself in wrath, pursued
                                  [us,
      slaughtered us without pity.

44   You have wrapped yourself in a cloud
      too thick for prayer to pierce.

45   You have reduced us to rubbish
      to the scourings of the nations.

*Pe*

46   Our enemies have opened their mouths
      in chorus against us.

47   Dread and pitfall have been our lot,
      ravage and ruin.

48   My eyes dissolve in torrents of tears
      over the ruin of the daughters of my people.

*Ain*

49   My eyes weep ceaselessly,
      without relief

50　until Yahweh looks down
　　and sees from heaven.

51　My eyes have grown sore
　　over all the daughters of my Citadel.

*Sade*

52　They hunted me, harried me like a bird,
　　they who hate me for no reason.

53　They tumbled my life into a pit,
　　they threw stones down on me.

54　The waters went over my head;
　　I said, "I am lost."

*Qoph*

55　Yahweh, I called on your name
　　from the deep pit.

56　You heard me crying, "Do not close your ear
　　to my prayer."

57　You came near that day when I called to you;
　　you said, "Do not be afraid."

*Resh*

58　You have defended the cause of my soul,
　　you have redeemed my life.

59　Yahweh, you have seen the wrong done to me;
　　grant me redress.

60　You have seen all their frenzy,
　　all their plots against me.

*Shin*

61　Yahweh, you have heard their insults,
　　all their plots against me,

62　my opponents slandering me
　　under their breath all day long.

63　Whether they sit, or whether they stand,
　　see, I am their butt.

*Tau*

64　Yahweh, repay them
　　as their deeds deserve.

65　Give them hardness of heart,
　　your curse be on them.

66　Pursue them in fury, root them out
　　from underneath your heavens.

## FOURTH LAMENTATION

*Aleph*

**1 4** Oh, how the old gold has tarnished,
        that gold so fine!
   The sacred stones now lie scattered
        at the corner of every street.

*Beth*

**2** The sons of Zion, as precious
        as finest gold,
   Oh, reckoned now no better than earthenware
                                    [pots
        made by the potter!

*Ghimel*

**3** The very jackals give the breast,
        and suckle their young:
   but the daughters of my people have grown
                                    [cruel
        like the ostriches of the desert.

*Daleth*

**4** The tongue of the baby at the breast
        sticks to his palate for thirst,
   little children go begging for bread;
        no one spares a scrap for them.

*He*

**5** Those who used to eat only the best,
        now lie dying in the streets;
   those who were reared in the purple
        claw at the rubbish heaps.

*Waw*

**6** The crimes of the daughter of my people have
                                    [outdone
        the sins of Sodom,
   which was overthrown in a moment,
        no time for a man to wring his hands.

*Zain*

**7** Once her young men were brighter than snow,
        whiter than milk;

rosier than coral their bodies,
    their hue as radiant as sapphire.

*Heth*

8 Now with faces darker than blackness itself
    they move unrecognizable through the streets.
The skin is shrunken against their bones,
    dry as a stick.

*Teth*

9 Happy were those killed by the sword,
    happier than those by hunger,
spent and sinking,
    deprived of the fruits of the fields.

*Yod*

10 With their own hands, tenderhearted women
    have boiled their children;
these have been their food
    in the disaster that fell on the daughter of my
                     [people.

*Kaph*

11 Yahweh has indulged his fury,
    has poured his anger out.
He has lit a fire in Zion
    that has devoured her foundations.

*Lamed*

12 The kings of the earth never believed,
    nor did all the inhabitants of the world,
that oppressor and enemy would ever penetrate
    the gates of Jerusalem.

*Mem*

13 It came through the sins of her prophets
    and the crimes of her priests,
who had shed the blood of the upright
    in the heart of the city.

*Nun*

14 Through the streets like blind men, they roamed
    polluted with blood,
so that no one dared to touch
    their clothes.

*Samek*

15 "Keep away! Unclean!" people shouted.
    "Keep away! Do not touch us!"

If they left and took refuge with the nations,
  they were not allowed to shelter there either.

*Pe*

16  The face of Yahweh dispersed them;
  he never spared a glance for them again.
People respected the priests no longer,
  they paid no attention to the prophets.

*Ain*

17  And still we wore out our eyes,
  watching for help—in vain.
From our towers we watched for a nation[a]
  which could not save us anyway.

*Sade*

18  Our enemies eyed our steps,
  and barricaded our squares.
Our end was near,
  our days were done.

*Qoph*

19  Our pursuers were swifter
  than eagles in the sky;
they dogged our steps in the mountains,
  they ambushed us in the desert.

*Resh*

20  The breath of our nostrils, Yahweh's anointed[b],
  was captured in their pits,
he of whom we said, "Under his shadow
  we shall live among the nations."

*Shin*

21  Rejoice, exult, daughter of Edom,
  as you dwell in Uz!
To you in turn the cup will pass;
  it will make you drunk, and you will show
            [your nakedness.

*Tau*

22  Your crime has been atoned for, daughter of
            [Zion;
    he will never banish you again.
  Your crime he will punish, daughter of Edom;
    he will lay bare your sins.

**4 a.** Egypt, ally of Judah in the reign of Zedekiah.
**b.** Zedekiah.

## FIFTH LAMENTATION

1 **5** Yahweh, remember what has happened to us;
　　　　look on us and see our degradation.

2　　Our inheritance has passed to aliens,
　　　　our homes to barbarians.

3　　We are orphans, we are fatherless;
　　　　our mothers are like widows.

4　　We drink our own water—at a price;
　　　　we have to pay for what is our own firewood.

5　　The yoke is on our necks; we are persecuted;
　　　　we are worked to death; no relief for us.

6　　We hold out our hands to Egypt,
　　　　or to Assyria, just to get enough bread.

7　　Our fathers have sinned; they are no more,
　　　　and we ourselves bear the weight of their
　　　　　　　　　　　　　　　　　　　　　　　[crimes.

8　　Slaves*a* rule us;
　　　　no one rescues us from them.

9　　At peril of our lives we earn our bread,
　　　　by risking the sword of the desert.

10　　Our skin is as hot as the oven,
　　　　such is the fever of famine.

11　　They have raped the women in Zion,
　　　　the virgins in the towns of Judah.

12　　Princes have been hanged at their hands;
　　　　the face of the old has not been respected.

13　　Youths have toiled at the mill;
　　　　boys have collapsed under loads of wood.

14　　The elders have deserted the gateway;
　　　　the young men have given up their music.

15　　Joy has vanished from our hearts;
　　　　our dancing has been turned to mourning.

**5 a.** The Chaldaean officials.

16    The garland has fallen from our heads.
      Woe to us, because we have sinned!

17    This is why our hearts are sick;
      this is why our eyes are dim:

18    because Mount Zion is desolate;
      jackals roam to and fro on it.

19    But you, Yahweh, you remain for ever;
      your throne endures from age to age.

20    You cannot mean to forget us for ever?
      You cannot mean to abandon us for good?

21    Make us come back to you, Yahweh, and we
                                [will come back.
      Renew our days as in times past,

22    unless you have utterly rejected us,
      in an anger that knows no limit.

# THE BOOK OF
# BARUCH

## I. INTRODUCTION

### Baruch and the Jews in Babylon

1 These are the words of the book written in Babylon by Baruch son of Neraiah, son of Mahseiah, son of 2 Zedekiah, son of Hasadiah, son of Hilkiah, ·in the fifth year,<sup>a</sup> on the seventh day of the month, at the time when the Chaldaeans captured Jerusalem and burned it down.

3 Baruch read the words of this book aloud to Jeconiah son of Jehoiakim, king of Judah, and to all the people 4 who had come to hear the reading, ·to the nobles and the sons of the king, and to the elders; to the whole people, that is, least no less than greatest, to all who 5 lived in Babylon beside the river Sud. ·On hearing it 6 they wept, fasted and prayed before the Lord; ·and 7 they collected as much money as each could afford ·and sent it to Jerusalem for the priest Jehoiakim son of Hilkiah, son of Shallum, and the other priests, and for 8 as many of the people as were with him in Jerusalem. ·It was Baruch who on the tenth day of Sivan had recovered the utensils of the house of the Lord, which had been removed from the Temple, to take them back to the land of Judah: these were silver utensils which Zedekiah son of Josiah, king of Judah, had had made 9 when Nebuchadnezzar king of Babylon had deported Jeconiah from Jerusalem to Babylon, together with the princes, the metalworkers, the men of rank and the common people.

10 With this—they wrote—we are sending you money with which to pay for holocausts, offerings for sin, and

1 a. The year 582, probably on the anniversary of the fall of Jerusalem.

incense; prepare oblations, and offer them on the altar
11 of the Lord our God. ·Pray for the long life of Nebuchadnezzar king of Babylon, and of his son Belshazzar,
and that their days on earth may endure as the heavens;
12 pray that the Lord may give us strength and clear
understanding so that we may lead our lives under the
protection of Nebuchadnezzar king of Babylon and of
his son Belshazzar, and by our long service win their
13 favor. ·Also pray to the Lord our God for us, because
we have sinned against him, and the anger, the fury
of the Lord, has still not been turned away from us.
14 Lastly, you are to read the book aloud which we send
you with this and so make public confession in the
house of the Lord on the feast day[b] and on days of
15 solemn assembly. ·You are to say:

## II. THE PRAYER OF THE EXILES

### Confession of sins

Integrity belongs to the Lord our God; to us the look
of shame we wear today, to us, the people of Judah
16 and the citizens of Jerusalem, ·to our kings and princes,
17 our priests, our prophets, as to our ancestors, ·because
18 we have sinned in the sight of the Lord, ·have disobeyed him, and have not listened to the voice of the
Lord our God telling us to follow the commandments
19 which the Lord had ordained for us. ·From the day
when the Lord brought our ancestors out of the land
of Egypt until today we have been disobedient to the
Lord our God, we have been disloyal, refusing to listen
20 to his voice. ·And so the disasters, and the curse which
the Lord pronounced through his servant Moses the
day he brought our fathers out of Egypt to give us a
land where milk and honey flow, have seized on us,
21 disasters we experience today. ·Despite all the words
of those prophets whom he sent us, we have not listened
22 to the voice of the Lord our God, ·but, each following
the dictates of his evil heart, we have taken to serving
alien gods, and doing what is displeasing to the Lord
our God.

1 And so the Lord has carried out the sentence which he passed on us, on our judges who governed Israel, on our kings and leaders, on the men of Israel
2 and of Judah; ·what he did to Jerusalem has never been paralleled under the wide heavens—all this in conformity with what was written in the Law of Moses;
3 we were all reduced to eating the flesh of our own sons
4 and daughters. ·Furthermore, he has handed them over into the power of all the kingdoms that surround us, to be loathed and avoided by all the neighboring na-
5 tions among whom he scattered them. ·Instead of being masters, they found themselves enslaved, because we had sinned against the Lord our God by not listening to his voice.

6 Integrity belongs to the Lord our God; to us the look
7 of shame we wear today, to us, as to our ancestors. ·All those disasters which the Lord pronounced against us
8 have now happened to us. ·And yet we have not tried to win the favor of the Lord by each one of us re-
9 nouncing the dictates of his own wicked heart; ·and so the Lord has watched for the right moment to bring disaster on us, since the Lord gives a just return for what we do of all that he has ordered us to do,
10 and we have not listened to his voice telling us to follow the commandments which the Lord had ordained for us.

### The prayer

11 And now, Lord, God of Israel, who brought your people out of the land of Egypt with a mighty hand, with signs and wonders, with great power and with outstretched arm, to win yourself a name renowned to-
12 day, ·we have sinned, we have been irreligious; Lord
13 our God, we have broken all your commandments. ·Let your anger turn from us since we are no more than a poor remnant among the nations where you have dis-
14 persed us. ·Listen, Lord, to our prayer, to our entreaty; deliver us for the sake of your honor and grant
15 us your favor for all our captors to see it, ·so that the whole world may know that you are the Lord our God,
16 since Israel and his descendants bear your name. ·Look

b. I.e., the feast of Tabernacles.

down, Lord, from your holy dwelling place and give a
17 thought to us, take heed of us and listen, ·look at us,
Lord, and consider; the dead down in Sheol, whose
breath has been taken from their bodies, are not the
ones to give glory and due observance to the Lord;
18 the person overcome with affliction, who goes his way
bowed down and frail, with failing eyes and hungering
soul, he is the one to give you glory, Lord, and due
observance.

19 We do not rely on the merits of our ancestors and
of our kings to offer you our humble plea, Lord our
20 God. ·No. You have sent down your anger and your
fury on us, as you promised through your servants the
21 prophets when they said, ·"The Lord says this: *Bend
your necks and submit to the king of Babylon, and you
will remain in the land which I gave your ancestors.*
22 But if you do not listen to the voice of the Lord and
23 submit to the king of Babylon, ·then *I will silence the
shouts of rejoicing and mirth and the voices of bridegroom and bride in the towns of Judah and in the
streets of Jerusalem, and the whole land will be reduced
24 to desert, without inhabitants."* ·But we did not listen
to your voice and submit to the king of Babylon, and
so you carried out what you had promised through
your servants the prophets: that the bones of our kings
and of our ancestors would be dragged from their rest-
25 ing places. ·They were indeed *tossed out to the heat
of the day and the frost of the night.* And people died
in dreadful agony, from famine, sword and plague.
26 And so, because of the wickedness of the House of
Israel and the House of Judah, you have made this
House, that bears your name, what it is today.

27 And yet, Lord our God, you have treated us in a
way worthy of all your goodness and boundless tender-
28 ness, ·just as you had promised through your servant
Moses, the day you told him to write your Law in the
29 presence of the sons of Israel, and said this, ·"If you
do not listen to my voice, this great and innumerable
multitude will certainly be reduced to a tiny few among
30 the nations among which I shall disperse them, ·and I
know very well that this people will not listen, it is so
stubborn. But in the country of their exile they will take
31 all this to heart ·and acknowledge that I am the Lord

their God. I will give them a heart and an attentive ear.
32 They will sing my praises in the country of their exile,
33 they will remember my name; ·they will not be stubborn any more, but, remembering what became of their ancestors who sinned in the sight of the Lord, will turn
34 from their evil deeds. ·Then I will bring them back to the land I promised on oath to Abraham, Isaac and Jacob, and make them masters in it. I will increase their
35 number: they shall not dwindle. ·And I will make an everlasting covenant with them; I will be their God and they shall be my people. And I will never again drive my people Israel out of the land that I have given them."

1 3 Almighty Lord, God of Israel, a soul in anguish, a
2 troubled heart now cries to you: ·Listen and have
3 pity, Lord, for we have sinned in your sight. ·You sit
4 enthroned for ever, while we perish continually. ·Almighty Lord, God of Israel, hear the prayer of the dead of Israel,[a] of the sons of those who have sinned against you and have not listened to the voice of the Lord their
5 God, hence the disasters that have seized on us. ·Do not call to mind the misdeeds of our ancestors, but
6 remember instead your power and your name. ·You are indeed the Lord our God and we long to praise
7 you, Lord, ·since you have put respect for you in our hearts to encourage us to call on your name. We long to praise you in our exile, for we have emptied our hearts of the evil inclinations of our ancestors who
8 sinned against you. ·Look on us today, still in exile where you have dispersed us as something execrable, accursed, condemned, in punishment for all the misdeeds of our ancestors who had abandoned the Lord our God.

## III. WISDOM, THE PREROGATIVE OF ISRAEL

9        Listen, Israel, to commands that bring life;
        hear, and learn what knowledge means.
10        Why, Israel, why are you in the country of your
        enemies,

3 a. Hyperbole: those brought near death.

11  growing older and older in an alien land,
sharing defilement with the dead,
reckoned with those who go to Sheol?

12  Because you have forsaken the fountain of
wisdom.

13  Had you walked in the way of God,
you would have lived in peace for ever.

14  Learn where knowledge is, where strength,
where understanding, and so learn
where length of days is, where life,
where the light of the eyes and where peace.

15  But who has found out where she lives,
who has entered her treasure house?

16  Where now are the leaders of the nations
and those who ruled even the beasts of earth,

17  who had the birds of heaven at their beck and
call,
who accumulated silver and gold
on which mankind relies,
and whose possessions had no limits,

18  those who displayed such artistry in silver
that their masterpieces beggar imagination?

19  They have vanished, gone down to Sheol.
Others have risen to their places,

20  more recent generations have seen the day
and peopled the earth in their turn:
but the way of knowledge is something they had
not known,

21  they have not recognized the paths she treads.
Nor have their sons had any grasp of her,
remaining far from her way.

22  Nothing has been heard of her in Canaan,
nothing has been seen of her in Teman;

23  the sons of Hagar in search of worldly wisdom,
the merchants of Midian and Tema,
the tale spinners and the philosophers
have none of them found the way to wisdom,
or discovered the paths she treads.

24  How great, Israel, is the house of God,
how wide his domain.

25  immeasurably wide,
infinitely lofty!

26    In it were born the giants, famous to us from
           antiquity,
       immensely tall, expert in war;

27    God's choice did not fall on these,
       he did not reveal the way to knowledge to them;

28    they perished for lack of wisdom,
       perished in their own folly.

29    Who has ever climbed the sky and caught her
       to bring her down from the clouds?

30    Who has ever crossed the ocean and found her
       to bring her back in exchange for the finest
           gold?

31    No one knows the way to her,
       no one can discover the path she treads.

32    But the One who knows all knows her,
       he has grasped her with his own intellect,
       he has set the earth firm for ever
       and filled it with four-footed beasts,

33    he sends the light—and it goes,
       he recalls it—and trembling it obeys;

34    the stars shine joyfully at their set times:

35    when he calls them, they answer, "Here we
           are";
       they gladly shine for their creator.

36    It is he who is our God,
       no other can compare with him.

37    He has grasped the whole way of knowledge,
       and confided it to his servant Jacob,
       to Israel his well-beloved;

38    so causing her to appear on earth
       and move among men.

1    **4**    This is the book of the commandments of God,
       the Law that stands for ever;
       those who keep her live,
       those who desert her die.

2    Turn back, Jacob, seize her,
       in her radiance make your way to light:

3    do not yield your glory to another,
       your privilege to a people not your own.

4    Israel, blessed are we:
       what pleases God has been revealed to us.

## IV. THE COMPLAINTS AND HOPES OF JERUSALEM

5    Take courage, my people,
constant reminder of Israel.[a]

6    You were sold to the nations,
but not for extermination.
You provoked God;
and so were delivered to your enemies,

7    since you had angered your creator
by offering sacrifices to demons, not to God.

8    You had forgotten the eternal God who reared
you.
You had also grieved Jerusalem who nursed
you,

9    for when she saw the anger fall on you
from God, she said:

Listen, you neighbors of Zion:
God has sent me great sorrow.

10    I have seen my sons and daughters taken into
captivity,
to which they have been sentenced by the
Eternal.

11    I had reared them joyfully;
in tears, in sorrow, I watched them go away.

12    Do not, any of you, exult over me,
a widow, deserted by so many;
I suffer loneliness because of the sins of my own
children,
who turned away from the Law of God,

13    who did not want to know his injunctions,
and would not follow the ways of his precepts,
or tread the paths of discipline as his justice directed.

14    Let them come here, those neighbors of Zion.
Let me remind you of the captivity of my sons
and daughters
to which they have been sentenced by the
Eternal:

15    how he brought a distant nation down on them,
a ruthless nation speaking a foreign language,

having neither respect for the aged,
nor pity for the child;

16  they carried off the widow's cherished sons,
they left her quite alone, bereft of her daughters.

17  For my part, how can I help you?

18  He who brought those disasters down on you,
he is the one to deliver you from the hands of
    your enemies.

19  Go, my children, go your way!
I must stay bereft and lonely;

20  I have taken off the clothes of peacetime,
and put on the sackcloth of entreaty;
I will cry to the Eternal all my life.

21  Take courage, my children, call on God:
he will deliver you from tyranny, from the
    hands of your enemies;

22  for I look to the Eternal for your rescue,
and joy has come to me from the Holy One
at the mercy soon to reach you
from your savior, the Eternal.

23  In sorrow and tears I watched you go away,
but God will give you back to me in joy and
    gladness for ever.

24  As the neighbors of Zion now witness your
    captivity,
so will they soon see you rescued by God,
who will intervene, in the great glory and
    splendor of the Eternal.

25  My children, patiently bear the anger brought
    on you by God.
Your enemy has persecuted you,
but soon you will witness his destruction
and set your foot on his neck.

26  My favorite children have traveled by rough
    roads,
carried off like a flock by a marauding enemy.

27  Take courage, my children, call on God:
he who brought disaster on you will remember
    you.

28  As by your will you first strayed away from
    God,

4 a. I.e., of Jacob.

so now turn back and search for him ten times
as hard;

29    for as he brought down those disasters on you,
so will he rescue you and give you eternal joy.

30    Take courage, Jerusalem:
he who gave you that name will console you.

31    Trouble will come to all who have ill-treated you
and gloated over your fall.

32    Trouble will come to the cities where your children were slaves;

trouble will come to the city which received
your sons,

33    for just as she rejoiced at your fall
and was happy to see you ruined,

so shall she grieve over her own desolation.

34    I will deprive her of that joy known to populous
cities,

her boasting shall be turned into mourning,

35    fire from the Eternal will burn in her for many
a day

and demons will dwell in her for ages.

36    Jerusalem, turn your eyes to the east,
see the joy that is coming to you from God.

37    Look, the sons you watched go away are on
their way home;

reassembled from east and west, they are on
their way home

at the command of the Holy One, jubilant at
the glory of God.

1 **5**    Jerusalem, take off your dress of sorrow and
distress,

put on the beauty of the glory of God for ever,

2    wrap the cloak of the integrity of God around
you,

put the diadem of the glory of the Eternal on
your head:

3    since God means to show your splendor to every
nation under heaven,

4    since the name God gives you for ever will be,
"Peace through integrity, and honor through de-
votedness."

5   Arise, Jerusalem, stand on the heights
and turn your eyes to the east:
see your sons reassembled from west and east
at the command of the Holy One, jubilant that
    God has remembered them.

6   Though they left you on foot,
with enemies for an escort,
now God brings them back to you
like royal princes carried back in glory.

7   For God has decreed the flattening
of each high mountain, of the everlasting hills,
the filling of the valleys to make the ground
    level
so that Israel can walk in safety under the glory
    of God.

8   And the forests and every fragrant tree will pro-
    vide shade
for Israel at the command of God;

9   for God will guide Israel in joy by the light of
    his glory
with his mercy and integrity for escort.

## V. THE LETTER OF JEREMIAH

A copy of the letter which Jeremiah sent to those
about to be led captive to Babylon by the king of the
Babylonians, to inform them of the instructions which
God had given him.

1 Because of the sins you have committed before God
you are to be deported to Babylon by Nebuchadnez-
2 zar king of the Babylonians. ·Once you have reached
Babylon you will stay there for many years, as long
as seven generations; after which I shall bring you home
3 in peace. ·Now in Babylon you will see gods made of
silver, of gold, of wood, being carried shoulder-high,
4 and filling the pagans with fear. ·Be on your guard.
Do not imitate the foreigners, do not have any fear of
5 their gods ·as you watch their worshipers flocking before and behind them. Instead, say in your hearts,
6 "Master, it is you that we have to worship." ·For my
angel is with you; your lives will be in his care.
7    Plated with gold and silver, their tongues polished

smooth by a craftsman, they are counterfeit and have
8 no power to speak. ·As though for a girl fond of finery,
these pagans take gold and make crowns for the heads
9 of their gods. ·Sometimes, the priests actually filch gold
and silver from their gods to spend themselves, even
10 using it on presents for the temple prostitutes. ·They
dress up these gods of silver, gold and wood, in clothes,
like human beings, although they cannot protect them-
11 selves either from tarnish or woodworm, ·in spite of
the purple cloaks they drape them in. Their faces
even have to be dusted, owing to the dust of the temple
12 which settles thick on them. ·One holds a scepter like
the governor of a province, yet is powerless to put any-
13 one who offends him to death; ·another holds sword
and ax in his right hand, yet is powerless to defend
14 himself against war or thieves. ·From this it is evident
that they are not gods; do not be afraid of them.

15      Just as a pot in common use becomes useless once
it is broken, so are these gods enshrined inside their
16 temples. ·Their eyes are full of dust raised by the feet
17 of those who enter. ·Just as the doors are locked on all
sides on the man who has offended the king and is
under sentence of death, so the priests secure the temples of these gods with gates and bolts and bars for
18 fear of burglary. ·They light more lamps than for them-
19 selves, and the gods cannot see one of them. ·They are
like one of the temple beams, gnawed away from
within, so they say, by termites which creep out of the
ground and eat them, and their fine clothes too. They
20 are unaware ·that their faces are blackened by the
21 smoke that rises from the temple. ·Bats, swallows, birds
of every kind flutter over their bodies and heads, and
22 cats prowl there. ·From all this you can see for yourselves that they are not gods: do not be afraid of them.

23      The gold with which they are plated is fine enough
to look at, but if someone does not rub off the tarnish,
these gods will not do much shining on their own. They
24 felt nothing while they were being cast. ·However
much was paid for them, there is still no breath of life
25 in them. ·Being unable to walk, they have to be carried
on men's shoulders, which shows how futile they are.
It is humiliating for their worshipers, too, who have to
26 stand them up again if they fall over. ·Once they have

been stood up, they cannot move on their own; if they
tilt askew, they cannot right themselves; offerings made
27 to them might as well be made to dead men. ·Whatever is sacrificed to them, the priests resell and pocket
the profit; while their wives salt down part of it, but
give nothing to the poor or to the helpless. As to the
sacrifices themselves, why, women during their periods
and women in childbed are not afraid to touch them!
28 As you can see from these examples that they are not
gods, do not be afraid of them.

29 Indeed, how can they even be called gods, when
women do the offering to these gods of silver, gold and
30 wood? ·In their temples, the priests stay sitting down,
their garments torn, heads and beard shaved and with
31 heads uncovered; ·they roar and shriek before their
32 gods as people do at funeral feasts. ·The priests take the
robes of the gods to clothe their own wives and chil-
33 dren. ·Whether these gods are treated badly or well,
they are incapable of paying back either treatment; as
34 incapable too of making or unmaking kings, ·equally
incapable of distributing wealth or money. If anyone
fails to honor a vow he has made to them, they cannot
35 call him to account. ·They can neither save a man from
36 death nor rescue the weak from the strong, ·nor restore sight to the blind, nor save someone in trouble,
37 nor take pity on a widow, nor be generous to an or-
38 phan. ·These wooden gods plated with gold and silver
are about as much use as rocks cut out of the mountain
39 side. Humiliation awaits their worshipers. ·So how can
anyone think or say that they are gods?

40 The Chaldaeans themselves do them no honor; if
they find someone who is dumb and cannot speak, they
present him to Bel, entreating him for the gift of speech,
41 as if he could hear them! ·And they are incapable of
drawing the conclusion and abandoning those gods—
42 such is their lack of commonsense. ·Women with
strings around their waists sit in the streets, burning
43 bran like incense; ·when one of these has been picked
up by a passer-by and been to bed with him, she then
twits her neighbor for not being singled out and for
44 not having her string broken. ·Everything going on
anywhere near these gods is spurious. So how can anyone think or say that they are gods?

45      Made by woodworkers and goldsmiths, they are only
46 what those workmen decide to make them. ·The makers have not long to live themselves, so how can the
47 things they make be gods? ·Their legacy to their descendants is nothing but illusion and disappointment.
48 If war or disasters occur, the priests discuss where best
49 to hide themselves and these gods; ·how can anyone fail to realize that they are not gods, if they cannot save
50 themselves from war or from disasters? ·And since in any case they are only made of wood plated with gold or silver, it must be obvious from all this that they are spurious; and plain to everyone, to nations as to kings, that they are not gods but the work of human hands, and that there is no divine activity in them.
51 Can there be anyone still unconvinced that they are not gods?

52      They can neither appoint a king over a country, nor
53 give rain to mankind, ·nor regulate their own affairs, nor rescue anyone who suffers a wrong; they are as
54 helpless as crows between sky and ground. ·If fire falls on the temple of these wooden gods plated with gold or silver, their priests fly to safety while they for their
55 part stay there like beams, to be burned. ·They cannot
56 put up any resistance to a king or to enemies. ·So how
57 can anyone think or say that they are gods? ·These wooden gods plated with gold or silver cannot evade thieves or marauders; violent men may rob them of their gold and silver and make off with the robes they are dressed in; yet they are powerless to help even
58 themselves. ·Better to be a king displaying his prowess, a household pot of use to its owner, than to be these false gods; or merely the door of a house, protecting what is inside, than these false gods; or a wooden pillar
59 in a palace than these false gods. ·The sun, the moon and the stars, which shine and have been given work
60 to do, are obedient; ·similarly, the lightning, as it flashes, is a fine sight; in the same way, the wind blows
61 across every country, ·the clouds execute the order God gives them to pass over the whole earth, and the fire, sent from above to consume mountain and forest,
62 carries out its orders. ·Now these gods are not their
63 equal, either in beauty or in power. ·So, no one can think or say that they are gods, powerless as they are

⁶⁴ to administer justice or to do men any good. ·Therefore, knowing that they are not gods, do not be afraid of them.

⁶⁵ ⁶⁶ They can neither curse nor bless kings, ·nor produce signs in heaven for the nations, nor shine like the sun,

⁶⁷ nor shed light like the moon. ·The animals are better off than they are, being able to make for cover and

⁶⁸ look after themselves. ·There is not the slightest shred of evidence that they are gods; do not be afraid of them!

⁶⁹ Their wooden gods plated with gold and silver are like a scarecrow in a melon patch—protecting nothing.

⁷⁰ Again, their wooden gods plated with gold and silver are like a thornbush in a garden—any bird may perch

⁷¹ on it—or like a corpse thrown into the dark. ·From the purple and fine linen rotting on their backs you will recognize that they are not gods; and in the end, eaten away themselves, they will be a disgrace to the country.

⁷² Better, then, a virtuous man who has no idols; disgrace will never come near him.

# INTRODUCTION
## TO THE BOOK OF
# EZEKIEL

According to the dates given inside the book, Ezekiel's ministry as a prophet was among the exiles in Babylon between
593 and 571. Nevertheless we find in chapters 4–24 a number
of reproaches and threats addressed to people living in Jerusalem, apparently before the siege; and following these, in
chapters 25–32, a series of oracles against "the nations,"
which belong to the same period. The remaining chapters,
33–48, plainly refer to the siege and the Exile, and indeed
look forward to the future re-establishment of the nation in
Palestine. Despite a certain amount of supplementary material, most of the prophecies are stamped with Ezekiel's own
style and teaching, and the details of the prophet's biography
remain a matter of debate and speculation.

Ezekiel was a priest; he was a prophet of action who made
himself "a sign" to Israel in elaborate symbolic miming. He
was also a visionary, as the four long violently imaginative
visions in the book show; these have the power of evoking
size and depth and the mysteriousness of God's working. His
teaching is centered on inner conversion: a new heart and
a new spirit, which will be given by God. By his visions,
he stands at the source of the apocalyptic tradition; for his
spiritual penetration, he has been called "the father of Ju-
daism."

# EZEKIEL

## INTRODUCTION

¹ ₁ In the thirtieth year, on the fifth day of the fourth month, as I was among the exiles on the bank of the river Chebar, heaven opened and I saw visions from ² God. ·On the fifth of the month—it was the fifth year ³ of exile for King Jehoiachin—·the word of Yahweh was addressed to the priest Ezekiel son of Buzi, in the land of the Chaldaeans, on the bank of the river Chebar.[a]

### The vision of the "Chariot of Yahweh"

⁴ There the hand of Yahweh came on me. ·I looked; a stormy wind blew from the north, a great cloud with light around it, a fire from which flashes of lightning darted, and in the center a sheen like bronze at the ⁵ heart of the fire. ·In the center I saw what seemed four animals. They looked like this. They were of human ⁶ form. ·Each had four faces, each had four wings. ⁷ Their legs were straight; they had hoofs like oxen, ⁸ glittering like polished brass. ·Human hands showed under their wings; the faces of all four were turned to ⁹ the four quarters.[b] ·Their wings touched each other; they did not turn as they moved; each one went straight ¹⁰ forward. ·As to what they looked like, they had human faces, and all four had a lion's face to the right, and all four had a bull's face to the left, and all four had ¹¹ an eagle's face. ·Their wings were spread upward; each had two wings that touched, and two wings that covered ¹² his body; ·and they all went straight forward; they went where the spirit urged them; they did not turn as they moved.

¹³ Between these animals something could be seen like flaming brands or torches, darting between the animals; the fire flashed light, and lightning streaked from ¹⁴ the fire. ·And the creatures ran to and fro like thunderbolts.

¹⁵ I looked at the animals; there was a wheel on the ground by each of them, one beside each of the four. ¹⁶ The wheels glittered as if made of chrysolite. All four looked alike, and seemed to be made one inside the ¹⁷ other. ·They went forward four ways and kept their ¹⁸ course unswervingly. ·Their rims seemed enormous when I looked at them and all four rims had eyes all ¹⁹ the way around. ·When the animals went forward, the wheels went forward beside them; and when the animals ²⁰ left the ground, the wheels too left the ground. ·Where the spirit urged them, there the wheels went, since the ²¹ spirit of the animal was in the wheels. ·When the animals moved on, they moved on; when the former halted, the latter halted; when the former left the ground, the wheels too left the ground, since the spirit ²² of the animal was in the wheels. ·Over the heads of the animals a sort of vault, gleaming like crystal, arched ²³ above their heads; ·under this vault their wings stretched out to one another, and each had two cover- ²⁴ ing his body. ·I heard the noise of their wings as they moved; it sounded like rushing water, like the voice of Shaddai, a noise like a storm, like the noise of a camp; ²⁵ when they halted, they folded their wings, ·and there was a noise.

²⁶ Above the vault over their heads was something that looked like a sapphire; it was shaped like a throne and high up on this throne was a being that looked like a ²⁷ man. ·I saw him shine like bronze, and close to and all around him from what seemed his loins upward was what looked like fire; and from what seemed his loins downward I saw what looked like fire, and a light all ²⁸ around ·like a bow in the clouds on rainy days; that is how the surrounding light appeared. It was something that looked like the glory of Yahweh. I looked, and prostrated myself, and I heard a voice speaking.

**1 a.** There seem to be two separate introductions in vv.1–3. The second of them dates Ezekiel's first vision in 593–592 and may be the introduction to the whole book; the other, v.1, is perhaps the introduction to the vision of the Chariot.
**b.** They are like the Assyrian "cherubs" whose effigies could be seen in Babylon.

### The vision of the scroll[a]

1 2 It said, "Son of man, stand up; I am going to speak
2 to you." ·As he said these words the spirit came into
me and made me stand up, and I heard him speaking to
3 me. ·He said, "Son of man, I am sending you to the
Israelites, to the rebels who have turned against me.
Till now they and their ancestors have been in revolt
4 against me. ·The sons are defiant and obstinate; I am
sending you to them, to say, 'The Lord Yahweh says
5 this.' ·Whether they listen or not, this set of rebels shall
6 know there is a prophet among them. ·And you, son of
man, do not be afraid of them, do not be afraid when
they say, 'There are thorns all around you and scorpi-
ons under you.' There is no need to be afraid either of
their words or of their looks, for they are a set of rebels.
7 You must deliver my words to them whether they listen
or not, for they are a set of rebels.

8      "You, son of man, listen to the words I say; do not
be a rebel like that rebellious set. Open your mouth
9 and eat what I am about to give you." ·I looked. A hand
was there, stretching out to me and holding a scroll.
10 He unrolled it in front of me; it was written on back
and front; on it was written "lamentations, wailings,
1 moanings." 3 He said, "Son of man, eat what is given
to you; eat this scroll, then go and speak to the House
2 of Israel." ·I opened my mouth; he gave me the scroll
3 to eat ·and said, "Son of man, feed and be satisfied by
the scroll I am giving you." I ate it, and it tasted
sweet as honey.

4      Then he said, "Son of man, go to the House of Israel
5 and tell them what I have said. ·You are not being
sent to a nation that speaks a difficult foreign language;
6 you are being sent to the House of Israel. ·Not to big
nations that speak difficult foreign languages, and
whose words you would not understand—if I sent you
7 to them, they would listen to you; ·but the House of
Israel will not listen to you because it will not listen to
me. The whole House of Israel is stubborn and ob-
8 stinate. ·But now, I will make you as defiant as they
9 are, and as obstinate as they are; ·I am going to make
your resolution as hard as a diamond and diamond is

harder than flint. So do not be afraid of them, do not be overawed by them for they are a set of rebels."

10 Then he said, "Son of man, remember everything
11 I say to you, listen closely, ·and go to your exiled countrymen and talk to them. Tell them, 'The Lord Yahweh says this,' whether they listen or not."

12 The spirit lifted me up, and behind me I could hear a tumultuous shouting, "Blessed be the glory of Yah-
13 weh in his dwelling place." ·This was the sound of the animals' wings beating against each other, and the sound of the wheels beside them; a tumultuous shouting.
14 The spirit lifted me up and took me; my heart, as I went, overflowed with bitterness and anger, and the
15 hand of Yahweh lay heavy on me. ·I came to Tel Abib, to the exiles beside the river Chebar where they were then living; and I stayed with them for seven days like a man stunned.

## The prophet as sentry

16 After seven days the word of Yahweh was addressed
17 to me as follows, ·"Son of man, I have appointed you as sentry to the House of Israel. Whenever you hear
18 a word from me, warn them in my Name. ·If I say to a wicked man: You are to die, and you do not warn him; if you do not speak and warn him to renounce his evil ways and so live, then he shall die for his sin,
19 but I will hold you responsible for his death. ·If, however, you do warn a wicked man and he does not renounce his wickedness and his evil ways, then he shall die for his sin, but you yourself will have saved
20 your life. ·When the upright man renounces his integrity to do evil and I set a trap for him, he too shall die; since you failed to warn him, he shall die for his sin and the integrity he practiced will no longer be remembered; but I will hold you responsible for his
21 death. ·If, however, you warn the upright man not to sin and he abstains from sinning, he shall live, thanks to your warning, and you too will have saved your life."

**2 a.** Probably Ezekiel's first vision; the vision of the Chariot is continued later, 3:12.

## I. BEFORE THE SIEGE OF JERUSALEM

### Ezekiel is struck dumb

22 While I was there the hand of Yahweh came on me;
he said, "Get up, go out into the valley; I am going to
23 speak to you." ·I got up and went out into the valley;
the glory of Yahweh was resting there, like the glory I
had seen by the river Chebar, and I prostrated myself.
24 The spirit of Yahweh then entered me, and made me
stand up, and spoke to me.

25 He said, "Go and shut yourself in your house. ·Son
of man, bonds are now about to be laid on you; you
will be bound with them and not be able to mix with
26 others. ·I am going to make your tongue stick to the
roof of your mouth; you will be dumb; you will stop
27 warning them, for they are a set of rebels. ·When I
speak to you, I shall open your mouth and you will tell
them, 'The Lord Yahweh says this.' Whoever will listen, let him listen; whoever will not, let him not; for
they are a set of rebels.

### The siege of Jerusalem foretold

1
2 **4** "Son of man, take a brick and lay it in front of you;
on it scratch a city, Jerusalem. ·You are then to
besiege it, trench around it, build earthworks, pitch
3 camps and bring up battering-rams all around. ·Then
take an iron pan and place it as if it were an iron wall
between you and the city. Then turn to it; it is being
besieged and you are besieging it. This is a sign for the
House of Israel.

4 "Lie down on your left side and take the sin of the
House of Israel on yourself. I am making you bear
5 their sin for as many days as you lie there. ·I myself
have set the years they will sin at a hundred and ninety
days; during these you are to bear the sin of the House
6 of Israel. ·And at the end of these days, you are to lie
down again on your right side and bear the sin of the
House of Judah for forty days. I have set the length

7 for you as one day for one year. ·And you are to turn toward the siege of Jerusalem, lift your bare arm and 8 prophesy against it. ·I have laid bonds on you, and you must not turn over until the period of your seclusion is finished.

9     "You must then take wheat, barley, beans, lentils, millet and spelt; put them all in the same pot and make yourself some bread. You are to eat it for as many days as you have been lying on your side, a hundred and 10 ninety days. ·As regards this food you are to measure out a daily portion of twenty shekels and make it last 11 the whole day. ·And you are to drink water sparingly; your drink is to be the sixth of a hin and to last the 12 whole day. ·Take this food in the shape of a barley cake baked where they can see you, over human dung. 13 And say, 'Yahweh, the God of Israel, says this: This is the way the Israelites will have to eat their defiled food, 14 wherever I disperse them among the nations.'" ·I then said, "Lord Yahweh, my soul is not defiled. From my childhood until now, I have never eaten an animal that has died a natural death or been savaged; no unclean 15 flesh has ever entered my mouth." ·"Very well," he said, "I grant you cow's dung instead of human dung; 16 you are to bake your bread on that." ·He then said, "Son of man, I mean to destroy the stock of bread in Jerusalem; in their distress they will eat bread strictly weighed; in terror they will drink water grudgingly 17 measured, ·since bread and water will be scarce; they will all pine and waste away as a result of their sins.

1 **5** "Son of man, take a sharp blade, sharp as a barber's razor; take it and use it on your head and beard. Then take scales and divide the hair you have cut off. 2 You are to set fire to a third in the center of the city, while the time of the siege is working itself out. Then take another third and toss it by swordpoint all around the city. The last third you are to scatter to the wind, 3 while I unsheathe the sword behind them. ·Then take a few hairs and wrap them in the folds of your cloak; 4 and of these again take a few, and throw them on the fire and burn them. From them will issue fire, and you 5 are to say to the entire House of Israel, ·'The Lord Yahweh says this: This is Jerusalem, which I have

placed in the middle of the nations, surrounded with
6 foreign countries. ·She is so perverse that she has rebelled more against my observances than the nations,
and more against my laws than the surrounding countries; for she has rejected my observances and refused
to keep my laws.

7　. Therefore, the Lord Yahweh says this: Since you
are more rebellious than the nations around you, since
you do not keep my laws or respect my observances,
and since you do not even respect the observances of
8 the surrounding nations, ·so then, the Lord Yahweh
says this: I have now set myself against you, I will inflict punishments upon you for all the nations to see.
9 On account of all your filthy practices I will do things
to you that I have never done before and that I will
10 never do again. ·Fathers among you will eat their children, and children eat their fathers. I will inflict punishments on you and disperse what remains of you to the
11 winds. ·Therefore, as I live—it is the Lord Yahweh who
speaks—as sure as you have defiled my sanctuary with
all your horrors and all your filthy practices, I too will
12 reject pitilessly; I will not spare, either. ·A third of your
inhabitants shall die of plague or starve to death inside
you; a third shall fall by the sword, outside you; a third
I will scatter to every wind, while I unsheathe the sword
13 behind them. ·My anger will be satisfied; I mean to
satisfy my fury against them and be avenged; they will
know that I, Yahweh, have spoken in my jealousy,
14 when I have exhausted my fury against them. ·I mean
to reduce you to a ruin, an object of contempt to sur-
15 rounding nations, in the eyes of all who pass by. ·You
will become an object of contempt and shame, an example and a thing of horror, to all the surrounding
nations, when I execute my judgments on you in anger
and fury, with bitter punishments. I, Yahweh, have
16 spoken. ·Against you I mean to send the deadly arrows
of starvation—which will destroy you, since I shall send
them to destroy you—and I will destroy your stock of
17 bread. ·Against you I mean to send famine and wild
animals, to rob you of your children; plague and bloodshed shall visit you. I will summon the sword against
you. I, Yahweh, have spoken.' "

### Against the mountains of Israel

1  6 The word of Yahweh was addressed to me as fol-
2  lows, ·"Son of man, turn toward the mountains of
3  Israel and prophesy against them. ·Say, 'Mountains of
   Israel, hear the word of the Lord Yahweh. The Lord
   Yahweh says this to mountains and hills and ravines
   and valleys: Listen; I am going to summon the sword
4  against you and destroy your high places. ·Your altars
   will be wrecked, and your incense burners smashed;
   your inhabitants are going to be cut to pieces and
5  thrown down in front of your idols, ·and their bones
6  spread all around your altars. ·Throughout your territory the towns will be destroyed and the high places
   wrecked, to the ruin and wrecking of your altars, the
   shattering and abolition of your idols, the smashing of
   your incense burners and the utter destruction of all
7  your works. ·Among you men will fall, and be cut to
   pieces; and so you will learn that I am Yahweh.
8     But I shall spare some of you; they will escape the
   sword and be dispersed by me among the nations.
9  Your survivors will remember me among the nations
   where they have been deported. I shall have broken
   their wanton hearts for having deserted me, and blinded
   their adulterous eyes for having fawned on idols. They
   will loathe themselves for all the wrong they have
10 caused by their filthy practices, ·and so they will learn
   that I am Yahweh; I have said, and I have meant it,
   that I am going to inflict all these disasters on them.

### The sins of Israel

11    The Lord Yahweh says this: Clap your hands, stamp
   your feet, and say: Alas! for all the abominable sins of
   the House of Israel, which is about to perish by sword,
12 famine and plague. ·Far off, they will die by plague;
   near at hand they will fall by the sword; those who are
   spared and besieged will die of hunger, since I mean to
13 satisfy my fury against them. ·You will know that I
   am Yahweh when their corpses, cut to pieces, lie there
   among their idols, all around their altars, on every high
   hill, on every mountain top, under every spreading
   tree, under every leafy oak, in fact wherever they offer
14 an appeasing fragrance to all their idols. ·I mean to

stretch out my hand against them and reduce the country to an empty wasteland from the desert to Riblah,[a] the length and breadth of the country; and so they will learn that I am Yahweh.'"

## The end is near

1 The word of Yahweh was addressed to me as fol-
2 lows, ·"Son of man, say, 'The Lord Yahweh says this to the land of Israel: Finished! The end is coming
3 for the four quarters of the land. ·Now all is over with you; I mean to unleash my anger on you, and judge you as your conduct deserves and force you to answer
4 for all your filthy practices. ·I mean to show you no pity, I will not spare you; I am going to call you to account for your conduct and for the filthy practices that you parade; and so you will learn that I am Yahweh.

5 The Lord Yahweh says this: Now disaster is going
6 to follow on disaster. ·The end is coming, the end is
7 coming for you; it is coming now. ·Now, it is your turn, you who live in this country. The time has come, the day is near; no joy now, only tumult, on the moun-
8 tains. ·Soon I am going to pour out my fury on you and exhaust my anger at you; I will judge you as your conduct deserves and call you to account for all your
9 filthy practices. ·I mean to show you neither pity nor mercy, since I am going to call you to account for your conduct and for the filthy practices which you parade; and so you will learn that I am Yahweh, and that I strike.

10 Here is the day! It has come; your turn has come, the
11 scourge is ready, pride is at its peak. ·Violence has
12 risen to become the scourge of wickedness . . . ·The time has come and the day is near. Let neither buyer rejoice, nor seller regret, for anger rages against all
13 alike. ·The seller will not recover what he has sold; they will all carry on sinning and be none the stronger
14 for it. ·The trumpet will sound, all will be ready; but no one will go into battle, since my anger rages against all alike.

## The sins of Israel

15 Outside, the sword; inside, plague and famine. Anyone who is found in the countryside will die by the

sword; anyone who is found in the city will be devoured
16 by famine and plague. ·Their fugitives will run away
and make for the mountains; I shall slaughter them all
17 like doves of the valleys, each for his sin. ·With limp
18 hands and quaking knees, ·they will put on sackcloth;
and shudder all over. All their faces will be red with
19 shame and every head will be shaved. ·They will throw
their silver down in the streets and their gold will fill
them with horror. Never again will they have enough
to eat, never again will they fill their bellies, since this
20 has been the cause of their crimes. ·They used to pride
themselves on the beauty of their jewelry, out of which
they made their loathsome images and idols. That is
21 why I mean to make it an object of horror to them. ·I
intend to hand it over to be the plunder of foreigners
22 and loot for local brigands, who will profane it. ·I shall
turn my face from them; my treasury will be profaned;
barbarians will force their way in and profane it.

23    Forge yourself a chain; for the country is filled with
24 bloody murders, the city is full of violent crime. ·I am
going to summon the cruelest of the nations to seize
their houses. I will break the pride of their grandees;
25 their sanctuaries will be profaned. ·Anguish is on its
way: they will look for peace and there will be none.
26 Disaster will follow on disaster, rumor on rumor; they
will pester the prophet for a vision; the priest will be at
a loss over the law and the elders on how to advise.
27 The king will go into mourning, the prince be plunged
in grief, the hands of the country people tremble. I
mean to treat them as their conduct deserves, and judge
them as their own verdicts merit; and so they will learn
that I am Yahweh.' "

### A vision of the sins of Jerusalem

1  8 In the sixth year, on the fifth day of the sixth
     month,[a] I was sitting at home and the elders of
Judah were sitting with me, when the hand of the Lord
Yahweh fell on me.
2    I looked and saw something that looked like a man.
Downward from what seemed to be his loins he was
fire; and upward from his loins he seemed to shine like

6 a. I.e., from the south of Palestine to the most northerly point.
8 a. September–October 592.

3 polished bronze. ·He stretched out what seemed to be
a hand and took me by the hair; and the spirit lifted me
into the air and, in visions from God, took me to Jerusalem, to the entrance of the inner north gate, where
4 the idol of Jealousy stands, provoking jealousy.[b] ·There
I saw the glory of the God of Israel, as I had seen it in
5 the valley. ·He said, "Son of man, raise your eyes to
the north." I raised my eyes to the north, and there, to
the north of the altar gate, stood this statue of Jealousy
6 at the entrance. ·He said, "Son of man, do you see
what they are doing? Do you see all the filth practiced
here by the House of Israel, to drive me out of my
sanctuary? You will see filthier practices yet."

7 He next took me to the entrance to the court. I
8 looked; there was a hole in the wall. ·He said, "Son of
man, break through the wall." I broke through the
9 wall; there was a door. ·He said, "Go in and look at
10 the filthy things they are doing inside." ·I went in and
looked: all sorts of images of snakes and repulsive animals and all the idols of the House of Israel drawn on
11 the wall all around. ·Seventy elders of the House of
Israel were standing in front of the idols, among them
Jaazaniah son of Shaphan, each one, censer in hand;
12 the fragrance of incense was rising. ·He said, "Son of
man, have you seen what the elders of the House of
Israel do in the dark, each in his painted room? They
say, 'Yahweh cannot see us; Yahweh has abandoned
13 the country.' " ·He said, "You will see them at filthier
practices still."

14 He next took me to the entrance of the north gate of
the Temple of Yahweh where women were sitting,
15 weeping for Tammuz.[c] ·He said, "Son of man, do you
see that? You will see even filthier things than that."

16 He then led me to the inner court of the Temple of
Yahweh. And there, at the entrance to the sanctuary
of Yahweh, between the porch and the altar, there were
about twenty-five men, with their backs to the sanctuary of Yahweh and their faces turned to the east.
17 They were bowing to the east, toward the sun. ·He
said to me, "Son of man, do you see that? Is it not bad
enough for the House of Judah to do the filthy things
that they are doing here? But they fill the country with
violence and provoke my anger further; look at them

18 now putting that branch to their nostrils. ·My anger
forces me to it; I will show neither pity nor mercy.
They may shout as loud as they like; I will not listen to
them."

### The punishment

1 Then as I listened he shouted, "Come here, you
scourges of the city, and bring your weapons of
2 destruction." ·Immediately six men advanced from the
upper north gate, each holding a deadly weapon. In
the middle of them was a man in white, with a scribe's
ink horn in his belt. They came in and halted in front
3 of the bronze altar. ·The glory of the God of Israel
rose off the cherubs where it had been and went up to
the threshold of the Temple. He called the man in
4 white with a scribe's ink horn in his belt ·and said,
"Go all through the city, all through Jerusalem, and
mark a cross on the foreheads of all who deplore and
5 disapprove of all the filth practiced in it." ·I heard him
say to the others, "Follow him through the city, and
6 strike. Show neither pity nor mercy; ·old men, young
men, virgins, children, women, kill and exterminate
them all. But do not touch anyone with a cross on his
forehead. Begin at my sanctuary." So they began with
7 the old men in front of the Temple. ·He said to them,
"Defile the Temple; fill the courts with corpses, and
go." They went out and hacked their way through the
city.
8 While they were hacking them down, I stayed behind; I fell face downward and exclaimed, "Ah, Lord
Yahweh, are you going to annihilate all that is left of
9 Israel as you turn your anger on Jerusalem?" ·He said,
"The guilt of the House of Israel and Judah is immense, boundless; the country is full of bloodshed, the
city overflows with wickedness, for they say, 'Yahweh
has abandoned the country, Yahweh cannot see.'
10 Right, then, I too will show no pity, I too will not
spare. I mean to call them to account for all their be-
11 havior." ·The man in white with the scribe's ink horn

b. Perhaps the statue of Astarte (Ishtar) set up by Manasseh,
2 K. 21:7, which would rouse the jealousy of Yahweh.
c. Adonis.

in his belt then came back and made his report, "I have
carried out your orders."

1 10 I looked, and I saw that above the vault over the
cherubs' heads there was something that looked
like a sapphire, and there showed above them the sem-
2 blance of a throne. ·He then said to the man in white,
"Go under the chariot, beneath the cherubs; take a
handful of burning coal from between the cherubs and
scatter it over the city." He went in as I watched.

3 The cherubs were on the right of the Temple as the
4 man went in, and the cloud filled the inner court. ·The
glory of Yahweh rose off the cherubs and up to the
threshold of the Temple; the Temple was filled with
the cloud and the court was filled with the brightness of
5 the glory of Yahweh. ·The noise of the cherubs' wings
could be heard even in the outer court, like the thun-
der of God Almighty when he speaks.

6 When he ordered the man in white to take the fire
from under the chariot, between the cherubs, the man
7 went and stopped by the wheel; ·one cherub stretched
his hand toward the fire which was between the cherubs, took some and put it into the hands of the man in
8 white, who took it and went off. ·I then saw that the
cherubs had what seemed to be a human hand under
9 their wings. ·I looked; there were four wheels at the
side of the cherubs, one wheel at the side of each
cherub, and the wheels glittered as if made of chryso-
10 lite. ·All four looked alike, and seemed to be one in-
11 side the other. ·They went forward four ways and kept
their course unswervingly, moving the way they faced
12 and never swerving off their course. ·Their bodies, their
backs, their hands, their wings, and the wheels—the
13 wheels of all four—were covered in eyes all over. ·I
14 heard that the wheels were called "galgal." ·Each
cherub had four faces: the first face was the face of
the cherub, the second face the face of a man, the
third the face of a lion, the fourth the face of an
15 eagle. ·The cherubs rose; this was the creature I had
16 seen by the river Chebar. ·As the cherubs went forward, the wheels went forward beside them; and the
wheels did not swerve even when the cherubs spread
17 their wings to leave the ground. ·When the former
stopped, the latter stopped; when the former rose, the

latter rose with them, since the spirit of the creature
was in them.

### The glory of Yahweh leaves the Temple

18 The glory of Yahweh came out from the Temple
19 threshold and paused over the cherubs. ·The cherubs
spread their wings and rose from the ground to leave,
and as I watched the wheels rose with them. They
paused at the entrance to the east gate of the Temple
of Yahweh, and the glory of the God of Israel hovered
20 over them. ·This was the creature that I had seen supporting the God of Israel beside the river Chebar, and
21 I was now certain that these were cherubs. ·Each had
four faces and four wings and what seemed to be hu-
22 man hands under their wings. ·Their faces were just
as I had seen them beside the river Chebar. Each
moved straight forward.

### The sins of Jerusalem (continued)

1 11 The spirit lifted me up and carried me to the east
gate of the Temple of Yahweh, the gate that looks
eastward. There at the entrance to the gate stood
twenty-five men, among whom I saw Jaazaniah son of
Azzur and Pelatiah son of Benaiah, leaders of the peo-
2 ple. ·Yahweh said, "Son of man, these are the wicked
schemers who are spreading their bad advice through
3 this city. ·They say, 'Shall we not soon be building
houses? Here is the cooking pot and we are the meat.'[a]
4 Therefore prophesy against them, prophesy, son of
5 man." ·The spirit of Yahweh fell on me, and he said
to me, "Say, 'Yahweh says this: I know what you are
saying, House of Israel, I know how insolent you are.
6 You have filled this city with more and more corpses of
murdered men, you have strewn its streets with your
7 victims. ·And so, the Lord Yahweh says this: The
corpses you have thrown into it are the meat, and the
city is the cooking pot; but I mean to drive you out.
8 You are afraid of the sword and I will summon it
9 against you—it is the Lord Yahweh who speaks. ·I shall
drive you from the city and hand you over to foreign-
10 ers, and I shall carry out my sentence on you; ·you

11 a. A proverb: "we are as safe inside our walls as meat in a
pot is safe from the fire."

will fall by the sword on the soil of Israel; I shall execute justice on you; and so you will learn that I am
11 Yahweh. ·This city will be no cooking pot for you, and
you will never be the meat inside; I am going to exe-
12 cute justice on you on the soil of Israel; ·and so you
will learn that I am Yahweh, whose laws you have not
obeyed and whose observances you have not kept; instead, you have adopted the manners of the nations
around you.'"

13    Now as I was prophesying, Pelatiah son of Benaiah
dropped dead. I prostrated myself and cried aloud, "Ah,
Lord Yahweh, are you going to wipe out all that is left
of Israel?"

## The new covenant promised to the exiles

14    The word of Yahweh was then addressed to me as
15 follows, ·"Son of man, your brothers, your kinsmen,
the whole House of Israel, these are told by the citizens
of Jerusalem, 'You have been sent away from Yahweh; it is to us that the land was given as our domain.'
16 Say therefore, 'The Lord Yahweh says this: Yes, I have
sent them far away among the nations and I have dispersed them to foreign countries; and for a while I
have been a sanctuary for them in the country to which
17 they have gone.' ·Then say, 'The Lord Yahweh says
this: I will gather you together from the peoples, I will
bring you all back from the countries where you have
been scattered and I will give you the land of Israel.
They will come and will purge it of all the horrors and
18 the filthy practices. ·I will give them a single heart and
19 I will put a new spirit in them; ·I will remove the heart
of stone from their bodies and give you a heart of
20 flesh instead, ·so that they will keep my laws and respect my observances and put them into practice. Then
21 they shall be my people and I will be their God. ·But
those whose hearts are set on their idols and their filthy
practices I will call to account for their conduct—it is
the Lord Yahweh who speaks.'"

## The glory of Yahweh leaves Jerusalem

22    The cherubs then spread their wings and the wheels
began to move with them, while the glory of the God
23 of Israel hovered over them. ·And the glory of Yah-

weh rose to leave the city and paused on the mountain
to the east of the city.
24    The spirit lifted me up in vision, in the spirit of God,
and took me to the Chaldaeans, away to the exiles, and
25 so the vision I had seen faded; ·and then I told the
exiles everything that Yahweh had shown me.

### The mime of the emigrant

1    12 The word of Yahweh was addressed to me as
2       follows, ·"Son of man, you are living with that
set of rebels who have eyes and never see, ears and
3 never hear, for they are a set of rebels. ·You, son of
man, pack an exile's bundle and emigrate by daylight
when they can see you, emigrate from where you are
to somewhere else while they watch. Perhaps they will
4 admit then that they are a set of rebels. ·You will pack
your baggage like an exile's bundle, by daylight, for
them to see, and leave like an exile in the evening,
5 making sure that they are looking. ·As they watch,
6 make a hole in the wall, and go out through it. ·As
they watch, you will shoulder your pack and go out
into the dark; you will cover your face so that you
cannot see the country, since I have made you a symbol for the House of Israel."
7    I did as I had been told. I packed my baggage like
an exile's bundle, by daylight; and in the evening I
made a hole through the wall with my hand. I went
out into the dark and shouldered my pack as they
watched.
8    The next morning the word of Yahweh was ad-
9 dressed to me as follows, ·"Son of man, did not the
House of Israel, did not that set of rebels, ask you what
10 you were doing? ·Say, 'The Lord Yahweh says this:
This oracle is directed against Jerusalem and the whole
11 House of Israel wherever they are living.' ·Say, 'I am a
symbol for you; the thing I have done will be done to
12 them; they will go into exile, into banishment.' ·Their
ruler will shoulder his pack in the dark and go out
through the wall; a hole will be made to let him out;
13 he will cover his face rather than see the country,[a] ·I

12 a. Perhaps a prophecy of two separate incidents in 2 K. 25:
the attempt of Zedekiah and his army to escape, and the putting
out of his eyes before he was led captive to Babylon.

shall throw my net over him and catch him in my mesh; I shall take him to Babylon, to the land of the Chaldaeans, though he will not see it; and there he will
14 die. ·And all those who form his court, his guards and all his troops, I shall scatter to all the winds and un-
15 sheathe the sword behind them. ·They will learn that I am Yahweh, when I scatter them throughout the na-
16 tions and disperse them in foreign countries. ·However, I intend to leave some of them unscathed by sword, famine and plague, to describe all their filthy practices to the peoples among whom they will go, so that these too may learn that I am Yahweh."

17 The word of Yahweh was addressed to me as fol-
18 lows, ·"Son of man, you are to tremble as you eat your bread and to behave restlessly and anxiously as you
19 drink your water, ·and you are to say to the people of the country, 'The Lord Yahweh says this to the citizens of Jerusalem scattered throughout Israel: They are going to eat their bread in anxiety, and drink their water in fear, until the country and those who live in it are
20 free of the violence of all its inhabitants. ·The inhabited towns are going to be destroyed and the country will be reduced to desert; and so you will learn that I am Yahweh.' "

## Popular proverbs

21 The word of Yahweh was addressed to me as fol-
22 lows, ·"Son of man, what do you mean by this proverb common throughout the land of Israel: Days go by and visions fade?

23 "Very well, tell them, 'The Lord Yahweh says this: I will put an end to this proverb; it shall never be heard in Israel again.' Instead, tell them:

'The day is coming when every vision will come
24 true.' ·From now on there will be no empty vision, no
25 deceitful prophecy in the House of Israel, ·since it is I, Yahweh, who will speak. What I say is said and will soon come true; since what I pronounce I will fulfill in your own lifetime, you set of rebels—it is the Lord Yahweh who speaks."

26 The word of Yahweh was addressed to me as fol-
27 lows, ·"Son of man, the House of Israel is saying, 'The vision that this man sees concerns the distant future;

28 he is prophesying for times far ahead.' ·Very well, tell them, 'The Lord Yahweh says this: There will be no further delay in the fulfilling of any of my words. What I say is said and will come true—it is the Lord Yahweh who speaks.' "

### Against the false prophets

1
2 13 The word of Yahweh was addressed to me as follows, ·"Son of man, prophesy against the prophets of Israel; prophesy, and say to those who make up prophecies out of their own heads, 'Hear the word
3 of Yahweh. ·The Lord Yahweh says this: Woe to the foolish prophets who follow their own spirit, without
4 seeing anything! ·Like jackals in a ruin, so are your prophets, Israel.

5     You have never ventured into the breach; you have never bothered to fortify the House of Israel, to hold
6 fast in battle on the day of Yahweh. ·They have empty visions and give lying prophecies and say: It is Yahweh who speaks, although Yahweh has not sent them; and
7 they are still waiting for their words to come true. ·Can you deny that you have only empty visions, that you utter only lying prophecies when you say: It is Yahweh who speaks, when I myself have not spoken?

8     Very well, the Lord Yahweh says this: Because of your empty words and lying visions, I have now set myself against you—it is the Lord Yahweh who speaks.
9 I am going to stretch my hand over the prophets who have empty visions and give lying predictions; they will not be admitted to the council of my people, their names will not be entered in the Book of the House of Israel, they will not set foot on the soil of Israel; and
10 you will learn that I am the Lord Yahweh, ·since they have misled my people by saying: Peace! when there is no peace. Instead of my people rebuilding the wall,
11 these men come and slap on plaster. ·Tell these plasterers: It will rain hard, it will hail, it will blow a gale,
12 and down will come the wall. Will not people ask:
13 Where is the plaster you slapped on it? ·Well then, the Lord Yahweh says this: I am going to unleash a stormy wind in my anger, torrential rain in my wrath, hail-
14 stones in my destructive fury. ·I mean to shatter the wall you slapped with plaster, to throw it down and lay

its foundations bare. It will fall and you will perish under it; and so you will learn that I am Yahweh.

15 When I have exhausted my anger against the wall and those who plastered it, I shall say to you: The wall is gone, and so are those who slapped it over with 16 plaster, ·these prophets of Israel who prophesy about Jerusalem and have visions of peace for her when there is no peace—it is the Lord Yahweh who speaks.'

### The false prophetesses

17 "And you, son of man, turn to the daughters of your people who make up prophecies out of their own heads; 18 prophesy against them. ·Say, 'The Lord Yahweh says this: Trouble is coming to the women who sew frills around wrists,ᵃ who make veils for people of all sizes, the better to ensnare lives! You ensnare the lives of the 19 men of my people while looking after your own. ·You dishonor me in front of my people for a few handfuls of barley, a few bits of bread, killing those who ought not to die and sparing those who ought not to live, lying to my people who love to listen to lies.

20 Well then, the Lord Yahweh says this. We shall see about these frills you use for snaring lives like birds. I intend to rip them off your arms, and free those lives 21 you try to snare like birds. ·I am going to rip your veils to pieces and rescue my people from you; they will no longer be fair game for you. And so you will learn that I am Yahweh.

22 Since you distress with lies the heart of the upright man whom I would never distress, and since you encourage the wicked man not to give up his wicked ways 23 and find life again, ·very well, you will have no more empty visions, and you will not make any more predictions. I mean to rescue my people from you, and then you will learn that I am Yahweh.'"

### Against idolatry

¹⁄₂ **14** When some elders of Israel had come to my house and sat down with me, the word of Yah- 3 weh was addressed to me as follows, ·"Son of man, these people have enshrined their own idols in their hearts, they cling to the cause of their sins; am I going 4 to let myself be consulted by them? ·Well then, speak

to them; tell them this, 'The Lord Yahweh says this:
Every member of the House of Israel who enshrines
his own idols in his heart, or who, clinging to the cause
of his sins, comes looking for the prophet, will get his
answer from me, Yahweh, on account of his hundreds
5 of idols'; ·and in this way I hope to touch the heart of
the House of Israel who have deserted me in favor of a
pack of idols.

6    "Say therefore to the House of Israel, 'The Lord
Yahweh says this: Come back, renounce your idols
7 and give up all your filthy practices; ·for if any member of the House of Israel—or even any foreigner living
in Israel—deserts me to enshrine his own idols in his
heart, and, clinging to the cause of his sins, then comes
looking for the prophet to consult me, he will get his
8 answer from me, Yahweh. ·I will turn against this man;
I will make him an example and a byword; I will cut
him off from my people; and you will learn that I am
9 Yahweh. ·If the prophet is led astray and speaks, it is
I, Yahweh, who have led that prophet astray; I will
stretch out my hand against him and will wipe him
10 out from my people Israel. ·They will bear the weight
of their faults, and the fault of the prophet will be as
11 grave as the fault of the man who consults him. ·So
the House of Israel will not desert me any more; it will
not defile itself with any more of these sins. They shall
be my people, and I will be their God—it is the Lord
Yahweh who speaks.' "

### Individual responsibility

12    The word of Yahweh was addressed to me as fol-
13 lows, ·"Son of man, if a country were to sin against
me by faithlessness, and if I were to stretch out my
hand against it and destroy its stock of bread and send
14 famine to it to kill its men and beasts, ·and if in that
country there were these three men, Noah, Danel and
Job,[a] these men would have their lives spared because
of their integrity—it is the Lord Yahweh who speaks.
15 Were I to unleash wild animals on that country to rob
it of its children and reduce it to such a desert that no

13 a. Presumably a magical or idolatrous practice.
14 a. Danel, famous for his goodness and wisdom, is known to
us from the Ras Shamra texts.

¹⁶ one would dare to cross it because of the animals, ·and if these three men were in that country, then, as I live —it is the Lord Yahweh who speaks—they would not be able to save either son or daughter; they alone would ¹⁷ be saved, and the country would become a desert. ·If I were to bring the sword into that country and say: Let the sword pass through the country; I will strike ¹⁸ down men and beasts with it, ·and if these three men were in that country, then, as I live—it is the Lord Yahweh who speaks—they would not be able to save either son or daughter; they alone would be saved. ¹⁹ If I were to send the plague into that country and satisfy my anger with them by bloodshed, cutting off men and ²⁰ beasts, ·if Noah and Danel and Job were in the country, as I live—it is the Lord Yahweh who speaks—they would not be able to save either son or daughter, though they would save their own lives because of their integrity.

²¹ "The Lord Yahweh says this: Now, if I do send my four dreadful scourges against Jerusalem—sword, famine, wild animals and plague—to cut off its men and ²² beasts, ·and if any survivors are left there to contrive the escape of son and daughter, they will come for you to see their conduct and actions and so be comforted in spite of the scourges I shall have brought on Jerusalem, in spite of everything I shall have brought ²³ on her. ·They will comfort you, when you see their conduct and actions, and so you will learn that I have not done all I have done against her for nothing—it is the Lord Yahweh who speaks."

### A parable of the vine

¹ **15** The word of Yahweh was addressed to me as follows:

²   "Son of man, how is the wood of the vine better than wood from the branch of a forest tree?

³   Do people use its wood to carve it into something?

   Do they make a peg out of it, and hang things on it?

⁴   There it is, thrown on the fire for fuel.
   The fire burns off both ends;

the middle is charred; is it fit for carving now?
5    While it was intact, it was impossible to carve;
     burned and charred, will it be now fit for
     carving?
6    Therefore, the Lord Yahweh says this:
     As the wood of the vine among the forest trees,
     which I have thrown on the fire for fuel,
     so have I treated the citizens of Jerusalem.
7    I have turned my face against them.
     They have escaped the fire, but the fire will
     devour them yet.
     And you will learn that I am Yahweh, when I
     turn my face against them.
8    I mean to reduce the country to desert, to pun-
     ish their faithlessness to me
     —it is the Lord Yahweh who speaks."

**An allegorical history of Israel**

1  **16** The word of Yahweh was addressed to me as
2         follows, ·"Son of man, confront Jerusalem with
3  her filthy crimes. ·Say, 'The Lord Yahweh says this:
   By origin and birth you belong to the land of Canaan.
   Your father was an Amorite and your mother a Hittite.
4  At birth, the very day you were born, there was no
   one to cut your navel string, or wash you in cleansing
   water, or rub you with salt, or wrap you in napkins.
5  No one leaned kindly over you to do anything like
   that for you. You were exposed in the open fields; you
   were as unloved as that on the day you were born.
6    I saw you struggling in your blood as I was passing,
7  and I said to you as you lay in your blood: Live, ·and
   grow like the grass of the fields. You developed, you
   grew, you reached marriageable age. Your breasts and
8  your hair both grew, but you were quite naked. ·Then
   I saw you as I was passing. Your time had come, the
   time for love. I spread part of my cloak over you and
   covered your nakedness; I bound myself by oath, I
   made a covenant with you—it is the Lord Yahweh who
9  speaks—and you became mine. ·I bathed you in water,
10 I washed the blood off you, I anointed you with oil. ·I
   gave you embroidered dresses, fine leather shoes, a
11 linen headband and a cloak of silk. ·I loaded you with
   jewels, gave you bracelets for your wrists and a neck-

¹² lace for your throat. ·I gave you nose ring and earrings;
¹³ I put a beautiful diadem on your head. ·You were loaded with gold and silver, and dressed in fine linen and embroidered silks. Your food was the finest flour, honey and oil. You grew more and more beautiful;
¹⁴ and you rose to be queen. ·The fame of your beauty spread through the nations, since it was perfect, because I had clothed you with my own splendor—it is the Lord Yahweh who speaks.

¹⁵ You have become infatuated with your own beauty; you have used your fame to make yourself a prostitute;
¹⁶ you have offered your services to all comers . . . . ·You have taken your clothes to brighten your high places
¹⁷ and there you have played the whore . . . . ·You have taken my presents of gold and silver jewelry and made
¹⁸ yourself human images to use in your whorings. ·You have taken your embroidered clothes and put them on the images, and the oil and incense which are rightly
¹⁹ mine you have offered to them. ·The bread I gave you, the finest flour, oil and honey with which I used to feed you, you have now offered to them as an appeasing fragrance.

You have even—it is the Lord Yahweh who speaks—
²⁰ taken the sons and daughters you bore me and sacrificed them as food to the images. Was it not enough
²¹ for you just to be a whore? ·You have slaughtered my children and handed them over as a burnt offering to
²² them, ·and in all your filthy practices and your whorings you have never remembered your youth or the time when you were quite naked and struggling in your own blood.

²³ To crown your wickedness—trouble for you, it is the
²⁴ Lord Yahweh who speaks—·you have built yourself a mound and made a high place at every crossroads.
²⁵ At the beginning of every road you have built a high place to defile your beauty there and to give your body to every comer; you have piled whoring on whoring.
²⁶ You have lain down for those big-membered neighbors, the Egyptians; you have piled whoring on whoring to
²⁷ provoke me, ·and now I have raised my hand against you. I have rationed your food, I have handed you over to the mercy of your enemies, the daughters of
²⁸ the Philistines, who are sick of your filthy ways. ·Still

unsatisfied, you have prostituted yourself to the Assyrians; you have played the whore and not been satis-
29 fied even then.ᵃ ·You have piled whoring on whoring
with Canaanite and Chaldaean, and even then not been
satisfied.

30    How easily led you were—it is the Lord Yahweh
who speaks—to behave no better than a bold-faced
31 whore! ·When you built yourself a mound at the beginning of every road and made a high place at every
crossroads, you were not, like the whore, out for
32 money: ·an adulteress welcomes strangers instead of
33 her husband; ·a prostitute is paid. But you, in your
whoring, have given your presents away to all your
lovers; you have offered them gifts to attract them from
34 everywhere. ·In your whoring you have done the exact
opposite from other women; no one was running after
you, so you went and paid them; they did not pay you
since your behavior was so outrageous.

35
36    Well then, whore, hear the word of Yahweh. ·The
Lord Yahweh says this: For having undressed and let
yourself be seen naked while whoring with your lovers
and with your filthy idols, and for giving them your
37 children's blood—·for all this, I am going to band together all the lovers who have pleasured you, both those
you liked and those you disliked, I am going to band
them together against you from all around; I will strip
you in front of them, and let them see you naked.
38 And I mean to punish you like women who commit
39 adultery and murder; ·I intend to hand you over to
fury and jealousy; I will hand you over to them; they
will level your mound and demolish your high places;
they will tear your clothes off, take your jewels and
40 leave you completely naked. ·They will then whip up
the crowd against you; you will be stoned and run
41 through with a sword; ·they will set your houses on
fire and execute justice on you with crowds of women
looking on; I will put an end to your whoring: no
42 more paid lovers for you. ·I will exhaust my fury
against you. My jealousy will then leave you; I shall
43 be appeased and my anger will stop. ·Since you have

16 a. Especially in the reign of Manasseh, Israel was unfaithful
in adopting the foreign gods of her allies.

never remembered your youth, since in all this you
have done nothing but provoke me, I in my turn intend
to bring your conduct down on your own head—it is
the Lord Yahweh who speaks. Have you not been dis-
gusting with all your filthy practices?

44 Now all the proverb makers will make up a proverb
45 about you: Like mother, like daughter. ·Yes; you are
a true daughter of your mother, who hated her husband and her children; a true sister of your sisters, who
hated their husbands and their children. Your mother
46 was a Hittite and your father an Amorite. ·Your elder
sister is Samaria, who lives on your left with her daughters. Your younger sister is Sodom, who lives on your
47 right with her daughters. ·You have not failed to copy
their behavior; throughout your career you have shown
48 yourself more corrupt than they were. ·As I live—it is
the Lord Yahweh who speaks—your sister Sodom and
her daughters have not been as bad as you and your
49 daughters. ·The crime of your sister Sodom was pride,
gluttony, arrogance, complacency; such were the sins
of Sodom and her daughters. They never helped the
50 poor and needy; ·they were proud and engaged in filthy
practices in front of me; that is why I have swept them
51 away as you have seen. ·And yet Samaria never committed half the crimes that you have.

You have done far filthier things than they did. By
your filthy practices you have made your sisters seem
52 almost innocent, ·and now you have to bear the shame
for all those faults of which you have cleared your
sisters; since the grossness of the sins for which you
bear the guilt is more horrible than theirs; they now
appear more virtuous than you are. Be ashamed, then;
bear the shame of having put your sisters in the right.
53 I will restore them. I will restore Sodom and her
daughters. I will restore Samaria and her daughters;
and, after that, I will restore you along with them,
54 that you may bear your shame and be ashamed of all
55 you have done, and so console them. ·Your sister
Sodom and her daughters will be restored to what they
were. Samaria and her daughters will be restored to
what they were. You and your daughters will be re-
56 stored to what you were. ·Did you not gloat over your
57 sister Sodom when you were still in your finery, ·before

you were stripped naked? Now the daughters of Edom
and all the women around are jeering at you, and the
daughters of the Philistines are treating you like something beneath them, and so are all your neighbors.
⁵⁸ You have brought it on yourself by your brazenness
and filth—it is the Lord Yahweh who speaks.
⁵⁹   For the Lord Yahweh says this: I will treat you as
you deserve, you who have despised your oath even to
⁶⁰ the extent of breaking a covenant, ·but I will remember
the covenant that I made with you when you were a
girl, and I will conclude a covenant with you that shall
⁶¹ last for ever. ·And you for your part will remember
your past behavior and be covered with shame when
I take your elder and younger sisters and make them
your daughters, although this was not included in this
⁶² covenant. ·I am going to renew my covenant with you;
⁶³ and you will learn that I am Yahweh, ·and so remember and be covered with shame, and in your confusion
be reduced to silence, when I have pardoned you for
all that you have done—it is the Lord Yahweh who
speaks.' "

**The allegory of the eagle**

1  ¹⁷ The word of Yahweh was addressed to me as
2       follows, ·"Son of man, ask them a riddle; pro-
3 pound a parable to the House of Israel. ·Say, 'The
Lord Yahweh says this:

> A large eagle,ᵃ with huge wings
> and a wide span,
> covered with speckled feathers,
> came to Lebanon.
> He took hold of the top of the cedar,
4 > plucked off the top branch,
> carried it off to the land of merchants,
> and set it down in a city of shopkeepers.
5 > Then he carried off a seedling vine,
> and planted it in fertile soil;
> by the side of a wide stream,
> as a border he set it.
6 > The seedling grew, and turned into a vine,
> not tall but well spread out;

**17 a.** Nebuchadnezzar; see interpretation in vv.12–18.

its branches grew up toward the eagle,
its roots grew down.
It turned into a vine;
it sent out stems and put out sprays.

7 There was another large eagle,
with huge wings and thickly feathered.
And now the vine twisted its roots toward him,
stretched its branches toward him
away from the bed where it was planted
for him to water them.

8 It was in a fertile field, by the side of a wide
stream,
that the vine had been planted,
to grow shoots, bear fruit
and become a noble vine.'

9 Say, 'The Lord Yahweh says this:
Will this vine thrive?
Will not the eagle break its roots,
and snap up the fruit,
so that all the new leaves will wither when they
shoot?
It will take no effort and no strong nation
to pull it up by the roots.

10 It is planted there; will it thrive?
Will it not shrivel when the east wind blows?
It will wither on the soil where it was growing.' "

11 The word of Yahweh was addressed to me as follows:
12 "Say to that set of rebels, 'Do you not know what
this means?' Say this, 'Listen; the king of Babylon came
to Jerusalem; he carried away the king and the princes,
13 and took them to where he lives in Babylon. •He took
a member of the royal family and made a treaty with
him, forcing him to swear loyalty, after having already
14 deported the chief men of the land, •so that the kingdom would remain modest and without ambition and
15 so maintain his treaty faithfully. •But the prince rebelled and sent envoys to Egypt, asking for horses and
a large number of troops. Is he going to thrive? Will
a man who has done this go unpunished? Can he
16 break a treaty and go unpunished? •As I live, I swear—
it is the Lord Yahweh who speaks: In Babylon, in the
country of the king who put him on the throne, whose
oath he has ignored, whose treaty he has broken, there

17 will he die. ·Despite the pharaoh's great army and
hordes of men, he will not be able to save him by fighting, however many earthworks are raised, however
18 many trenches dug to the loss of many lives. ·He has
ignored the oath and broken the treaty by which he
was bound. He has done all this and shall not go unpunished.

19      'And so, the Lord Yahweh says this: As I live, I
swear: my oath which he has ignored, my treaty which
he has broken, I will make them both recoil on his
20 own head. ·I mean to throw my net over him and catch
him in my mesh; I mean to take him to Babylon and
21 punish him there for breaking his oath to me. ·The pick
of his army will fall by the sword, and the survivors
be scattered to all the winds. And so you will learn that
I, Yahweh, have spoken.

22      'The Lord Yahweh says this:

> From the top of the cedar,
> from the highest branch I will take a shoot
> and plant it myself on a very high mountain.

23      I will plant it myself on the high mountain of
> Israel.
> It will sprout branches and bear fruit,
> and become a noble cedar.
> Every kind of bird will live beneath it,
> every winged creature rest in the shade of its
> branches.

24      And every tree of the field will learn that I,
> Yahweh, am the one
> who stunts tall trees and makes the low ones
> grow,
> who withers green trees and makes the withered
> green.
> I, Yahweh, have spoken, and I will do it.' "

## Individual responsibility

1   18 The word of Yahweh was addressed to me as
2      follows, ·"Why do you keep repeating this proverb in the land of Israel:

> The fathers have eaten unripe grapes;
> and the children's teeth are set on edge?

3      "As I live—it is the Lord Yahweh who speaks—there

will no longer be any reason to repeat this proverb in

4 Israel. ·See now: all life belongs to me; the father's
life and the son's life, both alike belong to me. The
man who has sinned, he is the one who shall die.

5/6    "The upright man is law-abiding and honest; ·he
does not eat on the mountains[a] or raise his eyes to the
idols of the House of Israel, does not seduce his neighbor's wife or sleep with a woman during her periods.

7 He oppresses no one, returns pledges, never steals, gives
his own bread to the hungry, his clothes to the naked.

8 He never charges usury on loans, takes no interest,
abstains from evil, gives honest judgment between man

9 and man, ·keeps my laws and sincerely respects my
observances—such a man is truly upright. It is Yahweh
who speaks.

10    "But if anyone has a son prone to violence and
11 bloodshed, who commits one of these misdeeds—·even
though the father never has—a son who dares to eat
on the mountains and to seduce his neighbor's wife,

12 who oppresses the poor and needy, steals, fails to return pledges, raises his eyes to idols, engages in filthy

13 practices, ·charges usury on loans and takes interest,
then this son shall certainly not live; having committed
all these appalling crimes he will have to die, and his
blood be on his own head.

14    "But if he in turn has a son who, in spite of seeing
all the sins that his father has committed, does not

15 imitate him, ·does not eat on the mountains or raise
his eyes to the idols of the House of Israel, does not

16 seduce his neighbor's wife, ·oppresses no one, takes
no pledges, never steals, gives his own bread to the

17 hungry, clothes to the naked, ·abstains from evil, does
not charge usury or take interest, respects my observances and keeps my laws, he will not die for his father's

18 sins, this son shall certainly live. ·Because the father
was violent, robbed others and never did good among

19 my people, be sure he shall die for his sins. ·But you
object, 'Why does the son not suffer for the sins of his
father?' The son, however, has been law-abiding and
honest, has kept all my laws and followed them, and

20 so he shall certainly live. ·The man who has sinned is
the one who must die; a son is not to suffer for the sins
of his father, nor a father for the sins of his son. To

the upright man his integrity will be credited, to the
wicked his wickedness.

21    "But if the wicked man renounces all the sins he has
committed, respects my laws and is law-abiding and
22  honest, he will certainly live; he will not die. ·All the
sins he committed will be forgotten from then on; he
shall live because of the integrity he has practiced.
23  What! Am I likely to take pleasure in the death of a
wicked man—it is the Lord Yahweh who speaks—and
not prefer to see him renounce his wickedness and
live?

24    "But if the upright man renounces his integrity, commits sin, copies the wicked man and practices every
kind of filth, is he to live? All the integrity he has practiced shall be forgotten from then on; but this is because he himself has broken faith and committed sin,
25  and for this he shall die. ·But you object, 'What the
Lord does is unjust.' Listen, you House of Israel: is
what I do unjust? Is it not what you do that is unjust?
26  When the upright man renounces his integrity to commit sin and dies because of this, he dies because of the
27  evil that he himself has committed. ·When the sinner
renounces sin to become law-abiding and honest, he
28  deserves to live. ·He has chosen to renounce all his
previous sins; he shall certainly live; he shall not die.
29  And yet the House of Israel objects, 'What the Lord
does is unjust.' Is what I do unjust, you House of Is-
30  rael? Is it not what you do that is unjust? ·House of
Israel, in future I mean to judge each of you by what
he does—it is the Lord Yahweh who speaks. Repent,
31  renounce all your sins, avoid all occasions of sin! ·Shake
off all the sins you have committed against me, and
make yourselves a new heart and a new spirit! Why
32  are you so anxious to die, House of Israel? ·I take no
pleasure in the death of anyone—it is the Lord Yahweh
who speaks. Repent and live!

**A lamentation over the rulers of Israel**

1  **19** "As for you, raise a dirge for the princes of
2        Israel. ·Say:

'What was your mother? A lioness
surrounded by lions;

**18 a.** In sacrificial meals on the "high places."

lying among the cubs
she nursed her whelps.

3 She reared one of her whelps
and it grew into a young lion;
he learned to tear his prey;
he became a man-eater.

4 The nations combined against him;
he was caught in their pit;
they dragged him off with hooks
to the land of Egypt.[a]

5 Her expectation thwarted,
her hope dashed,
she took another of her whelps
and made a young lion of him.

6 He grew to prowl with other lions,
and grew into a young lion;
he learned to tear his prey;
he became a man-eater.

7 He stormed their palaces,
and sacked their cities;
the country and its inhabitants were alarmed
by the sound of his roars.

8 The nations marched out against him
from the surrounding provinces;
they spread their net for him;
he was caught in their pit.

9 They caged him with hooks
(they took him to the king of Babylon);
they took him into a fortress,
so that his voice could never again be heard
on the mountains of Israel.[b]

10 'Your mother was like a vine
planted beside the water,
fruitful and leafy,
because the water flowed so full.

11 It put out strong branches
that turned to royal scepters;
they reached up, reached so high
they touched the clouds;
men admired them for their height
and their thick foliage.

12 But it was rooted up

and thrown on the ground;
the east wind dried up its fruit;
it was broken up;
its strong branch withered away;
fire consumed it all.
13  Now it has been transplanted into the desert,
the waterless country of drought;
14  fire has come out of its stem,
consumed its branches and fruit.
No more strong branch for her,
no more kingly scepter.' "

This is a dirge; it was used as such.

### An account of Israel's infidelities

1  20 In the seventh year, on the tenth day of the fifth
month,[a] some of the elders of Israel came to
2  consult Yahweh and sat down in front of me. ·The
3  word of Yahweh was addressed to me as follows, ·"Son
of man, speak to the elders of Israel. Say, 'The Lord
Yahweh says this: Have you come to consult me?' As
I live, I am not going to let myself be consulted by
4  them—it is the Lord Yahweh who speaks. ·Are you
ready to judge them? Are you ready to judge them,
son of man? Confront them with the filthy practices of
5  their fathers. ·Say, 'The Lord Yahweh says this: On
the day when I chose Israel, when I raised my hand
over the descendants of the House of Jacob, I told
them then in the land of Egypt; I raised my hand over
6  them and said: I am Yahweh your God. ·On that day
I raised my hand over them and swore to lead them out
of the land of Egypt and bring them into the land I had
chosen for them, a land where milk and honey flow,
7  and the noblest of them all. ·I said: Each one of you
must reject those horrors that attract you; do not pol-
lute yourselves with the idols of Egypt; I am Yahweh,
8  your God. ·But they rebelled against me and would
not listen to me. Not one of them rejected those horrors
that attracted them; they did not give up the idols of
Egypt. I resolved to discharge my anger on them and

19 a. King Jehoahaz, deposed and deported to Egypt in 609.
b. Jehoiachin, taken captive to Babylon in 597.
20 a. July–August 591.

⁹ exhaust my fury against them in Egypt. ·But respect
for my own name kept me from allowing it to be profaned in the opinion of the nations among whom they
were living, for I had given them my word that in the
sight of those nations I would lead my people out of
¹⁰ the land of Egypt. ·So I led them out of Egypt and
¹¹ into the wilderness. ·I gave them my laws and taught
them my observances, which must be practiced by all
¹² who want to live. ·I even gave them my sabbaths to be
a sign between me and them, so that they might learn
¹³ that I, Yahweh, am the one who sanctifies them. ·The
House of Israel, however, rebelled against me in the
wilderness; they refused to keep my laws, they scorned
my observances, which must be practiced by all who
wish to live, and they profaned my sabbaths. Then I
resolved to discharge my anger on them in the wilder-
¹⁴ ness and to destroy them. ·But respect for my own
name kept me from allowing it to be profaned in the
opinion of the nations, in whose sight I had brought
¹⁵ them out. ·However, I did raise my hand over them
in the wilderness and swear that I would not lead them
to the land which I had given them, a land where milk
¹⁶ and honey flow, the noblest of them all, ·since they
had scorned my observances, had refused to keep my
laws and had profaned my sabbaths, their hearts being
¹⁷ so attached to idols. ·In spite of this, I took pity on
them; I refrained from destroying them, and I did not
kill them all in the wilderness.
¹⁸    I said to their children in the wilderness: Do not live
by your ancestors' standards, do not practice the observances they practiced, do not defile yourselves with
¹⁹ their idols. ·I am Yahweh your God. Keep my laws,
²⁰ respect my observances and practice them. ·Keep my
sabbaths holy; let them be a sign between me and you,
so that men may learn that I am Yahweh your God.
²¹ The sons, however, rebelled against me; they refused
to keep my laws, they did not respect or practice my
observances, which must be practiced by all who want
to live; they profaned my sabbaths. I then resolved to
discharge my anger on them and exhaust my fury
²² against them in the wilderness. ·But I restrained my
hand; respect for my own name kept me from allowing
it to be profaned in the opinion of the nations, under

23 whose eyes I had brought them out. •Once again, however, I raised my hand over them in the wilderness, swearing to scatter them throughout the nations and
24 disperse them in foreign countries, •because they had not followed my observances but had rejected my laws and profaned my sabbaths, and because they had kept
25 their eyes fastened on their ancestors' idols. •I even gave them laws that were not good and observances
26 by which they could never live; •and I polluted them with their own offerings, making them sacrifice all their first-born; which was to punish them, so that they would learn that I am Yahweh.'

27    "For this reason, son of man, speak to the House of Israel. Say to them, 'The Lord Yahweh says this: Here is another way by which your ancestors outraged me,
28 behaving treacherously to me, •even though I led them into the land which I had solemnly sworn to give them. There they saw all sorts of high hills, all kinds of leafy trees, and there they performed their sacrifices and made offerings that provoked my anger; there they laid their appeasing fragrance and poured their libations.
29 I said to them: What is the name of the high place where you go? And they gave, and still give it, the
30 name of Bamah.'[b] •Very well, say to the House of Israel, 'The Lord Yahweh says this: Since you insist on defiling yourselves by behaving like your fathers, by
31 whoring with their idols, •by offering your gifts and by burning your children as sacrifices, polluting yourselves with your pack of idols to this very day, how can I let you consult me, House of Israel? As I live—it is the Lord Yahweh who speaks—I am not going to let myself
32 be consulted by you. •And that dream ever haunting your mind will never come true, when you say: We shall be like the nations, like foreign tribes worshiping
33 wood and stone. •As I live I swear it—it is the Lord Yahweh who speaks—I am the one who will reign over you, with a strong hand and outstretched arm, through
34 the discharge of my anger. •With a strong hand and outstretched arm, through the discharge of my anger, I will bring you out from the peoples and gather you

b. There is a pun in the Hebrew words for "high place" and "where you go."

together from foreign countries among which you have
³⁵ been scattered. ·I will lead you into the Desert of the
³⁶ Nations[c] and condemn you to your face. ·As I judged
your fathers in the desert of the land of Egypt, so will
³⁷ I judge you—it is the Lord Yahweh who speaks. ·I mean
to make you pass under my crook[d] and I will bring a
³⁸ few of you back; ·I will sort out the rebels who have
rebelled against me. I intend to bring them out of the
country where they are staying, but they shall not enter
the land of Israel, and you will learn that I am Yahweh.
³⁹ House of Israel, the Lord Yahweh says this: Go on,
all of you, worship your idols, but I swear that you will
hear me in the end. You will stop profaning my Holy
⁴⁰ Name with your offerings and your idols. ·For on my
holy mountain, on the high mountain of Israel—it is the
Lord Yahweh who speaks—is where the whole House
of Israel, resettled in the country, will worship me.
There I will welcome you, and there expect your presents, your choicest gifts and all your holy offerings.
⁴¹ I will welcome you like an appeasing fragrance when
I bring you out from among the peoples; I mean to
gather you together from the foreign countries in which
you have been scattered; through you I intend to display
⁴² my holiness for all the nations to see; ·and you will
learn that I am Yahweh, when I bring you back to the
soil of Israel, to the land I solemnly swore to give to
⁴³ your fathers. ·There you will remember your past behavior and all the misdeeds by which you have defiled
yourselves, and you will loathe yourselves for all the
⁴⁴ sins that you have committed. ·Then you will learn that
I am Yahweh, when I treat you as respect for my own
name requires, and not as your wicked behavior and
corrupt actions deserve, House of Israel. It is the Lord
Yahweh who speaks.' "

### The sword of Yahweh

¹
45.⅔46 **21** The word of Yahweh was addressed to me as
follows, ·"Son of man, turn to the right; utter
your word toward the south, prophesy against the forest
⅜47 land of the Negeb. ·Say to the forest of the Negeb,
'Hear the word of Yahweh. The Lord Yahweh says
this: Listen; I am about to kindle a fire in you that will
burn up every green tree as well as every dry one; it

will be an unquenchable blaze and every face will be
⁴/₄₈ scorched by it from the Negeb to the North. ·All mankind will see that it was I, Yahweh, who kindled
⁵/₄₉ it, and it will not be put out.'" ·I said, "Lord Yahweh,
21:⁶/₁ they say of me, 'What a storyteller this man is!'" ·The
⁷/₂ word of Yahweh was addressed to me as follows, ·"Son
of man, turn toward Jerusalem, curse their sanctuary
⁸/₃ and prophesy against the land of Israel. ·Say to the
land of Israel, 'Yahweh says this: Now I set myself
against you; I am about to unsheathe my sword and
⁹/₄ to kill both upright man and sinner. ·My sword will
leave its sheath to kill upright and sinful alike and turn
¹⁰/₅ against all mankind from the Negeb to the North. ·All
mankind is going to learn that I, Yahweh, am the one
who has drawn the sword from its sheath; it will not
go back again.'

¹¹/₆    "Son of man, groan as though your heart were breaking. Bitterly utter your groans where they can see you.
¹²/₇ And if they say, 'Why these groans?' reply, 'The news
has made all hearts sink, has numbed hands, troubled
spirits, caused knees to tremble. Now it has come, it
is here; it is the Lord Yahweh who speaks.'"

¹³    The word of Yahweh was addressed to me as fol-
¹⁴/₈,₉ lows, ·"Son of man, prophesy. Say, 'The Lord says
this.' Say:

> 'The sword, the sword
> sharpened and polished!
¹⁵/₁₀    Sharpened for slaughter,
> polished to flash like lightning . . .
¹⁶/₁₁    polished only to be wielded,
> sharpened and polished to fit the slaughterer's
> hand!
¹⁷/₁₂    Yes, shout and howl, son of man;
> it is meant for my people,
> for all the princes of Israel, doomed like my
> people to the sword.
¹⁸/₁₃    So beat your breast; ·this is no first attempt,
> and what would happen, were there no haughty
> scepter?
> —it is the Lord Yahweh who speaks.

c. The Syrian desert.
d. To be counted.

<sup>19</sup><sub>14</sub> Son of man, prophesy and clap your hands.
Let the sword be twice, three times, as cruel,
the butcher's sword,
the great sword of slaughter, menacing all
around.

<sup>20</sup><sub>15</sub> To make hearts sink and to increase the number
of victims
I have posted a sword at every gate
to flash like lightning, polished for havoc.

<sup>21</sup><sub>16</sub> Behind! To the right! To the left! In front!
<sup>22</sup><sub>17</sub> And I too will clap my hands;
I will exhaust my wrath.
I, Yahweh, have spoken.' "

### The king of Babylon at the crossroads

<sup>23</sup><sub>18</sub>  The word of Yahweh was addressed to me as fol-
<sup>24</sup><sub>19</sub> lows, ·"Son of man, mark out two roads for the sword
of the king of Babylon to come along, making both of
them begin from the same country. Put up a signpost
<sup>25</sup><sub>20</sub> where they begin, showing the way to a city, ·showing
the sword the way to Rabbah of the Ammonites, and
<sup>26</sup><sub>21</sub> the way to Judah, to the fortress of Jerusalem. ·For
the king of Babylon has halted at the fork where these
two roads diverge, to take the omens. He has shaken
the arrows, questioned the teraphim, inspected the liver.
<sup>27</sup><sub>22</sub> Into his right hand the lot for Jerusalem falls; there
he must set up battering-rams, give the word for slaugh-
ter, raise the war cry, level battering-rams against the
<sup>28</sup><sub>23</sub> gates, cast up earthworks, build entrenchments. ·The
citizens believe that these omens are idle, whatever
oaths have been sworn. But he is evidence of their
<sup>29</sup><sub>24</sub> crimes, and these will bring about their capture. ·And
so, thus says the Lord Yahweh. Since you give evidence
of your crimes by parading your sins and flaunting
your wickedness in everything you do, and since this
evidence is now produced against you, you will be pun-
<sup>30</sup><sub>25</sub> ished. ·As for you, prince of Israel, vile criminal on
<sup>31</sup><sub>26</sub> the last of whose crimes the day is about to dawn, ·the
Lord Yahweh says this: They will take away your tur-
ban and remove your crown; everything will be
changed; the low will be high and the high brought
<sup>32</sup><sub>27</sub> low. ·To ruin, and to ruin on ruin, am I going to bring
it, to such ruin as was never known before this man

came who is appointed to inflict the punishment which
I am determined to impose on it.

## The punishment of Ammon

33
28  "Son of man, prophesy and say, 'The Lord Yahweh
says this: To the Ammonites with their insults, say:
The sword, the sword is drawn for slaughter, polished
34
29  to destroy, to flash like lightning—while you have
empty visions and consult lying omens—to slaughter
the vile criminals on the last of whose crimes the day
35
30  is about to dawn. ·Put it back in the scabbard. In the
place where you were created, in the country where
36
31  you were born, there I will judge you; ·I am going to
discharge my anger on you, blow the flames of my fury
against you and hand you over to barbarous men whose
37
32  trade is destruction. ·You will be fuel to the fire, your
blood will flow through the country, you will leave no
memory behind you; for I, Yahweh, have spoken.'"

## The crimes of Jerusalem

1   **22** The word of Yahweh was addressed to me as
2       follows, ·"Son of man, are you prepared to
judge? Are you prepared to judge the murderous city?
3   Confront her with all her filthy crimes! ·Say, 'The Lord
Yahweh says this: City shedding blood inside yourself
to bring your hour closer, setting up idols on your soil
4   to defile yourself, ·you have incurred guilt by the blood
you have shed, you have defiled yourself with the idols
you have made, you have brought your hour closer,
you have come to the end of your time. And so I have
made you an object of scorn to the nations and a laugh-
5   ingstock to every country. ·Near and far, they will scoff
6   at you, the turbulent city with a tarnished name: ·where
all the princes of Israel live, each one busy shedding
7   blood, and a law to himself; ·where people despise their
fathers and mothers; where they ill-treat the settler;
8   where they oppress the widow and the orphan; ·where
you have no reverence for my sanctuaries and profane
9   my sabbaths; ·where informers incite to bloodshed;
where there are people who eat on the mountains and
10  couple promiscuously; ·where men uncover their
father's nakedness; where they force women in their
11  unclean condition; ·where one man engages in filthy

practices with his neighbor's wife, another defiles himself with his daughter-in-law, another violates his sister,
12 his own father's daughter; ·where people take bribes for shedding blood; you charge usury and interest, you rob your neighbor by extortion, you forget all about me—it is the Lord Yahweh who speaks.

13 'Now I will clap my hands at your acts of banditry
14 and the blood that flows in you. ·Will your heart be able to resist, will your hands be strong on the day I call you to account? I, Yahweh, have spoken, and I will do it.

15 'I mean to disperse you throughout the nations, to scatter you in foreign countries, and to take your foul-
16 ness from you. ·I shall be dishonored by you in the opinion of the nations; and so you will learn that I am Yahweh.' "

17 The word of Yahweh was addressed to me as fol-
18 lows, ·"Son of man, the House of Israel, as I see it, is base metal; they are all copper, tin, iron, lead, in the
19 melting pot; they are base metal. ·And so, the Lord Yahweh says this: Since you are all base metal, I will
20 collect you inside Jerusalem. ·As silver, copper, iron, lead and tin are thrown into the melting pot together, and the fire is stoked underneath to melt it all down, so I will collect you in my furious anger and melt you
21 down; ·I will collect you and stoke the fire of my fury
22 for you, and melt you down inside the city. ·As silver is melted in the melting pot, so you will be melted down inside the city; and thus you will learn that I, Yahweh, am the one who has discharged my anger on you."

23 The word of Yahweh was addressed to me as fol-
24 lows, ·"Son of man, say to her, 'You are a land that has not received rain or shower on the day of anger,
25 and whose princes are like a roaring lion tearing its prey inside her. They have eaten the people, seized
26 wealth and jewels and widowed many inside her. ·Her priests have violated my Law and desecrated my sanctuaries; they have drawn no distinction between sacred and profane, they have not taught people the difference between clean and unclean; they have turned their eyes away from my sabbaths and I have been dishonored
27 by them. ·Her leaders in the city are like wolves tearing their prey, shedding blood and killing people to steal

28 their possessions. ·Her prophets have whitewashed these
crimes with their empty visions and lying prophecies.
They have said: Yahweh says this; although Yahweh
29 has not spoken. ·The people of the country have taken
to extortion and banditry; they have oppressed the poor
30 and needy and ill-treated the settler for no reason. ·I
have been looking for someone among them to build
a wall and man the breach in front of me, to defend
the country and prevent me from destroying it; but I
31 have not found anyone. ·Hence I have discharged my
anger on them; I have destroyed them in the fire of my
fury. I have made their conduct recoil on their own
heads—it is the Lord Yahweh who speaks.'"

### An allegorical history of Jerusalem and Samaria

1 **23** The word of Yahweh was addressed to me as
2 follows, ·"Son of man, there were once two
3 women, daughters of the same mother. ·They became
prostitutes in Egypt, when they were girls. There their
nipples were handled, there their virgin breasts were
4 first fondled. ·Their names were: Oholah the elder,
Oholibah her sister. They belonged to me and bore
sons and daughters. As regards their names, Samaria
5 is Oholah, Jerusalem Oholibah. ·Now Oholah played
the whore, although she belonged to me; she lusted
6 for her lovers, her neighbors the Assyrians, ·dressed
in purple, governors and nobles, all of them young and
7 desirable, and skillful horsemen. ·She granted them her
favors—they were all the flower of the Assyrians—and
she defiled herself with all the idols of all those she
8 lusted for. ·She did not renounce the whoring begun
in Egypt, where men had slept with her from her girlhood, fondling her virgin breasts, debauching her.
9     "And that is why I have handed her over to her
10 lovers, to those Assyrians for whom she lusted. ·They
uncovered her nakedness, they seized her sons and
daughters and put her to the sword. She became no-
torious among women for the justice done on her.
11     "Though her sister Oholibah saw all this, her own
lust and whorings were even more shameful than her
12 sister's. ·She lusted for her neighbors the Assyrians,
governor and nobles, dressed in sumptuous clothes,
13 skillful horsemen, all young and desirable. ·I saw that

she was unchaste, that both sisters were as bad as each
14 other. ·She began whoring worse than ever; no sooner
had she seen wall carvings of men, paintings of Chal-
15 daeans colored vermilion, ·men with sashes around
their waists and elaborate turbans on their heads, all
so imperious of bearing, portraits of Babylonians from
16 Chaldaea, ·than she fell in love with them at first sight
17 and sent messengers to them in Chaldaea. ·The Babylonians came to her, shared her love bed and defiled
her with their debauchery. Once defiled she lost interest
18 in them. ·She flaunted her whoring, she stripped naked;
then I turned away from her as I had turned away
19 from her sister. ·She began whoring worse than ever,
remembering her girlhood, when she had played the
20 whore in the land of Egypt, ·when she had been infatuated by profligates big-membered as donkeys, ejacu-
lating as violently as stallions.
21     "You were hankering for the debauchery of your
girlhood, when they used to handle your nipples in
22 Egypt and fondle your young breasts. ·And so, Oholibah, the Lord Yahweh says this: I intend to call up
against you those of your lovers in whom you have
lost interest; I will bring them against you from every-
23 where, ·the Babylonians and all the Chaldaeans, the
men of Pekod and Shoa and Koa,ᵃ and all the Assyrians with them, young and desirable, all governors
24 and nobles, all famous officers and horsemen. ·They
will advance on you from the North, with chariots and
wagons, at the head of a horde of peoples. From every
side they will arm against you with shield, buckler and
helmet. I have told them to pass sentence on you; they
25 will pass sentence on you as they think fit. ·I shall
direct my jealousy against you; they will treat you with
fury; they will cut off your nose and ears, and what is
left of your family will fall by the sword; they will
seize your sons and daughters, and what is left of you
26 will be burned. ·They will strip off your garments and
27 rob you of your jewels. ·I mean to put an end to your
debauchery and to the whorings you began in Egypt;
you will not look to the Egyptians any more, you will
28 never think of them again. ·For the Lord Yahweh says
this: I now hand you over to those you hate, to those
29 in whom you have lost interest. ·They will treat you

with hatred, they will rob you of the fruit of your labors
and leave you completely naked. And thus your shameful whoring will be exposed. Your debauchery and your
30 whorings ·are the cause of these afflictions, since by
playing the whore with the nations you have defiled
31 yourself with their idols. ·As you have copied your
32 sister's behavior, I will put her cup in your hand. ·The
Lord Yahweh says this:

> You will drink your sister's cup,
> a cup that is wide and deep,
> leading to laughter and mockery,
> so ample the draught it holds.
33 You will be filled with drunkenness and sorrow.
> Cup of affliction and devastation,
> the cup of your sister Samaria,
34 you will drink it, you will drain it;
> then it will be shattered to pieces
> and lacerate your breast.

I have spoken—it is the Lord Yahweh who speaks.
35    "And so, the Lord Yahweh says this: Since you have
forgotten me and have turned your back on me, you
too will have to bear the weight of your debauchery
36 and whorings." ·And Yahweh said to me, "Son of
man, are you willing to judge Oholah and Oholibah
37 and charge them with their filthy crimes? ·They have
been adulteresses, their hands are dripping with blood,
they have committed adultery with their idols. As for
the children they had borne me, they have made them
38 pass through the fire to be consumed. ·And here is
something else they have done to me: they have defiled
my sanctuary the same day and have profaned my
39 sabbaths. ·The same day as sacrificing their children
to their idols, they have been to my sanctuary and
profaned it. Yes, this is what they have done in my
own house.
40    "Worse still, these men summoned from distant
countries, invited by messenger, arrived; you bathed
41 and painted your eyes, put on your jewels ·and sat on
a sumptuous bed, by which stood a table on which you
42 had put my incense and my oil. ·The revelry of a care-

23 a. Peoples from the east of Babylonia.

free company re-echoed because of the crowd of men brought in from the desert; they put bracelets on the women's arms and magnificent crowns on their heads. <sup>43</sup> I thought: The prostitutes are at work in the house of a woman worn out with adulteries. And she is still playing <sup>44</sup> the whore too, ·and men keep visiting her just like a prostitute, just as they went to those profligate women <sup>45</sup> Oholah and Oholibah. ·But upright men will judge them as adulteresses and murderesses are judged, since they are adulteresses and their hands are dripping with blood.

<sup>46</sup>    "The Lord Yahweh says this: Summon an assembly to deal with them, and hand them over to terror and <sup>47</sup> pillage; ·let the assembly stone them and hack them to death with the sword; let their sons and daughters <sup>48</sup> be slaughtered and their houses be set on fire. ·I mean to purge the land of debauchery; all the women will thus be warned, and ape your debauchery no more. <sup>49</sup> Your debauchery will recoil on your own heads, and you will bear the weight of your idolatrous sins; and so you will learn that I am the Lord Yahweh."

### A prophecy of the siege of Jerusalem

<sup>1</sup> **24** In the ninth year, on the tenth day of the tenth month,<sup>a</sup> the word of Yahweh was addressed to <sup>2</sup> me as follows, ·"Son of man, write down today's date, since this is the very day the king of Babylon has laid <sup>3</sup> siege to Jerusalem. ·So pronounce a parable for this set of rebels. Say, 'The Lord Yahweh says this:

> Put the pot on the fire;
> put it on; pour water into it.

<sup>4</sup>
> Put cuts of meat in too,
> the best cuts, leg and shoulder.
> Fill it with the best bones.

<sup>5</sup>
> Take the best of the flock.
> Then heap wood underneath;
> make the pot boil and bubble
> until even the bones are cooked.

<sup>6</sup>    For the Lord Yahweh says this:

> Trouble for the bloodstained city,
> that rusty cooking pot

whose rust can never be scoured away!
Empty it scrap by scrap, drawing no lots.

7  For her blood is in her;
she has put it on the naked rock;
she has not shed it on the ground to hide it in
dust.

8  To make my anger overflow, to take revenge,
I have put her blood on the naked rock, un-
hidden.

9  So, the Lord Yahweh says this:

Trouble for the bloodstained city!
I too plan to build a great fire.

10  Heap on the wood, light it,
cook the meat, prepare the spices,
let the bones burn.

11  Set the pot empty to heat on the coals;
let the bronze glow red-hot,
the filth inside melt away,
the rust inside be consumed.

12  But all that rust will not disappear in the flames. ·I
13  have tried to purge you of the filth of your debauchery,
but you would not let yourself be purged of your filth.
So now you will not be purged until my anger has been
14  exhausted against you. ·I, Yahweh, have spoken; my
word will come true; I shall act and not relent; I shall
show no pity, no compassion. I intend to judge you as
your conduct and actions deserve—it is the Lord Yahweh who speaks.' "

## The personal ordeals of the prophet

15  The word of Yahweh was addressed to me as fol-
16  lows, ·"Son of man, I am about to deprive you suddenly of the delight of your eyes. But you are not to
lament, not to weep, not to let your tears run down.
17  Groan in silence, do not go into mourning for the dead,
knot your turban around your head, put your sandals
on your feet, do not cover your beard, do not eat
18  common bread." ·I told this to the people in the morning, and my wife died in the evening, and the next

**24 a.** December 589–January 588.

¹⁹ morning I did as I had been ordered. ·The people then said to me, "Are you not going to explain what meaning
²⁰ these actions have for us?" ·I replied, "The word of
²¹ Yahweh has been addressed to me as follows, ·'Say to the House of Israel: The Lord Yahweh says this. I am about to profane my sanctuary, the pride of your strength, the delight of your eyes, the passion of your souls. Those of your sons and daughters whom you
²² have left behind will fall by the sword. ·And you are to do as I have done; you must not cover your beards
²³ or eat common bread; ·you must keep your turbans on your heads and your sandals on your feet; you must not lament or weep. You shall waste away owing to
²⁴ your sins and groan among yourselves. ·Ezekiel is to be a sign for you. You are to do just as he has done. And when this happens, you will learn that I am Yahweh.'

²⁵ "And, son of man, on the very day I deprive them of their sons and daughters who are their strength, their pride and glory, the delight of their eyes, the joy
²⁶ of their hearts, ·on that very day a fugitive will come
²⁷ and bring you news of this. ·On that day your mouth will be opened to speak to the fugitive; you will speak and not be dumb any more; you are to be a sign for them, and they will learn that I am Yahweh."

## II. ORACLES AGAINST THE NATIONS

### Against the Ammonites

¹ **25** The word of Yahweh was addressed to me as
² follows, ·"Son of man, turn toward the Am-
³ monites and prophesy against them. ·Say to the Ammonites, 'Hear the word of the Lord Yahweh. The Lord Yahweh says this:

You cried: Aha! over my sanctuary when it was profaned, and over the land of Israel when it was ravaged, and over the House of Judah when it went into
⁴ exile, ·and because of that I am going to hand you over to the sons of the East*ᵃ*; they will pitch their camps inside your frontiers, they will settle there. They are

5 going to eat your fruit, and drink your milk. ·I intend
to turn Rabbah into a camel yard and the towns of
Ammon into sheepfolds. And so you will learn that I
am Yahweh.

6     The Lord Yahweh says this: Since you have clapped
your hands and danced for joy, inwardly full of malice
7 against the land of Israel, ·I mean to stretch out my
hand against you for this; I will hand you over to be
looted by the peoples, obliterate you as a nation, wipe
you out as a country. I will reduce you to nothing,
and so you will learn that I am Yahweh.

### Against Moab

8     The Lord Yahweh says this:
Since Moab and Seir[b] have said: Look at the House
9 of Judah; it is no different from any other nation; ·very
well, I will strip the hillsides of Moab bare and destroy
her towns throughout the country, including her pride,
10 Beth-jeshimoth, Baal-meon and Kiriath-aim. ·I shall
hand her over to the sons of the East, the enemies of
the Ammonites; I shall hand her over so that the Am-
11 monites will not even be remembered as a nation. ·Thus
shall I punish Moab, and everyone will learn that I
am Yahweh.

### Against Edom

12     The Lord Yahweh says this:
Since Edom has taken revenge on the House of
13 Judah and committed great crimes in doing so, ·very
well, the Lord Yahweh says this: I will stretch out my
hand against Edom too and wipe out all the men and
animals in the country. I shall reduce it to desert; peo-
14 ple will be put to the sword from Teman to Dedan. ·I
shall unleash my revenge on Edom by means of my
people Israel. They will treat Edom as my anger and
fury dictate, and everyone will learn that this is my
vengeance—it is the Lord Yahweh who speaks.

### Against the Philistines

15     The Lord Yahweh says this:
Since the Philistines have acted in revenge and taken

25 a. The nomadic Arabs.
b. Edom.

revenge maliciously, and with persistent hatred have
16 done their best to destroy, ·very well, thus speaks the
Lord Yahweh: I will stretch out my hand against the
Philistines; I shall destroy the Cherethites*c* and wipe
17 out all the rest of the coastal peoples. ·I shall perform
frightful acts of vengeance and inflict furious punishments on them; and when I exact vengeance on them
they will learn that I am Yahweh.' "

## Against Tyre

1 **26** In the eleventh year, on the first of the month,*a*
the word of Yahweh was addressed to me as
follows:

2　　　"Son of man, since Tyre has jeered at Jerusalem,
　　　'Aha! It is shattered, that gate of nations;
　　　it is opening to me; its wealth is ruined,'
3　　　very well, the Lord Yahweh says this:
　　　Now, Tyre, I set myself against you.
　　　I mean to cause many nations to surge against
　　　　　you
　　　like the sea and its waves.
4　　　They will destroy the walls of Tyre,
　　　they will demolish her towers;
　　　I will sweep away her dust
　　　and leave her a naked rock.
5　　　She will be a drying ground in mid-ocean for
　　　　　fishing nets.
　　　For I have spoken—it is the Lord Yahweh who
　　　　　speaks—
　　　she will be the prey of the nations.
6　　　As for her daughters on the mainland,
　　　these will be put to the sword,
　　　and everyone will learn that I am Yahweh.
7　　　For the Lord Yahweh says this.
　　　From the North, I am sending Nebuchadnezzar,
　　　king of Babylon, king of kings, against Tyre
　　　with horses and chariots and horsemen,
　　　a horde of many races.
8　　　He will put your daughters
　　　on the mainland to the sword.
　　　He will build siegeworks against you,
　　　cast up a mound against you,
　　　raise a siege tower against you;

9     he will break down your walls with his
        battering-rams,
    and demolish your towers with his siege
        engines.[b]

10     His horses are so many their dust will hide you.
    Noise of his horsemen and his chariots and
        wagons
    will make your walls tremble as he rides through
        your gates
    like a man entering a conquered city.

11     His horses' hoofs will trample through your
        streets;
    he will put your people to the sword,
    and throw your massive pillars to the ground.

12     Your wealth will be seized, your merchandise
        looted,
    your walls razed, your luxurious houses shat-
        tered,
    your stones, your timbers, your very dust,
        thrown into the sea.

13     I will stop your music and songs;
    the sound of your harps will not be heard again.

14     I will reduce you to a naked rock,
    and make you into a drying ground for fishing
        nets,
    never to be rebuilt;
    for I, Yahweh, have spoken
    —it is the Lord Yahweh who speaks.

15 The Lord Yahweh says this to Tyre: When they hear
of your fall, the groans of your wounded and the havoc
16 inside your walls, will not the islands shake? ·The rulers
of the sea will all get off their thrones, lay aside their
cloaks and take off their embroidered robes. Dressed
in terror they will sit on the ground unable to stop
trembling, terrified at your fate.
17     "They will raise a dirge and say to you:

    'You are destroyed then, swept from the seas,
    city of pride,

c. Related to, and associated with, the Philistines.
26 a. The year 587–586.
b. The siege, begun by Nebuchadnezzar, lasted thirteen years.

you who were mighty on the sea,
you and your citizens,
who used to terrorize
the continent far and near.

18 Now the islands are trembling
on the day of your fall;
the islands of the sea are terrified by your end.'

19 "For the Lord Yahweh says this:

"When I make you as desolate as any depopulated
city, when I bring up the deep against you and the
20 ocean covers you, ·I will cast you down with those who
go down to the pit, down to the men of old; I will make
you live in the regions underground, in the eternal
solitudes, with those who go down to the pit, so that
you can never come back and be restored to the land
21 of the living. ·I will make you an object of terror; you
will not exist. People will look for you and never find
you again—it is the Lord Yahweh who speaks."

## A lamentation over the fall of Tyre

1 **27** The word of Yahweh was addressed to me as
2 follows, ·"Son of man, raise the dirge over Tyre.
3 Say to Tyre, that city standing at the edge of the sea,
doing business with the nations in innumerable islands,
'The Lord Yahweh says this:

Tyre, you used to say: I am a ship
perfect in beauty.
4 Your frontiers stretched far out to sea;
those who built you made you
perfect in beauty.
5 Cypress from Senir[a] they used
for all your planking.
They took a cedar from Lebanon
to make you a mast.
6 From the tallest ·oaks of Bashan
they made your oars.
They built you a deck of cedar inlaid with ivory
from the Kittim[b] isles.
7 Embroidered linen of Egypt was used for your
sail
and for your flag.

Purple and scarlet from the Elishah islands
formed your deck tent.

8   Men from Sidon and from Arvad<sup>c</sup>
were your oarsmen.
Your sages, Tyre, were aboard
serving as sailors.

9   The elders and craftsmen of Gebal<sup>d</sup> were there
to calk your seams.

All the ships of the sea and the sailors in them visited
10 you to trade with you. ·Men of Persia and Lud and
Put served in your army and were your warriors. They
hung up shield and helmet in you. They brought you
11 glory. ·The sons of Arvad and their army manned your
walls all around and kept watch from your bastions.
They hung their shields all around your walls and
12 helped to make your beauty perfect. ·Tarshish was your
client, profiting from your abundant wealth. People
paid you in silver and iron, tin and lead for your mer-
13 chandise. ·Javan, Tubal and Meshech<sup>e</sup> traded with you.
For your merchandise they bartered men and bronze
14 implements. ·The people of Beth-togarmah<sup>f</sup> traded you
15 horses, chargers, mules. ·The sons of Dedan traded
with you; many shores were your clients; you were
16 paid in ivory tusks and ebony. ·Edom was your client,
because of the variety and quantity of your goods; she
exchanged carbuncles, purple, embroideries, fine linen,
17 coral and rubies against your goods. ·Judah and the
land of Israel also traded with you, supplying you with
18 corn from Minnith, wax, honey, tallow and balm. ·Da-
mascus was your client, because of the plentifulness
of your goods and the immensity of your wealth, fur-
nishing you with wine from Helbon and wool from
19 Zahar. ·Dan and Javan, from Uzal onward, supplied
you with wrought iron, cassia and calamus in exchange
20 for your goods. ·Dedan traded with you in horsecloths.
21 Arabia and even the sheikhs of Kedar were all your

27 a. Hermon.
b. Cyprus; but here it also includes other islands and coastal
settlements.
c. Phoenician coastal towns.
d. Byblos.
e. Greeks.
f. Probably Armenia.

22 clients; they paid in lambs, rams and he-goats. ·The merchants of Sheba and Raamah traded with you; they supplied you with the best quality spices, precious stones
23 and gold against your goods. ·Haran, Canneh and Eden, traders of Sheba, Asshur and Chilmad*g* traded
24 with you. ·They traded rich clothes, embroidered and purple cloaks, multicolored materials and strong plaited
25 cords in your markets. ·The ships of Tarshish crossed the seas for your trade.

> Then you were rich and glorious
> surrounded by the seas.
>
> 26 Out to the open sea
> your oarsmen rowed you.
> The east wind has shattered you,
> surrounded by the seas.
>
> 27 Your riches, your goods, your cargo,
> your crew, your sailors,
> your calkers, your commercial agents,
> all the soldiers
> you carry with you, the whole host
> who are aboard:
> all will sink surrounded by the seas
> on the day of your shipwreck.
>
> 28 When they hear the cries of your sailors
> the coasts will tremble.
>
> 29 Then the oarsmen will all desert
> their ships.
> The sailors and seafaring people
> will stay ashore.
>
> 30 They will raise their voices for you,
> and weep bitterly.
> They will throw dust on their heads,
> and roll in ashes;
>
> 31 they will shave their heads for you,
> and put sackcloth around their waists.
> They will raise a bitter dirge over you,
> in their despair;
>
> 32 they will raise a dirge and mourn for you,
> they will bewail you:
> Who could compare with haughty Tyre
> surrounded by the seas?

33 When you unloaded your goods
to satisfy so many peoples,
you made the kings of the earth rich
with your excess of wealth and goods.

34 Now you are shattered by the waves,
surrounded by the seas.
Your cargo and all your crew
have foundered with you.

35 All those who live in the distant islands
have been horrified at your fate.
Their kings have been panic-stricken,
their faces quite cast down.

36 The traders of the nations
have whistled at your fate,
since you have become an object of dread,
gone for ever.' "

## Against the king of Tyre

1
2 **28** The word of Yahweh was addressed to me as
follows, ·"Son of man, tell the ruler of Tyre,
'The Lord Yahweh says this:

Being swollen with pride,
you have said: I am a god;
I am sitting on the throne of God,
surrounded by the seas.
Though you are a man and not a god,
you consider yourself the equal of God.

3 You are wiser now than Daniel;
there is no sage as wise as you.

4 By your wisdom and your intelligence
you have amassed great wealth;
you have piles of gold and silver
inside your treasure houses.

5 Such is your skill in trading,
your wealth has continued to increase,
and with this your heart has grown more
arrogant.

6 And so, the Lord Yahweh says this:
Since you consider yourself the equal of God,

7 very well, I am going to bring foreigners against
you,

g. Towns in the region of the Euphrates.

the most barbarous of the nations.
They will draw sword against your fine wisdom,
they will defile your glory;

8     they will throw you down into the pit
and you will die a violent death
surrounded by the seas.

9     Are you still going to say: I am a god,
when your murderers confront you?
No, you are a man and not a god
in the clutches of your murderers!

10     You will die like the uncircumcised
at the hand of foreigners.
For I have spoken—it is the Lord Yahweh who
speaks.' "

## The fall of the king of Tyre

11     The word of Yahweh was addressed to me as fol-
12 lows, ·"Son of man, raise a dirge over the king of Tyre.
Say to him, 'The Lord Yahweh says this:

You were once an exemplar of perfection,
full of wisdom,
perfect in beauty;

13     you were in Eden, in the garden of God.
A thousand gems formed your mantle.
Sard, topaz, diamond, chrysolite, onyx,
jasper, sapphire, carbuncle, emerald,
the gold of which your flutes and tambourines
are made,
all were prepared on the day of your creation.

14     I had provided you with a guardian cherub;
you were on the holy mountain of God;
you walked amid red-hot coals.

15     Your behavior was exemplary from the day of
your creation
until the day when evil was first found in you.

16     Your busy trading
has filled you with violence and sin.
I have thrown you down from the mountain of
God,
and the guardian cherub has destroyed you from
amid the coals.

17     Your heart has grown swollen with pride

on account of your beauty.
You have corrupted your wisdom
owing to your splendor.
I have thrown you to the ground;
I have made you a spectacle for other kings.

18 By the immense number of your sins,
by the dishonesty of your trading,
you have defiled your sanctuaries.
I have brought fire out of you to consume you.
I have made you ashes on the ground
before the eyes of all who saw you.

19 Of the nations, all who know you
are lost in amazement over you.
You are an object of terror;
gone for ever.' "

## Against Sidon[a]

20 The word of Yahweh was addressed to me as follows,
21 "Son of man, turn toward Sidon and prophesy against
22 her. ·Say, 'The Lord Yahweh says this:

Sidon, now I set myself against you;
I will show my glory through you.
Men shall learn that I am Yahweh,
since I will execute sentence on her
and display my holiness in her.

23 I will send the plague to her;
blood shall flow in her streets,
and in her the dead will fall
under the sword raised against her on all sides,
and so men will learn that I am Yahweh.

## Israel delivered from the nations

24 No more, for the House of Israel,
shall any of the hostile nations surrounding her
be a thorn that wounds or a briar that tears;
and so men will learn that I am Lord Yahweh.

25 The Lord Yahweh says this. When I gather the House
of Israel from the peoples among whom it is dispersed,
this is how I am going to display my holiness in the

---

**28 a.** Sidon, a city-state of Phoenicia, was a member of the alliance which led to the ruin of Judah, Jr. 27:3.

sight of the nations. They shall live on the soil that I
26 gave to my servant Jacob. ·They shall live there in
confidence, build houses, plant vineyards; they shall
live in confidence. When I inflict punishments on all
the hostile surrounding nations, then men will learn
that I am Yahweh their God.' "

## Against Egypt

1 **29** In the tenth year, on the twelfth day of the tenth
month,[a] the word of Yahweh was addressed to
2 me as follows, ·"Son of man, turn toward Pharaoh
king of Egypt and prophesy against him and against
3 the whole of Egypt. ·Speak to him and say, 'The Lord
Yahweh says this:

> Now I set myself against you, Pharaoh king of
>      Egypt,
> you great crocodile wallowing in your Niles,
> you have said: My Niles are mine, I made them.
4 I am going to put hooks through your jaws,
> make your Nile fish stick to your scales,
> and pull you out of your Niles
> with all your Nile fish sticking to your scales.
5 I shall drop you in the desert, with all your
>      Nile fish.
> You will fall on open ground
> and not be taken up or buried.
> I shall give you as food
> to the beasts of the earth and the birds of
>      heaven,
6 so that all the inhabitants of Egypt may learn
>      that I am Yahweh,
> since they have given no more support than a
>      reed to the House of Israel.
7 Whenever they grasped you, you broke in their
>      hands
> and cut their hands all over.
> Whenever they leaned on you, you broke
> and left their loins shaking.

8 For this reason, the Lord Yahweh says this: I am sending the sword against you, to kill your men and your
9 beasts. ·Egypt will be reduced to desert and desolation,
and men will learn that I am Yahweh. Since he has
10 said: The Nile is mine, I made it, ·very well, now I set

myself against you and your Niles. I mean to reduce
Egypt to desert and desolation, from Migdol to Syene
11 and beyond to the frontiers of Ethiopia.[b] •The feet of
men will not pass that way, the feet of animals will
not pass that way. For forty years it will remain un-
12 inhabited. •I intend to reduce the land of Egypt to a
waste among wasted countries; for forty years its cities
will be a waste among ruined cities. And I shall scatter
the Egyptians among the nations, dispersing them
13 throughout the peoples. •And the Lord Yahweh says
this: After forty years have passed, I will gather the
inhabitants of Egypt from the nations where they have
14 been scattered. •I will bring the Egyptian captives back
and reinstall them in the land of Pathros,[c] the land
they came from. There they will constitute a weak
15 kingdom. •Egypt will be the weakest of kingdoms and
no longer dominate other nations; I shall reduce her,
16 and she will not rule any more over the nations. •She
will no longer be anything for the House of Israel to
trust in, but will be living evidence of the sins of Israel
at the time when Israel turned to her for help. And
men will learn that I am the Lord Yahweh.' "

17    In the twenty-seventh year, on the first day of the first
month,[d] the word of Yahweh was addressed to me as
follows:

18    "Son of man, Nebuchadnezzar king of Babylon mo-
bilized his army for a great expedition against Tyre.
Their heads have all gone bald, their shoulders are all
chafed, but even so he has derived no profit from the
expedition mounted against Tyre either for himself or
19 for his army. •Since this is so, the Lord Yahweh says
this: I am going to hand Egypt over to Nebuchadnezzar
king of Babylon. He will levy his share of riches there
instead, will loot it and carry off the booty to pay his
20 army. •In reward for his efforts against Tyre I am
handing the land of Egypt over to him, since he has
been working for me—it is the Lord Yahweh who
speaks.

21    "On that day I will cause the House of Israel to

29 a. December 588–January 587.
b. From Migdol to Syene: i.e., from the north to the south of
Egypt.
c. Upper Egypt.
d. March–April 571.

sprout a horn, and I shall allow you to open your
mouth for all to hear. And so they will learn that I am
Yahweh."

## Against Egypt: the day of Yahweh

<sup>1</sup> **30** The word of Yahweh was addressed to me as
<sup>2</sup> follows, ·"Son of man, prophesy and say, 'The
<sup>3</sup> Lord Yahweh says this: Howl: Alas, the day! ·For the
day is near, the day of Yahweh is near; it will be a day
dark with cloud, the end of an epoch for the nations.

<sup>4</sup>     The sword will come on Egypt, and terror will visit
Ethiopia when the slaughtered fall in Egypt, when her
riches are carried away, when her foundations are de-
<sup>5</sup> stroyed. ·Cush and Put and Lud, the whole of Arabia
and Cub and the sons of my covenant will fall by the
sword along with them.

<sup>6</sup>     Yahweh says this:

The supports of Egypt will fall; the pride of her
strength will crumble; people will fall by the sword
from Migdol to Syene—it is the Lord Yahweh who
speaks.

<sup>7</sup>     They will be laid waste among wasted countries; her
<sup>8</sup> cities will rank with other ruined cities. ·They will learn
that I am Yahweh when I set fire to Egypt and all her
supports are shattered.

<sup>9</sup>     On that day messengers dispatched by me will set
out in boats to shake the complacency of Ethiopia.
Terror will run through her inhabitants on the day of
<sup>10</sup> Egypt—it is coming now! ·The Lord Yahweh says this:
I intend to destroy the huge population of Egypt at the
<sup>11</sup> hand of Nebuchadnezzar king of Babylon. ·He and his
people, most barbarous of nations, will be sent to ravage
the country. They will draw the sword against Egypt
<sup>12</sup> and fill the country with corpses. ·I am going to dry
up the arms of the Nile, hand the country over to
brigands, and lay the whole country waste and everything in it, at the hand of foreigners. I, Yahweh, have
spoken.

<sup>13</sup>     The Lord Yahweh says this: I mean to destroy the
idols, and take the rams away from Noph.<sup>a</sup> The land
of Egypt will be left with a ruler. I shall spread terror
<sup>14</sup> through the land of Egypt. ·I shall lay Pathros waste,
<sup>15</sup> set Zoan on fire, inflict my punishments on No. ·I shall

discharge my fury on Sin, the stronghold of Egypt; I
16 shall wipe out the crowding population of No. ·I shall
set fire to Egypt; Sin will be racked with anguish; there
17 will be a flood at No, the waters will inundate it. ·The
young men of On and Pi-beseth will fall by the sword
18 and the cities themselves go into captivity. ·At Tahpanhes day will turn to darkness when I shatter the
yoke of Egypt there, when the pride of her strength
ceases. A cloud will cover her, and her daughters will
19 go into captivity. ·Such will be the punishments that
I am going to inflict on Egypt. And so men will learn
that I am Yahweh.'"

20    In the eleventh year, on the seventh day of the first
month,[b] the word of Yahweh was addressed to me as
21 follows, ·"Son of man, I have broken the arm of
Pharaoh king of Egypt; you can see that no one has
bound up his wound to heal it, given it a bandage or a
dressing to make the arm strong enough to wield the
22 sword again. ·And so, the Lord Yahweh says this: Now
I set myself against Pharaoh king of Egypt; I intend
to break his arms, the sound one and the broken one,
23 and make the sword drop from his hand. ·I shall scatter
Egypt among the nations and disperse her throughout
24 the countries. ·I shall strengthen the arms of the king
of Babylon and put my sword in his hand. I shall break
Pharaoh's arms and, confronted with his enemy, he
25 will groan like a dying man. ·I shall strengthen the
arms of the king of Babylon, and the arms of Pharaoh
will fall. And so men will learn that I am Yahweh,
when I put my sword into the hands of the king of
26 Babylon and he wields it against the land of Egypt. ·I
mean to scatter Egypt among the nations and disperse
her throughout the countries; and men will learn that
I am Yahweh."

**The cedar**

1 **31** In the eleventh year, on the first day of the third
month, the word of Yahweh was addressed to

**30 a.** Memphis. Three of the Egyptian towns named in the following verses are more recognizable under their Greek names:
Zoan as Tanis, No as Thebes, On as Heliopolis.
**b.** March–April 587.

2 me as follows, ·"Son of man, say to Pharaoh king of Egypt and to all his subjects:

'To what shall I compare you in your greatness?

3 Surely, to a cedar of Lebanon
with noble branches, thickset needles and lofty trunk.
Its top pierces the clouds.

4 The waters have made it grow, the deep has made it tall,
pouring its rivers around the place where it is planted,
sending its streams to all the other trees.

5 This is why its trunk grew taller than all the other trees;
its branches increased in number, its boughs stretched wide,
because the plentiful waters reached it.

6 All the birds of heaven used to nest in its branches;
under its boughs all wild animals used to drop their young;
in its shade every kind of people sat.

7 It was beautiful in its size, in the span of its boughs;
its roots went deep into plentiful waters.

8 No cedar equaled it in the garden of God,
no cypress had branches such as these;
no plane tree could match its boughs,
no tree in the garden of God could rival its beauty.

9 I had made it lovely with branching green.
It was the envy of every tree in Eden, in the garden of God.

10 'Very well then, the Lord Yahweh says this:
Since it has raised itself to its full height, has lifted its top to the clouds, and has grown arrogant in its
11 height, ·I have handed it over to the prince of the nations,ᵃ to do with it as its wickedness deserves; I
12 have destroyed it. ·Foreigners, the most barbarous of the nations, have cut it down and felled it. On the mountains, in all the valleys, lie its branches; its broken boughs fill every ravine throughout the country; every-

body in the country has left its shade and deserted it.
13 On the wreckage perch all the birds of heaven; all the
wild animals have made their dens under its branches.
14     In future let no tree rise in pride beside the waters,
none push its top through the clouds, no well-watered
tree stretch its whole height toward them. For all of
them are doomed to death, to the regions underground, with the common run of mankind, with those
who go down to the pit.
15     The Lord Yahweh says this: On the day it went
down to Sheol, I closed the deep over it in sign of
mourning. I stopped its rivers, the plentiful waters dried
up; I made Lebanon dark for its sake, and all the trees
16 of the fields wilted for its sake. ·With the noise when
it fell I made the nations quake, as I hurled it down to
Sheol, with those who go down to the pit. In the regions underground all the trees of Eden took comfort,
all the noble and lovely trees of Lebanon nourished
17 by the waters. ·And with it went down to Sheol, to the
victims of the sword, all those nations who used to live
in its shade.
18     Was any one of all the trees of Eden your equal in
glory and size, for you to be hurled with the trees of
Eden down to the regions underground? With the uncircumcised there you lie; with the victims of the sword
lie Pharaoh and all his subjects—it is the Lord Yahweh
who speaks.' "

### The crocodile

1  **32** In the twelfth year, on the first day of the twelfth
month,[a] the word of Yahweh was addressed to
2 me as follows, ·"Son of man, raise the dirge for
Pharaoh king of Egypt. Say to him, 'Young lion of
nations, you have been wiped out.

> 'You were like a crocodile in the water;
> you snorted through your nostrils,
> you churned the water with your feet,
> you muddied its streams.

3     'The Lord Yahweh says this:

**31 a.** Nebuchadnezzar or one of his successors.
**32 a.** February–March 585.

I am going to throw my net over you in a great
    concourse of nations;
they will drag you ashore in my net.

4 I mean to leave you on land, drop you on the
    ground;
make all the birds settle on you,
glut all the beasts of the earth with you,

5 lay your carcass on the mountainside,
fill the valleys with your offal.

6 I intend to water the country with what flows
    from you,
with your blood, on the mountainsides,
and the ravines will be full of it.

7 When I extinguish you I will cover the skies,
and darken the stars.
I will cover the sun with clouds
and the moon will not give its light.

8 I will dim every luminary in heaven for you,
and cover your country in darkness
  —it is the Lord Yahweh who speaks.

9 I shall grieve the heart of many peoples when I lead
your captives among the nations, into countries un-
10 known to you. ·I shall stun many peoples with shock
at your fate; their kings will be panic-stricken at your
fate, when I brandish my sword before their eyes. On
the day of your fall, each will tremble continuously
11 for his life. ·For the Lord Yahweh says this: The
12 sword of the king of Babylon will follow you. ·I shall
make your throngs of subjects fall at the swords of my
warriors, who are the most barbarous of the nations.
They will annihilate the pride of Egypt, and her whole
13 population will be destroyed. ·I shall make all her cattle
perish too on the banks of the deep waters. The feet
of men will not muddy them again, the feet of animals
14 will not muddy them again. ·Then I shall calm her
waters; I shall make her rivers glide like oil—it is the
Lord Yahweh who speaks.

15 When I reduce Egypt to desert and the country is
stripped of its contents, when I strike all those who live
there, they will learn that I am Yahweh.

16 Such is the dirge that the daughters of the nations
will raise. They will raise it over Egypt and her huge

population. This is the dirge they will raise—it is the
Lord Yahweh who speaks.'"

## Egypt goes down to Sheol

17    In the twelfth year, on the fifteenth day of the first
month, the word of Yahweh was addressed to me as
18 follows, ·"Son of man, raise the dirge over the huge
population of Egypt; send them down, her and the
daughters of the nations in their majesty, to the regions
underground, with those who go down to the pit.

20    "With those who have fallen by the sword they too
21a will fall; her strength shall be totally extinguished. ·In
19 Sheol the greatest heroes will address her, ·'Do you
21b excel anyone in beauty now? ·Come down, make your
bed with the uncircumcised who have fallen by the
sword.'

22    "Assyria is there with all her warriors around her
23 tomb; all killed, all victims of the sword; ·their graves
have been made in the deepest part of the pit, with her
army around her tomb, all killed, all victims of the
sword, yet she once spread terror throughout the land
of the living.

24    "Elam is there, with all her troops around her tomb;
all killed, all victims of the sword, they have gone down
uncircumcised to the regions underground, yet she once
spread terror throughout the land of the living. They
endure the disgrace of those who go down to the pit.
25 In the middle of the slaughtered a bed has been made
for her, with all her troops around her tomb, all of
them uncircumcised, put to the sword, yet she once
spread terror throughout the land of the living. They
endure the disgrace of those who go down to the pit.
They have been put among the slaughtered.

26    "Meshech is there, and Tubal, with all her troops
around her tomb, all of them uncircumcised, put to the
sword for having spread terror throughout the land of
27 the living. ·They do not lie with the heroes who fell
long ago, those who went fully armed down to Sheol,
who had their swords laid under their heads and their
shields put under their bones, since the heroes inspired
28 the land of the living with terror. ·Instead, you shall
lie with the uncircumcised, with those who have fallen
to the sword.

29     "Edom is there, her kings and all her princes who, despite their valor, have been laid with those who have fallen by the sword. They lie with the uncircumcised, with those who go down to the pit.

30     "All the princes of the North and all the Sidonians are there, having gone down with the slaughtered, in spite of the terror their power inspired. Uncircumcised they lie with those who were victims of the sword. They endure the disgrace of those who go down to the pit.

31     "Pharaoh will see them and take comfort at the sight of such a host put to the sword, Pharaoh and his whole army—it is the Lord Yahweh who speaks.

32 He who once spread terror throughout the land of the living now lies with the uncircumcised, with those who were victims of the sword, Pharaoh and his whole army. It is the Lord Yahweh who speaks."

# III. DURING AND AFTER THE SIEGE OF JERUSALEM

### The prophet as sentry

1
2 **33** The word of Yahweh was addressed to me as follows, ·"Son of man, speak to the members of your nation. Say to them, 'When I send the sword against a country, the people of that country select one
3 of themselves and post him as a sentry; ·if he sees the sword coming against the country, he sounds his horn
4 to alert the people. ·If someone hears the sound of the horn, but pays no attention, the sword will overtake him and destroy him; he will have been responsible
5 for his own death. ·He has heard the sound of the horn and paid no attention; his death will be his own responsibility. But the life of someone who pays attention to the warning will be secure.
6     'If, however, the sentry has seen the sword coming but has not blown his horn, and so the people are not alerted and the sword overtakes them and destroys one of them, the latter shall indeed die for his sin, but I will hold the sentry responsible for his death.'
7     "Son of man, I have appointed you as sentry to the

House of Israel. When you hear a word from my
8 mouth, warn them in my name. ·If I say to a wicked
man: Wicked wretch, you are to die, and you do not
speak to warn the wicked man to renounce his ways,
then he shall die for his sin, but I will hold you re-
9 sponsible for his death. ·If, however, you do warn a
wicked man to renounce his ways and repent, and he
does not repent, then he shall die for his sin, but you
yourself will have saved your life.

**Conversion and perversity**

10     "Son of man, say to the House of Israel, 'You are
continually saying: Our sins and crimes weigh heavily
on us; we are wasting away because of them. How are
11 we to go on living?' ·Say to them, 'As I live—it is the
Lord Yahweh who speaks—I take pleasure, not in the
death of a wicked man, but in the turning back of a
wicked man who changes his ways to win life. Come
back, come back from your evil ways. Why are you
so anxious to die, House of Israel?'

12     "And you, son of man, say to the members of your
nation, 'The integrity of an upright man will not save
him once he has chosen to sin; the wickedness of a
wicked man will no longer condemn him once he renounces wickedness, nor will an upright man live on
the strength of his integrity once he has chosen to sin.
13 If I say to an upright man: You are to live, and then,
trusting in his own integrity, he turns to evil, all his
integrity will no longer be remembered; because he has
14 sinned, he shall die. ·If, however, I say to a wicked
man: You are to die, and he renounces his sins and
15 does what is lawful and right, ·if he returns pledges,
restores what he has stolen, keeps the laws that give
life and stops committing sin—he shall live, and will not
16 die. ·All his previous sins will no longer be remembered
—he has done what is lawful and right; he shall live.

17     'The members of your nation object: What the
Lord does is unjust; but it is what you do that is unjust.
18 When an upright man renounces his integrity and com-
19 mits sin, he dies for it. ·And when a wicked man renounces his wickedness and does what is lawful and
20 right, because of this he lives. ·You object: What the

Lord does is unjust; but I mean to judge each of you by what he does, House of Israel.'"

### The taking of the city

21 In the twelfth year of our captivity, on the fifth day of the tenth month,[a] a fugitive arrived from Jeru-
22 salem and said to me, "The city has been taken." ·Now the hand of the Lord had been on me the evening before the fugitive arrived; he had opened my mouth before the man came to me the next morning; my mouth had been opened and I was dumb no longer.[b]

### The ravaging of the country

23 The word of Yahweh was then addressed to me as
24 follows, ·"Son of man, the people living in those ruins in the land of Israel say, 'Abraham was alone when he was given possession of this land. Now we are many and we hold the country as our domain.'

25 "Very well, tell them, 'The Lord Yahweh says this: You eat blood, you raise your eyes to your idols, you shed blood; are you likely to keep possession of the
26 land? ·You rely on your swords, you engage in filthy practices, you each commit adultery with your neighbor's wife; are you likely to retain possession of the
27 land?' ·Tell them this, 'The Lord Yahweh says this: As I live, I swear it, those in the ruins will fall to the sword, those in the countryside I will give to wild animals to devour, those in strongholds and caves will die of
28 plague. ·I intend to reduce the land to desert and desolation and it will no longer take pride in its strength. The mountains of Israel will be deserted and
29 no one will pass that way again. ·And so men will learn that I am Yahweh, when I reduce the land to desert and desolation on account of all their filthy practices.'

### The results of the preaching

30 "Son of man, the members of your nation are talking about you on the ramparts and in doorways. They keep saying, 'Come and hear the word that has come
31 from Yahweh.' ·They throng toward you; my people sit down in front of you and listen to your words, but they do not act on them. They cannot tell the truth

³² and their hearts are set on dishonest gain. ·As far as
they are concerned, you are like a love song beautifully
sung to music. They listen to your words, but no one
³³ puts them into practice. ·When the thing takes place
—and it is beginning now—they will learn that there has
been a prophet among them."

### The shepherds of Israel

¹ **34** The word of Yahweh was addressed to me as
² follows, ·"Son of man, prophesy against the
shepherds of Israel; prophesy and say to them, 'Shepherds, the Lord Yahweh says this: Trouble for the
shepherds of Israel who feed themselves! Shepherds
³ ought to feed their flock, ·yet you have fed on milk,
you have dressed yourselves in wool, you have sacri-
⁴ ficed the fattest sheep, but failed to feed the flock. ·You
have failed to make weak sheep strong, or to care for
the sick ones, or bandage the wounded ones. You have
failed to bring back strays or look for the lost. On the
contrary, you have ruled them cruelly and violently.
⁵ For lack of a shepherd they have scattered, to become
the prey of any wild animal; they have scattered far.
⁶ My flock is straying this way and that, on mountains
and on high hills; my flock has been scattered all over
the country; no one bothers about them and no one
looks for them.
⁷ "Well then, shepherds, hear the word of Yahweh.
⁸ As I live, I swear it—it is the Lord Yahweh who speaks
—since my flock has been looted and for lack of a
shepherd is now the prey of any wild animal, since
my shepherds have stopped bothering about my flock,
since my shepherds feed themselves rather than my
⁹ flock, ·in view of all this, shepherds, hear the word of
¹⁰ Yahweh. ·The Lord Yahweh says this: I am going to
call the shepherds to account. I am going to take my
flock back from them and I shall not allow them to
feed my flock. In this way the shepherds will stop feeding themselves. I shall rescue my sheep from their
mouths; they will not prey on them any more.
¹¹ For the Lord Yahweh says this: I am going to look

33 a. December 586–January 585.
b. See 3:22f.

12 after my flock myself and keep all of it in view. ·As a shepherd keeps all his flock in view when he stands up in the middle of his scattered sheep, so shall I keep my sheep in view. I shall rescue them from wherever they have been scattered during the mist and darkness.

13 I shall bring them out of the countries where they are; I shall gather them together from foreign countries and bring them back to their own land. I shall pasture them on the mountains of Israel, in the ravines and in every

14 inhabited place in the land. ·I shall feed them in good pasturage; the high mountains of Israel will be their grazing ground. There they will rest in good grazing ground; they will browse in rich pastures on the moun-

15 tains of Israel. ·I myself will pasture my sheep, I myself will show them where to rest—it is the Lord Yah-

16 weh who speaks. ·I shall look for the lost one, bring back the stray, bandage the wounded and make the weak strong. I shall watch over the fat and healthy. I shall be a true shepherd to them.

17 As for you, my sheep, the Lord Yahweh says this: I will judge between sheep and sheep, between rams

18 and he-goats. ·Not content to graze in good pastures, you trample down the rest; not content to drink clear

19 water, you muddy the rest with your feet. ·And my sheep must graze on what your feet have trampled,

20 drink what your feet have muddied. ·Very well then, the Lord Yahweh says this: I myself am now about to

21 judge between fat sheep and lean sheep. ·Since you have butted all the weak sheep with your rump and shoulders and horns, until you have chased them away,

22 I am going to come and rescue my sheep from being cheated; I will judge between sheep and sheep.

23 I mean to raise up one shepherd, my servant David, and to put him in charge of them and he will pasture

24 them; he will pasture them and be their shepherd. ·I, Yahweh, will be their God, and my servant David shall

25 be their ruler. I, Yahweh, have spoken. ·I shall make a covenant of peace with them; I shall rid the country of wild animals. They will be able to live safely in the

26 wilderness and go to sleep in the woods. ·I shall settle them around my hill[a]; I shall send rain at the proper

27 time; it will be a fertile rain. ·The trees of the coun-tryside will yield their fruit and the earth its produce;

they will feel safe on their own farms. And men will learn that I am Yahweh when I break their yoke straps
28 and release them from their captors. ·No more will they be a prey to foreign countries, no more will they be eaten by wild animals in this country. They will live
29 without fear and no one will disturb them again. ·I shall make splendid vegetation grow for them; no more will they suffer from famine in this land; no more will
30 they have to bear the insults of other nations. ·And men will learn that I, their God, am with them and that they, the House of Israel, are my people—it is the
31 Lord Yahweh who speaks. ·And you, my sheep, are the flock I shall pasture, and I am your God—it is the Lord Yahweh who speaks.' "

## Against the mountains of Edom

1   **35** The word of Yahweh was addressed to me as
2 follows, ·"Son of man, turn toward the moun-
3 tain of Seir and prophesy against it. ·Say to it, 'The Lord Yahweh says this: Now I set myself against you, mountain of Seir; I am stretching out my hand against you; I am going to reduce you to desert and desolation,
4 I lay your towns in ruins, and make you a desolation,
5 and so you will learn that I am Yahweh. ·Since, nour-ishing a long-standing hatred, you betrayed the sons of Israel to the sword during their trouble, at the time of
6 their last crime, ·very well, as I live—it is the Lord Yahweh who speaks—I mean to hand you over to bloodshed, and bloodshed will pursue you. I swear it; you have sinned by shedding blood, and bloodshed will
7 pursue you. ·I intend to reduce the mountain of Seir to desert and desolation, and I will eliminate everyone
8 who travels up and down the country. ·I shall fill its mountains with corpses; people will fall, struck down by the sword on your hills, in your valleys, in every one
9 of your ravines. ·I am going to reduce you to desola-tion, for ever your towns will remain uninhabited, and so you will learn that I am Yahweh.
10     Since you said to the two nations, the two coun-tries[a]: You belong to me; we are going to take posses-

**34 a.** Zion.
**35 a.** After 587, Edom attempted to overrun not only the king-dom of Judah but the whole of Palestine.

11 sion here where Yahweh used to be: ·very well, as I live—it is the Lord Yahweh who speaks—in anger and fury I will do exactly what you did because you hated them. I shall make it clear that I am punishing you on 12 their behalf; ·then you will know that I, Yahweh, have overheard all the outrageous things you have said about the mountains of Israel, such as: They have been aban- 13 doned, they have been left for us to devour. ·You have talked arrogantly about me, too, you have repeatedly 14 slandered me; I have heard! ·The Lord Yahweh says this: To the joy of the whole country, I am going to 15 reduce you to desert. ·Since you rejoiced when the domain of the House of Israel became a desert, I will do the same to you, mountain of Seir; you will become a desert, and so will the whole of Edom; and so men will learn that I am Yahweh.'

## Oracle on the mountains of Israel

1 **36** "Son of man, prophesy this to the mountains of Israel. Say, 'Mountains of Israel, hear the word 2 of Yahweh.' ·The Lord Yahweh says this: Since the enemy has insulted you by saying, 'Aha! These eternal 3 heights have now become our domain,' ·you must prophesy. Say, 'The Lord Yahweh says this: Since you have been ravaged and seized on by surrounding coun- tries, and taken over by the rest of the nations, and 4 made the subject of people's talk and gossip, ·now, mountains of Israel, hear the word of the Lord Yah- weh: The Lord Yahweh says this to mountains and hills, to ravines and valleys, to abandoned ruins and the empty plundered cities that have become the laughing- 5 stock of all the surrounding nations. ·Yes, the Lord Yahweh says this: I swear it by the fierceness of my jealousy; I am speaking to the rest of the nations and to the whole of Edom who so exultantly and contemp- tuously took possession of my country and plundered it.'

6 "This being so, prophesy this about the land of Is- rael. Say to the mountains and hills, to the ravines and valleys, 'The Lord Yahweh says this: I am speaking in my jealousy and rage; because you are enduring the 7 insults of the nations, ·very well, the Lord Yahweh

says this: I raise my hand and I swear that the nations
around you shall have their own insults to bear.

8    Mountains of Israel, you will grow branches and
bear fruit for my people Israel, who will soon return.
9 Yes, I am coming to you, I have turned to you; you
10 will be tilled and sown. ·I shall multiply the men who
live on you, the whole House of Israel, yes, all. The
11 cities will be lived in again and the ruins rebuilt. ·I
shall multiply the men and animals that live on you;
there will be many of them and they will be fertile. I
shall repopulate you as you were before; I shall make
you more prosperous than you were before, and so
12 you will learn that I am Yahweh. ·Thanks to me, men
will tread your soil again, my people Israel; they will
have you for their own domain, and never again will
you rob them of their children.

13    The Lord Yahweh says this: Since people have said
of you: You are a man-eater, you have robbed your
14 nation of its children, ·very well, you will eat no more
men, never rob your nation of its children again—it is
15 the Lord Yahweh who speaks. ·I shall never again let
you hear the insults of the nations, you will never again
have to bear the taunts of the foreigners, you will never
again rob the nation of its children—it is the Lord
Yahweh who speaks.' "

16    The word of Yahweh was addressed to me as fol-
17 lows: ·"Son of man, the members of the House of
Israel used to live in their own land, but they defiled it
by their conduct and actions; to me their conduct was
18 as unclean as a woman's menstruation. ·I then discharged my fury at them because of the blood they
shed in their land and the idols with which they defiled
19 it. ·I scattered them among the nations and dispersed
them in foreign countries. I sentenced them as their
20 conduct and actions deserved. ·And now they have
profaned my holy name among the nations where they
have gone, so that people say of them, 'These are the
people of Yahweh; they have been exiled from his land.'
21 But I have been concerned about my holy name, which
the House of Israel has profaned among the nations
22 where they have gone. ·And so, say to the House of
Israel, 'The Lord Yahweh says this: I am not doing
this for your sake, House of Israel, but for the sake of

my holy name, which you have profaned among the
²³ nations where you have gone. ·I mean to display the
holiness of my great name, which has been profaned
among the nations, which you have profaned among
them. And the nations will learn that I am Yahweh—
it is the Lord Yahweh who speaks—when I display my
²⁴ holiness for your sake before their eyes. ·Then I am
going to take you from among the nations and gather
you together from all the foreign countries, and bring
²⁵ you home to your own land. ·I shall pour clean water
over you and you will be cleansed; I shall cleanse you
²⁶ of all your defilement and all your idols. ·I shall give
you a new heart, and put a new spirit in you; I shall
remove the heart of stone from your bodies and give
²⁷ you a heart of flesh instead. ·I shall put my spirit in
you, and make you keep my laws and sincerely respect
²⁸ my observances. ·You will live in the land which I
gave your ancestors. You shall be my people and I
²⁹ will be your God. ·I shall rescue you from all your
defilement. I shall summon the corn and make it plenti-
³⁰ ful, and no more bring famines on you. ·I shall increase the yield of fruit trees and fields so that you will
no longer have the ignominy of famine among the
³¹ nations. ·Then you will remember your evil conduct
and actions. You will loathe yourselves for your sins
³² and your filthy practices. ·I assure you that I am not
doing this for your sake—it is the Lord Yahweh who
speaks. Be ashamed and blush for your conduct, House
of Israel.

³³      The Lord Yahweh says this: On the day I cleanse
you from all your sins, I will repopulate the cities and
³⁴ cause the ruins to be rebuilt. ·Waste land, once desolate
for every passer-by to see, will now be farmed again.
³⁵ Everyone will say: This land, so recently a waste, is
now like a garden of Eden, and the ruined cities once
abandoned and leveled to the ground are now strong-
³⁶ holds with people living in them. ·And the nations left
around you will know that I, Yahweh, have rebuilt
what was destroyed and replanted what was ruined. I,
Yahweh, have spoken, and I will do it.

³⁷      The Lord Yahweh says this: To grant them further
favor, I shall encourage the House of Israel to look
for me, and shall increase them like a flock of men,

38 like a flock of sacrificial animals, like the flock in Jerusalem on her solemn feasts. And so your ruined cities will be filled with a human flock. And men will learn that I am Yahweh.' "

### The dry bones

1 37 The hand of Yahweh was laid on me, and he carried me away by the spirit of Yahweh and set me down in the middle of a valley, a valley full of
2 bones. ·He made me walk up and down among them. There were vast quantities of these bones on the ground the whole length of the valley; and they were
3 quite dried up. ·He said to me, "Son of man, can these
4 bones live?" I said, "You know, Lord Yahweh." ·He said, "Prophesy over these bones. Say, 'Dry bones, hear
5 the word of Yahweh. ·The Lord Yahweh says this to these bones: I am now going to make the breath[a] enter
6 you, and you will live. ·I shall put sinews on you, I shall make flesh grow on you, I shall cover you with skin and give you breath, and you will live; and you
7 will learn that I am Yahweh.' " ·I prophesied as I had been ordered. While I was prophesying, there was a noise, a sound of clattering; and the bones joined to-
8 gether. ·I looked, and saw that they were covered with sinews; flesh was growing on them and skin was cover-
9 ing them, but there was no breath in them. ·He said to me, "Prophesy to the breath; prophesy, son of man. Say to the breath, 'The Lord Yahweh says this: Come from the four winds, breath; breathe on these dead; let
10 them live!' " ·I prophesied as he had ordered me, and the breath entered them; they came to life again and stood up on their feet, a great, an immense army.
11     Then he said, "Son of man, these bones are the whole House of Israel. They keep saying, 'Our bones are dried up, our hope has gone; we are as good as
12 dead.' ·So prophesy. Say to them, 'The Lord Yahweh says this: I am now going to open your graves; I mean to raise you from your graves, my people, and lead you
13 back to the soil of Israel. ·And you will know that I am Yahweh, when I open your graves and raise you
14 from your graves, my people. ·And I shall put my spirit

**37 a.** In Hebrew the one word *ruah* means "breath" and "spirit."

in you, and you will live, and I shall resettle you on
your own soil; and you will know that I, Yahweh,
have said and done this—it is the Lord Yahweh who
speaks.'"

## Judah and Israel in one kingdom

15 The word of Yahweh was addressed to me as fol-
16 lows, ·"Son of man, take a stick and write on it, 'Judah
and those Israelites loyal to him.' Take another stick
and write on it, 'Joseph, the wood of Ephraim, and all
the House of Israel loyal to him.'

17 "Join one to the other to make a single piece of
18 wood, a single stick in your hand. ·And when the
members of your nation say, 'Tell us what you mean,'
19 say, 'The Lord Yahweh says this: I am taking the
stick of Joseph, now in the hand of Ephraim, and those
tribes of Israel loyal to him, and I am going to put the
stick of Judah with them. I shall make one stick out
of the two, and I shall hold them as one.'

20 "Keep the pieces of wood you have written on in
21 your hand where they can see, ·and say, 'The Lord
Yahweh says this: I am going to take the sons of Israel
from the nations where they have gone. I shall gather
them together from everywhere and bring them home
22 to their own soil. ·I shall make them into one nation in
my own land and on the mountains of Israel, and one
king is to be king of them all; they will no longer form
23 two nations, nor be two separate kingdoms. ·They will
no longer defile themselves with their idols and their
filthy practices and all their sins. I shall rescue them
from all the betrayals they have been guilty of; I shall
cleanse them; they shall be my people and I will be
24 their God. ·My servant David will reign over them, one
shepherd for all; they will follow my observances, re-
25 spect my laws and practice them. ·They will live in
the land that I gave my servant Jacob, the land in
which your ancestors lived. They will live in it, they,
their children, their children's children, for ever. David
26 my servant is to be their prince for ever. ·I shall make
a covenant of peace with them, an eternal covenant
with them. I shall resettle them and increase them; I
27 shall settle my sanctuary among them for ever. ·I shall
make my home above them; I will be their God, they

²⁸ shall be my people. ·And the nations will learn that I
am Yahweh the sanctifier of Israel, when my sanctuary
is with them for ever.'"

## Against Gog, king of Magog[a]

¹ **38** The word of Yahweh was addressed to me as
² follows, ·"Son of man, turn toward Gog and the
country of Magog, the prince of Rosh, Meshech and
³ Tubal, and prophesy against him. ·Say, 'The Lord Yahweh says this: I am against you, Gog, prince of Rosh,
⁴ Meshech and Tubal. ·I will turn you around, fixing
hooks in your jaws, and drag you and your troops
along, all the horses and well-armored horsemen, and
all that great army carrying shields and bucklers, and
⁵ wielding swords. ·Persia and Cush and Put are with
⁶ them, all with buckler and helmet; ·Gomer and all its
troops, northernmost Beth-togarmah and all its troops,[b]
⁷ and many nations with you. ·Be ready, be well prepared, you and all your troops and the others rallying
around you, and hold yourself at my service.

⁸ Many days will pass before you are given orders; in
years to come you will march against this country. Its
inhabitants will have been living undisturbed, remote
from all other peoples, since they escaped the sword
and were gathered in from various nations, here in the
⁹ long-deserted mountains of Israel. ·Like a storm you
will come up and onward, and cover the land like a
cloud, you, your army and many nations with you.

¹⁰ The Lord Yahweh says this: On that day, a thought
is going to enter your mind and you will work out a
¹¹ wicked plan. ·You will say: I will attack this unde-
fended country and march against this peaceful nation
living undisturbed. They all live in towns that have no
¹² walls or bars or gates. ·To plunder them for loot, I am
going to reach out my hand toward the ruins they live
in, against this nation gathered out of other nations,
these stockbreeders and tradesmen who live at the naval

**38 a.** Gog cannot be identified. Among the countries of which
he is called "the prince" in v.3, Meshech and Tubal can be recognized as nations from the far north, on the Black Sea borders,
and Gog is perhaps a type of the victorious barbarian from the
north.
**b.** Probably the Cimmerians.

¹³ of the earth.ᵒ ·Sheba and Dedan, the traders of Tarshish and all its young lions will ask you: Have you
come for plunder? Are you massing your troops with
a view to looting? To make off with gold and silver,
seize cattle and goods, and come away with unlimited
spoil?'

¹⁴      "And so, son of man, say in prophecy to Gog, 'The
Lord Yahweh says this: Is it not true that you are
planning to set out at a time when my people Israel is
¹⁵ living undisturbed? ·You plan to leave your home in
the far north, you and many nations with you, a great
¹⁶ army of countless troops all mounted. ·You plan to
invade Israel, my people. You will be like a cloud covering the earth. I myself am going to bring you in days
to come to attack my country, so that the nations may
learn what I am, when I have used you, Gog, to display my holiness to them.

¹⁷      The Lord Yahweh says this: it was of you that I
spoke in the past through my servants the prophets of
¹⁸ Israel, who prophesied and foretold your invasion. ·On
the day Gog attacks the land of Israel—it is the Lord
Yahweh who speaks—I shall grow angry. In my anger,
¹⁹ my jealousy and the heat of my fury I say it: I swear
that on that day there will be a fearful quaking in the
²⁰ land of Israel. ·At my presence the fish in the sea and
the birds of heaven, the wild beasts and all the reptiles
that crawl along the ground, and all men on earth, will
quake. Mountains will fall, cliffs crumble, walls col-
²¹ lapse, and ·I will confront him with every sort of terror
—it is the Lord Yahweh who speaks. His men will turn
²² their swords on each other, ·I will punish him with
plague and bloodshed and send torrential rain, hailstones, fire and brimstone against him and his hordes
²³ and against the many nations with him. ·I mean to
display my greatness and holiness and to compel the
many nations to acknowledge me; this is how they will
learn that I am Yahweh.'

¹ **39** "Son of man, prophesy against Gog. Say, 'The
Lord Yahweh says this: Now I set myself against
² you, Gog, prince of Rosh, Meshech and Tubal. ·I will
turn you around, lead you on, and bring you from the
³ farthest north to attack the mountains of Israel. ·I will
break the bow in your left hand and dash the arrows

4 out of your right. ·You will be killed on the mountains of Israel, you and all your hordes, and the nations with you. I shall make you food for carrion birds and wild
5 beasts. ·You will fall in the open countryside. I have
6 spoken—it is the Lord Yahweh who speaks. ·I will send fire to Magog and on those living undisturbed on
7 islands, and they will learn that I am Yahweh. ·I am going to see that my holy name is known among my people Israel, and I will no longer allow my holy name to be profaned; the nations shall learn that I am Yahweh, holy in Israel.

8 All this is going to happen, all this is going to take place—it is the Lord Yahweh who speaks. This is the day I predicted.

9 The citizens of the towns of Israel will go out and use these arms for firewood: shields and bucklers, bows and arrows, clubs and javelins. For seven years they
10 will feed the fire with them. ·Men will stop looking for wood in the countryside or cutting it in the forest; they will be feeding the fire with arms. They will plunder those who plundered them, and take spoil from those who despoiled them—it is the Lord Yahweh who speaks.

11 On that day, I shall give Gog a famous spot in Israel for his grave—the valley of the Abarim,*a* on the east of the Sea—the valley that turns back the traveler—and there Gog and his whole army will be buried, and it
12 shall be called the Valley of Hamon-gog. ·The House of Israel will take seven months to bury them and
13 cleanse the country. ·All the people of the country will dig their graves, and be honored for this on the day when I reveal my glory—it is the Lord Yahweh who
14 speaks. ·Men will be selected to go continually up and down the country to bury those left on the ground and cleanse it. For seven months they will go searching.
15 If one of them sees any human bones as they go up and down the country he will put a mark beside them until the gravediggers have buried them in the valley
16 of Hamon-gog—·the name of the town is to be Hamonah—and so have cleansed the country.'
17 "Son of man, the Lord Yahweh says this. Speak to

c. Jerusalem.
39 a. The Arnon.

every kind of bird and to all wild beasts, 'Muster, come
here, meet from everywhere around for the sacrifice
I am making for you, a great sacrifice on the mountains
18 of Israel; you will eat flesh and drink blood. ·You will
eat the flesh of heroes, you will drink the blood of the
princes of the world. They are all rams and lambs,
19 goats and fat bulls of Bashan. ·You will feed full on
fat, drink yourselves drunk with blood, at this sacrifice
20 I am making for you. ·You will glut yourselves at my
table on horses and chargers, on heroes and common
soldiers—it is the Lord Yahweh who speaks.'

### Conclusion

21     "That is how I shall display my glory to the nations,
and all nations will feel my sentence when I judge, and
22 feel my hand when I strike them. ·The House of Israel
will know that I am Yahweh their God, from that day
23 forward for ever. ·And the nations will learn that the
House of Israel was exiled for their sin in behaving so
treacherously to me that I had to avert my face from
them because they had rebelled against me, and to
hand them over to their enemies; and they all perished
24 by the sword. ·I treated them as their filthy sins de-
25 served and hid my face from them. ·And so, thus says
the Lord Yahweh: Now I am going to bring back the
captives of Jacob, now I am going to take pity on the
whole House of Israel and show myself jealous for my
holy name.
26     "They will forget the disgrace of having so often betrayed me when they were living safely in their own
27 land, with no one to disturb them. ·When I bring them
home from the peoples, when I bring them back from
the countries of their enemies, when I reveal my holi-
28 ness in them for many nations to see, ·they will know
that I am Yahweh their God, when I rescue the captives from the pagans and reunite them in their own
29 country, not leaving a single one behind. ·I shall never
hide my face from them again, since I shall pour out
my spirit on the House of Israel—it is the Lord Yahweh
who speaks."

## IV. THE TORAH OF EZEKIEL

### The future Temple

1 **40** In the twenty-fifth year of our captivity, at the beginning of the year, on the tenth day of the month, fourteen years after the destruction of the city,[a]
2 the hand of Yahweh came on me. ·In a divine vision he took me away to the land of Israel and put me down on a very high mountain, on the south of which there seemed to be built a city. ·He took me to it, and there
3 I saw a man who seemed to be made of bronze. He had a flax cord and a measuring rod in his hand and
4 was standing in the gateway. ·The man said to me, "Son of man, look carefully, listen closely and pay attention to everything I show you, since you have only been brought here for me to show it to you. Tell the House of Israel everything that you see."

### The outer wall

5 The Temple was surrounded with a wall, and the man was holding a measuring rod that was six cubits long, each cubit a forearm and a handbreadth. He measured the thickness of this construction—one rod; and its height—one rod.

### The east gate

6 He went to the east gate, climbed the steps and meas-
7 ured its threshold: one rod deep. ·Each guardroom one rod by one rod; and the walls between the guardrooms five cubits thick; and the threshold of the gate
9 inward from the porch of the gate: one rod. ·He measured the porch of the gate: eight cubits; its jambs: two cubits; the porch of the gate was at the inner end.
10 There were three guardrooms on each side of the east gate, all three the same size; the walls between them all
11 the same thickness each side. ·He measured the width of the entrance: ten cubits; and the width all down the

**40 a.** September–October 573.

¹² gateway: thirteen cubits. ·There was a rail in front of the guardrooms; each rail on either side was one cubit. And the guardrooms on either side were six cubits ¹³ square. ·He measured the width of the gate from the back wall of one guardroom to the back wall of the other; it was twenty-five cubits across from window to ¹⁴ window. ·He measured the porch: twenty cubits; after ¹⁵ the porch of the gate came the outer court. ·From the entrance end of the gate to the porch opposite: fifty ¹⁶ cubits. ·On each side of the gate there were splayed openings both in the guardrooms and in the spaces between, and there were openings all around inside the porch as well, and palm trees decorating the jambs.

### The outer court

¹⁷ He took me through to the outer court that had rooms and a paved terrace going all the way around; ¹⁸ there were thirty rooms on this terrace. ·This terrace, which came right up to the sides of the gates and ¹⁹ matched their depth, is the Lower Terrace. ·He measured across the outer court from the lower gate to the outside of the inner court: a hundred cubits on the eastern and northern sides.

### The north gate

²⁰ He measured the length and breadth of the north ²¹ gate of the outer court. ·It had three guardrooms on each side; the thickness of the walls between them, and its porch too, all measured the same as those of the ²² first gate: fifty cubits by twenty-five cubits. ·Its windows, its porch and its palm-tree decoration all measured the same as those of the east gate. There were seven steps up to it, and its porch was at the inner end. ²³ In the inner court there was, opposite the north gate, a gate like the one opposite the east gate. He measured the distance from one gate to the other: a hundred cubits.

### The south gate

²⁴ He took me to the south side where there was a south gate; he measured its guardrooms, wall thicknesses and porch; they were of the same dimensions as ²⁵ the others. ·All around it and its porch were windows,

like the other windows; it measured fifty cubits by
26 twenty-five cubits, ·and it had seven steps up to it; its
porch was at the inner end and had palm-tree decora-
27 tion on its jambs, one on each side. ·The inner court
had a south gate; he measured the distance southward
from one gate to the other: a hundred cubits.

### The inner court. The south gate

28 He then took me into the inner court by the south
gate; he measured the south gate which was the same
29 size as the others. ·Its guardrooms, wall thicknesses
and porch all measured the same as the others. It and
its porch had windows all around. It measured fifty
30 cubits by twenty-five cubits. ·Its porch, measured, in all,
31 all around, was twenty-five cubits by five cubits. ·The
porch gave on to the outer court. It had palm trees on
its jambs, each side, and eight steps leading up to it.

### The east gate

32 He took me to the east gate and measured it. It was
33 the same size as the others. ·Its guardrooms, the thickness of its walls, its porch all measured the same as the
others. It and its porch had windows all around. Its
34 area was fifty cubits by twenty-five cubits. ·Its porch
gave on to the outer court. There were palm trees on
its jambs on either side, and eight steps leading up to it.

### The north gate

35
36 He took me to the north gate and measured it. ·Its
guardrooms, the thickness of its walls and its porch all
measured the same as the others. It had windows all
around. Its area was fifty cubits by twenty-five cubits.
37 Its porch gave on to the outer court. There were palm
trees on its jambs on either side, and eight steps leading
up to it.

### Subsidiary buildings at the gate

38 There was a room entered from the porch of the
39 gates. It was here that they washed the holocaust. ·And
on either side of the porch of the gate there were two
tables for slaughtering the holocaust, the sacrifice for
40 sin and the sacrifice of reparation. ·Going northward
up to the gate, there were two tables outside and two

⁴¹ more tables at the porch end of the gate. ·Four tables on the inside and four tables on the outside of the porch; in all, eight tables on which the sacrifices were ⁴² offered. ·There were also four tables of dressed stone for holocausts, a cubit and a half long, a cubit and a half wide and a cubit high, on which all the things necessary for killing the holocaust and the sacrifices ⁴³ were put. ·Rims, a handbreadth broad, went all around the top, and on these tables was put the sacrificial flesh.

⁴⁴ He took me into the inner court; there were two lodges in the inner court, one at the side of the north gate, facing south, the other at the side of the south ⁴⁵ gate, facing north. ·He told me, "The lodge looking ⁴⁶ south is for the priests in charge of the Temple, ·and the lodge looking north is for the priests who serve the altar. These are the sons of Zadok, those of the sons of Levi who approach Yahweh to serve him."

### The inner court

⁴⁷ He measured the inner court. It was a quadrangle, a hundred cubits by a hundred cubits, with the altar in front of the Temple.

### The Temple.ᵇ The Ulam

⁴⁸ He took me to the Ulam of the Temple and measured its door jambs—five cubits each side; and the width of the entrance was fourteen cubits with a three-cubit ⁴⁹ wall each side. ·The Ulam was twenty cubits by twelve cubits. There were ten steps leading up to it, and there were columns by the door jambs, one on each side.

### The Hekal

¹ 41 He took me into the Hekal and measured its door jambs: six cubits deep on the one side, six cubits ² deep on the other. ·The width of the entrance was ten cubits. The walls each side of the entrance were five cubits on the one side and five cubits on the other. He measured its length: forty cubits; and its width: twenty cubits.

b. The Temple is on the plan of Solomon's Temple, and has three parts: The Ulam or Vestibule, the Hekal or Hall, and the Debir or Sanctuary (the "Holy of Holies").

### The Debir

3      He went in and measured the door jambs at the entrance: two cubits; then the entrance: six cubits; and
4 the walls each side of the entrance: seven cubits. ·He measured its length: twenty cubits; and its width measured across the end wall of the Hekal: twenty cubits. He then said to me, "This is the most holy place."

### The side cells

5      He measured the wall of the Temple: six cubits. The width of the side cells was four cubits, all around the
6 Temple. ·The cells were one above the other, thirty of them in three stories. The supports for the surrounding cells were fixed into the Temple wall, so that the cells
7 were not recessed into the wall of the Temple. ·The width of the cells increased, story by story, for they surrounded the Temple in the stories that went right
8 around it, and hence . . . ·Then I saw that there was a paved terrace all around the Temple. The height of this, which formed the base of the side cells, was a full
9 rod of six cubits. ·The outer wall of the side cells was five cubits thick and the pavement formed a verandah
10 outside the cells of the Temple. ·Beyond the rooms came an area twenty cubits wide right around the Tem-
11 ple. ·And for getting from the side cells on to the verandah there was one entrance on the north side and one entrance on the south side. The width of the verandah was five cubits right around.

### The building on the west side

12      The building to the west of this surrounding area was seventy cubits by ninety cubits, and the wall of the
13 building was five cubits thick, all around. ·He measured the length of the Temple: a hundred cubits. The length of the court plus the building and its walls: a hundred
14 cubits. ·The breadth of the façade of the Temple with
15 the quadrangle: a hundred cubits. ·He measured the length of the building plus the surrounding area at the back, plus the side depth of its door: a hundred cubits.

### Particulars of the Temple itself

     The inside of the Hekal and the porches of the court,
16 their thresholds, the window screens, the three sets of

doors, one at each threshold, were all paneled with
wood, from floor to windows, and the windows were
17 screened with latticework. ·From the door to the inner
part of the Temple, and right around the whole wall of
18 the inner room, outside and inside, were carved ·cher-
ubs and palm trees, palm trees and cherubs alternating;
19 each cherub had two faces—·the face of a man turned
toward the palm tree one side and the face of a lion
toward the palm tree the other side, all around the
20 Temple. ·The cherubs and palm trees were carved from
the floor to above the entrance, as also on the wall of
21 the hall. ·The pillars of the Temple were square.

### The wooden altar

22    In front of the Debir, there appeared to be ·a
wooden altar, three cubits high and two cubits square.
Its corners, base and sides were of wood. He said to
me, "This is the table in front of Yahweh."

### The doors

23    There was a double door for the Hekal, and a double
24 door for the Debir. ·These doors had two hinged leaves,
two leaves for the one door, two leaves for the other.
25 On them, on the doors of the Hekal, were carved cherubs and palm trees like those carved on the walls. A
wooden screen outside went across the front of the
26 Ulam. ·There were screened windows with flanking
palm trees on the walls of the Ulam, and of the cells to
the side of the Temple and on the screens.

### Outbuildings of the Temple

1    **42** He took me northward into the court and led
me to the rooms facing the outer court, those
2 to the north of the building. ·They were one hundred
3 cubits long on the north side and fifty cubits wide. ·On
the sides facing the porches of the inner court and
the paving of the outer court was a gallery in front of
4 the triple gallery, ·and in front of the rooms was a
walk, ten cubits broad measured inward and a hundred
5 cubits long; their doors looked north. ·The top-floor
rooms were narrow because the galleries took up part
of the width, being narrower than those on the ground
floor or those on the middle floor of the building,

6 since these were divided into three stories and had no columns such as the court had. Hence they were narrower than the ground-floor ones or the middle-floor
7 ones below them. ·The outer wall parallel to the rooms, facing them and giving on to the outer court, was fifty
8 cubits long, ·the length of the rooms facing the outer court being fifty cubits, while on the side facing the
9 Temple it was a hundred cubits. ·Beneath the rooms there was an entrance from the east, leading in from the outer court.

10 In the thickness of the wall of the court, on the south side fronting the court and the building, were rooms.
11 A walk ran in front of them, as with the rooms built on the north side; they were of the same length and breadth, and had similar design and doors in and out.
12 They were like the entrances of the southern rooms; one entrance at the end of each walk, fronting the
13 eastern wall, being the way in. ·He said to me, "The northern and southern rooms giving on to the court are the rooms of the Debir, in which the priests who approach Yahweh will eat the most holy things. In them will be placed the most holy things: the oblation, the sacrifice for sin and the sacrifice of reparation, since this
14 is a holy place. ·Once the priests have entered they will not go out of the holy place into the outer court without leaving their liturgical vestments there, since these vestments are holy; they will put on other clothes before going near places assigned to the people."

### Measurements of the court

15 When he had finished measuring the inside of the Temple, he took me out to the east gate and measured
16 the whole area of the court. ·He measured the east side with his measuring rod: a total of five hundred
17 cubits by the measuring rod. ·He then measured the north side: a total of five hundred cubits by the meas-
18 uring rod. ·He then measured the south side: five hun-
19 dred cubits by the measuring rod ·was the total. On the west side he measured five hundred cubits by the
20 measuring rod. ·He measured the entire enclosing wall on all four sides: length five hundred, breadth five hundred, separating the sacred from the profane.

## The return of Yahweh

1
2 **43** He took me to the gate, the one facing east.
I saw the glory of the God of Israel approach-
ing from the east. A sound came with it, like the sound
3 of the ocean, and the earth shone with his glory. ·This
vision was like the one I had seen when I had come
for the destruction of the city, and like the one I had
seen on the bank of the river Chebar. Then I prostrated
myself.

4    The glory of Yahweh arrived at the Temple by the
5 east gate. ·The spirit lifted me up and brought me into
the inner court; I saw the glory of Yahweh fill the
6 Temple. ·And I heard someone speaking to me from
7 the Temple while the man stood beside me. ·The voice
said, "Son of man, this is the dais of my throne, the
step on which I rest my feet. I shall live here among the
sons of Israel for ever; and the House of Israel, they
and their kings, will no longer defile my holy name with
8 their whorings and the corpses of their kings, ·setting
their threshold beside my threshold and their pillars
beside my pillars, with a party wall shared by them and
me. They used to defile my holy name by their filthy
practices, and this is why I destroyed them in my anger.
9 From now on they will banish their whorings and the
corpses of their kings from my presence and I shall live
among them for ever.

10    "Son of man, describe this Temple to the House of
Israel, to shame them out of their filthy practices. Let
11 them draw up the plan, ·and, if they are ashamed of
their behavior, show them the design and plan of the
Temple, its exits and entrances, its shape, how all of it
is arranged, the entire design and all its principles. Give
them all this in writing so that they can see and take
note of its design and the way it is all arranged and
12 carry it out. ·This is the charter of the Temple: all
the surrounding area on top of the mountain is a most
holy area. Such is the charter of the Temple."

## The altar

13    Here are the dimensions of the altar, in cubits each
of a cubit plus a handbreadth. The base: one cubit
high and one cubit wide. The ledge all around it: one
14 span. This is the height of the altar: ·from the ground

level of the base up to the lower plinth, two cubits
high and one cubit wide; from the lesser plinth to the
greater plinth, four cubits high and one cubit wide.
15 The altar hearth: four cubits high, with four horns
16 projecting from the hearth, ·the hearth being square:
17 twelve cubits by twelve cubits; ·and the square plinth:
fourteen cubits by fourteen cubits; and the ledge all
around: half a cubit; and the base: one cubit all around.
The steps were on the east side.

### The consecration of the altar

18    He said to me, "Son of man, the Lord Yahweh says
this: As regards the altar, this is how things are to be
done when it has been built for the offering of the
19 holocaust and for the pouring of blood. ·To those levitical priests of the race of Zadok who approach me to
serve me—it is the Lord Yahweh who speaks—you must
20 give a young bull as a sacrifice for sin. ·You are to
take some of its blood and put it on the four horns and
the four corners of the plinth and the surrounding
ledge. In this way you will purify it and make atone-
21 ment on it. ·Then take the bull of the sacrifice for sin
and burn it in that part of the Temple which is cut
22 off from the sanctuary. ·On the second day, you must
offer an unblemished he-goat as the sacrifice for sin,
and the altar is to be purified again as with the bull.
23 When you have finished the purification you must offer
a young bull without blemish and an unblemished ram
24 chosen from the flock. ·You are to present them before Yahweh, and the priests will sprinkle salt on them
25 and offer them as a holocaust to Yahweh. ·As a sacrifice
for sin, every day for seven days you must offer a he-
goat, a bull and an unblemished ram from the flock,
26 for a week. In this way the altar will be atoned for
27 and will be purified and inaugurated. ·At the end of
that time, on the eighth day and afterward, the priest
is to offer your holocausts and your communion sacrifices on the altar, and I will look kindly on you—it is
the Lord Yahweh who speaks."

### The use of the east gate

1    **44** He brought me back to the outer east gate of
2         the sanctuary. It was shut. ·Yahweh said to me,
"This gate will be kept shut. No one will open it or go

through it, since Yahweh the God of Israel has been
³ through it. And so it must be kept shut. ·The prince
himself, however, may sit there to take his meal in
the presence of Yahweh. He is to enter and leave
through the porch of the gate."

## Rules of admission to the Temple

⁴   He led me through the north gate to the front of
the Temple. I looked; I saw the glory of Yahweh filling
the Temple of Yahweh, and I prostrated myself.
⁵ Yahweh said to me, "Son of man, pay attention, look
carefully and listen closely to everything I explain; these
are all the arrangements of the Temple of Yahweh and
all its laws. Be careful about which men are admitted
to the Temple and which are excluded from the sanctu-
⁶ ary. ·And say to the rebels of the House of Israel,
'The Lord Yahweh says this: You have gone beyond
all bounds with all your filthy practices, House of Israel,
⁷ by admitting aliens, uncircumcised in heart and body,
to frequent my sanctuary and profane my Temple, while
you offer my bread, the fat and the blood, and break
⁸ my covenant with all your filthy practices. ·Instead of
performing your duties to me in the Holy Place, you
have deputed someone else to perform your duties in
⁹ my sanctuary. ·The Lord Yahweh says this: No alien,
uncircumcised in heart and body, is to enter my sanctuary, none of those aliens living among the Israelites.

## The Levites

¹⁰   As regards the Levites who abandoned me when
Israel strayed far from me to follow its idols, they must
¹¹ bear the weight of their own sin. ·They are to be
servants in my sanctuary, responsible for guarding the
Temple gates and serving the Temple. They will kill
the holocaust and the sacrifice for the people, and hold
¹² themselves at the service of the people. ·Since they
used to be at their service in front of their idols and
were an occasion of sin to the House of Israel, very
well, I raise my hand against them—it is the Lord Yahweh who speaks; they must bear the weight of their sin.
¹³ They are never to approach me again to perform the
priestly office in my presence, or to touch my holy
things and my most holy things; they must bear the

14 disgrace of their filthy practices. ·I shall give them the
responsibility of working in the Temple; I shall make
them responsible for serving it and for everything to
be done in it.

### The priests

15    As regards the levitical priests, the sons of Zadok,
who did their duty to me in the sanctuary when the
Israelites strayed far from me, they may still approach
me to serve me; they may stand in my presence to
offer me the fat and blood—it is the Lord Yahweh who
16 speaks. ·They may enter my sanctuary and approach
my table to serve me; they may perform my liturgy.
17 Once they enter the gates of the inner court, they are
to wear linen vestments; they are to wear no wool when
they serve inside the gates of the inner court and in the
18 Temple. ·They are to wear linen caps on their heads,
and linen breeches about their loins; they are not to
19 wear belts of . . . ·When they go out to the people in
the outer court, they are to remove the vestments in
which they have performed the liturgy and leave them
in the rooms of the Holy Place, and put on other
clothes, so as not to hallow the people with their vest-
20 ments. ·They are neither to shave their heads nor to
let their hair grow long, but must cut their hair to a
21 reasonable length. ·No priest is to drink wine on the
22 day he enters the inner court. ·They are not to marry
widows or divorced women, but only virgins of the
race of Israel; they may, however, marry widows, if
23 the widow of a priest. ·They are to teach my people
the difference between what is sacred and what is profane and make them understand the difference between
24 what is clean and what is unclean. ·They are to be
judges in disputes; they must judge in the spirit of my
statutes; they must follow my laws and ordinances at
25 all my feasts and keep my sabbaths holy. ·They are
not to go near a dead man, in case they become unclean, except in these permissible cases, that is, for
father, mother, daughter, son, brother or unmarried
26 sister. ·After one of them has been purified, seven
27 days must elapse; ·then, on the day when he enters the
Holy Place—enters the inner court to minister in the
Holy Place—he is to offer his sacrifice for sin—it is the

28 Lord Yahweh who speaks. •They are to have no inheritance; I myself will be their inheritance. You are
to give them no patrimony in Israel; I myself will be
29 their patrimony. •Their food is to be the oblation, the
sacrifice for sin and the sacrifice of reparation. Everything in Israel put under the ban shall be for them.
30 The best of all your first fruits, of every sort of due
and of all that you offer, is to go to the priests; and
the best of your dough you are also to give to the
priests, so that a blessing may rest on your house.
31 Priests are not to eat the flesh of anything that has
died a natural death or been savaged, neither of a bird
nor of any other creature.

## The division of the country. The portion for Yahweh

1 **45** When you divide the country into portions by
lot, you are to allocate the sacred portion of the
country to Yahweh: twenty-five thousand cubits long
and twenty thousand wide. The whole of this land is
2 to be sacred, •and of this an area five hundred by five
hundred cubits square is to be for the sanctuary, with
3 a boundary fifty cubits wide right around. •Out of this
area you are also to measure a section twenty-five thousand by ten thousand cubits, in which there shall stand
4 the sanctuary, the Holy of Holies. •This is to be the
sacred portion of the country; it shall belong to the
priests who officiate in the sanctuary and approach Yahweh to serve him. There they are to have their houses
5 and also a district set apart for the sanctuary. •An
area twenty-five thousand by ten thousand cubits is to
be kept for the Levites serving the Temple to own, with
6 towns to live in. •You are to give the city possession
of an area five thousand by twenty-five thousand cubits,
near the land belonging to the sanctuary; this is to be
for the whole House of Israel.

## The portion for the prince

7 The prince is to have a domain either side of the
land belonging to the Holy Place and of the land belonging to the city, and adjacent to the land belonging
to the Holy Place and the land belonging to the city,
stretching westward from the west and eastward from
the east, its size equal to one of the portions between

8 the west and the east frontiers[a] ·of the country. This is to be his possession in Israel. Then my princes will no longer oppress my people; they must leave the rest of the country for the House of Israel, for its tribes.

9 The Lord Yahweh says this: Let this be enough for you, princes of Israel! Give up your violence and plundering, practice justice and integrity, crush my people no more with taxation—it is the Lord Yahweh who speaks.

10 Have scales that are fair, a fair ephah, a fair bath.

11 Let the ephah and bath be equal, let the bath hold one tenth of a homer and the ephah one tenth of a

12 homer. Let the measures be based on the homer. ·The shekel is to be twenty gerahs. Twenty shekels, twenty-five shekels and fifteen shekels are to make one mina.

## Offerings for worship

13 "This is the offering that you are to levy: the sixth of an ephah for every homer of wheat, and the sixth of

14 an ephah for every homer of barley. ·The dues on oil: one bath of oil out of every ten baths or out of every cor (which is equal to ten baths or one homer,

15 since ten baths equal one homer). ·You are to levy one sheep on every flock of two hundred from the patrimony of Israel for the oblation, the holocaust and the communion sacrifice. This is to form your atone-

16 ment—it is the Lord Yahweh who speaks. ·Let all the people of the country be subject to this due for the

17 prince of Israel. ·The prince is to make himself responsible for providing the holocausts, oblation and libation for feasts, New Moons and sabbaths, for all the solemn festivals of the House of Israel. He is to provide the sacrifice for sin, oblation, holocaust and communion sacrifices atoning for the House of Israel.

## The feast of the Passover

18 The Lord Yahweh says this: On the first day of the first month, you must take a young bull without blem-

19 ish, to purify the sanctuary. ·The priest is to take blood

**45 a.** This plan provides an area about seven miles square at Jerusalem for the Temple, its precincts and towns for the priests and Levites; and on each side of it, a strip of the same width for the prince, to the Jordan on the east and to the Mediterranean on the west.

from the sacrifice for sin and put it on the doorposts
of the Temple, on the four corners of the altar plinth
and on the doorposts of the gates of the inner court.
20 You must do the same on the seventh of the month,
on behalf of anyone who has sinned through inadvert-
ence or ignorance. This is how you are to make atone-
21 ment for the Temple. ·On the fourteenth day of the
first month, you must celebrate the feast of the Passover.
For seven days everyone is to eat unleavened loaves.
22 On that day, the prince must offer a bull as a sacrifice
for sin, for himself and all the people in the country.
23 For the seven days of the feast, he must offer Yahweh
a holocaust of seven bulls and seven rams without
blemish, daily for a week, and one he-goat daily as a
24 sacrifice for sin, ·offering one ephah for each bull and
one ephah for each ram, and a hin of oil for every
ephah for the oblation.

## The feast of Tabernacles

25    For the feast that falls on the fifteenth day of the
seventh month, he must do the same for seven days,
offering the sacrifice for sin, the holocaust, oblation
and the oil.

## The sabbath and the New Moon

1  **46** Thus speaks the Lord Yahweh: The east gate of
        the inner court must be kept shut for the six
working days. On the sabbath day it is to be opened,
2 as also on the day of the New Moon; ·and the prince
is to go in through the porch of the outer gate and take
his position by the doorposts of the gate. The priests
must then offer his holocaust and his communion sacrifice. He must prostrate himself on the threshold of
the gate and go out, and the gate is not to be shut
3 again until the evening. ·The people of the country
are to prostrate themselves in the presence of Yahweh
at the entrance to the gate on sabbaths and days of the
4 New Moon. ·The holocaust offered to Yahweh by
the prince on the sabbath day is to consist of six un-
5 blemished lambs and one unblemished ram, ·and an
oblation of one ephah for the ram, and such oblation
as he pleases for the lambs, and a hin of oil for every
6 ephah. ·On the day of the New Moon it is to consist

of a young bull without blemish, six unblemished lambs
7 and one unblemished ram, ·when he must make an
oblation of one ephah for the bull and one ephah for
the ram, and what he pleases for the lambs, and a hin
of oil for every ephah.

### Miscellaneous regulations

8    When the prince goes in, he is to enter by the porch
of the gate, and he must leave by the same way.
9 When the people of the country come into the presence
of Yahweh at the solemn festivals, those who have come
in by the north gate to prostrate themselves are to go
out by the south gate, and those who have come in
by the south gate are to go out by the north gate; no
one is to turn back to leave through the gate by which
he entered but is to go out on the opposite side.
10 The prince is to come with them, coming in like them
11 and going out like them. ·On feast days and solemn
festivals the oblation must be one ephah for every bull,
one ephah for every ram, what he pleases for the lambs,
12 and a hin of oil for every ephah. ·When the prince
offers Yahweh a voluntary holocaust or a voluntary
communion sacrifice, the east gate is to be opened for
him, and he is to offer his holocaust and his communion
sacrifice as he does on the sabbath day; when he has
13 gone out, the gate is to be shut after him. ·Every day
he must offer an unblemished lamb one year old as a
holocaust to Yahweh; he must offer this every morning.
14 Every morning in addition he is to offer an oblation
of one sixth of an ephah and one third of a hin of oil,
for mixing with the flour. This is the oblation to Yah-
15 weh, an eternal law fixed in perpetuity. ·The lamb, the
oblation and the oil are to be offered morning after
morning for ever.
16    The Lord Yahweh says this: If the prince presents
his sons with part of his hereditary portion, the gift is
to pass into the ownership of his sons, and become
17 their hereditary property. ·If, however, he presents
part of his hereditary portion to one of his servants, it
shall only belong to the man until the year of libera-
tion[a] and is then to revert to the prince. Only his sons

**46 a.** The Jubilee year, occurring every fifty years; see Lv. 25:1.

¹⁸ may retain his hereditary portion. ·The prince may not take any part of the people's hereditary portion and thus rob them of their rightful possessions; he must provide the patrimony of his sons out of his own property, so that no member of my people is robbed of his rightful possessions.' "

¹⁹ He took me through the entrance at the side of the north gate that leads to the rooms of the Holy Place set apart for the priests. And there before us, to the

²⁰ west, was a space at the end. ·He said to me, "This is where the priests are to boil the slaughtered animals for the sacrifice for sin and the sacrifice of reparation, and where they are to bake the oblation, without having to carry them into the outer court and so run the risk

²¹ of hallowing the people." ·He took me into the outer court and led me to each of its four corners; in each

²² corner of the outer court was a compound; ·in other words, the four corners of the court contained four small compounds, forty cubits by thirty, all four being

²³ the same size. ·Each of the four was enclosed by a wall, with hearths all around the bottom of the wall.

²⁴ He said, "These are the kitchens where the Temple servants are to boil the sacrifices offered by the people."

### The spring in the Temple

¹ **47** He brought me back to the entrance of the Temple, where a stream came out from under the Temple threshold and flowed eastward, since the Temple faced east. The water flowed from under the right

² side of the Temple, south of the altar. ·He took me out by the north gate and led me right around outside as far as the outer east gate where the water flowed

³ out on the right-hand side. ·The man went to the east holding his measuring line and measured off a thousand cubits; he then made me wade across the stream; the

⁴ water reached my ankles. ·He measured off another thousand and made me wade across the stream again; the water reached my knees. He measured off another thousand and made me wade across again; the water

⁵ reached my waist. ·He measured off another thousand; it was now a river which I could not cross; the stream had swollen and was now deep water, a river impossible

⁶ to cross. ·He then said, "Do you see, son of man?" He

took me further, then brought me back to the bank of
7 the river. ·When I got back, there were many trees on
8 each bank of the river. ·He said, "This water flows
east down to the Arabah and to the sea; and flowing
9 into the sea it makes its waters wholesome. ·Wherever
the river flows, all living creatures teeming in it will
live. Fish will be very plentiful, for wherever the water
goes it brings health, and life teems wherever the river
10 flows. ·There will be fishermen on its banks. Fishing
nets will be spread from En-gedi to En-eglaim. The
fish will be as varied and as plentiful as the fish of the
11 Great Sea.*a* ·The marshes and lagoons, however, will
12 not become wholesome, but will remain salt. ·Along the
river, on either bank, will grow every kind of fruit
tree with leaves that never wither and fruit that never
fails; they will bear new fruit every month, because this
water comes from the sanctuary. And their fruit will
be good to eat and the leaves medicinal.

### The frontiers of the land

13    "The Lord Yahweh says this: Here are the frontiers
of the territories to be allotted between the twelve tribes
14 of Israel, with two portions for Joseph. ·You must share
it out equally between you, since I swore to your fathers
that I would give them this land which now falls to
15 you as your inheritance. ·Here are the frontiers of the
land. On the north, from the Great Sea by way of
Hethlon to the Pass of Hamath and on to Zedad,
16 Berothah, Sibraim lying between the territories of Damascus and Hamath—and to Hazer-hat-ticon on the
17 borders of Hauran. ·The frontier will extend from the
sea to Hazer-enon, marching with the frontier of Damascus to the north of it and the frontier of Hamath
also on the north; so much for the northern frontier.
18 On the east the Jordan will serve as frontier between
Hauran and Damascus, between Gilead and the land
of Israel, down to the Eastern Sea*b* as far as Tamar;
19 so much for the eastern frontier. ·On the south, from
Tamar southward to the waters of Meribah in Kadesh,
to the Wadi and the Great Sea; so much for the south-

47 a. The Mediterranean.
b. The Dead Sea.

20 ern frontier. ·On the west the Great Sea will serve as frontier up to the point opposite the Pass of Hamath; 21 so much for the western frontier. ·You are to share out this land among yourselves, between the tribes of 22 Israel. ·You are to divide it into inheritances for yourselves and the aliens settled among you who have begotten children with you, since you are to treat them as citizens of Israel. They are to draw lots with you 23 for their inheritance, with the tribes of Israel. ·You must give the alien his inheritance in the tribe in which he is living—it is the Lord Yahweh who speaks.

### The division of the land

1 **48** "This is the list of the tribes. In the far north by way of Hethlon to the Pass of Hamath, to Hazerenon, with the frontier of Damascus lying to the north, and marching with Hamath—the land from the eastern frontier to the western frontier: Dan, one portion. 2 Bordering Dan, from the eastern frontier to the western 3 frontier: Asher, one portion. ·Bordering Asher, from the eastern frontier to the western frontier: Naphtali, 4 one portion. ·Bordering Naphtali, from the eastern frontier to the western frontier: Manasseh, one portion. 5 Bordering Manasseh, from the eastern frontier to the 6 western frontier: Ephraim, one portion. ·Bordering Ephraim, from the eastern frontier to the western fron- 7 tier: Reuben, one portion. ·Bordering Reuben, from the eastern frontier to the western frontier: Judah, one 8 portion. ·Bordering Judah, from the eastern frontier to the western frontier, is the part you are to set aside, twenty-five thousand cubits wide, and as long as each of the other portions from the eastern frontier to the western frontier. The sanctuary will be in the center of it.

9 "The part you must set aside for Yahweh is to be twenty-five thousand cubits long and ten thousand cu- 10 bits wide. ·This consecrated portion is to belong to the priests, being, on the north side, twenty-five thousand cubits; on the west side ten thousand cubits wide, on the east side ten thousand cubits wide and on the south side twenty-five thousand cubits long, and the 11 sanctuary of Yahweh will be in the center of it. ·This is to belong to the consecrated priests, to those of the sons of Zadok who maintained my liturgy and did not

go astray with the straying Israelites, as the Levites went

12 astray. ·And so their portion is to be taken out of the most holy portion of the land, near the territory of the

13 Levites. ·The territory of the Levites, like the territory of the priests, is to be twenty-five thousand cubits long and ten thousand wide—the whole length being twenty-

14 five thousand and the width ten thousand. ·It will be illegal for them to sell or exchange any part of it, and the domain can never be alienated, since it is conse-

15 crated to Yahweh. ·As regards the remainder, an area of five thousand cubits by twenty-five thousand, this is to be for the common use of the city, for houses and

16 pastures. The city is to stand in the center. ·Here are its measurements: on the north side, four thousand five hundred cubits; on the south side, four thousand five hundred cubits; on the east side, four thousand five hundred cubits; on the west side, four thousand five

17 hundred cubits. ·And the city pastures are to extend two hundred and fifty cubits to the north, two hundred and fifty to the south, two hundred and fifty to the east,

18 two hundred and fifty to the west. ·One strip, contiguous to the consecrated portion, must be left over, consisting of ten thousand cubits to eastward and ten thousand to westward, marching with the consecrated portion; this will bring in a revenue for feeding the

19 municipal workmen. ·These municipal workpeople are

20 to be drawn from all the tribes of Israel. ·The portion is to have a total area of twenty-five thousand cubits by twenty-five thousand. You are to allocate a quarter

21 of the sacred portion to form the city. ·What is left over shall be for the prince, on either side of the sacred portion and of the common land belonging to the city, marching with the twenty-five thousand cubits to eastward to the eastern frontier, and marching with the twenty-five thousand cubits to westward to the western frontier—running parallel with the other portions and belonging to the prince. In the center will be the consecrated portion and the sanctuary of the Temple.

22 Thus, apart from the property of the Levites and the property of the city which lie inside the prince's portion, everything between the borders of Judah and the borders of Benjamin is to belong to the prince.

23     "Here are the rest of the tribes: from the eastern

frontier to the western frontier: Benjamin, one por-
²⁴ tion. ·Bordering Benjamin, from the eastern frontier
²⁵ to the western frontier: Simeon, one portion. ·Border-
ing Simeon, from the eastern frontier to the western
²⁶ frontier: Issachar, one portion. ·Bordering Issachar,
from the eastern frontier to the western frontier: Zebu-
²⁷ lun, one portion. ·Bordering Zebulun, from the eastern
frontier to the western frontier: Gad, one portion.
²⁸ The southern border of Gad will be formed by the
southern frontier running through Tamar to the waters
of Meribah in Kadesh, to the Wadi and the Great Sea.
²⁹ This is how you are to divide the land into patrimonies
for the tribes of Israel; and these are to be their portions—it is the Lord Yahweh who speaks.

### The gates of Jerusalem

³⁰     "Here are the ways out of the city. On the north
side, being four thousand five hundred cubits long,
³¹ three gates: the gate of Reuben, the gate of Judah, the
gate of Levi; the gates of the city are to be named after
³² the tribes of Israel. ·On the east side, being four thousand five hundred cubits long, three gates: the gate of
³³ Joseph, the gate of Benjamin, the gate of Dan. ·On
the south side, being four thousand five hundred cubits
long, three gates: the gate of Simeon, the gate of Is-
³⁴ sachar, the gate of Zebulun. ·On the west side, being
four thousand five hundred cubits long, three gates:
the gate of Gad, the gate of Asher, the gate of Naphtali.
³⁵ Total perimeter: eighteen thousand cubits.
     "The name of the city in future is to be: Yahweh-
is-there."

# INTRODUCTION
## TO THE BOOK OF
# DANIEL

The book of Daniel was written between 167 and 164 B.C., during the persecution under Antiochus Epiphanes and before the Maccabean revolt. The first six chapters relate the trials and perils of Daniel's life in the service of Nebuchadnezzar. The last six describe visions granted to Daniel under successors to Nebuchadnezzar in Babylon.

The aim of the book was to sustain faith and hope among the Jews in their persecutions by showing them the triumph of Daniel over his own severe ordeals and temptations of the same kind; and to hold before them the vision of a time to come when the wrath of God would be satisfied; and the kingdom of the saints would begin under a "Son of Man" whose reign would endure for ever.

The historical setting of the story undoubtedly disregards known facts, persons and dates and contains anachronisms in detail; the meaning of the book for its first readers was to be found in its insight into the present and the future in the purposes of God. It is the last expression of messianic prophecy in the Old Testament.

# DANIEL

## THE YOUNG HEBREWS
## AT THE COURT OF NEBUCHADNEZZAR

¹ In the third year of the reign of Jehoiakim king of
Judah, Nebuchadnezzar king of Babylon marched
² on Jerusalem and besieged it. ·The Lord delivered Jehoiakim king of Judah into his hands, with some of the
furnishings of the Temple of God. He took them away
to the land of Shinar, and stored the sacred vessels in
the treasury of his own gods.

³ The king ordered Ashpenaz, his chief eunuch, to
select from the Israelites a certain number of boys of
⁴ either royal or noble descent; ·they had to be without
any physical defect, of good appearance, trained in
every kind of wisdom, well informed, quick at learning,
suitable for service in the palace of the king. Ashpenaz
himself was to teach them the language and literature
⁵ of the Chaldaeans. ·The king assigned them a daily
allowance of food and wine from his own royal table.
They were to receive an education lasting for three
years, after which they were expected to be fit for the
⁶ king's society. ·Among them were Daniel, Hananiah,
⁷ Mishael and Azariah, who were Judaeans. ·The chief
eunuch gave them other names, calling Daniel Belteshazzar, Hananiah Shadrach, Mishael Meshach, and
⁸ Azariah Abednego. ·Daniel, who was most anxious
not to defile himself with the food and wine from the
royal table, begged the chief eunuch to spare him this
⁹ defilement; ·and by the grace of God Daniel met good
will and sympathy on the part of the chief eunuch.
¹⁰ But he warned Daniel, "I am afraid of my lord the
king: he has assigned you food and drink, and if he
sees you looking thinner in the face than the other
boys of your age, my head will be in danger with the

11 king because of you." ·At this, Daniel turned to the
guard whom the chief eunuch had assigned to Daniel,
12 Hananiah, Mishael and Azariah. He said, ·"Please allow your servants a ten days' trial, during which we
are given only vegetables to eat and water to drink.
13 You can then compare our looks with those of the
boys who eat the king's food; go by what you see, and
14 treat your servants accordingly." ·The man agreed to
do what they asked and put them on ten days' trial.
15 When the ten days were over they looked and were in
better health than any of the boys who had eaten their
16 allowance from the royal table; ·so the guard withdrew
their allowance of food and the wine they were to
17 drink, and gave them vegetables. ·And God favored
these four boys with knowledge and intelligence in
everything connected with literature, and in wisdom;
while Daniel had the gift of interpreting every kind of
18 vision and dream. ·When the period stipulated by the
king for the boys' training was over, the chief eunuch
19 presented them to Nebuchadnezzar. ·The king con-
versed with them, and among all the boys found none
to equal Daniel, Hananiah, Mishael and Azariah. So
20 they became members of the king's court, ·and on
whatever point of wisdom or information he might
question them, he found them ten times better than all
the magicians and enchanters in his entire kingdom.
21 Daniel remained there until the first year of King
Cyrus.


## NEBUCHADNEZZAR'S DREAM:

## THE COMPOSITE STATUE


### The king questions his sages

1  In the second year of the reign of Nebuchadnezzar,
2  Nebuchadnezzar had a series of dreams; his mind
was troubled, sleep deserted him. ·The king then had
magicians and enchanters, sorcerers and Chaldaeans[a]

2 a. I.e., diviners; the art of divination was believed to have
originated in Chaldaea.

summoned to tell the king what his dreams meant.
³ They arrived and stood in the king's presence. ·The
king said to them, "I have had a dream, and my mind
⁴ is disturbed by a desire to understand the dream." ·The
Chaldaeans answered the king:

"O king, live for ever! Tell your servants the dream,
⁵ and we will reveal its meaning for you." ·The king answered the Chaldaeans, "This is my firm resolve: if
you cannot tell me what my dream was, and what it
means, I will have you torn limb from limb and your
⁶ houses razed to the ground. ·If, on the other hand, you
can tell me what I dreamed and what it means, I will
give you presents, rewards and high honor. So tell me
⁷ what I dreamed and what it means." ·A second time
they said, "Let the king tell his dream to his servants,
⁸ and we will reveal its meaning." ·But the king retorted,
"It is plain to me that you are trying to gain time,
⁹ knowing my proclaimed and firm resolve. ·Your intention is not to interpret my dream, but to make me mis-
leading and tortuous speeches while the time goes by.
So tell me what my dream was, and I shall know
¹⁰ whether you can interpret it or not." ·The Chaldaeans
answered the king, "Nobody in the world could find
out the king's trouble; what is more, no other king,
governor or chief would think of putting such a ques-
¹¹ tion to any magician, enchanter or Chaldaean. ·The
question the king asks is difficult, and no one can find
the king an answer to it, except the gods, whose dwell-
¹² ing is not with creatures of flesh." ·At this the king flew
into a rage and ordered all the Babylonian sages to be
¹³ put to death. ·On publication of the decree to have the
sages killed, search was made for Daniel and his companions to have them put to death.

### Daniel intervenes

¹⁴     With shrewd and cautious words, however, Daniel
approached Arioch, commander of the king's execu-
tioners, when he was on his way to kill the Babylonian
¹⁵ sages. ·He said to Arioch, the royal marshal, "Why
has the king issued such an urgent decree?" Arioch
¹⁶ explained matters to Daniel, ·and Daniel went off to
ask the king for a stay of execution to give him the
opportunity of revealing his interpretation to the king.

17 Daniel then went home and told his friends Hananiah,
18 Mishael and Azariah what had happened, ·urging them
to beg the God of heaven to show his mercy in this
mysterious affair, so that Daniel and his friends might
19 be spared the fate of the other Babylonian sages. ·The
mystery was then revealed to Daniel in a night vision,
20 and Daniel blessed the God of heaven. ·This is what
Daniel said:

> "May the name of God
> be blessed for ever and ever,
> since wisdom and power are his alone.

21 His, to control the procession of times and sea-
sons,
> to make and unmake kings,
> to confer wisdom on the wise,
> and knowledge on those with wit to discern;

22 his, to uncover depths and mysteries,
> to know what lies in darkness;
> and light dwells with him.

23 To you, God of my fathers, I give thanks and
praise
> for having given me wisdom and intelligence:
> now you have shown me what we asked you,
> you have revealed the king's trouble to us."

24 So Daniel went to see Arioch whom the king had
made responsible for putting the Babylonian sages to
death. On going in he said, "Do not put the Babylonian
sages to death. Take me into the king's presence and I
25 will reveal the meaning to the king." ·Arioch lost no
time in bringing Daniel to the king. "Among the exiles from Judah," he said, "I have discovered a man
26 who can reveal the meaning to the king." ·The king
said to Daniel (who had been given the name Belteshazzar), "Can you tell me what my dream was, and
27 what it means?" ·Facing the king, Daniel replied,
"None of the sages, enchanters, magicians or wizards
has been able to tell the king the truth of the mystery
28 which the king propounded; ·but there is a God in
heaven who reveals mysteries, and who has shown
King Nebuchadnezzar what is to take place in the days
to come. These, then, are the dream and the visions
that passed through your head as you lay in bed:

<sup>29</sup>    "O king, on your bed your thoughts turned to what
would happen in the future, and the Revealer of Mys-
<sup>30</sup> teries disclosed to you what is to take place. ·This mys-
tery has been revealed to me, not that I am wiser than
any other man, but for this sole purpose: that the king
should learn what it means, and that you should understand your inmost thoughts.

<sup>31</sup>    "You have had a vision, O king; this is what you
saw: a statue, a great statue of extreme brightness,
<sup>32</sup> stood before you, terrible to see. ·The head of this
statue was of fine gold, its chest and arms were of silver,
<sup>33</sup> its belly and thighs of bronze, ·its legs of iron, its feet
<sup>34</sup> part iron, part earthenware. ·While you were gazing, a
stone broke away, untouched by any hand, and struck
the statue, struck its feet of iron and earthenware and
<sup>35</sup> shattered them. ·And then, iron and earthenware,
bronze, silver, gold all broke into small pieces as fine
as chaff on the threshing floor in summer. The wind
blew them away, leaving not a trace behind. And the
stone that had struck the statue grew into a great moun-
<sup>36</sup> tain, filling the whole earth. ·This was the dream; now
<sup>37</sup> we will explain to the king what it means. ·You, O
king, king of kings, to whom the God of heaven has
<sup>38</sup> given sovereignty, power, strength and glory—·the sons
of men, the beasts of the field, the birds of heaven,
wherever they live, he has entrusted to your rule, making you king of them all—you are the golden head.
<sup>39</sup> And after you another kingdom will rise, not so great
as you, and then a third, of bronze, which will rule the
<sup>40</sup> whole world. ·There will be a fourth kingdom, hard as
iron, as iron that shatters and crushes all. Like iron that
breaks everything to pieces, it will crush and break all
<sup>41</sup> the earlier kingdoms. ·The feet you saw, part earthen-
ware, part iron, are a kingdom which will be split in
two, but which will retain something of the strength of
iron, just as you saw the iron and the clay of the earth-
<sup>42</sup> enware mixed together. ·The feet were part iron, part
earthenware: the kingdom will be partly strong and
<sup>43</sup> partly weak. ·And just as you saw the iron and the
clay of the earthenware mixed together, so the two
will be mixed together in the seed of man[b]; but they
will not hold together any more than iron will blend
<sup>44</sup> with earthenware. ·In the time of these kings the God

of heaven will set up a kingdom which shall never be destroyed, and this kingdom will not pass into the hands of another race: it will shatter and absorb all the pre-
45 vious kingdoms, and itself last for ever—·just as you saw the stone untouched by hand break from the mountain and shatter iron, bronze, earthenware, silver and gold. The great God has shown the king what is to take place. The dream is true, the interpretation exact."

**The king's profession of faith**

46 At this, King Nebuchadnezzar fell prostrate before Daniel; he gave orders for Daniel to be offered an ob-
47 lation and a fragrant sacrifice. ·The king said to Daniel, "Your god must be the God of gods, the master of kings, and the Revealer of Mysteries, since you have
48 been able to reveal this mystery." ·The king conferred high rank on Daniel and gave him many handsome presents. He also made him governor of the whole province of Babylon and head of all the sages of Baby-
49 lon. ·At Daniel's request, however, the king entrusted the affairs of the province of Babylon to Shadrach, Meshach and Abednego; Daniel himself remained at court.


# THE ADORATION OF THE GOLDEN STATUE


**Nebuchadnezzar erects a golden statue**

1 3 King Nebuchadnezzar had a golden statue made, six cubits tall and three cubits wide, which he erected on the plain of Dura, in the province of
2 Babylon. ·King Nebuchadnezzar then summoned the satraps, prefects, governors, counselors, treasurers, judges, men of law, and all the provincial authorities to assemble and attend the dedication of the statue erected
3 by King Nebuchadnezzar. ·Then the satraps, prefects, governors, counselors, treasurers, judges, men of law and all the provincial authorities assembled for the

**b.** Probably alluding to the intermarriage of Seleucids and Ptolemies.

dedication of the statue erected by King Nebuchadnezzar; and they stood there in front of the statue which
4 King Nebuchadnezzar had erected. ·The herald then
made this proclamation: "Men of all peoples, nations,
5 languages! This is required of you: ·the moment you
hear the sound of horn, pipe, lyre, trigon, harp, bagpipe or any other instrument, you must prostrate yourselves and worship the golden statue erected by King
6 Nebuchadnezzar. ·Those who do not prostrate themselves and worship shall immediately be thrown into
7 the burning fiery furnace." ·And so, the instant the
people heard the sound of horn, pipe, lyre, trigon, harp,
bagpipe and all the other instruments, the men of all
peoples, nations and languages prostrated themselves
and worshiped the statue erected by King Nebuchadnezzar.

## The denunciation and condemnation of the Jews

8   Some Chaldaeans then came forward and laid in-
9 formation against the Jews. ·They said to King Nebu-
10 chadnezzar, "O king, live for ever! ·You have issued a
decree, O king, to the effect that everyone on hearing
the sound of horn, pipe, lyre, trigon, harp, bagpipe or
any other instrument is to prostrate himself and wor-
11 ship the golden statue; ·and that anyone who does not
prostrate himself and worship is to be thrown into the
12 burning fiery furnace. ·Now there are certain Jews to
whom you have entrusted the affairs of the province
of Babylon: Shadrach, Meshach and Abednego; these
men have ignored your command, O king; they do not
serve your gods, and refuse to worship the golden
13 statue you have erected." ·Furious with rage, Nebuchadnezzar sent for Shadrach, Meshach and Abednego. The men were immediately brought before the
14 king. ·Nebuchadnezzar addressed them, "Shadrach,
Meshach and Abednego, is it true that you do not
serve my gods, and that you refuse to worship the
15 golden statue I have erected? ·When you hear the
sound of horn, pipe, lyre, trigon, harp, bagpipe or any
other instrument are you prepared to prostrate yourselves and worship the statue I have made? If you refuse to worship it, you must be thrown straight away
into the burning fiery furnace; and where is the God

16 who could save you from my power?" ·Shadrach, Meshach and Abednego replied to King Nebuchadnezzar,
17 "Your question hardly requires an answer: ·if our God,
the one we serve, is able to save us from the burning
fiery furnace and from your power, O king, he will
18 save us; ·and even if he does not, then you must know,
O king, that we will not serve your god or worship the
19 statue you have erected." ·These words infuriated King
Nebuchadnezzar; his expression was very different now
as he looked at Shadrach, Meshach and Abednego.
He gave orders for the furnace to be made seven times
20 hotter than usual, ·and commanded certain stalwarts
from his army to bind Shadrach, Meshach and Abednego and throw them into the burning fiery furnace.
21 They were then bound, fully clothed, cloak, hose and
headgear, and thrown into the burning fiery furnace.
22 The king's command was so urgent and the heat of
the furnace was so fierce, that the men carrying Shadrach, Meshach, and Abednego were burned to death
23 by the flames from the fire; ·the three men, Shadrach,
Meshach and Abednego fell, still bound, into the burning fiery furnace.

### The song of Azariah in the furnace

24   And they walked in the heart of the flames, praising
25 God and blessing the Lord. ·Azariah stood in the heart
of the fire, and he began to pray:

26        "All honor and blessing to you, Lord, God of
              our ancestors,
          may your name be held glorious for ever.
27        In all that you have done your justice is ap-
              parent:
          your promises are always faithfully fulfilled,
          your ways never deviate,
          your judgments are always true.
28        You have given a just sentence
          in all the disasters you have brought down on us
          and on Jerusalem, the holy city of our ancestors,
          since it is for our sins that you have treated us
              like this,
          fairly and as we deserved.

29    Yes, we have sinned and committed a crime by
            deserting you,
      yes, we have sinned gravely;
      we have not listened to the precepts of your
            Law,
30    we have not observed them,
      we have not done what we were told to do
      for our own good.
31    Yes, all the disasters you have brought down on
            us,
      all that you have done to us,
      you have been fully justified in doing.
32    You have delivered us into the power of our
            enemies,
      of a lawless people, the worst of the godless,
      of an unjust king, the worst in the whole world;
33    today we dare not even open our mouths,
      shame and dishonor are the lot of those who
            serve and worship you.
34    Oh! Do not abandon us for ever,
      for the sake of your name;
      do not repudiate your covenant,
35    do not withdraw your favor from us,
      for the sake of Abraham, your friend,
      of Isaac your servant,
      and of Israel your holy one,
36    to whom you promised descendants as countless
            as the stars of heaven
      and as the grains of sand on the seashore.
37    Lord, now we are the least of all the nations,
      now we are despised throughout the world, to-
            day, because of our sins.
38    We have at this time no leader, no prophet, no
            prince,
      no holocaust, no sacrifice, no oblation, no in-
            cense,
      no place where we can offer you the first fruits
39    and win your favor.
      But may the contrite soul, the humbled spirit
            be as acceptable to you
40    as holocausts of rams and bullocks,
      as thousands of fattened lambs:
      such let our sacrifice be to you today,

and may it be your will that we follow you
    wholeheartedly,
since those who put their trust in you will not
    be disappointed.

41  And now we put our whole heart into following
    you,
into fearing you and seeking your face once
    more.

42  Do not disappoint us;
    treat us gently, as you yourself are gentle
and very merciful.

43  Grant us deliverance worthy of your wonderful
    deeds,
let your name win glory, Lord.

44  Confusion seize those who ill-treat your serv-
    ants:
may they be covered with shame,
deprived of all their power,
and may their strength be broken.

45  Let them learn that you alone are God and
    Lord,
glorious over the whole earth."

46  All this time the servants of the king who had thrown
the men into the furnace had been stoking it with
47  crude oil, pitch, tow and brushwood ·until the flames
rose to a height of forty-nine cubits above the furnace
48  and, leaping out, burned those Chaldaeans to death
49  who were standing around it. ·But the angel of the
Lord came down into the furnace beside Azariah and
his companions; he drove the flames of the fire out-
50  ward, ·and fanned in to them, in the heart of the furnace, a coolness such as wind and dew will bring, so
that the fire did not even touch them or cause them
any pain or distress.

**The song of the three young men**

51  Then all three in unison began to sing, glorifying
and blessing God, there in the furnace, in these words:

52      "May you be blessed, Lord, God of our an-
        cestors,
    be praised and extolled for ever.

Blessed be your glorious and holy name,
praised and extolled for ever.

53　May you be blessed in the Temple of your sacred
glory,

exalted and glorified above all else for ever:

54　blessed on the throne of your kingdom,

praised and exalted above all else for ever.

55　Blessed, you fathomer of the great depths, enthroned on the cherubs,

praised and glorified above all else for ever;

56　blessed in the vault of heaven,

exalted and glorified above all else for ever.

57　"All things the Lord has made, bless the Lord:

give glory and eternal praise to him.

58　Angels of the Lord! all bless the Lord:

give glory and eternal praise to him.

59　Heavens! bless the Lord:

give glory and eternal praise to him.

60　Waters above the heavens! bless the Lord:

give glory and eternal praise to him.

61　Powers of the Lord! all bless the Lord:

give glory and eternal praise to him.

62　Sun and moon! bless the Lord:

give glory and eternal praise to him.

63　Stars of heaven! bless the Lord:

give glory and eternal praise to him.

64　Showers and dews! all bless the Lord:

give glory and eternal praise to him.

65　Winds! all bless the Lord:

give glory and eternal praise to him.

66　Fire and heat! bless the Lord:

give glory and eternal praise to him.

67　Cold and heat! bless the Lord:

give glory and eternal praise to him.

68　Dews and sleet! bless the Lord:

give glory and eternal praise to him.

69　Frost and cold! bless the Lord:

give glory and eternal praise to him.

70　Ice and snow! bless the Lord:

give glory and eternal praise to him.

71　Nights and days! bless the Lord:

give glory and eternal praise to him.

72   Light and darkness! bless the Lord:
give glory and eternal praise to him.

73   Lightning and clouds! bless the Lord:
give glory and eternal praise to him.

74   Let the earth bless the Lord,
give glory and eternal praise to him.

75   Mountains and hills! bless the Lord:
give glory and eternal praise to him.

76   Every thing that grows on the earth! bless the
Lord:
give glory and eternal praise to him.

77   Springs of water! bless the Lord:
give glory and eternal praise to him.

78   Seas and rivers! bless the Lord:
give glory and eternal praise to him.

79   Sea beasts and everything that lives in water!
bless the Lord:
give glory and eternal praise to him.

80   Birds of heaven! all bless the Lord:
give glory and eternal praise to him.

81   Animals wild and tame! all bless the Lord:
give glory and eternal praise to him.

82   Sons of men! bless the Lord:
give glory and eternal praise to him.

83   Israel! bless the Lord:
give glory and eternal praise to him.

84   Priests! bless the Lord:
give glory and eternal praise to him.

85   Servants of the Lord! bless the Lord:
give glory and eternal praise to him.

86   Spirits and souls of the virtuous! bless the Lord:
give glory and eternal praise to him.

87   Devout and humblehearted men! bless the Lord:
give glory and eternal praise to him.

88   Ananiah, Azariah, Mishael! bless the Lord:
give glory and eternal praise to him.
For he has snatched us from the underworld,
saved us from the hand of death,
saved us from the burning fiery furnace,
rescued us from the heart of the flame.

89   Give thanks to the Lord, for he is good,
for his love is everlasting.

90   All you who worship him, bless the God of gods,

> praise him and give him thanks,
> for his love is everlasting."

## The king acknowledges the miracle

²⁴/₉₁ Then King Nebuchadnezzar sprang to his feet in amazement. He said to his advisers, "Did we not have these three men thrown bound into the fire?" They ²⁵/₉₂ replied, "Certainly, O king." ·"But," he went on, "I can see four men walking about freely in the heart of the fire without coming to any harm. And the fourth ²⁶/₉₃ looks like a son of the gods."ᵃ ·Nebuchadnezzar approached the mouth of the burning fiery furnace and shouted, "Shadrach, Meshach and Abednego, servants of the Most High God, come out, come here!" And from the heart of the fire out came Shadrach, Meshach ²⁷/₉₄ and Abednego. ·The satraps, prefects, governors and advisers of the king crowded around the three men to examine them: the fire had had no effect on their bodies: not a hair of their heads had been singed, their cloaks were not scorched, no smell of burning hung ²⁸/₉₅ about them. ·Nebuchadnezzar exclaimed, "Blessed be the God of Shadrach, Meshach and Abednego: he has sent his angel to rescue his servants who, putting their trust in him, defied the order of the king, and preferred to forfeit their bodies rather than serve or worship any ²⁹/₉₆ god but their own. ·I therefore decree as follows: Men of all peoples, nations and languages! Let anyone speak disrespectfully of the God of Shadrach, Meshach and Abednego, and I will have him torn limb from limb and his house razed to the ground, for there is no other ³⁰/₉₇ god who can save like this." ·Then the king showered favors on Shadrach, Meshach and Abednego in the province of Babylon.

# THE WARNING DREAM
# AND THE MADNESS OF NEBUCHADNEZZAR

³¹/₉₈ Nebuchadnezzar the king, to men of all peoples, nations and languages, throughout the world: "May peace ³²/₉₉ be always with you. ·It is my pleasure to make known

the signs and wonders with which the Most High God
has favored me.

<sup>33</sup>
<sub>100</sub>

> "How great are his signs,
>    how mighty his wonders!
> His sovereignty is an eternal sovereignty,
>    his empire lasts from age to age.

## Nebuchadnezzar describes his dream

1
2 **4** "I, Nebuchadnezzar, was living at ease at home,
prosperous in my palace. ·I had a dream; it appalled
me. Dread assailed me as I lay in bed; the visions that
3 passed through my head tormented me. ·So I decreed
that all the sages of Babylon be summoned to explain
4 to me what the dream meant. ·Magicians, enchanters,
Chaldaeans and wizards came, and I told them what I
had dreamed, but they could not interpret it for me.
5 Daniel, renamed Belteshazzar after my own god,[a] and
in whom the spirit of God Most Holy resides, then
came into my presence. I told him my dream:
6 "Belteshazzar, I said, chief of magicians, I know that
the spirit of God Most Holy resides in you and that no
mystery puts you at a loss. This is the dream I have
had; tell me what it means.
7 "The visions that passed through my head as I lay
in bed were these:

> "I saw a tree
>    in the middle of the world;
>    it was very tall.
8 The tree grew taller and stronger,
>    until its top reached the sky,
>    and it could be seen from the ends of the earth.
9 Its foliage was beautiful, its fruit abundant,
>    in it was food for all.
> For the wild animals it provided shade,
>    the birds of heaven nested in its branches,
>    all living creatures found their food on it.
10 I watched the visions passing through my head
>       as I lay in bed.
> Next a watcher, a holy one came down from
>       heaven.

3 a. The protecting angel.
4 a. Bel.

11
At the top of his voice he shouted,
'Cut the tree down, lop off its branches,
strip off its leaves, throw away its fruit;
let the animals flee from its shelter
and the birds from its branches.

12
But leave stump and roots in the ground
bound with hoops of iron and bronze
in the grass of the field.
Let him be drenched with the dew of heaven,
let him share the grass of the earth with the
    animals.

13
Let his heart turn from mankind,
let a beast's heart be given him
and seven times pass over him!

14
Such is the sentence proclaimed by the watchers,
the verdict announced by the holy ones,
that every living thing may learn
that the Most High rules over the kingship of
    men,
he confers it on whom he pleases,
and raises the lowest of mankind.'

15     "This is the dream I had, I, Nebuchadnezzar the king. Now it is for you, Belteshazzar, to pronounce on its meaning, since not one of the sages in my kingdom has been able to interpret it for me; you, however, will be able to, because the spirit of God Most Holy resides in you."

### Daniel interprets the dream

16     Daniel, known as Belteshazzar, hesitated for a moment in embarrassment. The king said, "Belteshazzar, do not be alarmed at the dream and its meaning." Belteshazzar answered, "My lord, may the dream apply
17 to your enemies, and its meaning to your foes! •The tree you saw that grew so tall and strong that it reached the sky and could be seen from the ends of the earth,
18 the tree with beautiful foliage and abundant fruit, with food for all in it, providing shade for the wild animals,
19 with the birds of heaven nesting in its branches, •that tree is yourself, O king, for you have grown tall and strong; your stature is now so great that it reaches the sky, and your rule extends to the ends of the earth.

20 "And the watcher seen by the king, the holy one coming down from heaven and saying, 'Cut the tree down and destroy it, but leave stump and roots in the ground, bound with hoops of iron and bronze in the grass of the field; let him be drenched with the dew of heaven, let him share with the wild animals until seven
21 times have passed over him': ·the meaning of this, O king, this decree of the Most High passed on my lord the king, is this:

22      "You are to be driven from human society,
        and live with the wild animals;
        you will feed on grass like the oxen,
        you will be drenched by the dew of heaven;
        seven times will pass over you
        until you have learned
        that the Most High rules over the kingship of
              men,
        and confers it on whom he pleases.

23 "And the order, 'Leave the stump and roots of the tree,' means that your kingdom will be kept for you until you come to understand that heaven rules all.
24 May it please the king to accept my advice: by virtuous actions break with your sins, break with your crimes by showing mercy to the poor, and so live long and peacefully."

### The dream comes true

25
26 This all happened to King Nebuchadnezzar. ·Twelve months later, while strolling on the roof of the royal
27 palace in Babylon, ·the king was saying, "Great Babylon! Imperial palace! Was it not built by me alone, by my own might and power to the glory of my majesty?"
28 The boast was not out of his mouth when a voice came down from heaven:

        "King Nebuchadnezzar, these words are for
              you!
        Sovereignty is taken from you,
29      you are to be driven from human society,
        and live with the wild animals;
        you will feed on grass like oxen,
        and seven times will pass over you

> until you have learned
> that the Most High rules over the kingship of
>     men,
> and confers it on whom he pleases."

30 The words were immediately fulfilled: Nebuchadnezzar was driven from human society and fed on grass like oxen, and was drenched by the dew of heaven; his hair grew as long as eagles' feathers, his nails became like birds' claws.

31 "When the time was over, I, Nebuchadnezzar, lifted up my eyes to heaven: my reason returned. And I blessed the Most High,

> "praising and extolling him who lives for ever,
> for his sovereignty is an eternal sovereignty,
> his empire lasts from age to age.

32 > The inhabitants of the earth count for nothing:
> he does as he pleases with the array of heaven,
> and with the inhabitants of the earth.
> No one can arrest his hand
> or ask him, 'What are you doing?'

33 "At that moment my reason returned, and, to the glory of my royal state, my majesty and splendor returned too. My counselors and noblemen acclaimed me; I was restored to my throne, and to my past greatness even more was added. •And now I, Nebuchadnezzar,

34

> "praise and extol and glorify the King of
>     heaven,
> his promises are always faithfully fulfilled,
> his ways are always just,
> and he has power to humble those who walk in
>     pride."

## BELSHAZZAR'S FEAST

1   King Belshazzar[a] gave a great banquet for his noblemen; a thousand of them attended, and he drank
2 wine in company with this thousand. •As he sipped his

wine, Belshazzar gave orders for the gold and silver
vessels to be brought which his father Nebuchadnezzar
had looted from the sanctuary in Jerusalem, so that the
king, his noblemen, his wives and his singing women
3 could drink out of them. ·The gold and silver vessels
looted from the sanctuary of the Temple of God in
Jerusalem were brought in, and the king, his noblemen,
his wives and his singing women drank out of them.
4 They drank their wine and praised their gods of gold
and silver, of bronze and iron, of wood and stone.
5 Suddenly the fingers of a human hand appeared, and
began to write on the plaster of the palace wall, directly
behind the lampstand; and the king could see the hand
6 as it wrote. ·The king turned pale with alarm: his
thigh joints went slack and his knees began to knock.
7 He shouted for his enchanters, Chaldaeans and wizards.
And the king said to the Babylonian sages, "Anyone
who can read this writing and tell me what it means
shall be dressed in purple, and have a chain of gold
put around his neck, and be third in rank in the king-
8 dom." ·The king's sages all crowded forward, but they
could neither read the writing nor explain to the king
9 what it meant. ·Greatly alarmed, King Belshazzar
turned even paler, and his noblemen were equally dis-
10 turbed. ·Then the queen, attracted by the noise made
by the king and his noblemen, came into the banqueting
hall. "O king, live for ever!" said the queen. "Do not
11 be alarmed, do not look so pale. ·In your kingdom
there is a man in whom lives the spirit of God Most
Holy. In your father's days, he was known for having
percipience, intelligence and wisdom comparable to that
of the gods. King Nebuchadnezzar, your father, made
him head of the magicians, enchanters, Chaldaeans
12 and wizards. ·Since such a marvelous spirit, and such
knowledge and intelligence in interpreting dreams, solv-
ing enigmas and unraveling difficult problems, live in
this man Daniel, whom the king had renamed Belteshazzar, send for Daniel: he will be able to tell you what
this means."
13    Daniel was brought into the king's presence; the king

5 a. Belshazzar ("May-Bel-protect-the-king") is a Babylonian
name, and there was a historical person bearing it; but he was
not a son of Nebuchadnezzar, nor was he a king.

said to Daniel, "Are you the Daniel who was one of the Judaean exiles brought by my father the king from

14 Judah? ·I am told that the spirit of God Most Holy lives in you, and that you are known for your percep-

15 tion, intelligence and marvelous wisdom. ·The sages and enchanters have already been brought to me to read this writing and tell me what it means, but they

16 have been unable to reveal its meaning. ·As I am told that you are able to give interpretations and to unravel difficult problems, if you can read the writing and tell me what it means, you shall be dressed in purple, and have a chain of gold put around your neck, and be third in rank in the kingdom."

17 Then Daniel spoke up in the presence of the king. "Keep your gifts for yourself," he said, "and give your rewards to others. I will read the writing to the king

18 without them, and tell him what it means. ·O king, the Most High God gave Nebuchadnezzar your father sov-

19 ereignty, greatness, glory, majesty. ·He made him so great that men of all peoples, nations and languages shook with dread before him: he killed whom he pleased, spared whom he pleased, promoted whom he

20 pleased, degraded whom he pleased. ·But because his heart grew swollen with pride, and his spirit stiff with arrogance, he was deposed from his sovereign throne

21 and stripped of his glory. ·He was driven from the society of men, his heart grew completely animal; he lived with the wild asses; he fed on grass like the oxen; his body was drenched by the dew of heaven, until he had learned that the Most High rules over the empire of men and appoints whom he pleases to rule it.

22 But you, Belshazzar, who are his son, you have not

23 humbled your heart, in spite of knowing all this. ·You have defied the Lord of heaven, you have had the vessels from his Temple brought to you, and you, your noblemen, your wives and your singing women have drunk your wine out of them. You have praised gods of gold and silver, of bronze and iron, of wood and stone, which cannot either see, hear or understand; but you have given no glory to the God who holds your

24 breath and all your fortunes in his hands. ·That is why he has sent the hand which, by itself, has written these

25 words. ·The writing reads: *Mene, Mene, Tekel* and

26 *Parsin.*[b] •The meaning of the words is this: *Mene:*
God has *measured* your sovereignty and put an end
27 to it; •*Tekel:* you have been *weighed* in the balance
28 and found wanting; •*Parsin:* your kingdom has been
*divided* and given to the Medes and the *Persians."*

29     At Belshazzar's order Daniel was dressed in purple,
a chain of gold was put around his neck and he was
proclaimed third in rank in the kingdom.

30     That same night, the Chaldaean king Belshazzar was
31 murdered, **6** and Darius the Mede[a] received the kingdom, at the age of sixty-two.


## DANIEL IN THE LION PIT


### The satraps resent Daniel's promotion

2
1     It pleased Darius to appoint a hundred and twenty
satraps over his kingdom for the various parts of the
3
2 kingdom, •and over them three presidents—of whom
Daniel was one—to whom the satraps were to be responsible. This was to ensure that no harm should come
4
3 to the king. •This Daniel, by virtue of the marvelous
spirit residing in him, was so evidently superior to the
presidents and satraps that the king considered appoint-
5
4 ing him to rule the whole kingdom. •The presidents and
satraps in consequence started hunting for some affair
of state by which they could discredit Daniel; but they
could find nothing to his discredit, and no case of negli-
gence; he was so punctilious that they could not find
6
5 a single instance of maladministration or neglect. •These
men then thought, "We shall never find a way of dis-
crediting Daniel unless we try something to do with
7
6 the law of his God." •The presidents and satraps then
went in a body to the king. "King Darius," they said,
8
7 "live for ever! •We are all agreed, the presidents of the
kingdom, the prefects, satraps, counselors and gover-

b. The literal meaning of the words is uncertain; possibly they are
the names of weights or coins—*mina, shekel* and *para* (half a *mina*)
have been suggested.
**6 a.** He is unknown to history.

nors, that the king should issue a decree enforcing the following regulation: whoever within the next thirty days prays to anyone, god or man, other than to yourself, O king, is to be thrown into the lions' den. ·O king, ratify the edict at once by signing this document, making it unalterable, as befits the law of the Medes and the Persians, which cannot be revoked." ·King Darius accordingly signed the document embodying the edict.

$^{9}_{8}$

$^{10}_{9}$

## Daniel's prayer

$^{11}_{10}$ When Daniel heard that the document had been signed, he retired to his house. The windows of his upstairs room faced toward Jerusalem. Three times each day he continued to fall on his knees, praying and $^{12}_{11}$ giving praise to God as he had always done. ·These men came along in a body and found Daniel praying $^{13}_{12}$ and pleading with God. ·They then came to the king and said, "Have you not just signed an edict forbidding any man for the next thirty days to pray to anyone, god or man, other than to yourself, O king, on pain of being thrown into the lions' den?" "The decision stands," the king replied, "as befits the law of the Medes $^{14}_{13}$ and the Persians, which cannot be revoked." ·Then they said to the king, "O king, this man Daniel, one of the exiles from Judah, disregards both you and the edict which you have signed: he is at his prayers three $^{15}_{14}$ times each day." ·When the king heard these words he was deeply distressed, and determined to save Daniel; he racked his brains until sunset to find some way out. $^{16}_{15}$ But the men came back in a body to the king and said, "O king, remember that in conformity with the law of the Medes and the Persians, no edict or decree can be altered when once issued by the king."

## Daniel is thrown to the lions

$^{17}_{16}$ The king then ordered Daniel to be fetched and thrown into the lion pit. The king said to Daniel, "Your God himself, whom you have served so faithfully, will $^{18}_{17}$ have to save you." ·A stone was then brought and laid over the mouth of the pit; and the king sealed it with his own signet and with that of his noblemen, so that there could be no going back on the original decision $^{19}_{18}$ about Daniel. ·The king returned to his palace, spent the night in fasting and refused to receive any of his

20
19 concubines. Sleep eluded him, ·and at the first sign of
21
20 dawn he was up, and hurried off to the lion pit. ·As
he approached the pit he shouted in anguished tones,
"Daniel, servant of the living God! Has your God,
whom you serve so faithfully, been able to save you
22
21 from the lions?" ·Daniel replied, "O king, live for ever!
23
22 My God sent his angel who sealed the lions' jaws, they
did me no harm, since in his sight I am blameless, and
I have never done you any wrong either, O king."
24
23 The king was overjoyed, and ordered Daniel to be released from the pit. Daniel was released from the pit,
and found to be quite unhurt, because he had trusted
25
24 in his God. ·The king sent for the men who had ac-
cused Daniel and had them thrown into the lion pit,
they, their wives and their children: and they had not
reached the floor of the pit before the lions had seized
them and crushed their bones to pieces.

### The king's profession of faith

26
25    King Darius then wrote to men of all nations, peoples
and languages throughout the world, "May peace be
27
26 always with you! ·I decree: in every kingdom of my
empire let all tremble with fear before the God of
Daniel:

> "He is the living God, he endures for ever,
> his sovereignty will never be destroyed
> and his kingship never end.

28
27
> He saves, sets free, and works signs and wonders
> in the heavens and on earth;
> he has saved Daniel from the power of the
> lions."

29
28    This Daniel flourished in the reign of Darius and the
reign of Cyrus the Persian.


## DANIEL'S DREAM: THE FOUR BEASTS


### The vision of the beasts

1 **7** In the first year of Belshazzar king of Babylon,
Daniel had a dream and visions that passed through
his head as he lay in bed. He wrote the dream down,

2 and this is how the narrative began: ·Daniel said, "I have been seeing visions in the night. I saw that the four winds of heaven were stirring up the great sea; 3 four great beasts emerged from the sea, each different 4 from the other. ·The first*a* was like a lion with eagle's wings; and as I looked its wings were torn off, and it was lifted from the ground and set standing on its feet 5 like a man; and it was given a human heart. ·The second beast I saw*b* was different, like a bear, raised up on one of its sides, with three ribs in its mouth, between its teeth. 'Up!' came the command. 'Eat quantities of 6 flesh!' ·After this I looked, and saw another beast,*c* like a leopard, and with four birds' wings on its flanks; 7 it had four heads, and power was given to it. ·Next I saw another vision in the visions of the night: I saw a fourth beast,*d* fearful, terrifying, very strong; it had great iron teeth, and it ate, crushed and trampled underfoot what remained. It was different from the previous beasts and had ten horns.

8     "While I was looking at these horns, I saw another horn sprouting among them, a little one*e*; three of the original horns were pulled out by the roots to make way for it; and in this horn I saw eyes like human eyes, 9 and a mouth that was full of boasts. ·As I watched:

**The vision of the "Ancient of Days" and of the son of man**

> "Thrones were set in place*f*
> and one of great age took his seat.
> His robe was white as snow,
> the hair of his head as pure as wool.
> His throne was a blaze of flames,
> its wheels were a burning fire.
10     A stream of fire poured out,
> issuing from his presence.
> A thousand thousand waited on him,
> ten thousand times ten thousand stood before
>      him.
> A court was held
> and the books were opened.

11     "The great things the horn was saying were still ringing in my ears, and as I watched, the beast was

killed, and its body destroyed and committed to the
12 flames. ·The other beasts were deprived of their power,
but received a lease of life for a season and a time.

13     "I gazed into the visions of the night.
    And I saw, coming on the clouds of heaven,
    one like a son of man.
    He came to the one of great age
    and was led into his presence.
14     On him was conferred sovereignty,
    glory and kingship,
    and men of all peoples, nations and languages
        became his servants.
    His sovereignty is an eternal sovereignty
    which shall never pass away,
    nor will his empire ever be destroyed.

## The interpretation of the vision

15     "I, Daniel, was deeply disturbed and the visions that
16 passed through my head alarmed me. ·So I approached
one of those who were standing by and asked him to
tell me the truth about all this. And in reply he revealed
17 to me what these things meant. ·"These four great beasts
18 are four kings who will rise from the earth. ·Those
who are granted sovereignty are the saints of the Most
High, and the kingdom will be theirs for ever, for ever
19 and ever.' ·Then I asked to know the truth about the
fourth beast, different from all the rest, very terrifying,
with iron teeth and bronze claws, eating, crushing and
20 trampling underfoot what remained; ·and the truth
about the ten horns on its head and why the other
horn sprouted and the three original horns fell, and
why this horn had eyes and a mouth that was full of
boasts, and why it made a greater show than the other

7 a. The Babylonian empire.
b. The kingdom of the Medes; the author sees the Medes as the
immediate successors to the Babylonians. Historically, the Persian
Cyrus had already conquered Media before he captured Babylon.
c. The Persian empire.
d. The empire of Alexander (d.323) and his successors. The ten
horns are kings of the Seleucid dynasty.
e. Antiochus IV Epiphanes (175–163) who came to power only
after getting rid of several rival claimants.
f. For judges.

²¹ horns. ·This was the horn I had watched making war
²² on the saints and proving the stronger, ·until the coming of the one of great age who gave judgment in favor
of the saints of the Most High, when the time came
²³ for the saints to take over the kingdom. ·This is what
he said:

> 'The fourth beast
> is to be a fourth kingdom on earth,
> different from all other kingdoms.
> It will devour the whole earth,
> trample it underfoot and crush it.

²⁴
> As for the ten horns: from this kingdom
> will rise ten kings, and another after them;
> this one will be different from the previous ones
> and will bring down three kings;

²⁵
> he is going to speak words against the Most
>      High,
> and harass the saints of the Most High.
> He will consider changing seasons and the
>      Law,ᵍ
> and the saints will be put into his power
> for a time, two times, and a half a time.ʰ

²⁶
> But a court will be held and his power will be
>      stripped from him,
> consumed, and utterly destroyed.

²⁷
> And sovereignty and kingship,
> and the splendors of all the kingdoms under
>      heaven
> will be given to the people of the saints of the
>      Most High.
> His sovereignty is an eternal sovereignty
> and every empire will serve and obey him.'

²⁸     "Here the narrative ends.
    "I, Daniel, was greatly disturbed in mind, and I grew
pale; but I kept these things to myself."

## DANIEL'S VISION: THE RAM AND THE HE-GOAT

### The vision

1  8 In the third year of King Belshazzar a vision appeared to me, Daniel, after the one that originally
2  appeared to me. ·I gazed at the vision, and as I gazed I found myself in Susa,[a] the citadel in the province of Elam; gazing at the vision, I found myself at the
3  Gate of the Ulai. ·I raised my eyes to look around me, and I saw a ram standing in front of the river. It had two horns; both were tall, but one taller than the other,
4  and the one that rose the higher was the second. ·I saw the ram thrust westward, northward and southward. No animal could stand up to it, nothing could escape it. It did as it pleased and grew very powerful.
5  This is what I observed: a he-goat came from the west, having covered the entire earth but without touching the ground, and between its eyes the goat had one
6  majestic horn. ·It advanced toward the ram with the two horns, which I had seen standing in front of the river, and charged at it with all the fury of its might.
7  I saw it reach the ram, and it was so enraged with the ram, it knocked it down, breaking both its horns, and the ram had not the strength to resist; it felled it to the ground and trampled it underfoot; no one was there to
8  save the ram. ·Then the he-goat grew more powerful than ever, but at the height of its strength the great horn snapped, and in its place sprouted four majestic horns, pointing to the four winds of heaven.
9  From one of these, the small one, sprang a horn which grew to great size toward south and east and

g. The Hellenizing policy of Antiochus Epiphanes included a ban on observance of the sabbath and feast days.

h. Three and a half years, the approximate duration of the persecution under Antiochus Epiphanes; but this period of time, also expressed as forty-two months, stands for "a temporary time of persecution with a limit set by God's providence."

8 a. One of the royal residences of the Achmenid dynasty; the Ulai river flows through the town.

¹⁰ toward the Land of Splendor.ᵇ ·It grew right up to the armies of heaven and flung armies and stars to the
¹¹ ground, and trampled them underfoot. ·It even challenged the power of that army's Prince; it abolished the perpetual sacrifice and overthrew the foundation of his
¹² sanctuary, ·and the army too; it put iniquity on the sacrifice and flung truth to the ground; the horn was active and successful.

¹³ I heard a holy one speaking, and another who said to the speaker, "How long is this vision to be—of perpetual sacrifice, disastrous iniquity, of santuary and
¹⁴ army trampled underfoot?" ·The first replied, "Until two thousand three hundred evenings and mornings have gone by: then the sanctuary shall have its rights restored."

## The angel Gabriel interprets the vision

¹⁵ As I, Daniel, gazed at the vision and tried to understand it, I saw someone standing before me who looked
¹⁶ like a man. ·I heard a man's voice cry over the Ulai,
¹⁷ "Gabriel, tell him the meaning of the vision!" ·He approached the place where I was standing; as he approached I was seized with terror, and fell prostrate. "Son of man," he said to me, "understand this: the
¹⁸ vision shows the time of the End." ·He was still speaking, when I fell senseless to the ground. He touched me,
¹⁹ however, and raised me to my feet. ·"Come," he said, "I will tell you what is going to happen when the wrath
²⁰ comes to an end; this concerns the appointed End. ·As for the ram that you saw, its two horns are the kings
²¹ of Media and of Persia. ·The hairy he-goat is the king of Javan, the large horn between its eyes is the first
²² king.ᶜ ·The horn that snapped and the four horns that sprouted in its place are four kingdoms rising from his nation but not having his power.

²³        "And at the end of their reign, when the measure of their sins is full,
       a king will arise, a proud-faced, ingenious-minded man.
²⁴        His power will gather strength—but not through power of his own—
       he will plot incredible schemes,

he will succeed in what he undertakes,
he will destroy powerful men
and the people of the saints.

25    Such will be his resourcefulness of mind
that all his treacherous activities will succeed.
He will grow arrogant of heart,
take many unawares and destroy them.
He will challenge the power of the Prince of
princes
but, no hand intervening,[d] shall himself be
broken.

26    This explanation of the vision of the mornings
and the evenings is true,
but you must keep the vision secret, for there
are still many days to go."

27    At this I, Daniel, lost consciousness; I was ill for
several days. Then I got up to discharge my duties in
the king's service, keeping the vision a secret, and not
understanding what it meant.

## THE PROPHECY OF THE SEVENTY WEEKS

### Daniel's prayer

1 **9** It was the first year of Darius son of Ahasuerus,
who was of Median stock and ruled the kingdom of
2 Chaldaea. ·In the first year of his reign I, Daniel, was
perusing the scriptures, counting over the number of
years—as revealed by Yahweh to the prophet Jeremiah
—that were to pass before the successive devastations
of Jerusalem would come to an end, namely seventy
3 years. ·I turned my face to the Lord God begging for
time to pray and to plead with fasting, sackcloth and
4 ashes. ·I pleaded with Yahweh my God and made this
confession:
"O Lord, God great and to be feared, you keep the

b. Palestine.
c. Alexander.
d. Antiochus died a natural death, see 1 M. 6.

covenant and have kindness for those who love you
5 and keep your commandments: ·we have sinned, we
have done wrong, we have acted wickedly, we have
betrayed your commandments and your ordinances
6 and turned away from them. ·We have not listened to
your servants the prophets, who spoke in your name
to our kings, our princes, our ancestors and to all the
7 people of the land. ·Integrity, Lord, is yours; ours the
look of shame we wear today, we, the people of Judah,
the citizens of Jerusalem, the whole of Israel, near and
far away, in every country to which you have dispersed
us because of the treason we have committed against
8 you. ·To us, Yahweh, the look of shame belongs, to our
kings, our princes, our ancestors, because we have
9 sinned against you. ·To the Lord our God mercy and
10 pardon belong, because we have betrayed him, ·and
have not listened to the voice of Yahweh our God nor
followed the laws he has given us through his servants
11 the prophets. ·The whole of Israel has flouted your
Law and turned away, unwilling to listen to your voice;
and the curse and imprecation written in the Law of
Moses, the servant of God, have come pouring down
12 on us—because we have sinned against him. ·He has
carried out the threats which he made against us and
against the princes who governed us—that he would
bring so great a disaster down on us that the fate of
Jerusalem would find no parallel in the whole of the
13 world. ·And now all this disaster has happened to us,
just as it is written in the Law of Moses; even so, we
have not tried to appease Yahweh our God by renounc-
ing our crimes and being guided by your truth.
14 Yahweh has watched for the right moment to bring
disaster on us, since Yahweh our God is just in all his
dealings with us, and we have not listened to his voice.
15 And now, Lord our God, who by your mighty hand
brought us out of the land of Egypt—the renown you
won then endures to this day—we have sinned, we have
16 done wrong. ·Lord, by all your acts of justice turn away
your anger and your fury from Jerusalem, your own
city, your holy mountain, for as a result of our sins
and the crimes of our ancestors, Jerusalem and your
own people have become a byword among all around
17 us. ·And now, our God, listen to the prayer and plead-

ing of your servant. For your own sake, Lord, let your
18 face smile again on your desolate sanctuary. ·Listen,
my God, listen to us; open your eyes and look on our
plight and on the city that bears your name. We are
not relying on our own good works but on your great
19 mercy, to commend our humble plea to you. ·Listen,
Lord! Lord, forgive! Hear, Lord, and act! For your
own sake, my God, do not delay, because they bear
your name, this is your city, this is your people."

## The angel Gabriel explains the prophecy

20    I was still speaking, still at prayer, confessing my
own sins and the sins of my people Israel and placing
my plea before Yahweh my God for the holy mountain
21 of my God, ·still speaking, still at prayer, when Gabriel, the being I had seen originally in a vision, flew
suddenly down to me at the hour of the evening sacri-
22 fice. ·He said to me, "Daniel, you see me; I have
23 come down to teach you how to understand. ·When
your pleading began, a word was uttered, and I have
come to tell you what it is. You are a man specially
chosen. Grasp the meaning of the word, understand
the vision:

24          "Seventy weeks are decreed[a]
          for your people and your holy city,
          for putting an end to transgression,
          for placing the seals on sin,
          for expiating crime,
          for introducing everlasting integrity,
          for setting the seal on vision and on prophecy,
          for anointing the Holy of Holies.
25          "Know this, then, and understand:
          from the time this message went out:
          'Return and rebuild Jerusalem'
          to the coming of an anointed Prince, seven
                    weeks
          and sixty-two weeks,
                    with squares and ramparts restored and rebuilt,
                    but in a time of trouble.
26          And after the sixty-two weeks

**9 a.** See v.25. The seventy "weeks of years" are from Jeremiah's
prophecy to the rebuilding of Jerusalem.

an anointed one will be cut off—and . . . will
    not be for him—
the city and the sanctuary will be destroyed
    by a prince who will come.
His end will come in catastrophe
and, until the end, there will be war
and all the devastation decreed.

27
He will make a firm covenant with many[b]
    for the space of a week;
and for the space of one half week
he will put a stop to sacrifice and oblation,
and on the wing of the Temple will be the dis-
    astrous abomination[c]
until the end, until the doom assigned to the
    devastator."


## THE GREAT VISION

### THE TIME OF WRATH

#### The vision of the man dressed in linen

1 **10** In the third year of Cyrus king of Persia a revelation was made to Daniel known as Belteshazzar,
a true revelation of a great conflict. He grasped the
meaning of the revelation; what it meant was disclosed
to him in a vision.
2 At that time, I, Daniel, was doing a three-week pen-
3 ance; ·I ate no rich food, touched no meat or wine,
and did not anoint myself, until these three weeks were
4 over. ·On the twenty-fourth day of the first month, as
5 I stood on the bank of that great river, the Tigris, ·I
raised my eyes to look about me, and this is what I saw:

A man dressed in linen, with a girdle of pure
    gold around his waist;
6
his body was like beryl,
his face shone like lightning,
his eyes were like fiery torches,
his arms and his legs had the gleam of burnished
    bronze,

the sound of his voice was like the noise of a
crowd.

7 I, Daniel, alone saw the apparition; the men who
were with me did not see the apparition, but so great
a trembling overtook them that they fled to hide.
8 I was left alone, gazing on this great apparition; I was
powerless, my appearance altered out of all recognition,
what strength I had deserted me.

### The apparition of the angel

9 I heard him speak, and at the sound of his voice I
10 fell unconscious to the ground. ·I felt a hand touching
11 me, setting my knees and my hands trembling. ·He
said, "Daniel, you are a man specially chosen; listen
carefully to the words that I am going to say; stand up;
I have been sent to you and here I am." He said this,
12 and I stood up trembling. ·He said then, "Daniel, do
not be afraid: from that first day when you resolved to
humble yourself before God, the better to understand,
your words have been heard; and your words are the
13 reason why I have come. ·The prince of the kingdom
of Persia has been resisting me for twenty-one days,
but Michael,*a* one of the leading princes, came to my
assistance. I have left him confronting the kings of Per-
14 sia ·and have come to tell you what will happen to
your people in the days to come. For here is a new
vision about those days."

15 When he had said these things to me I prostrated
16 myself on the ground, without saying a word; ·then
someone looking like a son of man came and touched
my lips. I opened my mouth to speak, and I said to
the person standing in front of me, "My lord, anguish
overcomes me at this vision, and what strength I had
17 deserts me. ·How can my lord's servant speak to my
lord now that I have no strength left and my breath
18 fails me?" ·Once again the person like a man touched

b. Probably the renegade Jews who renounced their obligations
and obeyed Antiochus Epiphanes.
c. Or "the blasphemous idol," here indicating Zeus to whom the
Temple was dedicated by Antiochus. The phrasing makes an allusion to the baals denounced by the prophets.
10 a. Michael ("Who-is-like-God?") is the guardian angel of the
people of God.

<sup>19</sup> me; he gave me strength. ·"Do not be afraid," he said, "you are a man specially chosen; peace be with you; play the man, be strong!" And as he spoke to me I felt strong again and said, "Let my lord speak, you have given me strength."

### The prelude to the prophecy

<sup>20a</sup> He said then, "Do you know why I have come to <sup>21a</sup> you? ·It is to tell you what is written in the Book of <sup>20b</sup> Truth. ·I must go back to fight against the prince of Persia: when I have done with him, the prince of Javan <sup>21b</sup> will come next. ·In all this there is no one to lend me <sup>1</sup> support except Michael your prince, **11** on whom I rely <sup>2</sup> to give me support and reinforce me. ·And now I will tell you the truth about these things.

### Early struggles between Seleucids and Ptolemies

"Three more kings are going to rise in Persia; a fourth will come and be richer than all the others, and when, thanks to his wealth, he has grown powerful, he <sup>3</sup> will challenge all the kingdoms of Javan. ·A mighty king will rise and reign over a vast empire and do what-<sup>4</sup> ever he pleases. ·But once he has come to power his empire will be broken up and parceled out to the four winds of heaven, though not to his descendants: it will not be ruled as he ruled it, for his sovereignty is going to be uprooted and pass to others than his own.

<sup>5</sup> "The king of the South<sup>a</sup> will grow powerful, but one of his princes<sup>b</sup> will grow more powerful still with <sup>6</sup> an empire greater than that of the former. ·Some years later, these will form an alliance and, to ratify the agreement, the daughter of the king of the South will go to the king of the North. Her arm will not, however, retain its strength, nor his posterity endure: she will be handed over, she, her escorts and her child, and he <sup>7</sup> who has had authority over her.<sup>c</sup> In due time ·a sprig from her roots will rise in his place, will march on the defenses, force the stronghold of the king of the North, <sup>8</sup> and succeed in overcoming them. ·He will even carry off all their gods, their statues, their precious gold and silver plate to Egypt. For some years he will leave the <sup>9</sup> king of the North in peace, ·but the latter will invade the kingdom of the king of the South, then retire to his

10 own country. ·His sons[d] will next be on the march, mustering a host of powerful forces; and he[e] will advance, deploy, break through and march on his strong-

11 hold once again. ·The king of the South will fly into a rage and set out to give battle to the king of the North who will have an immense army on his side, and this

12 army will be delivered into his hands. ·The army will be annihilated; he will be triumphant; he will overthrow

13 tens of thousands; yet he will have no strength. ·The king of the North will come back, having recruited an even larger army than before, and finally, when the time comes, he will advance with a great army and

14 plentiful supplies. ·In those times many will rebel against the king of the South; men of violence will also rebel from your own people, thus fulfilling the

15 vision; but they will fail. ·The king of the North will then come and throw up siegeworks to capture a strongly fortified city. The forces of the South will not stand their ground, its picked troops will not be strong

16 enough to resist. ·The invader will treat him as he pleases, no one will be able to resist him: he will take his stand in the Land of Splendor, destruction in his

17 hands. ·He will consider conquering his entire kingdom, but will then make a treaty with him and, to overthrow the kingdom, give him a woman's daughter[f]; but

18 this will not last or be to his advantage. ·He will next turn to the islands and conquer many of them, but a magistrate will put a stop to his outrages in such a way that he will be unable to repay outrage for outrage.[g]

19     "He will then turn on the strongholds of his own country, but will stumble, fall, and never be seen again.

11 a. Ptolemy I Soter of Egypt (306–285).
b. Seleucus I Nicator (301–281).
c. Antiochus II Theos married Ptolemy II's daughter Berenice about 252.
d. Seleucus III Ceraunus (227–223) and Antiochus III the Great (223–187).
e. The following verses describe the battles of Antiochus the Great with Ptolemy IV and Ptolemy V from 220 onward. V.15 mentions the siege of Gaza and v.16 the entry of Antiochus into Jerusalem.
f. Antiochus, foreseeing intervention from Rome, made an alliance with Egypt and married Ptolemy's daughter Cleopatra in 194.
g. Antiochus was defeated by Lucius Cornelius Scipio at Magnesia in 190.

20 In his place there will rise a man*ʰ* who will send an extortioner to despoil the royal splendor; in a few days he will be shattered, though neither publicly nor in battle.*ⁱ*

## Antiochus Epiphanes

21 "In his place there will rise a wretch*ʲ*: he will not be given royal honors, but will insinuate himself into them in his own time and gain possession of the king-
22 dom by intrigue. ·Armies will be utterly routed and crushed by him, the prince of the covenant too.*ᵏ*
23 Still conspiring, he will go from treachery to treachery, ever growing stronger despite the smallness of his fol-
24 lowing. ·In his own time he will invade the richest provinces, acting as his fathers or his fathers' fathers never acted, distributing plunder, spoil and wealth among them, plotting his stratagems against fortresses—for a time.

25 "He will rouse his strength and his heart against the king of the South with a great army. The king of the South will march to war with a huge and powerful army, but will offer no resistance, since he will be out-
26 witted by trickery. ·Those who shared his food will ruin him; his army will be swept away, many will fall in the slaughter.

27 "The two kings, seated at one table, hearts bent on evil, will tell their lies; but they will not have their way,
28 for the appointed time is still to come. ·He will return greatly enriched to his own country, his heart set against the holy covenant; he will take action, and next
29 return to his own country. ·In due time he will make his way southward again, but this time the outcome
30 will not be as before. ·The ships of Kittim*ˡ* will oppose him, and he will be worsted. He will retire and take furious action against the holy covenant and, as before, will favor those who forsake that holy covenant.
31 "Forces of his will come and profane the sanctuary citadel; they will abolish the perpetual sacrifice and in-
32 stall the disastrous abomination there. ·Those who break the covenant he will corrupt by his flatteries, but the people who know their God will stand firm and take
33 action. ·Those of the people who are learned will in-struct many; for some days, however, they will be

brought down by sword and flame, by captivity and by
34 plundering. ·And thus brought down, little help will
they receive, though many will be plotting on their side.
35 Of the learned some will be brought down, as a result
of which certain of them will be purged, purified and
made white—until the time of the End, for the appointed time is still to come.

36     "The king will do as he pleases, growing more and
more arrogant, considering himself greater than all the
gods; he will utter incredible blasphemies against the
God of gods, and he will thrive until the wrath reaches
bursting point; for what has been decreed will certainly
37 be fulfilled. ·Heedless of his fathers' gods, heedless of
the one whom women love,[m] heedless of any god what-
38 ever, he will ·consider himself greater than them all.
Instead of them, he will honor the god of fortresses,
will honor a god unknown to his ancestors with gold
39 and silver, precious stones and valuable presents. ·He
will use the people of an alien god[n] to defend the fortresses; he will confer great honors on those who will
acknowledge him, by giving them wide authority and
by farming out the land at a price.


### THE TIME OF THE END


#### The end of the persecutor

40     "When the time comes for the End, the king of the
South will try conclusions with him; but the king of the
North will come storming down on him with chariots,
cavalry, and a large fleet. He will invade countries,
41 overrun them and drive on. ·He will invade the Land
of Splendor, and many will fall; but Edom, Moab, and
what remain of the sons of Ammon will escape him.
42     "He will reach out to attack countries: the land of

h. Seleucus IV Philopator (187–175).
i. He was assassinated.
j. Antiochus IV Epiphanes (175–165).
k. Probably the high priest Onias III.
l. I.e., "from across the Mediterranean"; the Roman consul landed
at Alexandria.
m. Adonis.
n. Syrian and renegade Jewish troops.

43 Egypt will not escape him. ·The gold and silver treasures and all the valuables of Egypt will lie in his power.
44 Libyans and Cushites⁰ will be at his feet: ·but reports
coming from the East and the North will worry him,
and in great fury he will set out to bring ruin and
45 complete destruction to many. ·He will pitch the tents
of his royal headquarters between the sea and the
mountains of the Holy Splendor. Yet he will come to
his end—there will be no help for him.

**Resurrection and retribution**

1 **12** "At that time Michael will stand up, the great
prince who mounts guard over your people. There
is going to be a time of great distress, unparalleled
since nations first came into existence. When that time
comes, your own people will be spared, all those whose
2 names are found written in the Book. ·Of those who
lie sleeping in the dust of the earth many will awake,
some to everlasting life, some to shame and everlasting
3 disgrace. ·The learned will shine as brightly as the vault
of heaven, and those who have instructed many in virtue, as bright as stars for all eternity.
4 "But you, Daniel, must keep these words secret and
the book sealed until the time of the End. Many will
wander this way and that, and wickedness will go on
increasing."

**The sealed prophecy**

5 Then I, Daniel, looked on and saw two others standing, one on the near bank of the river, one on the
6 other. ·One said to the man dressed in linen who was
standing further up the stream, "How long until these
7 wonders take place?" ·I heard the man speak who was
dressed in linen, standing further up the stream: he
raised his right hand and his left to heaven and swore
by him who lives for ever, "A time and two times, and
half a time; and all these things are going to happen
when he who crushes the power of the holy people
8 meets his end." ·I listened but did not understand. Then
9 I said, "My lord, what is to be the outcome?" ·"Daniel," he said, "go away: these words are to remain se-
10 cret and sealed until the time of the End. ·Many will
be cleansed, made white and purged; the wicked will

go on doing wrong; the wicked will never understand;
11 the learned will understand. ·From the moment that
the perpetual sacrifice is abolished and the disastrous
abomination erected: one thousand two hundred and
12 ninety days. ·Blessed is he who stands firm and attains
13 a thousand three hundred and thirty-five days. ·But
you, go away and rest; and you will rise for your share
at the end of time."


## SUSANNA AND THE JUDGMENT OF DANIEL


1    13 In Babylon there lived a man named Joakim.
2       He had married Susanna daughter of Hilkiah, a
3 woman of great beauty; and she was God-fearing, ·be-
cause her parents were worthy people and had in-
4 structed their daughter in the Law of Moses. ·Joakim
was a very rich man, and had a garden attached to
his house; the Jews would often visit him since he was
5 held in greater respect than any other man. ·Two
elderly men had been selected from the people that
year to act as judges. Of such the Lord said, "Wickedness has come to Babylon through the elders and judges
6 posing as guides to the people." ·These men were often
at Joakim's house, and all who were engaged in litiga-
7 tion used to come to them. ·At midday, when everyone had gone, Susanna used to take a walk in her
8 husband's garden. ·The two elders, who used to watch
her every day as she came in to take her walk, gradu-
9 ally began to desire her. ·They threw reason aside, making no effort to turn their eyes to heaven, and forgetting
10 its demands of virtue. ·Both were inflamed by the same
passion, but they hid their desire from each other,
11 for they were ashamed to admit the longing to sleep
12 with her, ·but they still contrived to see her every day.
13 One day, having parted with the words, "Let us go
home, it is time for the midday meal," they went off
14 in different directions, ·only to retrace their steps and
find themselves face to face again. Obliged then to ex-

o. The peoples west and south of Egypt.

plain, they admitted their desire and agreed to look for
15 an opportunity of surprising her alone. ·So they waited
for a favorable moment; and one day Susanna came
as usual, accompanied only by two young maidservants.
The day was hot and she wanted to bathe in the garden.
16 There was no one about except the two elders, spying
17 on her from their hiding place. ·She said to the servants, "Bring me some oil and balsam and shut the gar-
18 den door while I bathe." ·They did as they were told,
shutting the garden door and going back to the house
by a side entrance to fetch what she had asked for;
they knew nothing about the elders, who were hiding.

19 Hardly were the servants gone than the two elders
20 were there after her. "Look," ·they said, "the garden
door is shut, no one can see us. We want to have you,
21 so give in and let us! ·Refuse, and we will both give
evidence that a young man was with you and that was
22 why you sent your maids away." ·Susanna sighed. "I
am trapped," she said, "whatever I do. If I agree, that
means my death; if I resist, I cannot get away from
23 you. ·But I prefer to fall innocent into your power
24 than to sin in the eyes of the Lord." ·Then she cried
out as loud as she could. The two elders began shouting
25 too, putting the blame on her, ·and one of them ran
26 to open the garden door. ·The household, hearing the
shouting in the garden, rushed out by the side entrance
27 to see what was happening; ·once the elders had told
their story the servants were thoroughly taken aback,
since nothing of this sort had ever been said of Susanna.

28 Next day a meeting was held at the house of her
husband Joakim. The two elders arrived, in their vin-
29 dictiveness determined to have her put to death. ·They
addressed the company: "Summon Susanna daughter
of Hilkiah and wife of Joakim." She was sent for,
30 and came accompanied by her parents, her children
31 and all her relations. ·Susanna was very graceful and
32 beautiful to look at; ·she was veiled, so the wretches
made her unveil in order to feast their eyes on her
33 beauty. ·All her own people were weeping, and so were
34 all the others who saw her. ·The two elders stood up,
with all the people around them, and laid their hands
35 on the woman's head.[a] ·Tearfully she turned her eyes
36 to heaven, her heart confident in God. ·The elders then

spoke. "While we were walking by ourselves in the garden, this woman arrived with two servants. She shut the
37 garden door and then dismissed the servants. ·A young
man who had been hiding went over to her and they
38 lay down together. ·From the end of the garden where
we were, we saw this crime taking place and hurried
39 toward them. ·Though we saw them together we were
unable to catch the man: he was too strong for us; he
40 opened the door and took to his heels. ·We did, however, catch this woman and ask her who the young man
41 was. ·She refused to tell us. That is our evidence."

Since they were elders of the people, and judges, the
assembly took their word: Susanna was condemned to
42 death. ·She cried out as loud as she could, "Eternal
God, you know all secrets and everything before it hap-
43 pens; ·you know that they have given false evidence
against me. And now have I to die, innocent as I am of
everything their malice has invented against me?"
44
45 The Lord heard her cry ·and, as she was being led
away to die, he roused the holy spirit residing in a
46 young boy named Daniel ·who began to shout, "I am
47 innocent of this woman's death!" ·At which all the
people turned to him and asked, "What do you mean
48 by these words?" ·Standing in the middle of the crowd
he replied, "Are you so stupid, sons of Israel, as to condemn a daughter of Israel unheard, and without trou-
49 bling to find out the truth? ·Go back to the scene of the
trial: these men have given false evidence against her."

50 All the people hurried back, and the elders said to
Daniel, "Come and sit with us and tell us what you
mean, since God has given you the gifts that elders
51 have." ·Daniel said, "Keep the men well apart from
52 each other for I want to question them." ·When the
men had been separated, Daniel had one of them
brought to him. "You have grown old in wickedness,"
he said, "and now the sins of your earlier days have
53 overtaken you, ·you with your unjust judgments, your
condemnation of the innocent, your acquittal of guilty
men, when the Lord has said, 'You must not put the
54 innocent and the just to death.' ·Now then, since you
saw her so clearly, tell me what tree you saw them

13 a. The formal preliminary to death by stoning.

lying under?" He replied, "Under a mastic tree."
⁵⁵ Daniel said, "True enough! Your lie recoils on your
own head: the angel of God has already received your
⁵⁶ sentence from him and will slash you in half." ·He
dismissed the man, ordered the other to be brought
and said to him, "Spawn of Canaan, not of Judah,
beauty has seduced you, lust has led your heart astray!
⁵⁷ This is how you have been behaving with the daughters
of Israel and they were too frightened to resist; but
here is a daughter of Judah who could not stomach
⁵⁸ your wickedness! ·Now then, tell me what tree you
surprised them under?" He replied, "Under a holm
⁵⁹ oak." ·Daniel said, "True enough! Your lie recoils on
your own head: the angel of God is waiting, with a
sword to drive home and split you, and destroy the
pair of you."
⁶⁰   Then the whole assembly shouted, blessing God, the
⁶¹ savior of those who trust in him. ·And they turned
on the two elders whom Daniel had convicted of false
⁶² evidence out of their own mouths. ·As prescribed in the
Law of Moses, they sentenced them to the same punishment as they had intended to inflict on their neighbor.
They put them to death; the life of an innocent woman
⁶³ was spared that day. ·Hilkiah and his wife gave thanks
to God for their daughter Susanna, and so did her
husband Joakim and all his relations, because she had
been acquitted of anything dishonorable.
⁶⁴   From that day onward Daniel's reputation stood
high with the people.


## BEL AND THE DRAGON

### Daniel and the priests of Bel

¹
² 14 When King Astyages joined his ancestors, Cyrus
of Persia succeeded him. ·Daniel was very close
to the king who thought more of him than of any other
³ of his friends. ·Now in Babylon there was an idol called
Bel,ᵃ to which twelve bushels of the finest flour, forty
sheep and six measures of wine were offered every day.

⁴ The king took part in this cult and used to go and worship the idol every day. Daniel, however, worshiped ⁵ his own God. ·"Why do you not worship Bel?" the king asked Daniel. "I do not worship idols made by the hands of men," Daniel replied. "I worship the living God who made heaven and earth and who has power ⁶ over all living creatures." ·"You believe, then," said the king, "that Bel is not a living god? Can you not ⁷ see how much he eats and drinks every day?" ·Daniel laughed. "My king," he said, "do not be taken in; he is clay inside, and bronze outside, and has never eaten ⁸ or drunk anything." ·This made the king angry; he summoned his priests, "Tell me who eats all this food," he said, "or die. Prove to me that Bel really eats it, and I will have Daniel put to death for blaspheming ⁹ him." ·Daniel said to the king, "Let it be as you say."

There were seventy of these priests, to say nothing of ¹⁰ their wives and children. ·The king went to the temple ¹¹ of Bel, taking Daniel with him. ·The priests of Bel said to him, "We are now withdrawing, as you can see; but we will leave you, O king, to set out food and prepare the wine and leave it there. Then you can shut the door and seal it with your own seal. If, when you return in the morning, you do not find that everything has been eaten by Bel, then let us be put to death; if not, ¹² then Daniel, that slanderer!" ·They were thinking—hence their confidence—of a secret entrance which they had made under the table, by which they came in daily ¹³ and took the offerings away. ·When the priests had ¹⁴ gone and the king had set out the food for Bel, ·Daniel made his servants bring ashes and spread them all over the temple floor, with no other witness than the king. Then they left the building, shut the door and, sealing ¹⁵ it with the king's seal, went away. ·That night, as usual, the priests came with their wives and children; they ate and drank everything.

¹⁶ The king was up very early next morning; so was ¹⁷ Daniel. ·"Daniel," said the king, "are the seals intact?" ¹⁸ "They are intact, O king," he replied. ·The king then opened the door and taking one look at the table he exclaimed, "You are great, O Bel! There is no decep-

**14 a.** Marduk, the god of Babylon.

19 tion in you!" ·But Daniel laughed. And restraining the king from going further in, he said, "Look at the floor
20 and examine these footprints." ·"I can see footprints of men, of women and of children," said the king,
21 and angrily ordered the priests to be arrested, with their wives and children. They showed him then the secret door through which they used to come and remove
22 what was on the table. ·The king had them put to death and handed Bel over to Daniel who destroyed both the idol and its temple.

### Daniel kills the dragon

23 There was a big dragon in Babylon, and this was
24 worshiped too. ·The king said to Daniel, "You are not going to tell me that this is no more than bronze? Look, it is alive; it eats and drinks; you cannot deny that this
25 is a living god; worship it, then." ·Daniel replied, "I worship the Lord my God; he is the living God. With your permission, O king, without using either sword or
26 club I will kill this serpent." ·"You have my permis-
27 sion," said the king. ·Whereupon Daniel took some pitch, some fat and some hair and boiled them up together, rolled the mixture into balls and fed them to the dragon; the dragon swallowed them and burst. Daniel said, "Now look at the sort of thing you wor-
28 ship!" ·The Babylonians were furious when they heard about this and began intriguing against the king. "The king has turned Jew," they said, "he has allowed Bel to be overthrown, and the dragon to be killed, and he
29 has put the priests to death." ·So they went to the king and said, "Hand Daniel over to us or else we will kill
30 you, and your family." ·They pressed him so hard that the king found himself forced to hand Daniel over to them.

### Daniel in the lion pit

31 They threw Daniel into the lion pit, and there he
32 stayed for six days. ·In the pit were seven lions, which were given two human bodies and two sheep every day; but for this period they were not given anything, to make sure they would eat Daniel.
33 Now the prophet Habakkuk was in Judaea: he had been making a stew, and breaking up bread small to

put in a basket. He was on his way to the fields, taking
34 this to the harvesters, ·when the angel of the Lord
spoke to him, "Take the meal you are carrying to Baby-
35 lon and give it to Daniel in the lion pit." ·"Lord,"
replied Habakkuk, "I have not even seen Babylon, and
36 know nothing about this pit." ·The angel of the Lord
seized his head and carried him off by the hair to Babylon where, with a great thrust of his spirit, he set Ha-
37 bakkuk down on the edge of the pit. ·"Daniel, Daniel," Habakkuk shouted, "take the meal that God has
38 sent you." ·And Daniel said, "You have kept me in
mind, O God; you have not deserted those who love
39 you." ·Rising to his feet he ate the meal, while the
angel of God lost no time in returning Habakkuk to
his own country.
40     On the seventh day the king came to lament over
Daniel; on reaching the pit he looked inside, and there
41 was Daniel, quite unperturbed. ·"You are great, O
Lord, God of Daniel," he exclaimed, "there is no god
42 but you!" ·Then he released Daniel from the pit and
had the plotters of Daniel's ruin thrown in instead,
where they were instantly eaten before his eyes.

INTRODUCTION TO

# THE MINOR PROPHETS

The twelve shorter books known as the "Minor Prophets"
appear in this edition of the Bible in their traditional order.
In these introductory notes, they are treated in what is most
probably their true historical order.

## Amos

Amos was a shepherd, called to prophesy for a brief period
in the reign of Jeroboam II, 783–743. The Northern Kingdom
was prosperous, a corrupt city life had developed, and the
military power of Assyria was a constant menace; in this
background, the prophet from the desert condemned the social injustices of his times and preached the coming "day of
Yahweh" as a visitation of wrath from which only a remnant
would be spared.

## Hosea

Hosea's ministry began under Jeroboam II and continued
under his successors, possibly until the fall of Samaria in 721.
A key to his prophecies is Hosea's own life with his unfaithful
wife, from which he was able to describe the love of Yahweh
for his people, whose unfaithfulness was plain from their
kings' policies of expedience, their unworthy priests, and their
worship of false gods.

## Micah

A contemporary of Isaiah, Micah too foresaw the ruin of
Israel as the punishment for a life of religious and social
corruption. Like other prophetic books, this book contains
some oracles which, from their character, appear to be of a
later time than that of the prophet named as the author.

## Zephaniah

Zephaniah prophesied in the reign of Josiah, before the religious reform of 622 B.C. In his understanding of a "day of retribution," Zephaniah echoes Amos; in his deep appreciation of sin as an offense against God, he anticipates Jeremiah.

## Nahum

The destruction of Nineveh is foretold with great poetic power in a prophecy made shortly before the capture of that city in 612. It is seen as the vindication of God's justice.

## Habakkuk

A poetic dialogue. If the oppressors who are cursed and finally routed are, as seems most likely, the Chaldaeans, the book should be dated between 605 and 597. The problem behind the prophet's questioning is that the God of goodness should choose the savage pagans as his instruments.

## Haggai

The first of the postexilic prophets. Haggai's four brief discourses urge the Jews, after the return from Babylon, to resume the work of rebuilding the Temple. They are dated precisely, in 520.

## Zechariah

Chapters 1–8 are dated between 520 and 517, and are the work of Zechariah, the prophet of national restoration. The rest of the chapters appear to be of various dates: Greeks appear among the oppressors of Israel together with the traditional Assyrians and Egyptians, and messianic expectation is strong; parts at least can be attributed to the late fourth century.

## Obadiah

This short book, half of which is a doublet of a passage in Jr. 49, seems to relate to the Edomite invasion after the destruction of Jerusalem, and should be dated in the fifth century.

## Malachi

"The book of my messenger"; six discourses which look forward to "the day of Yahweh." By its contents the book can be dated about the middle of the fifth century.

## Joel

The prophet sees a disastrous plague of locusts as a "sign," heralding the Judgment of the nations and the triumph of Yahweh and of Israel. The background is that of the postexilic community, and the book must have been written about 400 B.C.

## Jonah

A parable, written in the fourth century, but set in the remote past. It is written with a great freedom of imagination and teaches a clear lesson of God's mercy, his power and his universality.

# HOSEA

**1** The word of Yahweh that was addressed to Hosea son of Beeri when Uzziah, Jotham, Ahaz and Hezekiah were reigning in Judah, and Jeroboam son of Joash in Israel.[a]

## I. THE MARRIAGE OF HOSEA AND ITS SYMBOLISM

### Hosea's marriage: his three children

2 When Yahweh first spoke through Hosea, Yahweh said this to him, "Go, marry a whore, and get children with a whore, for the country itself has become nothing but a whore by abandoning Yahweh."

3 So he went; and he took Gomer daughter of Diblaim, 4 who conceived and bore him a son. ·"Name him Jezreel," Yahweh told him, "for it will not be long before I make the House of Jehu pay for the bloodshed at Jezreel[b] and I put an end to the sovereignty of the 5 House of Israel. ·When that day comes I will break Israel's bow in the Valley of Jezreel."[c]

6 She conceived a second time and gave birth to a daughter. "Name her Unloved," Yahweh told him. "No more love shall the House of Israel have from me 7 in future, no further forgiveness. ·(But my love shall go to the House of Judah and through Yahweh their God I mean to save them—but not by bow or sword or battle, horse or horseman.)"

8 She weaned Unloved, conceived again and gave 9 birth to a son. ·"Name him No-People-of-Mine," Yahweh said. "You are not my people and I am not your God."

### Yahweh and his unfaithful wife

⁴₂ **2** Denounce your mother, denounce her,
          for she is not my wife
          nor am I her husband.
          Let her rid her face of her whoring,
          and her breasts of her adultery,*a*
⁵₃        or else I will strip her naked,
          expose her as on the day she was born;
          I will make a wilderness of her,
          turn her into an arid land,
          and leave her to die of thirst.
⁶₄     I will not love her children,
          since they are the children of whoring.
⁷₅     Yes, their mother has played the whore,
          she who conceived them has disgraced herself.
          "I am going to court my lovers," she said,
          "who give me my bread and water,
          my wool, my flax, my oil and my drink."*b*
¹⁰₈    She would not acknowledge, not she,
          that I was the one who was giving her
          the corn, the wine, the oil,
          and who freely gave her that silver and gold
          of which they have made Baals.

¹¹₉    That is why, when the time comes, I mean to
                    withdraw my corn,
          and my wine, when the season for it comes.
          I will retrieve my wool, my flax,
          that were intended to cover her nakedness;
¹²₁₀   so will I display her shame before her lovers'
                    eyes
          and no one shall rescue her from my power.
¹⁴₁₂   I will lay her vines and fig trees waste,
          those of which she used to say,
          "These are the pay my lovers gave me";

**1 a.** More accurately, it was under the last four kings of Israel,
Menahem to Hoshea (743–724), that Hosea chiefly exercised his
prophetic ministry.
**b.** It was here that Jehu massacred the descendants of Omri.
**c.** Another name for Megiddo (Armageddon), one of the great
battlefields of Palestine.
**2 a.** Probably the amulets, tattooing and other distinctive marks
of the prostitute.
**b.** The Canaanite baals were gods of fertility.

I am going to make them into thickets
for the wild beasts to ravage.

13
11

I will put an end to all her rejoicing,
her feasts, her New Moons, her sabbaths
and all her solemn festivals.

15
13

I mean to make her pay for all the days
when she burned offerings to the Baals
and decked herself with rings and necklaces
to court her lovers,
forgetting me.
It is Yahweh who is speaking.

8
6

That is why I am going to block her way with
thorns,
and wall her in so that she cannot find her way;

9
7

she will chase after her lovers and never catch
up with them,
she will search for them and never find them.
Then she will say, "I will go back to my first
husband,
I was happier then than I am today."

16
14

That is why I am going to lure her
and lead her out into the wilderness
and speak to her heart.

17
15

I am going to give her back her vineyards,
and make the Valley of Achor[c] a gateway of
hope.
There she will respond to me as she did when
she was young,
as she did when she came out of the land of
Egypt.

18
16

When that day comes—it is Yahweh who
speaks—
she will call me "My husband,"
no longer will she call me "My Baal."[d]

19
17

I will take the names of the Baals off her lips,
their names shall never be uttered again.

20
18

When that day comes I will make a treaty on
her behalf with the wild animals,
with the birds of heaven and the creeping things
of the earth;

I will break bow, sword and battle in the
    country,
and make her sleep secure.

21
19
I will betroth you to myself for ever,
betroth you with integrity and justice,
with tenderness and love;

22
20
I will betroth you to myself with faithfulness,
and you will come to know Yahweh.

23
21
When that day comes—it is Yahweh who
    speaks—
the heavens will have their answer from me,
the earth its answer from them,

24
22
the grain, the wine, the oil, their answer from
    the earth,
and Jezreel his answer[e] from them.

25
23
I will sow him in the country,
I will love Unloved;

24
I will say to No-People-of-Mine, "You are my
    people,"
and he will answer, "You are my God."

**Hosea takes his unfaithful wife back and tests her fidelity. The symbol explained**

1 3 Yahweh said to me, "Go a second time, give your
love to a woman, loved by her husband but an
adulteress in spite of it, just as Yahweh gives his love
to the sons of Israel though they turn to other gods and
2 love raisin cakes." ·So I bought her for fifteen silver
3 shekels and a bushel and a half of barley, ·and said to
her, "For many days you must keep yourself quietly
for me, not playing the whore or offering yourself to
others; and I will do the same for you."

4 For the sons of Israel will be kept for many days
without a king, without a leader, without sacrifice or
5 sacred stone, without ephod or teraphim.[a] ·Afterward

c. "The Valley of Misery," one of the gorges near Jericho.
d. Strictly, "my master" or "my husband"; but the word had
taken on associations with the Canaanite gods.
e. The name Jezreel will no longer recall past crimes, see 1:4. Its
true meaning is "God sows."
3 a. I.e., without any visible link with Yahweh: the ephod was
the priest's amulet by which he determined the will of Yahweh;
the teraphim, a "household god" (of unknown form).

the sons of Israel will come back; they will seek Yahweh their God and David their king; they will come trembling to Yahweh, come for his good things in those days to come.

**The great future**

¹ **2**    And the number of the sons of Israel will be
                like the sand on the seashore,
         which cannot be measured or counted.
         In the place where they were told, "You are no
                people of mine,"
         they will be called, "The sons of the living God."
²    The sons of Judah and Israel will be one again
         and choose themselves one single leader,
         and they will spread far beyond their country;
         so great will be the day of Jezreel.
³    To your brother say, "People-of-Mine,"
         to your sister, "Beloved."

# II. THE CRIMES AND PUNISHMENT OF ISRAEL

**General corruption**

¹ **4**    Sons of Israel, listen to the word of Yahweh,
         for Yahweh indicts the inhabitants of the
                country:
²    there is no fidelity, no tenderness,
         no knowledge of God in the country,
²    only perjury and lies, slaughter, theft,
         adultery and violence, murder after murder.
³    This is why the country is in mourning, and all
                who live in it pine away,
         even the wild animals and the birds of heaven;
         the fish of the sea themselves are perishing.

**Against the priests**

⁴    But let no man denounce, no man rebuke;
         it is you, priest, that I denounce.
⁵    Day and night you stumble along,
         the prophet stumbling with you,

and you are the ruin of your people.

6 My people perish for want of knowledge.
As you have rejected knowledge
so do I reject you from my priesthood;
you have forgotten the teaching of your God,
I in my turn will forget your children.

7 Many as they are, all of them have sinned
against me,
they have bartered their glory for shame.

8 They feed on the sin of my people,
they are all greedy for their iniquity.

9 But as with the people, so let it be with the
priest:
I will make them pay for their conduct,
I will pay them out for their deeds.

10 They will eat but never be satisfied,
they will play the whore but still be sterile,
because they have deserted Yahweh

11 to give themselves up ·to whoring.

### Worship in Israel is not idolatrous and debauched

Wine, new wine addles the wits.

12 My people consult their block of wood,
a rod answers their questions[a];
for a prostituting spirit leads them astray,
they renounce their God to play the whore.

13 They offer sacrifice on the mountaintops,
burn their offerings on the hills,
under oak and poplar and terebinth,
so pleasant is their shade.
So, although your daughters prostitute themselves
and your sons' wives commit adultery,

14 I shall not be hard on your daughters for their
whoring
or on your sons' wives for their adultery,
when everyone else is wandering off with
whores
and offering sacrifice with sacred prostitutes.
Thus does a senseless people run to ruin.

4 a. The reference is to the sacred pole and the rod of a diviner.

### A warning to Judah

15
> Though you, Israel, play the whore,
> there is no need for Judah to sin too.
> Do not go to Gilgal,
> do not go up to Beth-aven,[b]
> do not take the oath "As Yahweh lives!"

### Israel the stubborn heifer

16
> Since Israel is as obstinate
> as a stubborn heifer,
> how can Yahweh pasture him
> like a lamb in rolling pastures?

17
> Ephraim is wedded to idols,

18
> they sprawl ·in the company of drunkards;
> whoring is all they care about,
> they barter their glory for shame.

19
> The wind will carry them off on its wings,
> then all their altars will bring them is disap-
> pointment.

### Priests, nobles and king are the ruin of the nation

1 **5**
> Listen to this, priests,
> attend, House of Israel,
> listen, royal household,
> you who are responsible for justice,
> for you have been a snare at Mizpah,
> and a net outspread on Tabor.

2
> They are entrenched in their deceitfulness
> and so I am going to punish them all.

3
> I know all about Ephraim,
> Israel has no secrets for me;
> yes Ephraim, you have played the whore,
> Israel has defiled himself.

4
> Their deeds do not allow them to return to
> their God,
> since a prostituting spirit possesses them;
> they do not know Yahweh.

5
> The arrogance of Israel is his own accuser,
> the iniquity of Ephraim knocks him down,
> and down comes Judah with him.

6
> Though they go in search of Yahweh with their
> sheep and oxen,

they do not find him;
for he has withdrawn from them.

7      They have proved unfaithful to Yahweh,
they have fathered bastards,
and now the destroyer will devour them, them
and their estates.

## The brothers' war

8      Sound the horn in Gibeah,
the trumpet in Ramah,
give the alarm at Beth-aven,
call Benjamin to arms!

9      Ephraim shall be laid waste when the day comes
for punishment;
I pronounce certain doom for the tribes of
Israel.[a]

10     The leaders of Judah are like men who displace
the boundary mark;
I mean to pour my anger out on them in a flood.

11     Ephraim is an oppressor, he tramples on justice,
so set is he on his pursuit of nothingness.

12     Very well, I myself will be the moth of
Ephraim,
the canker of the House of Judah.

## The folly of foreign alliances

13     Ephraim has seen how sick he is
and Judah the extent of his wound,
so Ephraim has turned to Assyria,
Judah has appealed to the Great King[b];
but he has no power to cure you
nor to heal your wound.

14     For I mean to be like a lion to Ephraim,
like a young lion to the house of Judah;
I, yes I, will tear to pieces, then go my way,
I will carry off my prey, and no one can snatch
it from me.

b. "House of nothing," a contemptuous name for Bethel.
5 a. This prophecy apparently relates to the Syro-Ephraimite
war (735–734), 2 K. 16–17.
b. Menahem paid tribute to Tiglath-pileser III of Assyria, 738;
Ahaz appealed to the same king for help, 735.

### Yahweh abandons his people

15

6:1

Yes, I am going to return to my dwelling place
until they confess their guilt and seek my face;
they will search for me in their misery.

### Israel's short-lived and shallow repentance

1

2

**6**

"Come, let us return to Yahweh.
He has torn us to pieces, but he will heal us;
he has struck us down, but he will bandage our
    wounds;

2
3

after a day or two he will bring us back to life,
on the third day he will raise us
and we shall live in his presence.

3a

Let us set ourselves to know Yahweh;
that he will come is as certain as the dawn;

5b

his judgment will rise like the light,

3b

he will come to us as showers come,
like spring rains watering the earth."

4

What am I to do with you, Ephraim?
What am I to do with you, Judah?
This love of yours is like a morning cloud,
like the dew that quickly disappears.

5a

This is why I have torn them to pieces by the
    prophets,
why I slaughtered them with the words from
    my mouth,

6

since what I want is love, not sacrifice;
knowledge of God, not holocausts.

### The past and present sins of Israel

7

But they have violated the covenant at Adam,
they have proved unfaithful to me there.

8

Gilead is a town of evildoers,
full of bloody footprints.

9

Like so many robbers in ambush
a band of priests commits murder on the road
    to Shechem—
appalling behavior, indeed!

10

I have seen horrors in Bethel;
that is where Ephraim plays the whore
and Israel defiles himself.

11

Judah, I intend a harvest for you, too,

when I restore the fortunes of my people.

**1 7** Whenever I want to heal Israel,
I am confronted by the guilt of Ephraim
and the wickedness of Samaria;
deceit is their principle of behavior,
thieves break into houses
and bandits raid outside.

2 They never pause to consider
that I know about all their wickedness;
yet their actions are all around them,
they stare me in the face.

## Conspiracy the order of the day in Israel

3 Such is their cunning, they beguile the king,
and the leaders too, such is their treachery.

4 But they breathe fury, all of them,
as fiery as an oven
which the baker does not need to stoke
from the time he has kneaded the dough until
it rises.

5 They addle the king and leaders with wine
fumes
as he mixes with these scoundrels.

6 Their hearts reach oven heat in the excitement
of the plot;
their fury smolders all night
and in the morning blazes like a fierce flame;

7 all burn at oven heat
and they consume the men who rule them.
Thus have all their kings fallen,
not one of them has ever called on me.[a]

## Israel ruined by relying on foreign powers

8 Ephraim mixes with the nations,
Ephraim is a half-baked cake.

9 Foreigners eat his strength away,
he is unconscious of it;
gray hairs are scattered on his head:
he is unconscious of it.

10 (The arrogance of Israel is his own accuser;

**7 a.** Seven of the kings of the Northern Kingdom had been murdered by the year 737.

they will not come back to Yahweh their God;
in spite of all this they will not seek him.)

11 Ephraim is like a silly, witless dove,
calling on Egypt, turning to Assyria.

12 Wherever they turn, I will spread my net over
them,
I mean to bring them down like the birds of
heaven,
I will punish them for their perversity.

### The ingratitude and punishment of Israel

13 Trouble is coming to them, for they have
strayed from me!
Ruin on them, for they have rebelled against
me!
I wanted to redeem them, but they tell lies about
me.

14 Theirs is no heartfelt cry to me
when they lament on their beds.
They gash themselves for the sake of corn and
wine,
yet they rebel against me.

15 I it was who gave strength to their arms,
yet all they do is make wicked plots against me.

16 They turn to Baal,
they are like a treacherous bow.
Their leaders will fall by the sword
because of their arrogant talk,
and how they will be laughed at in the land of
Egypt!

### Sound the alarm!

1 **8** Put the trumpet to your lips
like a watchman on duty at the house of Yahweh,
because they have violated my covenant
and rebelled against my Law.

2 Useless now to shout, "God of Israel, we acknowledge you."

3 Israel has rejected the good;
the enemy[a] will hunt him down.

## Civil anarchy and idolatry

4 They have set up kings, but not with my consent,
 and appointed princes, but without my knowledge.
 Out of their own silver and gold they have made idols,
 which are doomed to destruction.

5 I spurn your calf, Samaria,
 my anger blazes against it.
 (How long will it be before they purge themselves of this,

6 the sons of Israel?)
 A workman made the thing,
 this cannot be God!
 Yes, the calf of Samaria shall go up in flames.

7 They sow the wind, they will reap the whirlwind;
 their wheat will yield no ear,
 the ear will yield no flour,
 or, if it does, foreigners will swallow it.

## Israel ruined by relying on foreign powers

8 Israel himself has been swallowed,
 and is destined now to stay among the nations
 like a crock that no one wants,

9 for making approaches to Assyria
 —that wild ass living alone.
 Ephraim is renting lovers.

10 Right; let them rent them among the nations,
 I am going to disperse them this minute;
 that will soon put a stop to their anointing kings
 and leaders.

## Against the outward show of worship

11 Ephraim has built altar after altar,
 they have only served him as occasion for sin.

12 Were I to write out the thousand precepts of my Law for him,
 they would be paid no more attention than those of a stranger.

8 a. Assyria.

13
    They love sacrificing; right, let them sacrifice!
    They love meat; right, let them eat it!
    Yahweh takes no pleasure in these.
    He is now going to remember their iniquity
    and punish their sins;
    they will have to go back to Egypt.

### Against extravagance in building

14
    Israel has forgotten his Maker
    and has built palaces;
    Judah has built fortified town after fortified
        town;
    right, I will rain fire on his towns,
    it will devour his palaces.

### The sorrows of exile

1 **9**
    Let us have no rejoicing, Israel,
    no exulting like the other peoples;
    for you have deserted God to play the whore,
    you have enjoyed the prostitute's pay
    on every threshing floor.

2
    Neither floor nor vat will nourish them,
    the new wine will disappoint them.

3
    They will no longer live in the land of Yahweh,
    Ephraim will have to go back to Egypt,
    and in Assyria they will eat food that is unclean.

4
    They will pour libations of wine to Yahweh no
        longer,
    nor offer sacrifice to him;
    their bread will be like mourners' bread,
    all those who eat it will become unclean;
    for their bread will serve only for themselves,
    it must not enter the house of Yahweh.

5
    What will you do on the day of solemn festival,
    the day of the feast of Yahweh?

6
    Why, they will have gone, gone from the devas-
        tation.
    Egypt will receive them, Memphis bury them,
    nettles will inherit their treasures of silver,
    and brambles invade their tents.

### Persecution, the prophet's reward for foretelling the punishment

7       Now the days of reckoning have come,
           the days of reprisals are here.
           "The prophet is mad," Israel protests, "this inspired fellow is raving."
           —Ah yes, but only because your iniquity is so great,
           your apostasy so grave.

8       Ephraim watches the prophet's tent,
           traps are set for him on all his paths,
           in the house of his God enmity awaits him.

9       These men are as steeped in corruption
           as in the days of Gibeah;
           Yahweh will remember their iniquity,
           he will punish their sins.

### Punishment for the crime at Baal-peor

10      It was like finding grapes in the wilderness when I found Israel,
           like seeing early fruit on the fig tree when I saw your fathers;
           but when they reached Baal-peor they devoted themselves to shame
           and became as hateful as the thing they loved.

11      The glory of Ephraim will fly away like a bird:
           no giving birth, no pregnancy, no conceiving.

12      And if they rear sons, I will take these from them before they come to manhood;
           trouble for them indeed when I abandon them.

13      Ephraim, I see, has made his sons a prey,
           Ephraim must lead his sons to the slaughterhouse.

14      Give them, Yahweh—what are you to give?—
           give them wombs that miscarry, and dried-up breasts.

### Punishment for the crime at Gilgal

15      Their wickedness appeared in full at Gilgal,[a]
           there I came to hate them.
           Because of their wicked deeds

**9 a.** The monarchy was instituted there, 1 S. 13:7–14; 15:10–23.

I will drive them out of my house;
I will love them no longer,
for their leaders are all rebels.

16 Ephraim is cut down,
their roots are withered;
they will bear no fruit.
And if they bear children,
I will kill the darlings of their womb.

17 Because they have not listened to him, my God
will cast them off
and they will be wanderers throughout the nations.

## The destruction of Israel's cultic objects

1
**10**  Israel was a luxuriant vine
yielding plenty of fruit.
The more his fruit increased,
the more altars he built;
the richer his land became,
the richer he made the sacred stones.

2 Their heart is a divided heart;
very well, they must pay for it:
Yahweh is going to break their altars down
and destroy their sacred stones.

3 Then they will say,
"We have no king
because we have not feared Yahweh."
But what can a king do for us?

4 Words, words! False oaths! Alliances!
And judgment is only a poisonous weed that
thrives
in the furrows of the field.

5 The inhabitants of Samaria are trembling
for the calf of Beth-aven;
yes, its people mourn for it,
its so-called priests bewail its glory,
now this has vanished.

6 The calf itself shall be carried off to Assyria
as tribute to the Great King.
Ephraim will reap the shame,
and Israel blush for his idol.

7 Samaria has had her day.

Her king[a] is like a straw drifting on the water.

8   The idolatrous high places shall be destroyed—
that sin of Israel;
thorn and thistle will grow on their altars.
Then they will say to the mountains, "Cover
us!"
and to the hills, "Fall on us!"

## Against Gibeah

9   Ever since the days at Gibeah, Israel, you have
sinned.
Things are still the same.
And will not war overtake the guilty at Gibeah?
10  I shall come and punish them.
The nations will muster against them
to punish them for their double crime.

## Threats and an invitation to repentance

11  Ephraim is a well-trained heifer
that loves to tread the threshing floor;
very well, I myself mean to lay the yoke on
that fine neck of hers,
I am going to put Ephraim in harness,
Israel will have to plow,
Jacob must draw the harrow.
12  Sow integrity for yourselves,
reap a harvest of kindness,
break up your fallow ground:
it is time to go seeking Yahweh
until he comes to rain salvation on you.

## The end of Israel

13  Why have you plowed iniquity,
reaped injustice,
and eaten the produce, lies?
Because you have trusted in your chariots,
and in your host of warriors,
14  turmoil is going to break out in your towns,
and all your fortresses will be laid waste,
as Shalman[b] laid Beth-arbel waste

10 a. The calf.
b. Probably Salamanu, king of Moab.

on the day of the battle,
when mothers fell, dashed to pieces, on their
children.

15 That is what I mean to do to you, House of
Israel,
because of your great wickedness;

11:1 and in the storm the king of Israel is going to
disappear for ever.

### God's love despised: his vengeance

1 When Israel was a child I loved him,
and I called my son out of Egypt.

2 But the more I called to them, the further they
went from me;
they have offered sacrifice to the Baals
and set their offerings smoking before the idols.

3 I myself taught Ephraim to walk,
I took them in my arms;
yet they have not understood that I was the one
looking after them.

4 I led them with reins of kindness,
with leading strings of love.
I was like someone who lifts an infant close
against his cheek;
stooping down to him I gave him his food.

5 They will have to go back to Egypt,
Assyria must be their king,
because they have refused to return to me.

6 The sword will rage through their towns,
wiping out their children,
glutting itself inside their fortresses.

### God's love proves stronger than his vengeance

7 My people are diseased through their disloyalty;
they call on Baal,
but he does not cure them.

8 Ephraim, how could I part with you?
Israel, how could I give you up?
How could I treat you like Admah,
or deal with you like Zeboiim?[a]
My heart recoils from it,
my whole being trembles at the thought.

9 I will not give rein to my fierce anger,

> I will not destroy Ephraim again,
> for I am God, not man:
> I am the Holy One in your midst
> and have no wish to destroy.

## The return from exile

10
> They will follow behind Yahweh;
> he will be roaring like a lion—
> how he will roar!—
> and his sons will come speeding from the west;

11
> they will come speeding from Egypt like a bird,
> speeding from the land of Assyria like a dove,
> and I will settle them in their homes
> —it is Yahweh who speaks.

## Israel's religion and policy both alike perverse

$\frac{1}{12}$ **12**
> All around me are the lies of Ephraim
> and the deceit of the House of Israel.
> But God still recognizes Judah,
> and he is still called the people of the Holy
> One.

$\frac{2}{1}$
> Ephraim feeds on the wind,
> forever chasing the wind from the East,
> accumulating falsehood and fraud,
> making treaties with Assyria,
> sending oil to Egypt.

## Against Jacob

$\frac{3}{2}$
> Yahweh has a case against Israel,
> he will pay Jacob as his conduct merits,
> and will repay him as his deeds deserve.

$\frac{4}{3}$
> In the very womb he supplanted his brother,
> in maturity he wrestled against God.

$\frac{5}{4}$
> He wrestled with the angel and beat him,
> he wept and pleaded with him.
> He met him at Bethel
> and there God spoke to him.

$\frac{6}{5}$
> Yes, Yahweh God of Sabaoth, Yahweh is his
> name.

$\frac{7}{6}$
> Turn again, then, to your God,

**11 a.** Neighboring towns of Sodom and Gomorrah in Gn. 10:19; presumably overwhelmed by the same fate, according to the tradition followed here.

hold fast to love and justice,
and always put your trust in your God.

### Greed and the punishment of Israel

⁸/₇ Canaan holds fraudulent scales in his hands,
to defraud is his delight.

⁹/₈ "How rich I have become!" says Ephraim,
"I have amassed a fortune."
But he will keep nothing of all his profits,
because of the guilt that he has brought on
himself.

### The prospect of reconciliation between Yahweh and Israel

¹⁰/₉ I have been Yahweh, your God, since the days
in the land of Egypt.
I will make you live in tents again
as on the day of Meeting.ᵃ

¹¹/₁₀ I will speak to the prophets,
I will increase the visions
and through the prophets I will deal out death.

### New threats

¹²/₁₁ Gilead is nothing but iniquity,
they are falsehood, nothing else;
at Gilgal they sacrifice to bulls;
their altars shall be reduced to heaps of stones
in a plowed field.

### Against Jacob and Ephraim

¹³/₁₂ Jacob fled to the plains of Aram,
Israel worked to win a wife,
to win a wife he looked after sheep.

¹⁴/₁₃ But Yahweh brought Israel out of Egypt by a
prophet,
and a prophet looked after Israel.

¹⁵/₁₄ Ephraim has given bitter provocation
and Yahweh means to bring his bloodshed down
on him,
his Lord will repay him for his insults.

### Idolatry punished

¹ **13** When Ephraim spoke, all trembled,
so great was he in Israel,

but through Baal he brought guilt on himself
    and perished.
And now they add sin to sin,
they smelt images from their silver,
idols of their own manufacture,
smith's work, all of it.
"Sacrifice to them," they say.
Men blow kisses to calves!

3    Therefore they will be like morning mist,
like the dew that quickly disappears,
like the chaff whirled from the threshing floor,
like smoke escaping through the window.

## The punishment for ingratitude

4    Yet I am Yahweh, your God since the days in
        the land of Egypt;
you know no God but me,
there is no other savior.

5    I pastured you in the wilderness;
in the land of drought

6    I pastured them, and they were satisfied;
once satisfied, their hearts grew proud,
and so they came to forget me.

7    Very well, I will be a lion to them,
a leopard lurking by the way;

8    like a bear robbed of her cubs I will pounce on
        them,
and tear the flesh around their hearts;
the dogs shall eat their flesh,
the wild beasts tear them to pieces.

## The end of the monarchy

9    I mean to destroy you, Israel;
who can come to your help?

10    Your king, where is he now, to save you,[a]
where are your leaders to champion you?
Those of whom you used to say,
"Give me a king and leaders."

**12 a.** At Sinai, Ex. 5:3.
**13 a.** Possibly an ironic allusion to Hoshea, whose name means
"Yahweh-is-savior." He was imprisoned at the beginning of the
siege of Samaria, see 14:1.

11
In my anger I gave you a king
and in my wrath I take him away.

### The inevitability of ruin

12
The iniquity of Ephraim is carefully hoarded,
his sin is safely stored away.

13
Pangs as of childbirth overtake him,
and a stupid child it is,
its time is up but it does not leave the womb.

14
And am I to save them from the power of
Sheol?
Am I to rescue them from Death?
Where is your plague, Death?
Where are your scourges, Sheol?
I have no eyes for pity.

15
Ephraim may flourish among the reeds,
but the wind from the East will come,
the breath of Yahweh will rise from the desert
to dry his water sources, to parch his springs,
to strip his land of all its treasures.

1
**14**
Samaria must atone
for rebelling against her God.
They shall fall by the sword,
their little children be dashed to pieces,
their pregnant women disemboweled.

## III. THE REPENTANCE AND RECONCILIATION OF ISRAEL. A PROMISE OF FUTURE HAPPINESS

### The sincere conversion of Israel to Yahweh

2
Israel, come back to Yahweh your God;
your iniquity was the cause of your downfall.

3
Provide yourself with words
and come back to Yahweh.
Say to him, "Take all iniquity away
so that we may have happiness again
and offer you our words of praise.

4
Assyria cannot save us,
we will not ride horses any more,[a]

or say, 'Our God!' to what our own hands have
made,
for you are the one in whom orphans find
compassion."

5     —I will heal their disloyalty,
I will love them with all my heart,
for my anger has turned from them.

6     I will fall like dew on Israel.
He shall bloom like the lily,
and thrust out roots like the poplar,

7     his shoots will spread far;
he will have the beauty of the olive
and the fragrance of Lebanon.

8     They will come back to live in my shade;
they will grow corn that flourishes,
they will cultivate vines
as renowned as the wine of Helbon.

9     What has Ephraim to do with idols any more
when it is I who hear his prayer and care for
him?
I am like a cypress ever green,
all your fruitfulness comes from me.

### Concluding admonition

10     Let the wise man understand these words.
Let the intelligent man grasp their meaning.
For the ways of Yahweh are straight,
and virtuous men walk in them,
but sinners stumble.

**14 a.** "Ride horses"; possibly "conclude an alliance with Egypt,"
for the sake of the mounted troops for which Egypt was famous.

# JOEL

1 1     The word of Yahweh that was addressed to
Joel son of Pethuel.


## I. THE PLAGUE OF LOCUSTS


### A. A LITURGY OF MOURNING AND ENTREATY


#### a. Lamentation over the ruin of the country

2     Listen to this, you elders;
all inhabitants of the country, attend.
Has anything like this ever happened in your
day,
or in your fathers' days?

3     Tell it to your sons,
let your sons tell it to their sons,
and their sons to a generation after them.

4     What the gnawer has left, the grown locust has
devoured,
what the grown locust has left, the hopper has
devoured,
what the hopper has left, the shearer has devoured.[a]

5     Awake, drunkards, and weep!
All you who drink wine, lament
for that new wine: it has been dashed from your
lips.

6     For a nation has invaded my country,
mighty and innumerable;

**1 a.** The locust invasion has included insects in four distinct
stages of growth.

its teeth are the teeth of lions,
it has the fangs of a lioness.

7    It has laid waste my vines
and torn my fig trees to pieces;
it has stripped them clean and cut them down,
their branches have turned white.

8    Mourn like a virgin wearing sackcloth
for her young man betrothed to her.

9    Oblation and libation[b] have vanished
from the house of Yahweh.
The priests, the ministers of Yahweh,
are in mourning.

10   Wasted lie the fields,
the fallow is in mourning.
For the corn has been laid waste,
the wine fails,
the fresh oil dries up.

11   Stand dismayed, you farmers,
wail, you vinedressers,
for the wheat, for the barley;
the harvest of the field has been ruined.

12   The vine has withered,
the fig tree wilts away;
pomegranate, and palm, and apple,
every tree in the field is drooping.
Yes, gladness has faded
among the sons of men.

### b. A call to repentance and prayer

13   Priests, put on sackcloth and lament.
Ministers of the altar, wail.
Come, pass the night in sackcloth,
you ministers of my God.
For the house of our God has been deprived
of oblation and libation.

14   Order a fast,
proclaim a solemn assembly;
elders, call together
all the inhabitants of the country
to the house of Yahweh your God.
Cry out to Yahweh,

15   "Oh, what a day!

> For the day of Yahweh is near,
> it comes as a devastation from Shaddai."[c]

16    Has not the food disappeared
before our eyes?
Have not joy and gladness vanished
from the house of our God?

17    Seeds shrivel
under their clods;
the barns are broken down,
the granaries lie in ruins,
for lack of harvest.

18    What mourning from the beasts!
The herds of cattle wander bewildered
because they have no pasture.
Even the flocks of sheep must bear their punishment.

19    To you, Yahweh, I cry:
fire has devoured the pastures on the heath,
flame has burned up
every tree in the orchard.

20    Even the wild beasts wait anxiously for you,
for the watercourses have run dry,
and fire has devoured the pastures on the heath.

### c. The day of Yahweh and the present calamity

### The alarm

1   **2**    Sound the trumpet in Zion,
give the alarm on my holy mountain!
Let all the inhabitants of the country tremble,
for the day of Yahweh is coming,
yes, it is near.

2    Day of darkness and gloom,
day of cloud and blackness.
Like the dawn there spreads across the mountains
a vast and mighty host,
such as has never been before,

**b.** The daily offerings from the produce of the soil: corn, wine and oil, as listed in v.10.
**c.** There is a Hebrew pun on the word for "devastation" and Shaddai (one of the names of God).

such as will never be again
to the remotest ages.

## The invading army

3
In their van the fire devours,
in their rear a flame consumes.
The country is like a garden of Eden ahead of
them
and a desert waste behind them.
Nothing escapes them.

4
They look like horses,
like chargers they gallop on,

5
with a racket like the clatter of chariots
they hurtle over the mountain tops,
with a crackling like a blazing fire
devouring the stubble,
a mighty army in battle array.

6
At the sight of them the peoples are appalled
and every face grows pale.

7
Like fighting men they press forward,
like warriors scale the walls,
each marching straight ahead,
not turning from his path;

8
they never jostle each other,
each marches straight ahead:
arrows fly, they still press forward,
without breaking ranks.

9
They hurl themselves at the city,
they leap on to its walls,
climb to the housetops,
and make their way through windows
like marauders.

## A vision of the day of Yahweh

10
As they come on, the earth quakes,
the skies tremble,
sun and moon grow dark,
the stars lose their brilliance.

11
Yahweh makes his voice heard
at the head of his army,
and indeed his regiments are innumerable,

all powerful is the one that carries out his
    orders,
for great is the day of Yahweh,
and very terrible—who can face it?

#### d. A call to repentance

12      "But now, now—it is Yahweh who speaks—
        come back to me with all your heart,
        fasting, weeping, mourning."
13      Let your hearts be broken, not your garments
            torn,
        turn to Yahweh your God again,
        for he is all tenderness and compassion,
        slow to anger, rich in graciousness,
        and ready to relent.
14      Who knows if he will not turn again, will not
            relent,
        will not leave a blessing as he passes,
        oblation and libation
        for Yahweh your God?

15      Sound the trumpet in Zion!
        Order a fast,
        proclaim a solemn assembly,
16      call the people together,
        summon the community,
        assemble the elders,
        gather the children,
        even the infants at the breast.
        Let the bridegroom leave his bedroom
        and the bride her alcove.
17      Between vestibule and altar let the priests,
        the ministers of Yahweh, lament.
        Let them say,
        "Spare your people, Yahweh!
        Do not make your heritage a thing of shame,
        a byword for the nations.
        Why should it be said among the nations,
        'Where is their God?' "

## B. THE PRAYER ANSWERED

18
> Then Yahweh, jealous on behalf of his land,
> took pity on his people.

### The plague ceases

19
> Yahweh spoke in answer to his people,
> "Now I send you
> corn and wine and oil,
> until you have enough.
> Never again shall I make you
> a thing of shame for the nations.

20
> I will drive the invader from the north far away
>     from you
> and drive him into an arid, desolate land,
> his vanguard to the eastern sea,
> his rearguard to the western sea.
> He will give off a stench,
> give off a foul stink."
> (For he has done great things.)

### A vision of plenty

21
> O soil, do not be afraid;
> be glad, rejoice,
> for Yahweh has done great things.

22
> Beasts of the field, do not be afraid;
> the pastures on the heath are green again,
> the trees bear fruit,
> vine and fig tree yield abundantly.

23
> Sons of Zion, be glad,
> rejoice in Yahweh your God;
> for he has given you
> the autumn rain, since he is just,
> and has poured the rains down for you,
> the autumn and spring rain as before.

24
> The threshing floors will be full of grain,
> the vats overflow with wine and oil.

25
> "I will make up to you for the years
> devoured by grown locust and hopper

> by shearer and young locust,
> my great army
> which I sent to invade you."

26
> You will eat to your heart's content, will eat
>     your fill,
> and praise the name of Yahweh your God
> who has treated you so wonderfully.
> (My people will not be disappointed any more.)

27
> And you will know that I am in the midst of
>     Israel,
> that I am Yahweh your God, with none to
>     equal me.
> My people will not be disappointed any more.

## II. THE NEW AGE AND THE DAY OF YAHWEH

### A. THE OUTPOURING OF THE SPIRIT

$28^1$ **3**
> "After this
> I will pour out my spirit on all mankind.
> Your sons and daughters shall prophesy,
> your old men shall dream dreams,
> and your young men see visions.

$29^2$
> Even on the slaves, men and women,
> will I pour out my spirit in those days.

$30^3$
> I will display portents in heaven and on earth,
> blood and fire and columns of smoke."

$31^4$
> The sun will be turned into darkness,
> and the moon into blood,
> before the day of Yahweh dawns,
> that great and terrible day.

$32^5$
> All who call on the name of Yahweh will be
>     saved,
> for *on Mount Zion there will be some who have
>     escaped,*[a]
> as Yahweh has said,

**3 a.** Ob. 17.

and in Jerusalem some survivors whom Yahweh
will call.


## B. THE JUDGMENT OF THE NATIONS

### The judgment announced

1
3
4

"For in those days and at that time,
when I restore the fortunes of Judah and Jerusalem,

2

I am going to gather all the nations
and take them down to the Valley of Jehosh-
aphat;
there I intend to put them on trial
for all they have done to Israel, my people and
my heritage.
For[a] they have scattered them among the nations
and have divided up my land among themselves.

3

They have cast lots for my people;
they have bartered the boys for prostitutes,
have sold the girls for wine and drunk it."

### Charges against the Phoenicians and Philistines

4

"And you, Tyre and Sidon, what do you expect
from me?
You too, regions of Philistia?
Do you want to take revenge on me?
If you were to take revenge on me,
I would make it recoil promptly and swiftly on
your own heads.

5

You who have taken my silver and my gold,
who have carried off my rich treasures to your
temples,

6

you who have sold to the people of Javan[b]
the sons of Judah and Jerusalem,
to remove them far from their own frontiers.

7

Now I mean to summon them from wherever
you have sold them,
now I intend to make your crime recoil on your
own heads.

8   I am going to sell your sons and daughters
     into the hands of the sons of Judah,
     and they will sell them to the Sabaeans,[c]
     to a distant nation;
     Yahweh has spoken!"

### A summons to the nations

9   "Proclaim this among the nations.
     'Prepare for war!
     Muster the champions!
     Warriors, advance,
     quick march!
10   Hammer your plowshares into swords,
     your sickles into spears,
     let the weakling say, "I am a fighting man."
11   Come quickly,
     all you surrounding nations,
     assemble there!'
     (Yahweh, send down your champions!)

12   "Let the nations rouse themselves, let them
      march
     to the Valley of Jehoshaphat,
     for I am going to sit in judgment there
     on all the nations around.
13   Put the sickle in:
     the harvest is ripe;
     come and tread:
     the winepress is full,
     the vats are overflowing,
     so great is their wickedness!"

14   Host on host
     in the Valley of Decision!
     For the day of Yahweh is near
     in the Valley of Decision!

### The day of Yahweh

15   Sun and moon grow dark,
     the stars lose their brilliance.

**4 a.** After the siege of Jerusalem in 597 there were deportations
to Babylon. There was a further deportation in 586.
**b.** Greece.
**c.** Of South Arabia.

16       Yahweh roars from Zion,
      makes his voice heard from Jerusalem;
      heaven and earth tremble.

      But Yahweh will be a shelter for his people,
      a stronghold for the sons of Israel.

17       "You will learn then that I am Yahweh your
            God,
      dwelling in Zion, my holy mountain.
      Jerusalem will be a holy place,
      no alien will ever pass through it again."


## C. THE GLORIOUS FUTURE OF ISRAEL

18       When that day comes,
      the mountains will run with new wine
      and the hills flow with milk,
      and all the river beds of Judah
      will run with water.
      A fountain will spring from the house of Yah-
            weh
      to water the wadi of Acacias.
19       Egypt will become a desolation,
      Edom a desert waste
      on account of the violence done to the sons of
            Judah
      whose innocent blood they shed in their coun-
            try.
20       But Judah will be inhabited for ever,
      Jerusalem from age to age.
21       "I will avenge their blood and let none go un-
            punished,"
      and Yahweh shall make his home in Zion.

# AMOS

### Title

¹ 1 Words of Amos who was one of the shepherds of Tekoa. The visions he had about Israel in the time of Uzziah king of Judah and of Jeroboam$^a$ son of Joash, king of Israel, two years before the earthquake.

### Introduction

² He said:

> Yahweh roars from Zion,
> and makes his voice heard from Jerusalem;
> the shepherds' pastures mourn,
> and the crown of Carmel withers.

## I. JUDGMENT ON THE NEIGHBORS OF ISRAEL AND ON ISRAEL ITSELF

### Damascus

³ Yahweh says this:

> For the three crimes, the four crimes,$^b$ of Damascus
> I have made my decree and will not relent:
> because they have thrashed Gilead with iron threshing sledges,
⁴
⁵ > I am going to hurl fire on the House of Hazael
> to burn up Ben-hadad's$^c$ palaces;
> I am going to break the gate bars of Damascus,

**1 a.** Jeroboam II of Israel, 783–743.
**b.** In the manner of the "numerical proverbs," the two consecutive numbers indicate an indefinite number.
**c.** King Hazael of Damascus and his son Ben-hadad III were bitter enemies of Israel.

and cut down the one enthroned at Bikath-aven
and the sceptered one at Beth-eden[d];
and the people of Aram shall go captive to Kir,
    says Yahweh.

### Gaza and Philistia

6 Yahweh says this:

For the three crimes, the four crimes, of Gaza
I have made my decree and will not relent:
because they have deported entire nations
    as slaves to Edom,
7      I am going to hurl fire on the walls of Gaza
to burn up her palaces.
8      I am going to cut down the one enthroned at
    Ashdod
and the sceptered one at Ashkelon;
I am going to turn my hand against Ekron
until the last of the Philistines is dead,
    says Yahweh.

### Tyre and Phoenicia

9 Yahweh says this:

For the three crimes, the four crimes, of Tyre
I have made my decree and will not relent:
because they have deported entire nations as
    slaves to Edom
and have not remembered the covenant of
    brotherhood,
10      I am going to hurl fire on the walls of Tyre
to burn up her palaces.

### Edom

11 Yahweh says this:

For the three crimes, the four crimes, of Edom
I have made my decree and will not relent:
because he has persecuted his brother with the
    sword,
stifling his pity,
persistently nursing his fury
and ever cherishing his rage,
12      I am going to hurl fire on Teman[e]
to burn up the palaces of Bozrah.

## Ammon

13 Yahweh says this:

> For the three crimes, the four crimes, of the
>     sons of Ammon
> I have made my decree and will not relent:
> because they have disemboweled the pregnant
>     women of Gilead
> in order to extend their own frontiers,

14
> I am going to light a fire against the wall of
>     Rabbah
> to burn up her palaces,
> to the sound of war cries on the day of battle,
> amid storms on a day of hurricane;

15
> and their king shall go into exile,
> he and his princes with him,
> says Yahweh.

## Moab

1 2 Yahweh says this:

> For the three crimes, the four crimes, of Moab
> I have made my decree and will not relent:
> because they have burned the bones of the
>     king[a] of Edom for lime,

2
> I am going to hurl fire on Moab
> to burn up the palaces of Kerioth,
> and Moab shall die in tumult,
> to the sound of war cries and the blare of
>     trumpets;

3
> I will cut down the chieftain inside her
> and slaughter all her princes with him,
> says Yahweh.

## Judah

4 Yahweh says this:

> For the three crimes, the four crimes, of Judah
> I have made my decree and will not relent:

d. The two place names (meaning "valley of wickedness" and "house of pleasure") stand for Damascus.
e. A tribal name or place name.
2 a. Thus ensuring the suffering of the soul.

> because they have rejected the Law of Yahweh
> and failed to keep his precepts,
> because the false gods which their ancestors
>     followed
> have led them astray,
> 5 I am going to hurl fire on Judah
> to burn up the palaces of Jerusalem.

### Israel

6 Yahweh says this:

> For the three crimes, the four crimes, of Israel
> I have made my decree and will not relent:
> because they have sold the virtuous man for
>     silver
> and the poor man for a pair of sandals,
> 7 because they trample on the heads of ordinary
>     people
> and push the poor out of their path,
> because father and son have both resorted to
>     the same girl,<sup>b</sup>
> profaning my holy name,
> 8 because they stretch themselves out by the side
>     of every altar
> on clothes acquired as pledges,
> and drink the wine of the people they have fined
> in the house of their god . . .
> 9 Yet it was I who overthrew the Amorites when
>     they attacked,
> men tall as cedars and strong as oaks,
> I who destroyed them,
> both fruit above ground
> and root below.
> 10 It was I who brought you out of the land of
>     Egypt
> and for forty years led you through the
>     wilderness
> to take possession of the Amorite's country.
> 11 I raised up prophets from your sons
> and nazirites from your young men.
> Is this not true, sons of Israel?
> —it is Yahweh who speaks.
> 12 But you have forced the nazirites to drink wine

and given orders to the prophets,
"Do not prophesy."

13 See then how I am going to crush you into the ground
as the threshing sledge crushes when clogged by straw;

14 flight will not save even the swift,
the strong man will find his strength useless,
the mighty man will be powerless to save himself.

15 The bowman will not stand his ground,
the fast runner will not escape,
the horseman will not save himself,

16 the bravest warriors will run away naked that day.
It is Yahweh who speaks.


## II. ISRAEL WARNED AND THREATENED


### Election and punishment

1 **3** Listen, sons of Israel, to this oracle Yahweh speaks against you, against the whole family I brought out of the land of Egypt:

2 You alone, of all the families of earth, have I acknowledged,
therefore it is for all your sins that I mean to punish you.


### The prophetic call cannot be resisted

3 Do two men take the road together
if they have not planned to do so?

4 Does the lion roar in the jungle
if no prey has been found?
Does the young lion growl in his lair
if he has captured nothing?

5 Does the bird fall to the ground
if no trap has been set?

**b.** Sacred prostitution was a feature of Canaanite worship.

Does the snare spring up from the ground
if nothing has been caught?
6 Does the trumpet sound in the city
without the populace becoming alarmed?
Does misfortune come to a city
if Yahweh has not sent it?
7 No more does the Lord Yahweh do anything
without revealing his plans to his servants the
prophets.
8 The lion roars: who can help feeling afraid?
The Lord Yahweh speaks: who can refuse to
prophesy?

## Samaria will perish for her corruption

9 Proclaim it in the palaces of Assyria
and in the palaces in the land of Egypt;
saying, "Assemble on Samaria's mountain
and see what great disorder there is in that city,
what oppression is found inside her."
10 They know nothing of fair dealing
—it is Yahweh who speaks—
they cram their palaces full by harshness and
extortion.
11 Therefore, the Lord Yahweh says this:
An enemy[a] is going to invade the country,
your power will be brought low,
your palaces looted.
12 Yahweh says this:
Like a shepherd rescuing a couple of legs or a
bit of an ear
from the lion's mouth,
so will these sons of Israel
be rescued, who now loll in Samaria
on the corner pillows of their divans.

## Against Bethel and domestic luxury

13 Listen, and then testify it against the House of
Jacob
—it is the Lord Yahweh who speaks, the God of
Sabaoth:
14 On the day I punish Israel for his crimes
I will punish the altars of Bethel;
the horns of the altar are going to be broken off

and dropped on the ground.

15    I mean to pull down both winter houses and
summer houses,
the houses of ivory will be destroyed,
the houses of ebony will vanish.
It is the Lord Yahweh who speaks.

## Against the women of Samaria

1    Listen to this word, you cows of Bashan
living in the mountain of Samaria,
oppressing the needy, crushing the poor,
saying to your husbands, "Bring us something
to drink!"

2    The Lord Yahweh swears this by his holiness:
The days are coming to you now
when you will be dragged out with hooks,
the very last of you with prongs.

3    Out you will go, each by the nearest breach in
the wall,
to be driven all the way to Hermon.[a]
It is Yahweh who speaks.

## The self-deception, obstinacy and punishment of Israel

4    Go to Bethel, and sin,
to Gilgal, and sin your hardest!
Offer your sacrifices each morning
and your tithes on the third day,

5    burn leavened dough as a sacrifice with praise,
announce your voluntary offerings, make them
public,
for this is what makes you happy, sons of Israel.
It is the Lord Yahweh who speaks.

6    And that is why I left your teeth clean in all
your towns,
left you without bread in all your villages;
and yet you never came back to me.
It is Yahweh who speaks.

7    I kept your rain back with harvest still three
months away;

3 a. Assyria.
4 a. I.e., toward Assyria.

I let rain fall on one town and none on another,
one field was rained on and the next dried up
    because I sent it no rain;
two towns, three towns, went tottering to the
    next for drinking water,
but their thirst had to stay unquenched;
and yet you never came back to me.
It is Yahweh who speaks.

9

I struck you with burning and scorching,
and withered your gardens and vineyards;
the locusts devoured your fig trees and olives;
and yet you never came back to me.
It is Yahweh who speaks.

10

I sent you a plague like Egypt's plague;
I slaughtered your young men with the sword,
while your horses were captured for plunder;
I filled your nostrils with the stench of your
    camps;
and yet you never came back to me.
It is Yahweh who speaks.

11

I overthrew you as God overthrew Sodom and
    Gomorrah,[b]
and you were like a brand snatched from the
    blaze;
and yet you never came back to me.
It is Yahweh who speaks.

12

This therefore, Israel, is what I plan to do to
    you,
and because I am going to do this to you,
Israel, prepare to meet your God!

### Doxology

13

For he it was who formed the mountains, cre-
    ated the wind,
reveals his mind to man,
makes both dawn and dark,
and walks on the top of the heights of the world;
Yahweh, God of Sabaoth, is his name.

## Lament for Israel

1 **5** Listen to this oracle I speak against you,
it is a dirge, House of Israel:

2 She is down and will rise no more,
the virgin of Israel.
There she lies all alone on her own soil,
with no one to lift her up;

3 for thus says the Lord Yahweh to the House of
Israel:
The town which used to put a thousand in the
field
will be left with a hundred,
and the one which used to put a hundred
will be left with ten.

## No salvation without repentance

4 For Yahweh says this to the House of Israel.
Seek me and you shall live.

5 Do not seek Bethel,
do not go to Gilgal,
do not journey to Beersheba,
since Gilgal is going to be exiled
and Bethel brought to nothing.

6 Seek Yahweh and you shall live,
or else he will rush like fire on the House of
Joseph
and burn it up, with none at Bethel able to put
out the flames.

## Doxology

8 It is he who made the Pleiades and Orion,
who turns the dusk to dawn
and day to darkest night.
He summons the waters of the sea
and pours them over the land.
Yahweh is his name.

9 He blazes out ruin on the stronghold
and brings destruction to the fortress.

**b.** Perhaps the earthquake of 1:1.

### Threats

7
> Trouble for those who turn justice into worm-
> wood,
> throwing integrity to the ground;

10
> who hate the man dispensing justice at the city
> gate
> and detest those who speak with honesty.

11
> Well then, since you have trampled on the poor
> man,
> extorting levies on his wheat—
> those houses you have built of dressed stone,
> you will never live in them;
> and those precious vineyards you have planted,
> you will never drink their wine.

12
> For I know that your crimes are many,
> and your sins enormous:
> persecutors of the virtuous, blackmailers,
> turning away the needy at the city gate.

13
> No wonder the prudent man keeps silent,
> the times are so evil.

### Exhortation

14
> Seek good and not evil
> so that you may live,
> and that Yahweh, God of Sabaoth, may really
> be with you
> as you claim he is.

15
> Hate evil, love good,
> maintain justice at the city gate,
> and it may be that Yahweh, God of Sabaoth,
> will take pity
> on the remnant of Joseph.

### Impending punishment

16
> Therefore Yahweh says this,
> the God of Sabaoth, the Lord.
> In every public square there will be lamentation,
> in every street wails of "Alas! Alas!"
> Peasants will be called on to lament
> as well as the professional mourners

17
> and there will be wailing in every vineyard,
> for I am going to pass through you,
> says Yahweh.

### The day of Yahweh

18    Trouble for those who are waiting so longingly
              for the day of Yahweh!
      What will this day of Yahweh mean for you?
      It will mean darkness, not light,
19    as when a man escapes a lion's mouth,
              only to meet a bear;
      he enters his house and puts his hand on the
              wall,
              only for a snake to bite him.
20    Will not the day of Yahweh be darkness, not
              light?
      It will all be gloom, without a single ray of light.

### Against formalism in religion

21    I hate and despise your feasts,
      I take no pleasure in your solemn festivals.
22    When you offer me holocausts,
      . . . . . . . . . . . . . . . . . . .
      I reject your oblations,
      and refuse to look at your sacrifices of fattened
              cattle.
23    Let me have no more of the din of your
              chanting,
      no more of your strumming on harps.
24    But let justice flow like water,
      and integrity like an unfailing stream.
25    Did you bring me sacrifice and oblation in the
              wilderness
      for all those forty years, House of Israel?
26    Now you must shoulder Sakkuth your king
      and Kaiwan your god,
      those idols you have made for yourselves[a];
27    for I mean to take you far beyond Damascus
              into exile,
      says Yahweh—God of Sabaoth is his name.

### Against the self-indulgent and their false sense of security

1    6    Woe to those ensconced so snugly in Zion
              and to those who feel so safe on the mountain
              of Samaria,

**5 a.** Presumably the names are those of Babylonian gods.

those famous men of this first of nations
to whom the House of Israel goes as client.

2     Make a journey to Calneh and look,
go on from there to Hamath the great,
then down to Gath in Philistia.[a]
Are they any better off than these kingdoms?
Is their territory larger than yours?

3     You think to defer the day of misfortune,
but you hasten the reign of violence.

4     Lying on ivory beds
and sprawling on their divans,
they dine on lambs from the flock,
and stall-fattened veal;

5     they bawl to the sound of the harp,
they invent new instruments of music like David,

6     they drink wine by the bowlful,
and use the finest oil for anointing themselves,
but about the ruin of Joseph[b] they do not care
        at all.

7     That is why they will be the first to be exiled;
the sprawlers' revelry is over.

### The punishment and its horrors

8     The Lord Yahweh swears it by his own self
—it is the Lord Yahweh who speaks, the God of
        Sabaoth.
I detest the pride of Jacob,
I hate his palaces.
I mean to abandon the city[c] and all it contains.

9     And if ten men are left in a single house, they
        shall die.

10    Only a few will escape
to carry the bones out of the house;
and if a man should say to another one in a
        corner of the house,
"Is there anyone left with you?"
he will reply, "No! Hush! The name of Yahweh
        must not
be mentioned."

11    For see, Yahweh himself orders it;
as he strikes, the great house falls to pieces,
the small house crumbles.

12      Do horses gallop on rocks,
        do men plow the sea with oxen,
        for you to change justice into poison,
        and the fruit of integrity into wormwood?

13      You rejoice over Lo-debar,[d]
        "Was it not by our own strength," you say,
        "that we took Karnaim?"

14      Now see, you House of Israel, how I am stirring
                up against you
        —it is Yahweh who speaks, the God of Sabaoth—
        a nation that will harry you
        from the Pass of Hamath
        right down to the wadi of the Arabah.[e]


## III. THE VISIONS


### First vision: the locusts

1       This is what the Lord Yahweh showed me:
        it was a swarm of locusts
        at the time when the second crop was starting
                to grow,
        a swarm of full-grown locusts, when the king's
                cutting was over.

2       They were about to devour all the greenstuff in
                the land,
        but I said, "Lord Yahweh, forgive, I beg you.
        How can Jacob survive, being so small?"

3       And Yahweh relented;
        "This shall not happen," said Yahweh.


### Second vision: the drought

4       This is what the Lord Yahweh showed me:
        the Lord Yahweh himself summoning fire in
                punishment;


6 a. Three cities already in ruins.
b. The impending collapse of Israel.
c. Samaria; possibly standing for all the towns of the Northern
Kingdom.
d. Lo-debar and Karnaim, in Transjordania, had been recon-
quered.
e. I.e., from the north boundary to the south.

it had devoured the great Abyss<sup>a</sup>
and was already encroaching on the land.

5    Then I said, "Stop, Lord Yahweh, I beg you.
How can Jacob survive, being so small?"

6    And Yahweh relented;
"This will not happen either," said the Lord
Yahweh.

### Third vision: the plumb line

7    This is what the Lord Yahweh showed me:
a man standing by a wall,
plumb line in hand.

8    "What do you see, Amos?" Yahweh asked me.
"A plumb line," I said.
Then the Lord said to me,
"Look, I am going to measure my people Israel
by plumb line;
no longer will I overlook their offenses.

9    The high places of Isaac are going to be ruined,
the sanctuaries of Israel destroyed,
and, sword in hand, I will attack the House of
Jeroboam."

### The intervention of Amaziah: Amos expelled from Bethel

10   Amaziah the priest of Bethel then sent word to
Jeroboam king of Israel as follows. "Amos is plotting
against you in the heart of the House of Israel; the
country can no longer tolerate what he keeps saying.
11 For this is what he says, 'Jeroboam is going to die by
the sword, and Israel go into exile far from its coun-
12 try.'" ·To Amos, Amaziah said, "Go away, seer; get
back to the land of Judah; earn your bread there, do
13 your prophesying there. ·We want no more prophesying in Bethel; this is the royal sanctuary, the national
14 temple." ·"I was no prophet, neither did I belong to
any of the brotherhoods of prophets," Amos replied
to Amaziah. "I was a shepherd, and looked after syca-
15 mores: ·but it was Yahweh who took me from herding
the flock, and Yahweh who said, 'Go, prophesy to my
16 people Israel.' ·So listen to the word of Yahweh. You
say:

'Do not prophesy against Israel,

utter no oracles against the House of Isaac.'

17  Very well, this is what Yahweh says,
'Your wife will be forced to go on the streets,
your sons and daughters will fall by the sword,
your land be parceled out by measuring line,
and you yourself die on unclean soil
and Israel will go into exile far distant from its
    own land.' "

## Fourth vision: the basket of ripe fruit

1  **8**  This is what the Lord Yahweh showed me:
a basket of ripe fruit:

2  "What do you see, Amos?" he asked.
"A basket of ripe fruit," I said.
Then Yahweh said,
"My people Israel is ripe for destruction;
I will no longer overlook its offenses.

3  The palace singing girls will wail that day
—it is the Lord Yahweh who speaks—
so many will be dead,
all thrown down anywhere. Hush!"

## Against swindlers and exploiters

4  Listen to this, you who trample on the needy
and try to suppress the poor people of the
    country,

5  you who say, "When will New Moon be over
so that we can sell our corn,
and sabbath, so that we can market our wheat?
Then by lowering the bushel, raising the shekel,
by swindling and tampering with the scales,

6  we can buy up the poor for money,
and the needy for a pair of sandals,
and get a price even for the sweepings of the
    wheat."

7  Yahweh swears it by the pride of Jacob,
"Never will I forget a single thing you have
    done."

8  Is this not the reason for the earthquakes,
for its inhabitants all mourning,
and all of it heaving, like the Nile,
then subsiding, like the river of Egypt?

**7 a.** "The waters under the earth" from which the rain and rivers
come.

### Prediction of a mysterious punishment: darkness and mourning

9
> "That day—it is the Lord Yahweh who speaks—
> I will make the sun go down at noon,
> and darken the earth in broad daylight.

10
> I am going to turn your feasts into funerals,
> all your singing into lamentation;
> I will have your loins all in sackcloth,
> your heads all shaved.
> I will make it a mourning like the mourning for
> an only son,
> as long as it lasts it will be like a day of
> bitterness.

### Famine and drought of the word of God

11
> "See what days are coming—it is the Lord Yah-
> weh who speaks—
> days when I will bring famine on the country,
> a famine not of bread, a drought not of water,
> but of hearing the word of Yahweh.

12
> They will stagger from sea to sea,
> wander from north to east,
> seeking the word of Yahweh
> and failing to find it.

### Fresh prediction of punishment

13
> That day, delicate girl
> and stalwart youth shall faint from thirst.

14
> All who swear by Samaria's Ashimah,
> those who swear, 'By your god's life, Dan!'[a]
> and, 'By your Beloved's life, Beersheba!'
> these shall all fall, never to rise again."

### Fifth vision: the fall of the sanctuary

1 **9**
> I saw the Lord standing at the side of the altar.
> "Strike the capitals," he said, "and let the roof
> tumble down!
> I mean to break their heads, every one,
> and all who remain I will put to the sword;
> not one shall get away,
> not one escape.

2
> Should they burrow their way down to Sheol,
> my hand shall haul them out;

should they scale the heavens,
I will drag them down;
3        should they hide on Carmel's peak,
there I will track them down and catch them;
should they hide from my sight on the sea bed,
I will tell the Dragon to bite them there;
4        should they go into exile driven before their
                enemies,
I will order the sword to slaughter them there;
and my eyes will be on them
for their misfortune, not their good."

## Doxology

5        The Lord Yahweh of Sabaoth—
he touches the earth and it melts,
and all its inhabitants mourn;
it all heaves, like the Nile,
and subsides, like the river of Egypt.
6        He has built his high dwelling place in the
                heavens
and supported his vault on the earth;
he summons the waters of the sea
and pours them over the land.
Yahweh is his name.

## No special privileges for Israel

7        "Are not you and the Cushites[a] all the same to
                me,
sons of Israel?—it is Yahweh who speaks.
Did not I, who brought Israel out of the land
                of Egypt,
bring the Philistines from Caphtor, and the Ara-
                maeans from Kir?
8        Now, my eyes are turned on the sinful kingdom,
to wipe it off the face of the earth.

## Only sinners will perish

"Yet I am not going to destroy
the House of Jacob completely—it is Yahweh
                who speaks.

8 a. At Dan, Jeroboam had set up a golden calf.
9 a. Ethiopians, instanced as a distant and foreign nation.

9
    For now I will issue orders
    and shake the House of Israel among all the
        nations,
    as you shake a sieve
    so that not one pebble can fall on the ground.

10
    All the sinners of my people are going to perish
        by the sword,
    all those who say,
    'No misfortune will ever touch us, nor even
        come anywhere near us.'

## IV. PROSPECTS OF RESTORATION
## AND OF IDYLLIC PROSPERITY

11
    "That day I will re-erect the tottering hut of
        David,
    make good the gaps in it, restore its ruins
    and rebuild it as it was in the days of old,

12
    so that they can conquer the remnant of Edom
    and all the nations that belonged to me.
    It is Yahweh who speaks, and he will carry this
        out.

13
    "The days are coming now—it is Yahweh who
        speaks—
    when harvest will follow directly after plowing,
    the treading of grapes soon after sowing,
    when the mountains will run with new wine
    and the hills all flow with it.

14
    I mean to restore the fortunes of my people
        Israel;
    they will rebuild the ruined cities and live in
        them,
    plant vineyards and drink their wine,
    dig gardens and eat their produce.

15
    I will plant them in their own country,
    never to be rooted up again
    out of the land I have given them,
    says Yahweh, your God."

# OBADIAH

### Title and prologue

1a  Vision of Obadiah: about Edom.

1c  I have received a message from Yahweh,
a herald has been sent throughout the nations,
"Up! Let us march against this people.
Into battle!"

### Sentence pronounced on Edom

1b  The Lord Yahweh says this:
2  Now I am going to reduce you among the
nations,
and make you utterly despised.

3  Your pride of heart has led you astray,
you whose home is in the holes in the rocks,[a]
who make the heights your dwelling,
who say in your heart,
"Who will bring me down to the ground?"

4  Though you soared like the eagle,
though you set your nest among the stars,
I would still fling you down again—it is Yahweh
who speaks.

### The annihilation of Edom

5  If robbers came to you,
or plunderers at night,
they would steal to their heart's content.
If grape gatherers came to you,
they would leave no gleanings behind them.

How you have been pillaged!
6  How Esau has been looted,
his hidden treasures rifled!
7  They have driven you right to the frontiers,
they have misled you, all your allies.

a. The capital of Edom was named "the Rock" (Petra).

They have deceived you, your fine friends.
Those who ate your bread now set traps for you,
"He has no intelligence now."

8

When that day comes—it is Yahweh who
    speaks—
shall I not deprive Edom of sages,
the Mount of Esau of intelligence?

9

Your warriors, Teman,[b] will be seized with
    terror
until not a single one is left
in the Mount of Esau.

### The guilt of Edom

10

For the slaughter, ·for the violence
done to your brother Jacob,[c]
shame will cover you
and you will vanish for ever.

11

On the day you stood by
as strangers carried off his riches,
as barbarians passed through his gate
and cast lots for Jerusalem,
you behaved like the rest of them.

12

Do not gloat over your brother
on the day of his misfortune.
Do not exult over the sons of Judah
on the day of their ruin.
Do not play the braggart
on the day of distress.

13

Do not pass through the gate of my people
on the day of its misfortune.
Do not, in your turn, gloat over its disaster
on the day of its misfortune.
Do not lay a finger on its treasures
on the day of its misfortune.

14

Do not take your stand at the crossroads
to cut off its fugitives.
Do not hand over its survivors
on the day of distress.

15

For the day of Yahweh is near
for all the nations.

As you have done, so will it be done to you:
your deeds will recoil on your own head.

## The day of Yahweh. Israel revenged on Edom

16    [d]Yes, as you have drunk on my holy mountain,
so will all the nations drink unsparingly;
they will drink, and drink deep,
and will be as if they had never been.

17    But on Mount Zion there will be some who
have escaped
—it shall become a holy place—
and the House of Jacob will despoil
its own despoilers.

18    The House of Jacob shall be a fire,
the House of Joseph[e] a flame,
the House of Esau stubble.
They will set it alight and burn it up,
and no member of the House of Esau shall
survive.
Yahweh has spoken.

## The new Israel

19    Men from the Negeb will occupy the Mount of
Esau,
men from the Lowlands the country of the Philistines;
they will occupy the land of Ephraim and the
land of Samaria,
and Benjamin will occupy Gilead.

20    The exiles from this army, the sons of Israel,
will occupy Canaan[f] as far as Zarephath;
and the exiles from Jerusalem now in Sepharad
will occupy the towns of the Negeb.

21    Victorious, they will climb Mount Zion
to judge the Mount of Esau,
and the sovereignty shall belong to Yahweh.

b. Northern district of Edom.
c. The land of Judah.
d. The rest of the prophecy is addressed to Israel.
e. The Northern Kingdom.
f. Phoenicia; Zarephath was between Tyre and Sidon.

# JONAH

## Jonah rebels against his mission

1 ¹ The word of Yahweh was addressed to Jonah son
2  of Amittai: ·"Up!" he said, "Go to Nineveh, the
great city, and inform them that their wickedness has
3 become known to me." ·Jonah decided to run away
from Yahweh, and to go to Tarshish.ᵃ He went down
to Joppa and found a ship bound for Tarshish; he paid
his fare and went aboard, to go with them to Tarshish,
4 to get away from Yahweh. ·But Yahweh unleashed a
violent wind on the sea, and there was such a great
5 storm at sea that the ship threatened to break up. ·The
sailors took fright, and each of them called on his own
god, and to lighten the ship they threw the cargo over-
board. Jonah, however, had gone below and lain down
6 in the hold and fallen fast asleep. ·The boatswain came
upon him and said, "What do you mean by sleeping?
Get up! Call on your god! Perhaps he will spare us a
7 thought, and not leave us to die." ·Then they said to
each other, "Come on, let us draw lots to find out who
is responsible for bringing this evil on us." So they
8 cast lots, and the lot fell to Jonah. ·Then they said to
him, "Tell us, what is your business? Where do you
come from? What is your country? What is your na-
9 tionality?" ·He replied, "I am a Hebrew, and I worship
Yahweh, the God of heaven, who made the sea and
10 the land." ·The sailors were seized with terror at this
and said, "What have you done?" They knew that he
was trying to escape from Yahweh, because he had
11 told them so. ·They then said, "What are we to do
with you, to make the sea grow calm for us?" For the
12 sea was growing rougher and rougher. ·He replied,
"Take me and throw me into the sea, and then it will
grow calm for you. For I can see it is my fault this
13 violent storm has happened to you." ·The sailors rowed
hard in an effort to reach the shore, but in vain, since

1 a. "The end of the world": Tartessos in Spain.

14 the sea grew still rougher for them. ·They then called
on Yahweh and said, "O Yahweh, do not let us perish
for taking this man's life; do not hold us guilty of innocent blood; for you, Yahweh, have acted as you
15 have thought right." ·And taking hold of Jonah they
threw him into the sea; and the sea grew calm again.
16 At this the men were seized with dread of Yahweh;
they offered a sacrifice to Yahweh and made vows.

### Jonah is saved

1 Yahweh had arranged that a great fish should be
2 there to swallow Jonah; and Jonah remained in the
belly of the fish for three days and three nights. ·From
the belly of the fish he prayed to Yahweh, his God;
he said:

3
> "Out of my distress I cried to Yahweh
> and he answered me;
> from the belly of Sheol I cried,
> and you have heard my voice.

4
> You cast me into the abyss, into the heart of
> the sea,
> and the flood surrounded me.
> All your waves, your billows,
> washed over me.

5
> And I said: I am cast out
> from your sight.
> How shall I ever look again
> on your holy Temple?

6
> The waters surrounded me right to my throat,
> the abyss was all around me.
> The seaweed was wrapped around my head

7
> at the roots of the mountains.
> I went down into the countries underneath the
> earth,
> to the peoples of the past.
> But you lifted my life from the pit,
> Yahweh, my God.

8
> While my soul was fainting within me,
> I remembered Yahweh,
> and my prayer came before you
> into your holy Temple.

9       Those who serve worthless idols
        forfeit the grace that was theirs.

10      "But I, with a song of praise,
        will sacrifice to you.
        The vow I have made, I will fulfill.
        Salvation comes from Yahweh."

11      Yahweh spoke to the fish, which then vomited Jonah
        on to the shore.

### The conversion of Nineveh and God's pardon

1    **3** The word of Yahweh was addressed a second time
2       to Jonah: ·"Up!" he said, "Go to Nineveh, the
3    great city, and preach to them as I told you to." ·Jonah
     set out and went to Nineveh in obedience to the word
     of Yahweh. Now Nineveh was a city great beyond com-
4    pare: it took three days to cross it. ·Jonah went on into
     the city, making a day's journey. He preached in these
     words, "Only forty days more and Nineveh is going
5    to be destroyed." ·And the people of Nineveh believed
     in God; they proclaimed a fast and put on sackcloth,
6    from the greatest to the least. ·The news reached the
     king of Nineveh, who rose from his throne, took off
7    his robe, put on sackcloth and sat down in ashes. ·A
     proclamation was then promulgated throughout Nine-
     veh, by decree of the king and his ministers, as follows:
     "Men and beasts, herds and flocks, are to taste nothing;
8    they must not eat, they must not drink water. ·All are
     to put on sackcloth and call on God with all their might;
     and let everyone renounce his evil behavior and the
9    wicked things he has done. ·Who knows if God will
     not change his mind and relent, if he will not renounce
10   his burning wrath, so that we do not perish?" ·God
     saw their efforts to renounce their evil behavior. And
     God relented: he did not inflict on them the disaster
     which he had threatened.

### The grievance of the prophet and God's answer

1    **4** Jonah was very indignant at this; he fell into a rage.
2       He prayed to Yahweh and said, "Ah! Yahweh, is
     not this just as I said would happen when I was still at
     home? That was why I went and fled to Tarshish: I
     knew that you were a God of tenderness and compas-

sion, slow to anger, rich in graciousness, relenting from
3 evil. ·So now Yahweh, please take away my life, for I
4 might as well be dead as go on living." ·Yahweh re-
5 plied, "Are you right to be angry?" ·Jonah then went
out of the city and sat down to the east of the city.
There he made himself a shelter and sat under it in the
6 shade, to see what would happen to the city. ·Then
Yahweh God arranged that a castor-oil plant should
grow up over Jonah to give shade for his head and
soothe his ill-humor; Jonah was delighted with the
7 castor-oil plant. ·But at dawn the next day, God arranged that a worm should attack the castor-oil plant—
8 and it withered. ·Next, when the sun rose, God arranged that there should be a scorching east wind; the
sun beat down so hard on Jonah's head that he was
overcome and begged for death, saying, "I might as
9 well be dead as go on living." ·God said to Jonah, "Are
you right to be angry about the castor-oil plant?" He
replied, "I have every right to be angry, to the point of
10 death." ·Yahweh replied, "You are only upset about
a castor-oil plant which cost you no labor, which you
did not make grow, which sprouted in a night and has
11 perished in a night. ·And am I not to feel sorry for
Nineveh, the great city, in which there are more than a
hundred and twenty thousand people who cannot tell
their right hand from their left, to say nothing of all the
animals?"

# MICAH

<sup>1</sup> **1** The word of Yahweh that was addressed to Micah of Moresheth in the time of Jotham, Ahaz and Hezekiah, kings of Judah.

His visions of Samaria and Jerusalem.


## I. ISRAEL ON TRIAL


### THREAT AND CONDEMNATION


#### The judgment of Samaria<sup>a</sup>

2
> Listen, you peoples, all of you.
> Attend, earth, and everything in it.
> Yahweh is going to give evidence against you,
> the Lord, as he sets out from his sacred palace.

3
> For look, Yahweh sets out from his holy place,
> he comes down, he treads the heights of earth.

4
> The mountains melt as he goes,
> the valleys are torn apart,
> like wax before the fire,
> like water poured out on a steep place.

5
> All this is because of the crime of Jacob,
> the sin of the House of Israel.
> What is the crime of Jacob?
> Is it not Samaria?
> What is the sin of the House of Judah?
> Is it not Jerusalem?

6
> I mean to make Samaria a ruin in the open
>     country,
> a place where vines will be planted.
> I will set her stones rolling into the valley,
> I will lay her foundations bare.

**1 a.** Before the fall of the city in 721.

7
    All her images are going to be shattered,
      all her earnings consumed by fire,
      all her idols broken in pieces,
      for they have been collected with prostitutes'
         earnings
    and prostitutes' earnings they will be again.

### Lament for the lowland cities[b]

8
    This is why I am going to mourn and lament,
      go barefoot and naked,
    howl like the jackals,
    wail like the ostriches.

9
    For there is no healing for the blow Yahweh
        strikes;
    it reaches into Judah,
    it knocks at the very door of my people,
    reaches even into Jerusalem.

10
    *Do not announce it in Gath,*[c]
    in . . . shed no tears.
    In Beth-leaphrah
    roll in the dust.

11
    Sound the horn,
      you who live in Shaphir.
    She has not left her city,
      she who lives in Zaanan.
    Beth-ezel is torn from its foundations,
      from its strong supports.

12
    What hope has she of happiness,
      she who lives in Maroth?
    For doom has come down from Yahweh
      to the very gate of Jerusalem.

13
    Harness the horse to the chariot,
      you who live in Lachish.
    (This was the beginning of sin for the daughter
        of Zion,
    for Israel's crimes were to be found in you.)

14
    So you must provide a dowry
      for Moresheth-gath.
    Beth-achzib will prove a snare
      for the kings of Israel.

15
    The plunderer will come to you again,
      you who live in Mareshah.

> . . . to Adullam will go
> the glory of Israel.

16      Off with your hair, shave your head,
>      for the sons that were your joy.
>      Make yourselves bald like the vulture,
>      for they have gone from you into exile.

### Against the tyranny of the rich

1 2      Woe to those who plot evil,
>      who lie in bed planning mischief!
>      No sooner is it dawn than they do it
>      —their hands have the strength for it.

2      Seizing the fields that they covet,
>      they take over houses as well,
>      owner and house they confiscate together,
>      taking both man and inheritance.

3      So Yahweh says this:
>      Now it is I who plot
>      such mischief against this breed
>      as your necks will not escape;
>      nor will you be able to walk proudly,
>      so evil will the time be.

4      On that day they will make a satire on you,
>      sing a dirge and say,
>      "We are stripped of everything;
>      my people's portion is measured out and shared,
>      no one will give it back to them,
>      our fields are awarded to our despoiler."

5      Therefore you will have no one
>      to measure out a share
>      in the community of Yahweh.

### The prophet of misfortune

6      "Do not rave," they rave,
>      "do not rave like this.
>      No shame is going to overtake us.

b. Twelve towns to the southwest of Judah; one is the prophet's home, Moresheth (1:1), and six of the others can be identified; one name is missing from the text. The prophecy about each of the towns is a play on its name, and the whole refers to Sennacherib's invasion of 701.
c. 2 S. 1:20.

7
> Can the House of Jacob be accursed?
> Has Yahweh lost patience?
> Is that his way of going to work?
> Surely his words are words of kindness
> for his people Israel?"

8
> It is you who play the enemy
> to my people.
> From the innocent man you snatch his cloak,
> on the man who thinks himself safe you inflict
> the damage of war.

9
> The women of my people you drive out
> from the homes they loved;
> their children you rob for ever
> of the honor I gave them,

10
> "Get up! Be off! There is no resting here."
> For a worthless thing, you exact
> an extortionate pledge.

11
> Were there a man of inspiration who would
> invent this lie,
> "I prophesy you wine and strong drink,"
> he would be the prophet for a people like this.

## Promises of restoration

12
> Yes, I am going to gather all Jacob together,
> I will gather the remnant of Israel,
> bring them together like sheep in the fold;
> like a flock in its pasture
> they will fear no man.

13
> He who walks at their head will lead the way
> in front of them;
> he will walk at their head, they will pass through
> the gate and go out by it;
> their king will go on in front of them,
> Yahweh at their head.

## Against the rulers who oppress the people

1 **3**
> Then I said:
> Listen now, you princes of the House of Jacob,
> rulers of the House of Israel.
> Are you not the ones who should know what is
> right,

2
> you, enemies of good and friends of evil?

3    When they have devoured the flesh of my
people
and torn off their skin
and crushed their bones;
when they have shredded them like flesh in a pot
and like meat in a caldron,
4    then they will cry out to Yahweh.
But he will not answer them.
He will hide his face at that time
because of all the crimes they have committed.

## Against venal prophets

5    Yahweh says this against the prophets
who lead my people astray:
So long as they have something to eat
they cry "Peace."
But on anyone who puts nothing into their
mouths
they declare war.
6    And so the night will come to you: an end of
vision;
darkness for you: an end of divination.
The sun will set for the prophets,
the day will go black for them.
7    Then the seers will be covered with shame,
the diviners with confusion;
they will all cover their lips,
because no answer comes from God.
8    Not so with me, I am full of strength
(of the breath of Yahweh),
of justice and courage
to declare Jacob's crime to his face
and Israel's to his.

## To the guilty ones: prophecy of the ruin of Zion

9    Now listen to this, you princes of the House of
Jacob,
rulers of the House of Israel,
you who loathe justice
and pervert all that is right,
10    you who build Zion with blood,
Jerusalem with crime.
11    Her princes pronounce their verdict for bribes,

her priests take a fee for their rulings,
her prophets make divinations for money.
And yet they rely on Yahweh. They say,
"Is not Yahweh in our midst?
No evil is going to overtake us."

12  Because of this, since the fault is yours,
Zion will become plowland,
Jerusalem a heap of rubble,
and the mountain of the Temple a wooded
    height.


## II. PROMISES TO ZION


### The future reign of Yahweh in Zion[a]

1  **4**  In the days to come
the mountain of the Temple of Yahweh
will be put on top of the mountains
and be lifted higher than the hills.
The peoples will stream to it,

2  nations without number will come to it; and they
    will say,
"Come, let us go up to the mountain of Yah-
    weh,
to the Temple of the God of Jacob
so that he may teach us his ways
and we may walk in his paths;
since from Zion the Law will go out,
and the oracle of Yahweh from Jerusalem."

3  He will wield authority over many peoples
and arbitrate for mighty nations;
they will hammer their swords into plowshares,
their spears into sickles.
Nation will not lift sword against nation,
there will be no more training for war.

4  Each man will sit under his vine and his fig
    tree,
with no one to trouble him.
The mouth of Yahweh Sabaoth has spoken it.

5
    For all the peoples go forward, each in the
        name of its god;
    but we, we go forward in the name of Yahweh,
        our God,
    for ever and evermore.

## The gathering of the scattered flock in Zion

6
    That day—it is Yahweh who speaks—
    I will finally gather in the lame,
    and bring together those that have been led
        astray
    and those that have suffered at my hand.

7
    Out of the lame I will make a remnant,
    and out of the weary a mighty nation.
    Then will Yahweh reign over them
    on the mountain of Zion
    from now and for ever.

8
    And you, Tower of the Flock,
    Ophel of the daughter of Zion,[b]
    to you shall be given back your former sov-
        ereignty,
    and royal power over the House of Israel.

## The siege, exile and liberation of Zion

9
    Why are you crying aloud?
    Is there no king within you?
    Are your counselors lost
    that pains should grip you like a woman in
        labor?

10
    Writhe, cry out, daughter of Zion,
    like a woman in labor,
    for now you have to leave the city
    and live in the open country.
    To Babylon you must go
    and there you will be rescued;
    there Yahweh will ransom you
    out of the power of your enemies.

## The pagans crushed on the threshing floor in Zion

11
    Now many nations

4 a. The same oracle as Is. 2:2–4.
b. Ophel is the district where the king lived.

are mustered against you.
"Let her be desecrated," they say,
"let our eyes feast on the ruins of Zion."

12 But they do not know Yahweh's thoughts,
they have failed to understand his purpose,
he has collected them like sheaves on the threshing floor.

13 Up, daughter of Zion, and thresh;
for I will give you horns of iron,
hoofs of bronze,
for you to trample down many peoples.
You will dedicate their plunder to Yahweh,
their treasures to the Lord of the whole earth.

## The distress and glory of the Davidic dynasty

14
1  Now look to your fortifications, Fortress.
They have laid siege against us;
with a rod they strike on the cheek
the judge of Israel.

1
2  **5** But you, (Bethlehem) Ephrathah,
the least of the clans of Judah,
out of you will be born for me
the one who is to rule over Israel;
his origin goes back to the distant past,
to the days of old.

2
3  Yahweh is therefore going to abandon them
till the time when she who is to give birth[a] gives
birth.
Then the remnant of his brothers will come
back
to the sons of Israel.

3
4  He will stand and feed his flock
with the power of Yahweh,
with the majesty of the name of his God.
They will live secure, for from then on he will
extend his power
to the ends of the land.

4a
5a  He himself will be peace.

3b
6b  He will deliver us from Assyria should it invade
our country,
should it set foot inside our frontiers.

### The confidence of the people of Judah

4b
5b
As for Assyria, should it invade our country,
should it set foot on our soil,
we will raise seven shepherds against it,
eight leaders of men;

5a
6a
they will shepherd Assyria with the sword,
and the land of Nimrod with the sword blade.

### The future role of the remnant among the nations

6
7
Then among the many peoples,
the remnant of Jacob will be
like a dew from Yahweh,
like raindrops on the grass,
putting no hope in men,
expecting nothing from mankind.

7
8
Then among the many peoples,
the remnant of Jacob will be
like a lion among beasts of the forest,
like a young lion among flocks of sheep
trampling as he goes,
mangling his prey which no one takes from him.

### Yahweh will withdraw the temptation to rely on men

8
9
Let your hand be raised against your foes
and all your enemies shall be cut off.

9
10
This is how it will be, that day
—it is Yahweh who speaks—
I will tear away your horses from you,
and destroy your chariots;

10
11
tear the towns of your country from you,
bring down all your strongholds;

11
tear the charms from your hands,
and you will have no more soothsayers;

12a
tear from you your images
and your pillars;

13
tear from you your sacred poles,
and demolish your idols;

12b
and no longer will you bow down
before the work of your hands.

5 a. Probably the "maiden" of Isaiah's prophecy about thirty
years earlier, Is. 7:14.

14
    I will take revenge in anger and fury
    on the nations that would not obey.


## III. ISRAEL ON TRIAL


### DENUNCIATION AND THREAT

### Yahweh puts his people on trial

1

6

    Now listen to what Yahweh is saying:
    Stand up and let the case begin in the hearing
        of the mountains
    and let the hills hear what you say.

2
    Listen, you mountains, to Yahweh's accusation,
    give ear, you foundations of the earth,
    for Yahweh is accusing his people,
    pleading against Israel:

3
    My people, what have I done to you,
    how have I been a burden to you? Answer me.

4
    I brought you out of the land of Egypt,
    I rescued you from the house of slavery;
    I sent Moses to lead you,
    with Aaron and Miriam.

5
    My people, remember:
    what did Balak plot, that king of Moab?
    What did Balaam answer, that son of Beor?

    . . . . . . . . . . . . . . . . . .
    . . . from Shittim to Gilgal,
    for you to know the rightness of the ways of
        Yahweh.

6
    —"With what gift shall I come into Yahweh's
        presence
    and bow down before God on high?
    Shall I come with holocausts,
    with calves one year old?

7
    Will he be pleased with rams by the thousand,
    with libations of oil in torrents?
    Must I give my first-born for what I have done
        wrong,
    the fruit of my body for my own sin?"

8   —What is good has been explained to you, man;
this is what Yahweh asks of you:
only this, to act justly,
to love tenderly
and to walk humbly with your God.

## Against tricksters in the city

9   The voice of Yahweh. He is calling to the city:
Listen, tribe, and assembly of the city
12   whose rich men are crammed with violence,
whose citizens are liars.
10   Must I put up with fraudulent measure,
or that abomination the short-weight bushel?
11   Must I hold the man honest who measures with
false scales
and a bag of faked weights?
13   I have therefore begun to strike you down,
to bring you to ruin for your sins.
15   You will sow but never reap,
press the olive but never rub yourself with oil,
press the grape but never drink wine from it;
14   you will eat but never be satisfied,
store away but never preserve—
and what is preserved I shall give to the sword.

## The example of Samaria

16   You keep the laws of Omri
and follow all the practices of the House of
Ahab[a];
you are guided by their standards,
and they force me to make a terrible example
of you,
and to turn your inhabitants into a laughingstock,
to suffer the scorn of the peoples.

## Universal injustice

1  7   I am in trouble! I have become
like a harvester in summertime,

6 a. Omri and his son Ahab were two of the kings of Israel listed
1 K. among those who led the people into the worship of Canaanite idols.

like a gleaner at the vintage:
not a single cluster to eat,
not one of the early figs I so long for.

2    The devout have vanished from the land:
there is not one honest man left.
All are lurking for blood,
every man hunting down his brother.

3    Their hands are skilled in evil:
the official demands . . . ,
the judge gives judgment for a bribe,
the man in power pronounces as he pleases.

5    Put no trust in a neighbor,
have no confidence in a friend;
to the woman who shares your bed
do not open your mouth.

6    For son insults father,
daughter defies mother,
daughter-in-law defies mother-in-law;
a man's enemies are those of his own household.

4    . . . among them, the best is like a briar,
the most honest a hedge of thorn.
Today will come their ordeal from the North,
now is the time for their confusion.

7    For my part, I look to Yahweh,
my hope is in the God who will save me;
my God will hear me.[a]


# IV. HOPE FOR THE FUTURE


## Zion insulted by her enemy

8    Do not gloat over me, my enemy:
though I have fallen, I shall rise;
though I live in darkness,
Yahweh is my light.

9    I must suffer the anger of Yahweh,
for I have sinned against him,

**7 a.** Possibly the conclusion of the book of Micah; the additional
poems that follow seem to date from the Exile.

until he takes up my cause
and rights my wrongs;
he will bring me out into the light
and I shall rejoice to see the rightness of his
ways.

10 When my enemy sees it,
she will be covered with shame,
she who said to me, "Where is Yahweh your
God?"
My eyes will gloat over her;
she will be trampled underfoot
like mud in the streets.

## An oracle of restoration

11 The day is coming for rebuilding your walls.
Your frontiers will be extended that day,
12 men will come to you that day
from Assyria as far as to Egypt,
from Tyre as far as to the river,
from sea to sea, from mountain to mountain.
13 The earth will become a desert
by reason of its inhabitants, in return for what
they have done.

## A prayer for the confusion of the pagans

14 With shepherd's crook lead your people to pasture,
the flock that is your heritage,
living confined in a forest
with meadowland all around.
Let them pasture in Bashan and Gilead
as in the days of old.
15 As in the days when you came out of Egypt
grant us to see wonders.
16 The pagans, seeing it, will be confounded
for all their power;
they will lay their hands to their mouths,
their ears will be deafened by it.
17 They will lick the dust like serpents,
like things that crawl on the earth.
They will come trembling from their lairs,
in terror and fear before you.

### A plea for God's forgiveness

18
What god can compare with you: taking fault
away,
pardoning crime,
not cherishing anger for ever
but delighting in showing mercy?

19
Once more have pity on us,
tread down our faults,
to the bottom of the sea
throw all our sins.

20
Grant Jacob your faithfulness,
and Abraham your mercy,
as you swore to our fathers
from the days of long ago.

# NAHUM

1 **1** Oracle on Nineveh. Book of the vision of Nahum
of Elkosh.

## PRELUDE

### Psalm. The wrath of Yahweh

    *Aleph*
2    Yahweh is a jealous and vengeful God,
    Yahweh avenges, he is full of wrath;
    Yahweh takes vengeance on his foes,
    he stores up fury for his enemies.
3    Yahweh is slow to anger but immense in power.
    Most surely Yahweh will not leave the guilty
                    [unpunished.

    *Beth*
    In storm and whirlwind he takes his way,
    the clouds are the dust stirred up by his feet.

    *Ghimel*
4    He rebukes the sea and drains it,
    he dries up all the rivers.

    *Daleth*
    . . . Bashan and Carmel wither,
    the green of Lebanon fades.

    *He*
5    The mountains tremble before him,
    the hills reel;

    *Waw*
    the earth collapses before him,
    the world and all who live in it.

    *Zain*
6    His fury—who can withstand it?
    Who can endure his burning wrath?

*Heth*
His anger pours out like fire
and the rocks break to pieces before him.

*Teth*

7    Yahweh is good; he is a stronghold
in the day of distress;

*Yod*

8    he calls to mind those who trust in him
when the flood overtakes them.

*Kaph*
Those who defy him he will destroy utterly,
he will pursue his foes into the darkness.

## Prophecies addressed alternately to Judah and Nineveh

*to Judah*

9    How do you imagine Yahweh?
He it is who utterly destroys:
oppression will not lift its head a second time.

10    They will be consumed like a thicket of thorns,
like dry straw, utterly.

*to Assyria*

11    From you has sprung
one who plots evil against Yahweh,
a man with the mind of Belial.*

*to Judah*

12    Yahweh says this:
Equipped and many though they be,
they are going to be cut down, annihilated.
Though I have disciplined you,
I will discipline you no more.

13    And now I am going to break that yoke of his
                        [that weighs you down,
and I will burst your chains.

*to the king of Nineveh*

14    For you, here is Yahweh's decree:
There will be no more offspring to bear your
                        [name;
from the temple of your gods I mean to take
                        [away
the carved and the cast image,
and I intend to make your tomb an object of
                        [shame.

*to Judah*

15 **2** See, over the mountains the messenger hurries!
"Peace!" he proclaims.
Judah, celebrate your feasts,
carry out your vows,
for Belial will never pass through you again;
he is utterly annihilated.

3
2
Yes, Yahweh is restoring the vineyard of Jacob
and the vineyard of Israel.
For the plunderers had plundered them,
they had broken off their branches.


# THE FALL OF NINEVEH


## The assault

2
A destroyer advances against you.
Mount guard on the rampart,
watch the road, tuck up your cloaks;
muster all your forces.

4
3
The shields of his fighting men show red,
his warriors are dressed in scarlet;
all the steel of the chariots flashes
as they are thrown into battle;
the horsemen are impatient for action;

5
4
the chariots storm through the streets,
they hurtle across the squares;
they look like blazing flames,
like lightning they dash to and fro.

6
5
The picked troops are called out;
the columns clash,
they hurl themselves against the rampart,
the mantelet is already in place.

7
6
The gates that give on the river are opened,
in the palace all is panic.

8
7
The Lady[a] is carried off, taken into exile,
her handmaids raise the dirge, with sighs
like the moaning of doves,

1 a. This is probably Sennacherib, 2 K. 18–19.
2 a. Probably the statue of Ishtar.

and beat their breasts.

$\frac{9}{8}$ Nineveh is like a pool
whose waters are draining away.
"Stop! Stop!"
But no one turns back.

$\frac{10}{9}$ "Plunder the silver! Plunder the gold!"
There are endless treasures,
tons of valuables.

$\frac{11}{10}$ Raid and ravage and ruin!
Heart fails and knees give way,
fear is in the loins of all
and every face grows pale.

## The Lion of Assyria threatened

$\frac{12}{11}$ Where is the lions' den,
the cave of the lion's whelps?
When the lion made his foray the lioness stayed
behind,
the lion's cubs too; and no one molested them.

$\frac{13}{12}$ The lion clawed enough for his whelps,
and tore up prey for his lionesses;
he filled his caves with his spoil,
and his dens with the prey.

$\frac{14}{13}$ I am here! Look to yourself!—It is Yahweh Sabaoth who speaks.
I mean to send your chariots up in smoke;
the sword shall devour your lion's whelps.
I will wipe the earth clean of your plunder,
the voice of your envoys shall be heard no
more.

## Nineveh threatened for its crimes

1 **3** Woe to the city soaked in blood,
full of lies,
stuffed with booty,
whose plunderings know no end!

2 The crack of the whip!
The rumble of wheels!
Galloping horse,
jolting chariot,

3 charging cavalry,
flash of swords,
gleam of spears . . .

a mass of wounded,
hosts of dead,
countless corpses;
they stumble over the dead.

4    So much for all the whore's debauchery,
for that wonderful beauty, for that cunning
    witch
who enslaved nations by her debauchery
and tribes by her spells.

5    I am here! Look to yourself! It is Yahweh Sab-
    aoth who speaks.
I mean to lift your skirts as high as your face
and show your nakedness to nations,
your shame to kingdoms.

6    I am going to pelt you with filth,
shame you, make you a public show.

7    And all who look on you
will turn their backs on you and say,
"Nineveh is a ruin."
Could anyone pity her?
Where can I find anyone to comfort her?

## The lesson of Thebes

8    Are you mightier than No-amon[a]
who had her throne beside the river,
who had the sea for outer wall,
the waters for rampart?

9    Her strength was Ethiopia,
Egypt too; she had no boundaries.
Men of Put and the Libyans were her auxilia-
    ries.

10   And yet she was forced into exile,
she went into captivity;
her little ones, too, were dashed to pieces
at every crossroad;
lots were drawn for her nobles,
all her great men were loaded with chains.

11   You too will be encircled,
you will be overwhelmed;
you too will have to search
for a refuge from the enemy.

**3 a.** Thebes, "the city of Amon," sacked in 663.

### Nineveh's preparations useless

12

> Your fortresses are all fig trees
> laden with early-ripening figs:
> shake, and they fall
> into any mouth that wants to eat them.

13

> Look at your people:
> your inhabitants are women.
> The gates of your country
> stand wide open to the foe;
> fire has burned up your locking beams.

14

> Draw water for the siege,
> strengthen your bulwarks,
> tread the mud, tread down the clay,
> set your hand to the brick mold.

15

> There the fire will burn you up,
> the sword will cut you down.

### The locusts fly away

> Increase like the locust,
> increase like the grasshopper;

16a

> multiply your traders

17a

> to exceed the stars of heaven;
> your guards are like grasshoppers,
> your scribes like a cloud of insects.
> They settle on the walls
> when the day is cold.
> The sun appears,

16b

> and the locusts spread their wings; they fly away,

17b

> they are gone, no one knows where.

### A funeral lament

18

> Alas! ·Are your shepherds asleep, then,
> king of Assyria?
> Your picked troops slumber,
> your people are scattered on the mountains
> with no one to rally them.

19

> There is no remedy for your wound,
> your injury is past healing.
> All who hear the news of you
> clap their hands at your downfall.
> For who has not felt
> your unrelenting cruelty?

# HABAKKUK

1 **1** The oracle that Habakkuk the prophet received in
a vision.


## I. DIALOGUE BETWEEN THE PROPHET AND HIS GOD


### First complaint of the prophet: lawlessness prevails

2    How long, Yahweh, am I to cry for help
while you will not listen;
to cry "Oppression!" in your ear
and you will not save?

3    Why do you set injustice before me,
why do you look on where there is tyranny?
Outrage and violence, this is all I see,
all is contention, and discord flourishes.

4    And so the law loses its hold,
and justice never shows itself.
Yes, the wicked man gets the better of the upright,
and so justice is seen to be distorted.

### First oracle. The Chaldaeans the instrument of God's justice

5    Cast your eyes over the nations, look,
and be amazed, astounded.
For I am doing something in your own days
that you would not believe if you were told of it.

6    For now I am stirring up the Chaldaeans,
that fierce and fiery people
who march miles across country
to seize the homes of others.

7
> A people feared and dreaded,
>> from their might proceeds their right, their
>> greatness.

8
> Their horses are swifter than leopards,
> fiercer than wolves in the dark;
> their horsemen gallop on,
> their horsemen advance from afar,
> swooping like an eagle to stoop on its prey.

9
> They come for plunder, all of them,
> their faces scorching like an east wind;
> they scoop up prisoners like sand.

10
> They are a people that scoff at kings,
> and laugh at princes.
> They make light of all fortresses:
> they heap up earth and take them.

11
> Then the wind changes and is gone . . .
> Sinful, he who makes his own strength his god.

### Second complaint of the prophet: the tyranny of the conqueror

12
> Are not you, from ancient times Yahweh,
> my God, my Holy One, who never dies?
> Yahweh, you have made this people an instru-
>> ment of justice,
> set it firm as a rock in order to punish.

13
> Your eyes are too pure to rest on wickedness,
> you cannot look on at tyranny.
> Why do you look on while men are treacherous,
> and stay silent while the evil man swallows a
>> better man than he?

14
> You treat mankind like fishes in the sea,
> like creeping, masterless things.

15
> A people, these, who catch all on their hook,
> who draw them with their net,
> in their dragnet gather them,
> and so, triumphantly, rejoice.

16
> At this, they offer a sacrifice to their net,
> and burn incense to their dragnet,

for providing them with luxury
and lavish food.

17      Are they then to empty their net unceasingly,
slaughtering nations without pity?

### Second oracle: the upright man will live by faithfulness

1       I will stand on my watchtower,
and take up my post on my battlements,
watching to see what he will say to me,
what answer he will make to my complaints.

2       Then Yahweh answered and said,
"Write the vision down,
inscribe it on tablets
to be easily read,

3       since this vision is for its own time only:
eager for its own fulfillment, it does not deceive;
if it comes slowly, wait,
for come it will, without fail.

4       "See how he flags, he whose soul is not at rights,
but the upright man will live by his faithfulness."

## II. CURSES ON OPPRESSORS

### Prelude

5       Wealth is indeed a treacherous thing.
Haughty and unable to rest is he
who is as greedy as Sheol,
who is like death, insatiable,
who assembles all the nations for his own ends,
collects all the peoples to his own advantage.

6       On him, will not all men make satires,
and turn an epigram against him?
They will say:

### Five imprecations

I

Trouble is coming to the man who amasses
goods that are not his,

(for how long?)
and loads himself with pledges.

7    Will not your creditors suddenly rise,
will not your duns awake?
Then you will be their victim.

8    Since you have plundered many nations,
all that remains of the peoples will plunder you;
for you have shed men's blood and ravished the
      country,
the city and all who live in it.

## II

9    Trouble is coming to the man who grossly ex-
      ploits others for the sake of his House,
to fix his nest on high
and so evade the hand of misfortune.

10    You have contrived to bring shame on your
      House;
by making an end of many peoples
you have worked your own ruin.

11    For the stone from the very walls cries out,
and the beam responds from the framework.

## III

12    Trouble is coming to the man who builds a
      town with blood
and founds a city on crime.

13    Is it not the will of Yahweh Sabaoth
that the laboring of peoples should end in fire,
and the toiling of nations come to nothing?

14    *For the country shall be filled with the knowl-*
      *edge of the glory of Yahweh*
*as the waters swell the sea.*[a]

## IV

15    Trouble is coming to the man who makes his
      neighbors drink,
who pours his poison until they are drunk,
to look at their nakedness.

16        You are drunk with ignominy, not with glory.

          Your turn now to drink and show your foreskin.
          The cup from Yahweh's right hand comes
              around to you,
          and disgrace will overshadow your glory.

17        For the violence done to Lebanon is going to
              overwhelm you,
          so will the slaughter of terrified beasts,
          for you have shed men's blood and ravished the
              country,
          the city and all who live in it.

                          V

19        Trouble is coming to the man who says to the
              piece of wood, "Wake up!"
          to the dumb stone, "On your feet!"
          (And that is the oracle.)
          Plated it may be with gold and silver,
          but not a breath of life inside it.

18        What is the use of a carved image, or for its
              maker to carve it at all?
          It is a thing of metal, a lying oracle.
          What is the use of its maker trusting this
          and fashioning dumb idols?

20        But Yahweh is in his holy Temple:
          let the whole earth be silent before him.


## III. PLEA TO YAHWEH FOR DELIVERANCE

1   **3**  A prayer[a] of Habakkuk the prophet; tone as for
          dirges.

2         Yahweh, I have heard of your renown,
              your work, Yahweh, inspires me with dread.
          Repeat it in our own time,

2 a. Is. 11:9.
3 a. The note at the end of this chapter and the three rubrics
marking pauses show that this psalm was used in the liturgy.

reveal it in our time.
For all your wrath, remember to be merciful.

3
Eloah is coming from Teman,
and the Holy One from Mount Paran.[b]   *Pause*
His majesty veils the heavens,
the earth is filled with his glory.

4
His brightness is like the day,
rays flash from his hands,
that is where his power lies hidden.

5
Plague goes in front of him,
fever follows on his heels.

6
When he stands up he makes the earth tremble,
with his glance he makes the nations quake.

Then the ancient mountains are dislodged,
the everlasting hills sink down,
his pathway from of old.

7
I have seen the tents of Cushan terrified,
the pavilions of the land of Midian shuddering.[c]

8
Yahweh, is your anger blazing against the
    rivers,
or your fury against the sea,
that you come mounted on your horses,
on your victorious chariots?

9
You uncover your bow,
you ply its string with arrows.      *Pause*

10
You trench the soil with torrents;
the mountains shiver when they see you;
great floods sweep on their way,
the abyss[d] roars aloud,
high it lifts its hands.

11
Sun and moon stay in their houses,
avoiding the flash of your arrows,
the gleam of your glittering spear.

12
Raging, you stride the earth,
in anger you trample the nations.

13    You have marched to save your people,
      to save your own anointed;
      you have beaten down the wicked man's house,
      bared its foundations to the rock.         *Pause*

14    With your shafts you have pierced the leader of
           his warriors
      who stormed out with shouts of joy to scatter us,
      as if they meant to devour some poor wretch
           in their lair.

15    You have trampled the sea with your horses,
      the surge of great waters.

16    I have heard. My whole body trembles,
      my lips quiver at the sound;
      decay creeps into my bones,
      my steps falter beneath me.

      Calmly I await the day of anguish
      which is dawning on the people now attacking
           us.

17    (For the fig tree is not going to blossom,
      nor will there be any fruit on the vine,
      the yield of the olive will fail,
      the fields afford no food;
      the sheep will vanish from the fold,
      nor will there be any cattle in the stalls.)

18    But I will rejoice in Yahweh,
      I will exult in God my savior.

19    Yahweh my Lord is my strength,
      he makes my feet as light as a doe's,
      he sets my steps on the heights.

For the choirmaster; on stringed instruments.

**b.** Eloah is an ancient name for God. The place names are in
Edom, and the coming of Yahweh is described in terms of an
advancing storm.
**c.** Midian is to the south of Edom; Cushan appears to be the
same region.
**d.** "The waters under the earth" rise to join the rain.

# ZEPHANIAH

1 ¹ The word of Yahweh that was addressed to Zephaniah son of Cushi, son of Gedaliah, son of Amariah, son of Hezekiah, in the reign of Josiah son of Amon, king of Judah.

## I. THE DAY OF YAHWEH FOR JUDAH

### Prelude: judgment on all creation

2
> I mean to sweep away everything
> off the face of the earth
> —it is Yahweh who speaks.

3
> I mean to sweep away men and beasts,
> the birds of the air and the fish of the sea,
> I mean to send the wicked staggering,
> and wipe man off the face of the earth
> —it is Yahweh who speaks.

### Against the worship of alien gods

4
> I am going to raise my hand against Judah
> and against all the inhabitants of Jerusalem,
> and from this place I will wipe out Baal,
> to the very last vestige of him,
> even to the name of his spurious priests,

5
> those who prostrate themselves on the roofs
> before the array of heaven,
> those who prostrate themselves before Yahweh
> but swear by Milcom,ᵃ

6
> those who turn aside from Yahweh,
> who do not seek Yahweh,
> who will not bother with him.

7
> Silence before the Lord Yahweh!
> For the day of Yahweh is near.

**1 a.** God of the Ammonites.

> Yes, Yahweh has prepared a sacrifice,
> he has consecrated his guests.

## Against the dignitaries of the court[b]

8
> On the day of Yahweh's sacrifice,
> I will punish the ministers,
> the royal princes,
> and all those who dress themselves
> in foreign style.

9
> On that day I mean to punish
> all those who are near the throne,
> those who fill the palace of their lord
> with violence and deceit.

## Against the merchants of Jerusalem

10
> On that day—it is Yahweh who speaks—
> a shout will be raised from the Fish Gate,
> from the new town, howls,
> from the hills, a great uproar.

11
> Men of the Mortar, howl!
> For the whole brood of Canaan[c] has been de-
> stroyed,
> the weighers of silver are all wiped out.

## Against unbelievers

12
> When that time comes
> I will search Jerusalem by torchlight,
> and punish the men
> who are stagnating on their lees,
> those who say in their hearts,
> "Yahweh has no power
> for good or for evil."

13
> Then their wealth will be given up to looting,
> their households to plundering.
> They built houses, did they? They will not live
> in them.
> They planted vineyards, did they? They will not
> drink their wine.

## The day of Yahweh

14
> The great day of Yahweh is near,
> near, and coming with all speed.
> How bitter the sound of the day of Yahweh,

      the day when the warrior shouts his cry of war.

15     A day of wrath, that day,
      a day of distress and agony,
      a day of ruin and of devastation,
      a day of darkness and gloom,
      a day of cloud and blackness,

16     a day of trumpet blast and battle cry
      against fortified town
      and high corner tower.

17     I am going to bring such distress on men
      that they will grope like the blind
      (because they have sinned against Yahweh);
      their blood will be scattered like dust,
      their corpses like dung.

18     Neither their silver nor their gold
      will have any power to save them.

      On the day of the anger of Yahweh,
      in the fire of his jealousy,
      all the earth will be consumed.
      For he means to destroy, yes, to make an end
      of all the inhabitants of the earth.

## Conclusion: a call to conversion

1 **2**   . . . . . . . . . . . . . . . . . . .
      nation without desire,

2     before you are driven
      like chaff that is blown away in a day,
      before there descends on you
      the fierce anger of Yahweh
      (before there descends on you
      the day of the anger of Yahweh).

3     Seek Yahweh,
      all you, the humble of the earth,
      who obey his commands.
      Seek integrity,
      seek humility:
      you may perhaps find shelter
      on the day of the anger of Yahweh.

b. The regents during the minority of King Josiah.
c. "Canaanites" is a term for the merchants.

## II. AGAINST THE PAGANS

### The enemy to the west: the Philistines

4
Yes, Gaza is going to be reduced to desert,
Ashkelon to waste.
Ashdod will be stormed in broad daylight,
and Ekron rooted out.

5
Woe to the members of the Confederacy of the
Sea,
to the nation of the Cherethites!
This is the word of Yahweh against you:
I mean to bring you down, land of the Philis-
tines,
I am going to ruin you, empty you of inhabit-
ants;

6
and you will be reduced to pasture land,
to grazing grounds for the shepherds,
to folds for the sheep.

7
It will be included in the property
of the remnant of the House of Judah;
they will lead flocks there to pasture;
among the houses of Ashkelon they will rest at
evening;
for Yahweh their God is going to deal kindly
with them
and restore their fortunes.

### The enemies to the east: Moab and Ammon

8
I have heard the taunts of Moab
and the insults of the sons of Ammon
as they laughed at my people,
and boasted of their own domains.

9
For this, as I live—it is Yahweh Sabaoth who
speaks,
the God of Israel—
Moab shall become like Sodom
and the sons of Ammon like Gomorrah:
a realm of nettles, a heap of salt,
a desolation for ever.

What is left of my people will plunder them,
those of my nation who survive will take their
heritage.

10 This will be the price of their pride,
of their taunts, of their boasts
against the people of Yahweh Sabaoth.

11 Full of terror will Yahweh be for them.
When he has utterly destroyed all the gods of
the earth,
the nations will prostrate themselves before him,
each on its own soil,
all the islands of the nations.

### The enemy to the south: Ethiopia[a]

12 And as for you, Ethiopians:
They will be run through with my sword.

### The enemy to the north: Assyria

13 He is going to raise his hand against the north
and bring Assyria down in ruins;
he will make Nineveh a waste,
dry as the desert.

14 In the middle of her the flocks will rest;
all the beasts of the valley,
even the pelican and the heron
will roost around her cornices at night;
the owl will hoot at the window
and the raven croak on the doorstep.

. . . . . . . . . . . . . . . . . . .

15 Is this the joyful city,
so confident on her throne,
who said in her heart,
"Here am I, with none to equal me?"
What a ruin she is now,
a lair for beasts!
All those who pass by her
whistle and shake their fists.

**2 a.** In this fragmentary oracle, "Ethiopia" stands for Egypt,
where an Ethiopian dynasty had ruled from 715 to 663.

## III. AGAINST JERUSALEM

### Against the leaders of the people

1   3     Trouble is coming to the rebellious, the defiled,
             the tyrannical city!
2        She would never listen to the call,
        would never learn the lesson;
        she has never trusted in Yahweh,
        never drawn near to her God.
3        The leaders she harbors
        are roaring lions,
        her judges, wolves at evening
        that have had nothing to gnaw that morning;
4        her prophets are braggarts,
        they are impostors;
        her priests profane the holy things,
        they do violence to the Law.

5        Yahweh is in her, he is just and honorable;
        he never does wrong;
        morning by morning he makes his law known,
        each dawn unfailingly;
        he knows no injustice.

### The pagans punished

6        I have wiped out nations,
        their corner towers lie in ruins;
        I have emptied their streets,
        no one walks there;
        their towns have been sacked:
        no one left there, no more inhabitants.
7        "At least," I used to say, "you will fear me now,
        you will learn the lesson;
        she cannot lose sight
        of the many times I have punished her."
        But no, it only made them more anxious
        to see that all they did was corrupt.

8        Therefore, expect me—it is Yahweh who
        speaks—

on the day I stand up to make my accusation;
for I am determined to gather the nations,
to assemble the kingdoms,
and to pour out my fury on you,
the whole heat of my anger.


## IV. PROMISES


### Conversion of the pagans

9    Yes, I will then give the peoples
lips that are clean,
so that all may invoke the name of Yahweh
and serve him under the same yoke.

10    From beyond the banks of the rivers of Ethiopia my suppliants
will bring me offerings.


### The humble remnant of Israel

11    When that day comes
you need feel no shame for all the misdeeds
you have committed against me,
for I will remove your proud boasters
from your midst;
and you will cease to strut
on my holy mountain.

12    In your midst I will leave
a humble and lowly people,

13    and those who are left in Israel will seek refuge
in the name of Yahweh.
They will do no wrong,
will tell no lies;
and the perjured tongue will no longer
be found in their mouths.
But they will be able to graze and rest
with no one to disturb them.


### Psalms of joy in Zion

14    Shout for joy, daughter of Zion,
Israel, shout aloud!

Rejoice, exult with all your heart,
daughter of Jerusalem!

15      Yahweh has repealed your sentence;
he has driven your enemies away.
Yahweh, the king of Israel, is in your midst;
you have no more evil to fear.

16      When that day comes, word will come to Jerusalem:
Zion, have no fear,
do not let your hands fall limp.

17      Yahweh your God is in your midst,
a victorious warrior.
He will exult with joy over you,
he will renew you by his love;
he will dance with shouts of joy for you

18      as on a day of festival.

## Return of the exiles

I have taken away your misfortune,
no longer need you bear the disgrace of it.

19      I am taking action here and now
against your oppressors.
When that time comes I will rescue the lame,
and gather the strays,
and I will win them praise and renown
when I restore their fortunes.

20      When that time comes, I will be your guide,
when that time comes, I will gather you in;
I will give you praise and renown
among all the peoples of the earth
when I restore your fortunes under your own
eyes,
says Yahweh.

# HAGGAI

## The movement to rebuild the Temple

1 ¹ In the second year of King Darius, on the first day
of the sixth month,[a] the word of Yahweh was addressed through the prophet Haggai to Zerubbabel son
of Shealtiel, high commissioner of Judah, and to
Joshua son of Jehozadak, the high priest, as follows,
² "Yahweh Sabaoth says this, 'This people says: The
time has not yet come to rebuild the Temple of Yah-
³ weh. ·(And the word of Yahweh was addressed
⁴ through the prophet Haggai, as follows:) ·Is this a
time for you to live in your paneled houses, when this
⁵ House lies in ruins? ·So now, Yahweh Sabaoth says
this: Reflect carefully how things have gone for you.
⁶ You have sown much and harvested little; you eat but
never have enough, drink but never have your fill, put
on clothes but do not feel warm. The wage earner gets
his wages only to put them in a purse riddled with
⁸ holes. ·So go to the hill country, fetch wood, and rebuild the House: I shall then take pleasure in it, and
⁷ be glorified there, says Yahweh. ·Yahweh Sabaoth says
this: Reflect carefully how things have gone for you.
⁹ The abundance you expected proved to be little. When
you brought the harvest in, my breath spoiled it. And
why?—it is Yahweh Sabaoth who speaks. Because while
my House lies in ruins you are busy with your own,
¹⁰ each one of you. ·That is why the sky has withheld the
¹¹ rain and the earth withheld its yield. ·I have called
down drought on land and hills, on wheat, on new
wine, on oil and on all the produce of the ground, on
man and beast and all their labors.'"

¹² Now Zerubbabel son of Shealtiel, Joshua son of
Jehozadak, the high priest, and all the remnant of the
people, paid attention to the voice of Yahweh their
God and to the words of the prophet Haggai, Yahweh
having sent him to them. And the people were filled

**1 a.** August 520.

<sup>13</sup> with fear before Yahweh. ·Haggai, the messenger of Yahweh, passed on the message of Yahweh to the people, as follows, "I am with you—it is Yahweh who

<sup>14</sup> speaks." ·And Yahweh roused the spirit of Zerubbabel son of Shealtiel, high commissioner of Judah, the spirit of Joshua son of Jehozadak, the high priest, and the spirit of all the remnant of the people; and they came and set to work on the Temple of Yahweh Sabaoth their

<sup>15</sup> God. ·This was on the twenty-fourth day of the sixth month.

## The glory that is to come to the Temple

<sup>1</sup>    In the second year of King Darius, **2** on the twenty-first day of the seventh month,[a] the word of Yahweh was addressed through the prophet Haggai, as follows,

<sup>2</sup> "You are to speak to Zerubbabel son of Shealtiel, the high commissioner of Judah, to Joshua son of Jehozadak, the high priest, and to all the remnant of

<sup>3</sup> the people. Say this, ·'Who is there left among you that saw this Temple in its former glory? And how does it look to you now? Does it seem nothing to you?

<sup>4</sup> But take courage now, Zerubbabel—it is Yahweh who speaks. Courage, High Priest Joshua son of Jehozadak! Courage, all you people of the country!—it is Yahweh who speaks. To work! I am with you—it is Yahweh

<sup>5</sup> Sabaoth who speaks—·and my spirit remains among

<sup>6</sup> you. Do not be afraid! ·For Yahweh Sabaoth says this: A little while now, and I am going to shake the heav-

<sup>7</sup> ens and the earth, the sea and the dry land. ·I will shake all the nations and the treasures of all the nations shall flow in, and I will fill this Temple with glory,

<sup>8</sup> says Yahweh Sabaoth. ·Mine is the silver, mine the

<sup>9</sup> gold!—it is Yahweh Sabaoth who speaks. ·The new glory of this Temple is going to surpass the old, says Yahweh Sabaoth, · and in this place I will give peace—it is Yahweh Sabaoth who speaks.' "

## The prophet consults the priests

<sup>10</sup>    On the twenty-fourth day of the ninth month, in the second year of Darius,[b] the word of Yahweh was ad-

<sup>11</sup> dressed to the prophet Haggai as follows, ·"Yahweh Sabaoth says this: Ask the priests for a decision on this

<sup>12</sup> question, ·'If a man carries consecrated meat in the fold of his gown and with this fold touches bread,

broth, wine, or food of any kind, does such food become holy?' " The priests answered, "No, it does not."
13 Haggai then said, "If a man made unclean by contact with a corpse touches any of this, does it become unclean?"
14 The priests answered, "Yes, it does." ·Haggai then spoke out. "It is the same with this people," he said, "the same with this nation as I see it—it is Yahweh who speaks—the same with everything they turn their hands to; and what they offer here is unclean.

## A promise of agricultural prosperity

15 "Reflect carefully from today onward. Before one stone had been laid on another in the sanctuary of
16 Yahweh, ·what state were you in? A man would come to a twenty-measure heap and there would be ten; he would come to a vat to draw fifty measures and there
17 would be twenty. ·I struck with blight and mildew and hail everything you turned your hands to. And still you
18 would not return to me—it is Yahweh who speaks. ·Reflect carefully from today onward (from the twenty-fourth day of the ninth month, from the day the foundation of the sanctuary of Yahweh was laid, think
19 carefully) ·if grain is still short in the barn, and if vine and fig tree, pomegranate and olive, still bear no fruit. From today onward I intend to bless you."

## The promise to Zerubbabel

20 On the twenty-fourth day of the month the word of Yahweh was addressed a second time to Haggai, as
21 follows, ·"Speak to Zerubbabel, the high commissioner of Judah. Say this, 'I am going to shake the heavens
22 and the earth. ·I will overturn the thrones of kingdoms and destroy the power of the kings of the nations. I will overthrow the chariots and their charioteers; horses and their riders will be brought down; they shall fall,
23 each to the sword of his fellow. ·When the day comes—it is Yahweh Sabaoth who speaks—I will take you, Zerubbabel son of Shealtiel, my servant—it is Yahweh Sabaoth who speaks—and make you like a signet ring. For I have chosen you—it is Yahweh Sabaoth who speaks.' "

**2 a.** October 520, the last day of the feast of Tabernacles.
**b.** December 520.

# ZECHARIAH

## FIRST PART

### A summons to conversion

1 ¹ In the second year of Darius, in the eighth month,ᵃ the word of Yahweh was addressed to the prophet Zechariah (son of Berechiah),ᵇ son of Iddo, as follows, ³ "Cry out to the remnant of this people and say to them, 'Yahweh Sabaoth says this: Return to me, and I will ⁴ return to you, says Yahweh Sabaoth. ·Do not be like your ancestors, to whom the prophets in the past cried: Yahweh Sabaoth says this: Turn back from your evil ways and evil deeds. But—it is Yahweh who speaks— ⁵ they would not listen or pay attention to me. ·Where are your ancestors now? Are those prophets still alive? 6a Did not my words and my orders, with which I charged my servants the prophets, overtake your ancestors? ² Yahweh was stirred to anger against your ancestors.'" 6b This reduced them to such confusion that they said, "Yahweh Sabaoth has treated us as he resolved to do, and as our ways and deeds deserved."

### First vision: the horsemen

7 On the twenty-fourth day of the eleventh month (the month of Shebat), in the second year of Darius,ᶜ the word of Yahweh was addressed to the prophet Zecha- ⁸ riah (son of Berechiah), son of Iddo, as follows, ·"I saw a vision during the night. It was this: a man was standing among the deep-rooted myrtles; behind him ⁹ were horses, red and sorrel and black and white. ·I said: What are these, my lord? (And the angel who was talking to me said, 'I will explain to you what they

**1 a.** October–November 520.
**b.** A gloss suggested by Is. 8:2. According to Ezr. 5:1 and Ne. 12:16, Zechariah was the son of Iddo.
**c.** February 519.

10 are.') ·The man standing among the myrtles answered,
'They are those whom Yahweh has sent to patrol
11 throughout the world.' ·They then spoke to the angel
of Yahweh standing among the myrtles; they said, 'We
have been patroling the world, and see, the whole world
12 is at peace and rest.' ·The angel of Yahweh then spoke
and said, 'Yahweh Sabaoth, how long will you wait
before taking pity on Jerusalem and the cities of Judah,
on which you have inflicted your anger for the past
13 seventy years?' ·Yahweh then replied with very con-
14 soling words to the angel who was talking to me. ·The
angel who was talking to me then said to me, 'Make
this proclamation: Yahweh Sabaoth says this: I feel
15 most jealous love for Jerusalem and Zion, ·but very
bitter anger against the proud nations; for my part I
was only a little angry, but they have overstepped all
16 limits. ·Yahweh, then, says this. I turn again in compassion to Jerusalem; my Temple there shall be rebuilt
—it is Yahweh Sabaoth who speaks—and the measuring
17 line will be stretched over Jerusalem. ·Make this proclamation too: Yahweh Sabaoth says this: My cities are
once more going to be very prosperous. Yahweh will
again take pity on Zion, again make Jerusalem his very
own.' "

## Second vision: the horns and the smiths

1/18   2   Then, raising my eyes, I saw a vision. It was this:
2/19       there were four horns. ·I said to the angel who was
talking to me, "What are these horns, my lord?" He
said to me, "These are the horns which have scattered
3/20  Judah (Israel) and Jerusalem." ·Yahweh then showed
4/21  me four smiths. ·And I said, "What are these coming
to do?" He said to me, "(Those are the horns which
have so scattered Judah that no one has dared to raise
his head; but) these have come to lay them low (to
strike down the horns of the nations who lifted their
hands against the land of Judah, in order to scatter it)."

## Third vision: the measurer

5/1   Then, raising my eyes, I saw a vision. It was this:
6/2   there was a man with a measuring line in his hand. ·I
asked him, "Where are you going?" He said, "To measure Jerusalem, to find out her breadth and her length."

7
3
8
4
And then, while the angel who was talking to me stood
still, another angel came forward to meet him. ·He said
to him, "Run, and tell that young man this, 'Jerusalem
is to remain unwalled, because of the great number of
9
5
men and cattle there will be in her. ·But I—it is Yahweh
who speaks—I will be a wall of fire for her all around
her, and I will be her glory in the midst of her.'"

### Two exhortations to the exiles

10
6
Up, up, and leave the land of the North (it is
Yahweh who speaks)!
(For to the four winds of heaven
I have scattered you—it is Yahweh who speaks.)

11
7
Zion, up! Dweller in Babylon, flee!

12
8
For Yahweh Sabaoth says this
(he whose glory has sent me here)
as regards the nations who despoiled you
(for whoever touches you touches the apple of
my eye):

13
9
See now, I raise my hand over them,
for them to be plunder for their slaves.
(And you will know that Yahweh Sabaoth has
sent me.)

14
10
Sing, rejoice,
daughter of Zion;
for I am coming
to dwell in the middle of you
—it is Yahweh who speaks.

15
11
Many nations will join Yahweh,
on that day;
they will become his people.
(But he will remain among you,
and you will know that Yahweh Sabaoth has
sent me to you.)

16
12
But Yahweh will hold Judah
as his portion in the Holy Land,
and again make Jerusalem his very own.

17
13
Let all mankind be silent before Yahweh!
For he is awaking and is coming from his holy
dwelling.

## Fourth vision: the investiture of Joshua

1 3 He[a] showed me Joshua the high priest, standing before the angel of Yahweh, with Satan standing 2 on his right to accuse him. ·The angel of Yahweh said to Satan, "May Yahweh rebuke you, Satan, may Yahweh rebuke you, he who has made Jerusalem his very own. Is not this man a brand snatched from the fire?"[b] 3 Now Joshua was dressed in dirty clothes[c] as he stood 4a before the angel of Yahweh. ·The angel said these words to those who stood before him, "Take off his dirty clothes and clothe him in splendid robes of state, 5 and put a clean turban on his head." They clothed him in splendid robes of state and put a clean turban on his head.[d] The angel of Yahweh was standing there 4b and said to him, ·"Look, I have taken away your 6 iniquity from you." ·The angel of Yahweh then pro- 7 claimed to Joshua: ·"Yahweh Sabaoth says this, 'If you walk in my ways and keep my ordinances, you shall govern my house, you shall watch over my courts, and I will give you free access among those who stand here. 9a For this is the stone which I am placing before Joshua; on this single stone there are seven eyes; and I myself intend to cut the inscription on it—it is Yahweh Sabaoth who speaks.

## The coming of the "Branch"

8 'Now listen, High Priest Joshua, you and the friends who sit before you—for you are men of good omen. I 9b now mean to raise my servant Branch, ·and I intend 10 to put aside the iniquity of this land in a single day. ·On that day—it is Yahweh Sabaoth who speaks—you will entertain each other under your vine and fig tree.' "

## Fifth vision: the lampstand and the olive trees

1 4 The angel who was talking to me came back and 2 roused me as a man is roused from his sleep. ·And he asked me, "What can you see?" I answered, "As I look, this is what I see: there is a lampstand entirely of gold with a bowl at the top of it; seven lamps are on the lampstand, and seven lips for the lamps on it. 3 By it are two olive trees, one to the right of it and one 4 to the left." ·Speaking again, I said to the angel who

was talking to me, "What do those things mean, my
5 lord?" ·The angel who was talking to me replied, "Do
you not know what these things mean?" I said, "No,
6a my lord." ·He then gave me this answer, ·"These seven
10b are the eyes of Yahweh; they cover the whole world."
11 In reply to this I asked him, "What is the meaning of
these two olive trees, to the right and to the left of the
12 lampstand?" ·(Speaking again, I asked him, "What is
the meaning of the two olive branches pouring the oil
13 through the two golden pipes?") ·He replied, "Do you
not know what these things mean?" I said, "No, my
14 lord." ·He said, "These are the two anointed ones who
stand before the Lord of the whole world.[a]

### Three sayings about Zerubbabel

6b      "This is the word of Yahweh with regard to Zerubbabel, 'Not by might and not by power, but by my
spirit, says Yahweh Sabaoth.
7      'What are you, you great mountain? Before Zerubbabel, be a plain! He will pull out the keystone to shouts
of: Blessings on it, blessings on it!'"
8      The word of Yahweh was addressed to me as follows,
9 "The hands of Zerubbabel have laid the foundation of
this Temple; his hands will finish it. (And you will learn
10a that Yahweh Sabaoth has sent me to you.) ·A day for
little things, no doubt, but who would dare despise it?
People will rejoice when they see the chosen stone in
the hands of Zerubbabel."

### Sixth vision: the flying scroll

1  5 Again I raised my eyes, and this is what I saw: a
2  flying scroll. ·The angel who was talking to me said,
"What can you see?" I replied, "I can see a flying scroll;
3 it is twenty cubits long and ten cubits broad." ·He then
said to me, "This is the Curse sweeping across the face
of the whole country. According to what it says, every
thief will be banished; according to what it says, every-

3 a. Yahweh.
b. The high priest represents the Jewish people.
c. Sign of mourning or national calamity.
d. The national mourning is over.
4 a. Joshua, the high priest; and Zerubbabel, the High Commissioner, seen as the anointed king.

one who swears falsely by my name will be banished.
⁴ I am going to let it loose—it is Yahweh Sabaoth who
speaks—to enter the house of the thief and the house
of anyone who swears falsely by my name, to settle in
his house and to consume it, timber, stone and all."

## Seventh vision: the woman in the bushel

⁵    The angel who was talking to me came forward and
said to me, "Raise your eyes, and see what this is,
⁶ moving forward." ·I said, "What is it?" He said, "This
is a bushel moving forward." He went on, "This is
⁷ their iniquity throughout the country." ·At this, a disc
of lead was raised, and I saw a Woman sitting inside
⁸ the bushel. ·He said, "This is Wickedness." And he
forced her back into the bushel and closed its mouth
⁹ with the mass of lead. ·I raised my eyes, and this is
what I saw: two women appearing. The wind caught
their wings—they had wings like a stork's; they raised
¹⁰ the bushel midway between earth and heaven. ·I then
said to the angel who was talking to me, "Where are
¹¹ they taking the bushel?" ·He replied, "They mean to
build a temple for it in the land of Shinar, and to make
a plinth on which to place it."[a]

## Eighth vision: the chariots

¹    Again I raised my eyes, and this is what I saw: four
6    chariots coming out between the two mountains,
² and the mountains were mountains of bronze. ·The
first chariot had red horses, the second chariot had
³ black horses, ·the third chariot had white horses and
⁴ the fourth chariot had (vigorous) piebald horses. ·I
asked the angel who was talking to me, I said, "What
⁵ is the meaning of these, my lord?" ·The angel answered,
"These are going out to the four wings of heaven after
⁶ standing before the Lord of the whole world. ·The red
horses are going out to the country of the East; the
black horses are going out to the country of the North;
the white are going out to the country of the West and
the piebald are going out to the country of the South."
⁷ They came out vigorously, eager to patrol the world.
He said to them, "Go and patrol the world." And they
⁸ patroled the world. ·He called me and said to me, "See,
those going northward will make the spirit of Yahweh

15 descend on the country of the North.[a] •And those who
   are far away will come and rebuild the sanctuary of
   Yahweh. (And you will learn that Yahweh Sabaoth has
   sent me to you.) (This will happen if you listen carefully to the voice of Yahweh your God.)"

## The votive crown

9   And the word of Yahweh was addressed to me as
10 follows, •"Take the offerings of the captives,[b] of Hel-
    dai, Tobijah and Jedaiah, and go to the house of Josiah
11 son of Zephaniah, who has arrived from Babylon. •Take
    the silver and gold, make a crown and set it on the
12 head of Joshua son of Jehozadak, the high priest.[c] •And
    say this to him, 'Yahweh Sabaoth says this: Here is a
    man whose name is Branch; where he is, there will be
    a branching out (and he will rebuild the sanctuary of
13 Yahweh). •It is he who is going to rebuild the sanctuary
    of Yahweh. It is he who is going to wear the royal
    insignia. He will sit on his throne as ruler. And a priest
    shall be at his right hand. Perfect peace will reign be-
14 tween these two; •while the crown will be a glorious
    memorial to Heldai, Tobijah and Jedaiah, and to Josiah,
    son of Zephaniah, in the sanctuary of Yahweh.'"

## A question on fasting

1  7 In the fourth year of King Darius (the word of
      Yahweh was addressed to Zechariah), on the fourth
   day of the ninth month[a] (the month of Chislev),
2  Bethel sent Sharezer and his men to entreat the favor
3  of Yahweh •and to say to the priests in the Temple
   of Yahweh Sabaoth, and to his prophets, "Ought I to
   go on mourning and fasting in the fifth month as I
   have been doing for so many years past?"[b]

5 a. Wickedness is banished to Babylon, where it is worshiped.
6 a. Where there are still some exiles.
b. Of the captives who have returned from captivity.
c. It is evident that the original text read "Zerubbabel," see vv.
12–13. "Joshua son of Jehozadak" is a "modernization" by a
later hand.
7 a. November 518.
b. The destruction of the Temple in 587 had been commemorated
by a fast in the month of July; now rebuilding has begun. The
answer to this question is in ch. 8. The oracle which follows in
the next paragraph seems to have been attached merely because
it too mentions fasting, and the second fast to which it alludes
was the commemoration of the murder of Gedaliah, 2 K. 25.

### The nation's past surveyed

⁴ Then the word of Yahweh Sabaoth was addressed
⁵ to me as follows, ·"Say to all the people of the country,
and to the priests, 'While you have been fasting and
mourning in the fifth and seventh months for the past
seventy years, was it for my sake you fasted so rigor-
⁶ ously? ·And when you were eating and drinking, were
⁷ not you the eaters and you the drinkers? ·Do you not
know the words which Yahweh proclaimed through
the prophets in the past, when Jerusalem was inhabited
and secure, with her surrounding towns, and when the
⁸ Negeb and the Lowlands were inhabited? (·The word
of Yahweh was addressed to Zechariah as follows:
⁹ Yahweh Sabaoth says this.) He said: Apply the law
fairly, and practice kindness and compassion toward
¹⁰ each other. ·Do not oppress the widow and the orphan,
the settler and the poor man, and do not secretly plan
¹¹ evil against one another. ·But they would not pay attention; they turned a petulant shoulder; they stopped
¹² their ears rather than hear; ·they made their hearts
adamant rather than listen to the teaching and the
words that Yahweh Sabaoth had sent by his spirit
through the prophets in the past. This aroused great
¹³ anger on the part of Yahweh Sabaoth. ·And this is
what happened, since he kept calling them and they
would not listen (similarly they will call and I shall
¹⁴ not listen, says Yahweh Sabaoth): ·he scattered them
throughout nations unknown to them; hence the country was reduced to desolation behind them, and no one
came or went. They turned a land of delights into a
desert.' "

### A prospect of messianic salvation

¹ **8** The word of Yahweh Sabaoth was addressed to me
as follows:

²
> "Yahweh Sabaoth says this.
> I am burning with jealousy for Zion,
> with great anger for her sake.

³
> "Yahweh Sabaoth says this.
> I am coming back to Zion
> and shall dwell in the middle of Jerusalem.

Jerusalem will be called Faithful City
and the mountain of Yahweh Sabaoth, the Holy
Mountain.

4     "Yahweh Sabaoth says this.
Old men and old women will again sit down
in the squares of Jerusalem;
every one of them staff in hand
because of their great age.

5     And the squares of the city will be full
of boys and girls
playing in the squares.

6     "Yahweh Sabaoth says this.
If this seems a miracle
to the remnant of this people (in those days),
will it seem one to me?
It is Yahweh Sabaoth who speaks.

7     "Yahweh Sabaoth says this.
Now I am going to save my people
from the countries of the East
and from the countries of the West.

8     I will bring them back
to live inside Jerusalem.
They shall be my people
and I will be their God
in faithfulness and integrity.

9     "Yahweh Sabaoth says this. Let your hands be
strong, you who here and now listen to these words
from the mouths of the prophets who have been
prophesying since the day when the Temple of Yahweh
Sabaoth had its foundation laid for the rebuilding of
10 the sanctuary. ·For before the present day men were
not paid their wages and nothing was paid for the
animals either; and because of the enemy there was
no security for a man to go about his business; I had
11 set every man against everyone else. ·But now, with
the remnant of this people, I am not as I was in the
12 past. It is Yahweh Sabaoth who speaks. ·For I mean
to spread peace everywhere; the vine will give its fruit,
the earth its increase, and heaven its dew. I am going
to bestow all these blessings on the remnant of this
13 people. ·Just as once you were a curse among the

nations, you House of Judah (and House of Israel), so I mean to save you for you to become a blessing. Do not be afraid; let your hands be strong.

14 For Yahweh Sabaoth says this. Just as I once resolved to inflict evil on you when your ancestors provoked me—says Yahweh Sabaoth—and as I did not then 15 relent, ·so now I have another purpose, and I intend in the present day to confer benefits on Jerusalem and on the House of Judah. Do not be afraid.

16 "These are the things that you must do. Speak the truth to one another; let the judgments at your gates 17 be such as conduce to peace; ·do not secretly plot evil against one another; do not love false oaths; since all this is what I hate. It is Yahweh who speaks."

### The answer to the question on fasting

18 The word of Yahweh Sabaoth was addressed to me as follows:

19 "Yahweh Sabaoth says this. The fast of the fourth month, the fast of the fifth, the fast of the seventh and the fast of the tenth are to become gladness and happiness and days of joyful feasting for the House of Judah.[a] But love the truth and peace!

### A prospect of messianic salvation

20 "Yahweh Sabaoth says this. There will be other peo-
21 ples yet, and citizens of great cities. ·And the inhabitants of one city will go to the next and say, 'Come, let us go and entreat the favor of Yahweh, and seek
22 Yahweh Sabaoth; I am going myself.' ·And many peoples and great nations will come to seek Yahweh Sabaoth in Jerusalem and to entreat the favor of Yahweh.
23 "Yahweh Sabaoth says this. In those days, ten men of nations of every language will take a Jew by the sleeve and say, 'We want to go with you, since we have learned that God is with you.'"

## SECOND PART

**1** **9** An oracle.

### The new promised land[a]

Yahweh has passed
through the land of Hadrach
and Damascus is his dwelling place;
for the cities of Aram belong to Yahweh
no less than all the tribes of Israel;

**2**   Hamath too, which borders on it,
(Tyre) and Sidon also, despite her acumen.

**3**   Tyre has built herself a rampart,
has heaped up silver like dust
and gold like the dirt of the streets.

**4**   And now the Lord is going to take possession
of her;
he will topple her power into the sea;
she herself will be consumed by fire.

**5**   Seeing this, Ashkelon will be terrified,
and Gaza be seized with trembling,
so will Ekron, at the ruin of her prospects;
the king will vanish from Gaza
and Ashkelon remain unpeopled,

**6**   but the bastard[b] will live in Ashdod!
I mean to destroy the arrogance of the Philistine;

**7**   I intend to take his blood out of his mouth
and his abomination from between his teeth.[c]
He too will become a remnant for our God

**8 a.** This answer abolishes the two fasts already mentioned, and
those of the fourth and tenth months, which commemorated the
breaching of the walls and the beginning of the siege.
**9 a.** The new Promised Land is larger than Israel and includes
Aramaean, Phoenician and Philistine cities. A victorious cam-
paign against these territories, probably that of Alexander in 333,
is seen as the action of Yahweh.
**b.** A population of mixed races.
**c.** Philistines followed the pagan practice of eating meat with the
blood in it, and eating the forbidden meats, such as pork.

and be like a family in Judah:
Ekron shall be like the Jebusite.[d]

8

Near my house I will take my stand
like a watchman on guard against prowlers;
the tyrant shall pass their way no more,
because I have now taken notice of its distress.

## The Messiah

9

Rejoice heart and soul, daughter of Zion!
Shout with gladness, daughter of Jerusalem!
See now, your king comes to you;
he is victorious, he is triumphant,
humble and riding on a donkey,
on a colt, the foal of a donkey.

10

He will banish chariots from Ephraim
and horses from Jerusalem;
the bow of war will be banished.
He will proclaim peace for the nations.
His empire shall stretch from sea to sea,
from the River to the ends of the earth.

## The restoration of Israel

11

As for you, because of the blood of your
    covenant
I am sending back your prisoners from the pit
(in which there is no water).

12

To you, daughter of Zion,
the hopeful captives will return.
In compensation for your days of banishment
I will give you back double.

13

For I bend my bow; it is Judah;
I make Ephraim its arrow.
I am going to brandish your children, Zion,
(against your children, Javan)[e];
I mean to make you like the sword of a hero.

14

Yahweh will appear above them
and his arrow will flash out like lightning.
(The Lord) Yahweh will sound the trumpet
and advance in the storms of the south.

15

Yahweh (Sabaoth) will protect them!
They will trample sling stones underfoot,
they will drink blood like wine,

they will be soaked in it like the horns of an
    altar.

16      Yahweh their God will give them victory
    when that day comes;
    he will pasture his people like a flock
    (like the flashing jewels of a diadem)
    on his land.

17      What joy and what beauty shall be theirs!
    Corn will make the young men flourish,
    and sweet wine the maidens.

### Faithfulness to Yahweh

1 **10**  Ask Yahweh for rain
    at the time of the spring rains.
    For it is Yahweh who sends the lightning
    and gives the showers of rain;
    he gives bread to man,
    and grass to the cattle.

2      Because the teraphim utter futile words
    and the diviners have lying visions[a]
    and publish empty dreams
    and voice misleading nonsense,
    naturally the people stray like sheep;
    they wander because they have no shepherd.

### Israel's deliverance and return

3      "My anger burns against the shepherds,
    and I mean to punish the he-goats."
    Yes, Yahweh (Sabaoth) will take care of his
        flock
    (the House of Judah),
    he will make it his proud steed (in battle).

4      From him will issue Cornerstone and Tent peg,[b]
    from him the Bow of battle,
    from him all the Leaders.

5      Together ·they will be like heroes
    trampling the dirt of the streets (in battle);

d. I.e., incorporated into Israel.
e. This gloss refers to the conquest of the Persian empire ("Ja-van"—the Greeks) by Alexander.
10 a. Teraphim, often the word for a household god, here means instruments of divination.
b. Future leaders who will rise from the people.

they will fight, since Yahweh is with them,
and the riders of horses will be thrown into
    confusion.

6     And I will make the House of Judah mighty,
and the House of Joseph victorious.
I am going to restore them, because I have taken
    pity on them,
and they shall be as though I had never cast
    them off
(for I am Yahweh their God and I mean to
    answer their prayer).

7     Ephraim will be like a hero.
Their hearts will be cheered as though by wine.
Their sons will look on this in gladness,
their hearts will exult in Yahweh.

8     I am going to whistle to them and gather
    them in
(for I have redeemed them);
they will be as numerous as they used to be.

9     I have scattered them among the peoples
but from far away they will remember me
(they will teach their sons, and these will re-
    turn).

10     I mean to bring them back from the land of
    Egypt,
and gather them from Assyria;
I shall lead them into the land of Gilead (and
    Lebanon),
and even that will not be large enough for them.

11     They will pass through the sea of Egypt
(and he will strike the waves on the sea);
all the depths of the Nile will be dried up.
The arrogance of Assyria will be cast down
and the scepter of Egypt be taken away.

12     Their strength will be in Yahweh;
in his name they will glory:
it is Yahweh who speaks.

1 **11** Open your gateways, Lebanon,
and let the fire burn down your cedars.
2     (Wail, cypress,
for felled is the cedar,

the mighty ones have been brought low!)
Wail, oaks of Bashan,
for the impenetrable forest has been felled!

3  The wailing of the shepherds is heard;
their glorious pastures have been ruined.
The roaring of the young lions is heard;
the thickets of the Jordan have been laid waste.

### The two shepherds

4    This is how Yahweh spoke to me, "Pasture the sheep
5 bred for slaughter, ·whose buyers kill them and go unpunished, whose sellers say of them, 'Blessed be Yahweh; now I am rich!' and their shepherds handle[a] them
6 without kindness. ·(For no longer am I going to show
kindness to the inhabitants of the world—it is Yahweh
who speaks. But instead I mean to hand over every
man to the next, and to his king. They shall devastate
the world and I will not deliver them from their
7 hands.)" ·Then I began to pasture these sheep bred
for slaughter for the sheep dealers. I took two staves:
one I called Goodwill, the other Union. And so I began
8 to pasture the sheep. ·I dismissed the three shepherds
in one month.[b] But I began to dislike the sheep, and
9 they equally detested me. ·I then said, "I am going to
pasture you no longer; let those that wish to die, die;
let those that wish to perish, perish; and let those that
10 are left devour each other's flesh!" ·I then took my
staff, Goodwill, and broke it in half, to break the cove-
11 nant Yahweh had made with all the peoples.[c] ·When
it was broken, that day the dealers, who were watching
me, realized that this had been a word of Yahweh.
12 I then said to them, "If you think it right, give me my
wages; if not, never mind." And they weighed out my
13 wages: thirty shekels of silver.[d] ·But Yahweh told me,
"Throw it into the treasury, this princely sum at which
they have valued me." Taking the thirty shekels of
silver, I threw them into the Temple of Yahweh, into

11 a. Buyers and sellers are the Jewish ruling classes; the shepherds are the priests.
b. Alluding to a succession of high priests deposed.
c. Yahweh no longer undertakes to protect the Jewish nation from
its neighbors.
d. The price of a slave.

14 the treasury. ·I then broke my second staff, Union, in half, to break the brotherhood between Judah and Israel.*

15 Next, Yahweh said to me, "Now take the gear of
16 an incompetent shepherd. ·For I am now going to raise an incompetent shepherd in this country. He will not bother about the lost; he will not look for the stray; he will not heal the wounded; he will not support the weary; but he will only eat the flesh of the fat beasts and tear off their hoofs.

17          "Trouble is coming to the worthless shepherd
          who deserts the flock!
          May the sword strike his arm
          and his right eye!
          May his arm wither entirely,
          may his eye be totally blinded!"

## The deliverance and restoration of Jerusalem

1 12 An oracle. The word of Yahweh about Israel. It is Yahweh who speaks, who spread out the heaven and founded the earth and formed the spirit of man within him:

2 "Look, I am going to make Jerusalem an intoxicating cup to all the surrounding peoples . . .

3 "When that day comes, I mean to make Jerusalem a stone to be lifted by all the peoples; all who try to lift it will hurt themselves severely. (And all the nations
4 of the earth will mass against her.) ·When that day comes—it is Yahweh who speaks—I intend to strike all the horses with confusion and their riders with madness. (But on the House of Judah I will open my eyes.) And I will strike all the horses of the peoples with blindness.
5 Then the clans of Judah will say in their hearts, 'Strength for the citizens of Jerusalem is in Yahweh
6 Sabaoth their God.' ·When that day comes I mean to make the clans of Judah like a brazier burning in a pile of wood, like a flaming torch in stubble; and they will consume the peoples around them to right and left.
7 And Jerusalem shall stand firm in her place. ·Yahweh will save the tents of Judah first to forestall the arrogance of the House of David and the arrogance of the citizens of Jerusalem from rising to the detriment of

8 Judah. ·When that day comes, Yahweh will spread his protection over the citizens of Jerusalem; the one among them who was about to fall will be like David on that day, and the House of David will be like God (like the angel of Yahweh) at their head.

9     "When that day comes, I shall set myself to destroy
10 all the nations who advance against Jerusalem. ·But over the House of David and the citizens of Jerusalem I will pour out a spirit of kindness and prayer. They will look on the one whom they have pierced; they will mourn for him as for an only son, and weep for
11 him as people weep for a first-born child. ·When that day comes, there will be great mourning in Judah, like the mourning of Hadad-rimmon in the plain of Me-
12 giddo. ·And the country will mourn clan by clan; the clan of the House of David apart, with their wives by
13 themselves; ·the clan of the House of Nathan apart, with their wives by themselves; the clan of the House of Levi apart, with their wives by themselves; the clan
14 of Shimei apart, with their wives by themselves. ·All the clans that remain, clan by clan, with their wives
1 by themselves. **13** When that day comes, a fountain will be opened for the House of David and the citizens of Jerusalem, for sin and impurity.

2     "When that day comes—it is Yahweh (Sabaoth) who speaks—I am going to root out the names of the idols from the country, and they shall never be mentioned again; and I will also rid the country of the prophets,
3 and of the spirit of impurity. ·If anyone still wants to prophesy, his father and the mother who gave him birth shall say to him, 'You have no right to live, since you utter lies in the name of Yahweh.' And while he is prophesying, his father and the mother who gave him
4 birth shall run him through. ·When that day comes, every prophet shall be ashamed of his prophetic vision; they will no longer put on their hair cloaks to utter their
5 lies, ·but they will all say, 'I am no prophet. I am a peasant; the land has been my living ever since I was a
6 boy.' ·And if anyone asks him, 'Then what are these

**e.** Probably the schism of the Samaritans, who built a rival temple on Mount Gerizim in 328.

wounds on your body?' he will reply, 'These I received in the house of my friends.'

### Invocation to the sword; the new people

7
"Awake, sword, against my shepherd
and against the man who is my companion—
it is Yahweh Sabaoth who speaks.
I am going to strike the shepherd
so that the sheep may be scattered,
and I will turn my hand against the weak.

8
And it will happen throughout this territory—
it is Yahweh who speaks—
that two thirds in it will be cut off ("will be killed")
and the remaining third will be left.

9
I will lead that third into the fire,
and refine them as silver is refined,
test them as gold is tested.
They will call on my name
and I shall listen;
and I shall say: These are my people;
and each will say, 'Yahweh is my God!' "

### The eschatological battle; the splendor of Jerusalem

1 **14** See, a day is coming for Yahweh when the spoils taken from you will be divided among you.
2 Yahweh will gather all the nations to Jerusalem for battle. The city will be taken, the houses plundered, the women ravished. Half the city will go into captivity, but the remnant of the people will not be cut off
3 from the city. ·Then Yahweh will take the field; he will fight against these nations as he fights in the day of
4 battle. ·On that day, his feet will rest on the Mount of Olives, which faces Jerusalem from the east. The Mount of Olives will be split in half from east to west, forming a huge gorge; half the Mount will recede northward,
5 the other half southward. ·And the Vale of Hinnom will be filled up from Goah to Jasol; it will be blocked as it was by the earthquake in the days of Uzziah king of Judah. Yahweh your God will come, and all the holy ones with him.
6 When that day comes, there will be no more cold,
7 no more frost. ·It will be a day of wonder—Yahweh

knows it—with no alternation of day and night; in the
8 evening it will be light. ·When that day comes, running
waters will issue from Jerusalem, half of them to the
eastern sea, half of them to the western sea; they will
9 flow summer and winter. ·And Yahweh will be king
of the whole world. When that day comes, Yahweh
10 will be unique and his name unique. ·The entire country will be transformed into plain, from Geba to Rim-
mon in the Negeb. And Jerusalem will be raised higher,
though still in the same place; from the Gate of Benjamin to the site of the First Gate, that is to say to the
Gate of the Corner and from the Tower of Hananel
11 to the king's winepress, ·people will make their homes.
The ban will be lifted; Jerusalem will be safe to live in.
12     And this is the plague with which Yahweh will strike
all the nations who have fought against Jerusalem; their
flesh will molder while they are still standing on their
feet; their eyes will rot in their sockets; their tongues
14 will rot in their mouths. ·And such will be the plague
on the horses and mules, camels and donkeys, and all
13 the animals to be found in that camp. ·When that day
comes, a great terror will fall on them from Yahweh;
each man will grab his neighbor's hand and they will
14 hit out at each other. ·Even Judah will fight against
Jerusalem. The wealth of all the surrounding nations
will be heaped together: gold, silver, clothing, in vast
quantity.
16     All who survive of all the nations that have marched
against Jerusalem will go up year by year to worship
the King, Yahweh Sabaoth, and to keep the feast of
17 Tabernacles. ·Should one of the races of the world
fail to go up to Jerusalem to worship the King, Yahweh
18 Sabaoth, there will be no rain for that one. ·Should
the race of Egypt fail to go up and pay its visit, on it
will fall the plague which Yahweh will inflict on each
one of those nations that fail to go up to keep the feast
19 of Tabernacles. ·Such shall be the punishment for
Egypt and for all the nations that fail to go up to keep
20 the feast of Tabernacles. ·When that day comes, the
horse bells will be inscribed with the words, "Sacred
to Yahweh," and in the Temple of Yahweh the very
cooking pots will be as fine as the sprinkling bowls at
21 the altar. ·And every cooking pot in Jerusalem and in

Judah shall become sacred to Yahweh Sabaoth; all who want to offer sacrifice will come and help themselves from them for their cooking; there will be no more traders in the Temple of Yahweh Sabaoth, when that day comes.

# MALACHI

## 1

<sup>1</sup> An oracle.
The word of Yahweh to Israel through the ministration of Malachi.[a]

## The love of Yahweh for Israel

<sup>2</sup> I have shown my love for you, says Yahweh. But you ask, "How have you shown your love?" Was not Esau[b] Jacob's brother?—it is Yahweh who speaks; yet <sup>3</sup> I showed my love for Jacob ·and my hatred for Esau. I turned his towns into a wilderness and his heritage <sup>4</sup> into desert pastures. ·Should Edom say, "We have been struck down but we will rebuild our ruins," this is the reply of Yahweh Sabaoth: Let them build! I will pull down. They shall be known as Unholy Land and <sup>5</sup> Nation-with-which-Yahweh-is-angry-for-ever. ·Your eyes are going to see this and you will say, "Yahweh is mighty beyond the borders of Israel."

## An indictment of the priests

<sup>6</sup> The son honors his father, the slave respects his master. If I am indeed father, where is my honor? If I am indeed master, where is my respect? Yahweh Sabaoth asks this of you, priests, you who despise my name. <sup>7</sup> You ask, "How have we despised your name?" ·By putting polluted food on my altar. You ask, "How have we polluted it?" By holding the table of Yahweh in <sup>8</sup> contempt. ·When you bring blind animals for sacrifice, is that not wrong? When you bring the lame and the diseased, is that not wrong? Try offering them to your high commissioner, and see if he is pleased with this <sup>9</sup> or receives you graciously, says Yahweh Sabaoth. ·Now try pleading with God to take pity on us (this is your own fault); do you think he will receive you graciously? <sup>10</sup> says Yahweh Sabaoth. ·Oh, is there no one among you

---

**1 a.** "Malachi" means "my messenger" and is probably not a proper name.
**b.** The ancestor of Edom.

who will shut the doors and stop you from lighting useless fires on my altar? I am not pleased with you, says Yahweh Sabaoth; from your hands I find no of-
11 ferings acceptable. ·But from farthest east to farthest west my name is honored among the nations and everywhere a sacrifice of incense is offered to my name, and a pure offering too, since my name is honored among
12 the nations, says Yahweh Sabaoth. ·But you, you profane it by thinking of the Lord's table as defiled and by
13 holding in contempt the food placed on it. ·"How tiresome it all is!" you say; and you sniff disdainfully at me, says Yahweh Sabaoth. You bring a stolen, lame or diseased animal, you bring that as an offering! Am I to accept this from your hand? says Yahweh Sabaoth.
14 Cursed be the rogue who owns a male which he has vowed to offer from his flock, and instead sacrifices a blemished animal to me! For I am a great king, says Yahweh Sabaoth, and my name is feared throughout
1 the nations. 2 And now, priests, this warning is for you.
2 If you do not listen, if you do not find it in your heart to glorify my name, says Yahweh Sabaoth, I will send the curse on you and curse your very blessing.ᵃ Indeed I have already cursed it, since there is not a single one
3 of you who takes this to heart. ·Now watch how I am going to paralyze your arm and throw dung in your face—the dung from your very solemnities—and sweep
4 you away with it. ·Then you shall learn that it is I who have given you this warning of my intention to abolish
5 my covenant with Levi, says Yahweh Sabaoth. ·My covenant was with him: it stood for life and peace, and these were what I gave him; it stood for fear and trembling, and he respected me and stood in awe of
6 my name. ·The teaching of truth was in his mouth, falsehood was not to be found on his lips; he walked with me in integrity and virtue; he converted many
7 from sinning. ·The lips of the priest ought to safeguard knowledge; his mouth is where instruction should be sought, since he is the messenger of Yahweh Sabaoth.
8 But you, you have strayed from the way; you have caused many to stumble by your teaching. You have destroyed the covenant of Levi, says Yahweh Sabaoth.
9 And so I in my turn have made you contemptible and vile in the eyes of the whole people in repayment for

the way you have not kept to my paths but have shown partiality in your administration.

## Mixed marriage and divorce

10 Have we not all one Father? Did not one God create us? Why, then, do we break faith with one another, 11 profaning the covenant of our ancestors? ·Judah has broken faith: a detestable thing has been done (in Israel and) in Jerusalem. Yes, Judah has profaned the sanctuary that Yahweh loves. He has married the 12 daughter of an alien god. ·The man who does this— whoever he be—may Yahweh cut him off from the tents of Jacob and from the company of those who 13 present the offering to Yahweh Sabaoth. ·And here is something else you do: you cover the altar of Yahweh with tears, with weeping and wailing, because he now refuses to consider the offering or to accept it from 14 your hands. ·And you ask, "Why?" It is because Yahweh stands as witness between you and the wife of your youth, the wife with whom you have broken faith, even though she was your partner and your wife by 15 covenant. ·Did he not create a single being that has flesh and the breath of life? And what is this single being destined for? God-given offspring. Be careful for your own life, therefore, and do not break faith with 16 the wife of your youth. ·For I hate divorce, says Yahweh the God of Israel, and I hate people to parade their sins on their cloaks, says Yahweh Sabaoth. Respect your own life, therefore, and do not break faith like this.

## The day of Yahweh

17 You weary Yahweh with your talk. You ask, "How do we weary him?" When you say, "Any evildoer is good as far as Yahweh is concerned; indeed he likes them best"; or when you say, "Where is the God of 1 justice now?" 3 Look, I am going to send my messenger to prepare a way before me. And the Lord you are seeking will suddenly enter his Temple; and the angel of the covenant whom you are longing for, yes,

2 a. The "blessing" of the priests is the levitical revenue.

² he is coming, says Yahweh Sabaoth. ·Who will be able
to resist the day of his coming? Who will remain standing when he appears? For he is like the refiner's fire
³ and the fullers' alkali. ·He will take his seat as refiner
and purifier; he will purify the sons of Levi and refine
them like gold and silver, and then they will make the
⁴ offering to Yahweh as it should be made. ·The offering of Judah and Jerusalem will then be welcomed by
⁵ Yahweh as in former days, as in the years of old. ·I
mean to visit you for the judgment and I am going to
be a ready witness against sorcerer, adulterer and
perjurer, against those who oppress the wage earner,
the widow and the orphan, and who rob the settler of
his rights—no need for you to be afraid of me, says
Yahweh Sabaoth.

## Temple tithes

⁶ No; I, Yahweh, do not change; and you, sons of
⁷ Jacob, you are not ruined yet! ·Since the days of your
ancestors you have evaded my statutes and not observed them. Return to me and I will return to you,
says Yahweh Sabaoth. You ask, "How are we to return?
⁸ Can a man cheat God?" Yet you are cheating me. You
ask, "How are we cheating you?" In the matter of
⁹ tithes and dues. ·The curse lies on you because you,
¹⁰ yes you the whole nation, are cheating me. ·Bring the
full tithes and dues to the storehouse so that there may
be food in my house, and then see if I do not open the
floodgates of heaven for you and pour out blessing for
¹¹ you in abundance. ·For your sake I will lay a strict
injunction on the locust not to destroy the fruits of
your soil nor to make the vine in your fields barren,
¹² says Yahweh Sabaoth. ·All the nations will call you
blessed, for you will be a land of delights, says Yahweh
Sabaoth.

## The triumph of the virtuous on the day of Yahweh

¹³ You say harsh things about me, says Yahweh. You
¹⁴ ask, "What have we said against you?" ·You say, "It
is useless to serve God; what is the good of keeping
his commands or of walking mournfully before Yah-
¹⁵ weh Sabaoth? ·Now we have reached the point when
we call the arrogant blessed; yes, they prosper, these

evildoers; they try God's patience and yet go free."
16 This is what those who fear Yahweh used to say to
one another. But Yahweh took note and heard them:
a book of remembrance was written in his presence
recording those who fear him and take refuge in his
17 name. ·On the day which I am preparing, says Yahweh Sabaoth, they are going to be my own special
possession. I will make allowances for them as a man
18 makes allowances for the son who obeys him. ·Then
once again you will see the difference between an upright man and a wicked one, between the one who
19 serves God and the one who does not serve him. ·For
4:1 the day is coming now, burning like a furnace; and all
the arrogant and the evildoers will be like stubble. The
day that is coming is going to burn them up, says Yah-
20 weh Sabaoth, leaving them neither root nor stalk. ·But
2 for you who fear my name, the sun of righteousness
will shine out with healing in its rays; you will leap
21 like calves going out to pasture. ·You will trample on
3 the wicked, who will be like ashes under your feet on
the day I am preparing, says Yahweh Sabaoth.

**Appendices**

22 Remember the Law of my servant Moses to whom
4 at Horeb I prescribed laws and customs for the whole
23 of Israel. ·Know that I am going to send you Elijah
5 the prophet before my day comes, that great and ter-
24 rible day. ·He shall turn the hearts of fathers toward
6 their children and the hearts of children toward their
fathers, lest I come and strike the land with a curse.

# NOTES